Charles Munch

Charles Munch

D. Kern Holoman

OXFORD
UNIVERSITY PRESS

OXFORD

UNIVERSITY PRESS

Oxford University Press, Inc., publishes works that further
Oxford University's objective of excellence
in research, scholarship, and education.

Oxford   New York
Auckland   Cape Town   Dar es Salaam   Hong Kong   Karachi
Kuala Lumpur   Madrid   Melbourne   Mexico City   Nairobi
New Delhi   Shanghai   Taipei   Toronto

With offices in
Argentina   Austria   Brazil   Chile   Czech Republic   France   Greece
Guatemala   Hungary   Italy   Japan   Poland   Portugal   Singapore
South Korea   Switzerland   Thailand   Turkey   Ukraine   Vietnam

Published by Oxford University Press, Inc.
198 Madison Avenue, New York, New York 10016

www.oup.com

Oxford is a registered trademark of Oxford University Press

Holoman, D. Kern, 1947–
Charles Munch / D. Kern Holoman.
p.   cm.
Includes bibliographical references and index.
ISBN 978-0-19-977270-4
1. Munch, Charles, 1891–1968. 2. Conductors (Music)—Biography. I. Title.
ML422.M9H65   2011
784.2092—dc22
[B]
2011004243

9 8 7 6 5 4 3 2 1

Printed in the United States of America
on acid-free paper

Charles Munch was born on September 26, 1891,
in Strasbourg
and died on November 6, 1968,
in Richmond, Virginia.

CONTENTS

LIST OF ILLUSTRATIONS

ACKNOWLEDGMENTS

In the end, I realized, I was telling this story especially to Munch's nephew, Jean-Philippe Schweitzer, and to Lita Starr, his companion of the last decades, and this book is thus fondly dedicated to them both with my deep and lasting thanks.

Similar thanks go to other family members: Ernest Munch, Veronique Schweitzer, Agnès Schoeller, and Jérôme and Annie Kaltenbach. I am also grateful to Geneviève Honegger in Strasbourg, who might just as well be a member of the family.

My thanks also go to others in France: Frédéric Blin and the staff of the Bibliothèque Nationale et Universitaire in Strasbourg, Gilles Cantagrel, Jean Daltroff, Jean Douay, Georges-François Hirsch and the staff of the Orchestre de Paris, Pascale Honegger, Harry Lapp, Catherine Massip and the staff of the Bibliothèque Nationale's Music Division, Jean-Michel Nectoux, Gérard Neuvecelle, Alena Parthonnaud at the Médiathèque Musicale Mahler in Paris, and the staff of the Documentation Musicale office at Radio-France.

I extend my thanks to several people in and around Boston: Bridget Carr, archivist of the Boston Symphony Orchestra, and the BSO staff in general; Sarah Funke Donovan; Margaretta Fulton (with whom I first planned the project); Francis Hauert, Gus Manos, Margo Miller; Diane Ota and the Boston Public Library; Sylvia Sandeen; Caldwell Titcomb; and any number of BSO musicians I had the pleasure of interviewing, notably Lorna Cooke de Varon, Doriot Anthony Dwyer, Vic Firth, Roger Shermont, and Roger Voisin.

I also thank Frank Villella, archivist, Rosenthal Archives of the Chicago Symphony Orchestra; Carol S. Jacobs, archivist, Cleveland Orchestra; Ronald Desmarais; Paul Ganson, Detroit Symphony Orchestra; Karen Schnackenberg, Dallas Symphony Orchestra; Steven Lacoste, archives of the Los Angeles Philharmonic Orchestra; Paul Gunther, Minnesota Orchestra; Judy Ross; Paul Ryder, Saint Louis Symphony Orchestra; and Thomas Tierney and Che Williams, Sony Music Archives Library.

Tim Day of the BBC Written Archives in the British Library and Françoise Davoine of Radio-Canada were also of help.

Heartfelt thanks go, as well, to Michael Gray and James H. North, who simply turned over their databases of information on the Munch recordings and helped me begin to understand the industry.

For particular factual contributions I thank Elizabeth Crist, Dan Flanagan, and Brian Salter.

Readers of the manuscript drafts included several of the aforementioned, as well as David Cairns, Beth Levy, Hugh Macdonald, Michael Malone, Martin Neary, Michael Steinberg, and the unnamed but fastidious and provocative reviewers of the manuscript. At Oxford University Press both author and subject found a warm, comforting welcome from Suzanne Ryan, Nancy Toff, Caelyn Cobb, Norm Hirschy, Carol Hoke, and Erica Woods Tucker.

My colleagues in the Department of Music at the University of California, Davis shared in every stage of the gestation; those who contributed directly include Rhio Barnhart, Ross Bauer, Anna Maria Busse Berger, Jonathan Elkus, Nataliya Kornetova, Beth Levy, David Nutter, Jessie Ann Owens, Christopher Reynolds, and Don Roth. A graduate seminar in musicology worked through the first full draft, then went on to flesh out particular areas and write papers of their own: Jessica Bejarano, Katerina Frank, Chantal Frankenbach, Fawzi Haimor, Hernán Mouro, and Beverly Wilcox. I was fortunate to hold the Barbara K. Jackson Chair in Orchestral Conducting at UC Davis during the period in which this work emerged and will always be deeply grateful to Mrs. Jackson for all she has meant to my professional and personal life and to the University of California in general.

The same must surely be said of the UC Davis Symphony Orchestra, which I had the privilege of conducting for more than three decades. While the orchestra members must surely have tired of hearing Munch stories and being sent to RCA Living Stereo discs, they never said as much and indeed presented a wonderful Charles Munch program in my last season, notably including his excerpts from act III of *Die Meistersinger*. Philip Daley, my longtime associate in concert management and production, supported every aspect of bringing this project to fruition.

At home the children gave me my first iPod, which, like my second, was soon filled to overflowing with the recorded legacy of Charles Munch. My wife, Elizabeth, summoned once again the wherewithal to confect a life in which research and writing mingled successfully with family, students, concerts, and events unexpected in what can only be called a Good Life.

INTRODUCTION

"Pas nécessaire!" he would often mutter to his players, skipping to the next movement.

You need spend only an hour or two reviewing the legacy of Charles Munch to learn two things: his adamant opposition to superfluous rehearsal and the corresponding spontaneity he believed essential to a living performance. No two readings would, or could, be the same.

The usual anecdote is that Munch would be leading a pick-up rehearsal of a program already well known to the players. "Anybody want to rehearse *La Mer?*" he would ask. "*Non? Bon.* I have confidence in you." This goes on as he leafs through one score after another. Finally he asks for a particular passage "just for me." "That's OK," comes a voice from the orchestra, "we have confidence in you."[1]

Nor would players object to arriving at the workplace for a rehearsal, only to encounter their colleagues leaving a canceled practice. In Boston, after Serge Koussevitzky's long and idiosyncratic reign, what seemed to the musicians a player-centric approach had immediate positive effect. "Now we can play without ulcers," a Boston Symphony Orchestra (BSO) musician told the press in so many words, and the Providence newspaper reported a few weeks into the Munch tenure that: "They're crazy about him to a man."[2] So, too, were audiences crazy about him, almost without exception, and most living composers he played and the majority of critics who heard him, though quicker to identify his foibles, had little trouble elevating Charles Munch to the ranks of the great conductors.

That every concert he led—and there were more than two thousand—deserved its unique marks of vitality was for Munch a matter of faith, the root of his understanding of the transactions that take place among composer, musician, and listener at any given moment in a live performance. One searches without much success for a Munch "sound" or, say, the "definitive" performance of the *Fantastique* (of which there are eight published recordings and several radio broadcasts in circulation). Nevertheless, even if a particular reading is too fast or too loud or not quite ready—common Munch limitations—there are always dazzlingly perceptive passages and, what is more, viable and often haunting arguments as to what the work is actually all about.

Hence a third area of accord—from the musicians who played for him, to the composers whose work he created, to the public privileged to have heard Charles Munch in live surroundings—is that once he began to hear his own inner voice, a certain magic took wing that amounted to the very essence of music in concert. It was as though (and this is a trait shared by many, perhaps most, great recreative artists) the circumstances of public performance loosed facets of character and artistry and poetry otherwise muffled by timidity and simple disinclination to say much.

This was noted early on by thoughtful observers. To Pierre Hiégel, pondering how Munch could let himself be swept away by the music while still appearing to maintain detailed control of his reflexes, "it was almost like a sort of wizardry."[3] Francis Poulenc, not always an admirer of the Munch style, says much the same of the premiere of the *Gloria:*

> Saturday night was OK. Very good, very lovely, a success, but Munch less inspired than usual. Yesterday, by contrast, with the critics there [Sunday, 22 January 1961, the Friday night having been snowed out], a *sublime performance.* Charlie in a trance, but careful; the chorus amazing, La Addison *unbelievable,* and thus ovation on ovation. They tell me this morning that the press was excellent. Marlene Dietrich was there: kisses, photos, and all.[4]

To Marcel Landowski, architect of the Orchestre de Paris and of the overall government approach to classical music in France, "He was one of those exceptional people who understand above all the voices of the heart, who present to the audience the impression that their rhetoric is the reflection of an internal song. His musical ambition, which is to say his life's ambition, was to have the audience grasp the mysterious song hidden within the music."[5] Landowski's notion that Charles Munch was defined, in the French fashion, by his concept of *métier* is correct. I think, too, that his ideas of success and fame were a good deal humbler than we typically associate with the top-tier maestro: "To a reserved, withdrawn, and timid person," he wrote in assessment of his own career, conducting "offers the chance to realize his dreams in sound."[6]

By the time the Munch mystique had won over a community of listeners, his mere appearance on taking the stage was enough to trigger a kind of collective paroxysm of the public, the spell extended to the players by a particular grin that conveyed, at once, shared anticipation, inner contentment, and an undeniable hint of collusion as though conductor and players keep secrets that outsiders must never know. Only then would the music begin.

Though "imperfect and fragmentary" (to use the words of the flutist Michel Debost),[7] the plentiful audio and video tapes of Munch concerts coalesce into a

good composite portrait. Take, as a single example, a 1963 performance of
Daphnis et Chloé, Suite 2, with the Philadelphia Orchestra and a chorus.[8] Here,
in a favorite composition he had led several hundred times by this point in his
career, one is struck by the specifics: how the sonority—the richness of the
strings, the solo winds rather less prominent than in Boston—and balance are
those one associates more with Philadelphia than with Munch and how the bac-
chanal seems defined by the way this particular chorus treats its role. As usual in
a Munch performance, the tempo accelerates toward the end, but here not so
much with a sharp lurch: Rather, the effect is of all the elements—volume and
speed, of course, but also the way the falls become less and less distinguishable
from glissandi—gathering around the chorus in its ecstasy. The roar that bursts
from the public during the last chord seems a calculated component of the climax. Certainly, here and elsewhere, it was cultivated.

Charles Munch was for all intents and purposes solely dedicated to the symphony orchestra. He became a conductor in middle age, after some two
decades as an orchestral violinist and concertmaster. Any structured course of
study he may have lacked had been counterbalanced by then with the experience of daily life under influential conductors in accomplished ensembles.
(Virgil Thomson reminds us that "the greatest interpreters of them all," in
which number he included Munch, "did not come to conducting through
early mastery of the conservatory routines. They bought, muscled, or
impressed their way in and then settled down to learn their job. They succeeded gloriously." The French critic Claude Samuel thought much the same,
suggesting that both Munch and Boulez were conductors "by accident."[9])
Munch had an elevated understanding of orchestral structure and purpose, of
the things he should leave to others, and of the matters only he could control.
The daily life of an orchestra was second nature to him. His sense of programming (the "confection" of programs, as it was thought of in French) was impeccable both for individual concerts and at the season level. In Paris and in
Boston, when Munch was around, there was always something happening in
the concert hall to attract the attention and stimulate the mind. By limiting
himself, with very rare exceptions, to that venue, he was able to focus on its
particular priorities and philosophies, especially where they concerned the
needs of living composers and the opportunities these artists afforded to
advance orchestral practice.

    About the living composer he had strong personal conviction. It was a fun-
damental of his worldview that young composers and local ones must be heard
day in and day out, and this was as true in Hungary, Holland, Israel—and
Egypt—as it was in Paris of the 1930s or Boston in the '50s. He tried to put a
work of his time or place on every week's program, and even in an epoch when

many good composers were still writing symphonies and concertos, that was an aggressive stance. Some of these works, like *Medea's Meditation and Dance of Vengeance* by Samuel Barber, achieved a place on his list of favorites. (He was fond of a number of American composers before he ever left Paris.) Helping the BSO choose its seventy-fifth-anniversary commissions was one of the great joys of his life, and he jealously guarded his right to conduct the premieres even for those works that arrived after his official reign was over.

He took these positions, as was his habit, without much by way of polemic. On one (and, so far as I can tell, only one) occasion, the Boston Symphony released his written response to a patron who had complained about his weekly programming of contemporary music.[10] Still, the apparently docile public reception of a concerto for *ondes Martenot* and orchestra in the second week of his Boston tenure remains a thing of wonder—especially as Cyrus Durgin, dean of the local critics, had blistering things to say about Messiaen's *Turangalîla-Symphonie*, as premiered that same month by Bernstein.[11] But Bostonians became accustomed to the approach, and they stayed with it.

There were many reasons for Munch to have left the Société des Concerts after World War II, but the fundamental issue was his disagreement with the orchestra's general manager over precisely this kind of programming. Munch rode out the end of his career, it is true, with the most popular works in the French canon: the *Fantastique, Daphnis et Chloé, La Valse,* a little Bizet, a little Fauré. His early reputation, however, was as a promoter of new music, and his original passions for Albert Roussel and Guy Ropartz and Arthur Honegger gathered into an ongoing commitment toward building the European repertoire that finds him as interested as ever, in the 1960s, in promoting the new work of Poulenc, Jacques Ibert, Bohuslav Martinu, and especially the famous Second Symphony of Henri Dutilleux. He had also been, it is important to note, a primary agent in winning the French over to Brahms—fifty years later than any other culture.

Except for excerpts in the concert hall and a single *Pelléas et Mélisande* in Florence at the end of his career, Munch did not conduct opera. This was as much a matter of upbringing as anything else: The Munch children were not sent to the theater for their entertainment, and employment in pit orchestras was something that one needed to escape. He counteracted his apparent aversion to opera with his deep spiritual connection to works with biblical and liturgical texts, notably the Bach passions and cantatas.

On the podium Munch was arresting (many thought seductive) in appearance, an effect emphasized in later years by what was usually, enviously, described as the "silver thatch" of his hair. He conducts with a long, pliable baton similar to the style preferred also by his countrymen Pierre Monteux and Paul Paray. His most characteristic gesture is the enormous arc traced by the baton when the right hand moves from bent above the head to fully extended by the knee. (I like to think of this as a "French" stroke, since Habeneck—another violinist/ conductor—and his bow are pictured in the same starting position.) The left hand points, shapes, accentuates, and provides nuance in more or less the modern manner—though rather less than more. The face is a veritable catalogue of encouragement, desire, pleasure, insistence, and, when circumstances demand, apotheosis—or its infernal opposite. Debost writes of *allégresse, angoisse, fatalité,* and *tendresse,* admiring especially the willingness to be vulnerable in public.[12]

From the waist down Munch was immobile, a stance that he insisted his conducting students follow. (One of the Tanglewood students, Zubin Mehta, complained that the only thing Munch ever said to him was "Keep your feet together."[13]) For rehearsals he would perch on a stool, and in later years he occasionally sat during concerts. At his most loquacious his verbal instructions were minimal: "*Vibrez . . . Plus vite!*" and sometimes poetic: "*Et maintenant, aussi souple que les hanches d'une danseuse*" ("as supple as a ballerina's hips").[14] In central Europe these would be delivered in German, and he would always respond to German crosstalk in that language. In the United States he would mutter phrases in whatever language came first to mind. (He was quick, too, to summon a certain chauvinism to get what he wanted: "You are, after all, French." "This is the Boston Symphony.") Partly it was a matter of efficient communication in an increasingly English-speaking world by a person who had learned the language late in life. His taciturnity was also, however, a matter of theory. Conductors should be seen and not heard.

At the beginning he attracted a good deal of attention in the press for conducting from memory, still at that time considered to be a major feat. Other corners of his technique were more significant to his results, for instance the bowing habits he brought from his years as violinist in quartets and orchestras. Composers including Roussel sought him out for help with bowing, and it was through a misunderstanding of bowing strategy that he first made friends with Toscanini. He believed it was incumbent on the conductor to have thoroughly mastered a score before introducing it to an ensemble, and he was given to long, restless nights before beginning a new work with his players. There are few anecdotes suggesting legendary memory for detail but many threads of evidence that he knew his texts flawlessly and often proffered corrections to manuscript scores and sometimes suggestions for their improvement.

It is also worth noting the diligence with which he went about perfecting relationships with his constituents around the world. He was even comfortably resigned, for the most part, to the necessity of critics: "I have been assassinated many times, but I am still among the living."[15]

What women remembered about Charles Munch was his undeniable sex appeal—the smile and the hair, of course, but also the eyes, which to many conveyed mischief or even outright desire. In his early middle age, he was a matinee idol. "*Ah, qu'il était beau!*" remarked one of his principal players, a half century later, with a sigh. In Boston he was fondly and often called "le beau Charles" or "Charles le beau"—Charles the good-looking. In the late 1930s *Elle* magazine polled a hundred thousand female readers, asking, with a *pudeur* appropriate to the era: "*Avec qui aimeriez-vous dîner ce soir?*" (What man would you like to have dinner with tonight?). Winston Churchill was first, and Munch was the runner-up. Jean Marais, President Auriol, Gary Cooper—and Stalin— were further down the list. Shortly after the article appeared, Munch took his teen-aged niece to the Bon Marché department store to buy a handbag, and they were swamped with excited salesgirls clamoring for a glimpse. (The niece didn't like the purse either: "Black alligator. And I was just a girl. He had his very particular ideas about fashion." Then she added: "Music sometimes bored him, but never the flattery of pretty girls."[16])

Others remember his sense of pleasure, again in the French sense of the word: games of *belote* with his musicians, naughty charades, pranks. He went to great length, for instance, to send one of his stuffier musicians a picture postcard from one of the less reputable Paris *boîtes de nuit*. After work, but only then, he enjoyed a fine meal—sometimes simple, frequently in very high style. Few came away from his table unimpressed by the cuisine and hospitality.

Still others recall demonstrations of exceptional personal warmth, how thoroughly "gentle, protective, and personally generous" he was to his musicians.[17] Players who were very young at the time tend to remember how kind he was to them during their audition, whatever its result. Often, when he was together with others from his inner circle, he would organize joint letters to loved ones conspicuous by their absence.

His financial largesse was considerable, measured by the frequency with which he waived his own fee on behalf of a worthy cause, rounded off the proceeds to next higher level, and quietly paid some unmet need of his orchestra. We will look carefully at the evidence of his quiet heroism during the Occupation of Paris. In 1950 he joined Yehudi Menuhin and Igor Stravinsky to meet the cost of a new cortisone therapy it was hoped would cure the pianist Dinu Lipatti of leukemia. His was the (largely unmentioned) lead gift to rebuilding the Shed at Tanglewood in 1956, and he left the Boston Symphony with an endowed Charles Munch Fund on his retirement.[18]

As a visually oriented person, he surrounded himself with things of beauty, from canvasses of celebrated painters to the works of master photographers and artisans. Friend and patron of Raoul Dufy, he was in part responsible for Dufy's interest in the orchestra and allowed him to sketch from the percussion section during rehearsals.[19] He collected fine porcelain and silver—and heirloom violins—and was well known by Boston antiquarians for his furtive visits to their shops. Works of Monet and Pisarro hung in his study. He does not appear to have been widely or deeply read in literature and poetry but knew his European history well enough and a certain amount about the beginnings of the orchestra and its repertoire.

The preponderance of the evidence, then, suggests a simple but urbane, kind but courageous individual whose personality and work people found easy to like. Three American presidents, Truman, Eisenhower, and Kennedy, knew and admired him, as did government officials in France (notably including André Malraux, though Munch appears to have loathed Charles de Gaulle) and not a few kings and queens. A generation of the most influential Bostonians adored him—including, again, the Kennedys. For a man who was, so far as we can tell, oblivious to *amour-propre*, Munch was recognized with dozens of major honors and awards, including the Legion of Honor in France and near-simultaneous doctor's degrees from Harvard, Boston College, Tufts, and (later) the New England Conservatory. Proper Bostonians thought of him and addressed him as "Dr. Munch."

American families tuned in as faithfully to the Boston Symphony nationwide radio broadcasts as they had to the NBC Symphony just preceding them—and as they would, soon after, to the televised Young People's Concerts of the New York Philharmonic with Leonard Bernstein. The Boston Symphony Transcription Trust circulated performances all over the country. Introduced by the familiar patrician voice of William Pierce, they are a sometimes overlooked high point of the radio age. Countless students in the 1950s and '60s learned Munch's corner of the repertoire (Berlioz, Saint-Saëns, Debussy, Ravel) from the great RCA stereophonic recordings made in Symphony Hall, just as they learned Dvořák and Brahms from Szell, Wagner from Solti, and Mahler from Bernstein.

Charles Munch remains enigmatic on several scores. For a man who came from and was surrounded by distinguished lineages—he was related to Albert Schweitzer and Jean-Paul Sartre and had grown to adulthood at the center of Strasbourg's most gifted musical dynasty—he lived a private life of remarkable solitude. A current of sadness permeated his life, and everybody noticed that, too. "*Je suis bien seul dans la vie*," he remarks with indescribable poignancy.[20]

After him there was neither a widow nor children, and, lacking them, little of the myth-making apparatus left behind by Toscanini (through his son, Walter, and daughter, Wanda Toscanini Horowitz) and Koussevitzky and Monteux (who were survived by spirited wives). All three of these, incidentally, adopted the United States with more enthusiasm than Munch ever did. His celebrated older brother Fritz was focused on Strasbourg, and his beloved heirs, Nicole Henriot-Schweitzer and her husband, the admiral, also had major careers of their own. The same could be said of his three protégés, Jean Martinon, Charles Dutoit, and Seiji Ozawa, who all acknowledge their debt to him but were too occupied to go into the question in any detail.

Nor did his own personality favor the building of legends. Notoriously private, he would flee worshipful crowds and even admiring, powerful trustees by various prearrangements with his chauffeur—hoping to dine at home or with a handful of intimates and working above all to keep Mrs. Koussevitzky at bay. One journalist noted that he had devoted as much energy to avoiding publicity as he had to earning it honestly as a musician. The facts had to be pried loose from him. He did not talk much about music even to his friends, preferring to chat about fine wines and other luxuries to savor in life—a love of life, Claude Samuel remarked, that he nevertheless brought to his concerts and recordings.[21]

Once he came to the United States, this apparent reserve was accentuated by his minimal English. He had no reason to know languages beyond French and German until he was more than forty years old, and he began to use English every day only as he approached fifty. His spoken English remained halting to the end, though after the second season in Boston it would have been impossible to mistake his meaning. In an interview during the intermission of a 1967 concert with the New York Philharmonic—his last engagement there—he sounds very old indeed, with a voice made deep and gravelly by time and tobacco. You can sense when he smiles or is about to chuckle, and when the Occupation is brought up with reference to Honegger's Second Symphony, there is a marked darkening of the atmosphere as he follows every line of the interviewer's winding question. One cannot help but enjoy his inadvertently comic response: "I make in New York the creation of this symphony.... The Swiss peoples are not happy if you say that Honegger is a Frenchman." Of the New York Philharmonic he says, "I have the great pleasure to play with these peoples."[22]

Though he must have had to attend to an enormous correspondence merely to keep up with daily life, his personal letters are sparsely preserved, and one of his greatest admirers said in the *Boston Globe* that he was the worst correspondent he had ever met.[23] Nevertheless, there is much to be learned from his exchanges with his composer friends . . . and still more from his book-length reflections on his *métier,* called in English *I Am a Conductor* (1955). This fascinating volume suggests an author who has at the very least reflected deeply enough on his profession to have formulated a comprehensive theory of it and who—even if he worked with an associate on a manuscript that was subsequently rewritten in one or both languages—has developed a stylish ring. It also belies the notion that Munch did not think deeply about his work: "Spontaneous" and "intuitive" approaches are not thoughtless ones.

That he was not by nature a committed intellectual means that we find him at the sidelines of the great aesthetic debates that fill the pages of the journals of the time. He was instead a man of action and for much of his life almost limitless energy. When his world fell apart for the second time in the 1930s, pitting his two native cultures against each other, he stayed on the scene and adroitly steered, protected, and provided for an orchestra of a hundred French citizens while less overtly seeing to any number of other interests of his country and compatriots. While politicians pushed and pulled in the Middle East, Munch went to Palestine (considerably before Leonard Bernstein did) to conduct what is now the Israel Philharmonic, with whom he developed a close and ongoing relationship. Next came the Baalbeck Festival, where he was decorated by the president of Lebanon, and eventually Nasser's Cairo. He arranged goodwill tours to the Soviet Union, Eastern Europe, and Japan. When Boulez was at odds with the entire French establishment and making headlines every day, Munch, very obviously in physical decline, abandoned what little retirement he had achieved to oversee the organization of the Orchestre de Paris, the *orchestre de prestige* he believed was essential to his nation's artistic standing. There is every indication he did not expect to last long as founding conductor.

Here is as good a place as any to point out that a certain number of his most vexatious characteristics—incessant worrying over contractual details, for instance, even as he was accruing real wealth—have to do with his determination not to repeat mistakes of committing to arrangements he disliked. Often he failed to understand the implications of language he did not much want to read in the first place. What people sometimes thought to be evidence of boredom and routine in his daily work was usually instead real, life-threatening fatigue brought about by one of the several conditions from which he suffered and which his managers and physicians routinely, though without much success, warned him against incurring. By the same token we will have occasion, too, to encounter tragedies in his personal life that he never took the time to overcome.

To take Charles Munch as a representative of music in the mid-twentieth century is to grapple with the conspicuous internationalization of orchestral practice that took place between the 1920s and the 1970s and with the emergence of what is now generally known as the "maestro" concept of conducting. It is to observe the canonization of a part of the French repertoire—Berlioz, Debussy, and Ravel—and the loss of another, perhaps larger, portion. It is to witness any number of steps in the Franco-American experience and especially how Francophilia helped compensate for the sudden disincentives toward playing the "German" repertoire.

And it is to try to understand why, in the long run, only Monteux and Munch were recognized internationally as the voices of French music. After all, Munch had the enormous good fortune to have been raised in an elevated musical and intellectual milieu where the diet was Bach, Mozart, Beethoven, and Brahms.

Any number of conductors were working just as hard as he was on behalf of French music, some of whom—notably Paul Paray and Roger Désormière— were well established in Paris before he first took the podium there. It cannot have been indefatigability, long residence in the United States, or amusingly French personality traits, for Paray in Detroit had all of those, too.

The pages that follow address all of these questions and suggest answers for many others. In the first portion we will find Munch claiming his place at the pinnacle of the French musical establishment, then making the pivotal decision not to emigrate but to stay in Paris throughout the war and Occupation to do what he could to lead French music to its rightful place in whatever modern culture might mean. Then we examine Munch's abrupt departure to the New World and his arrival there as the major conduit in transmitting French orches- tral literature forward into the postwar period, an accomplishment virtually unrivaled in the case of Berlioz, Roussel, and Honegger. Munch will give us much to think about as to an orchestra's essence and how it serves its many con- stituencies. As an orchestral patriarch, he had few peers indeed.

My personal involvement with Charles Munch follows three main channels. Like most others in my generation, I learned the Berlioz Requiem and *La dam- nation de Faust* and *Roméo et Juliette* from the Boston Symphony recordings on RCA, and he thus played a major role in my career decisions to become a con- ductor and to write about Berlioz. The turning point in my personal experience of Munch—from awareness to a certain form of discipleship—was my oppor- tunity, as a very young man, to hear him conduct the *Fantastique*. When Charles Munch came to Raleigh with the new Orchestre de Paris in November 1968, several students from Duke University in nearby Durham organized an expedi- tion to hear the concert in the Friends of the College series at North Carolina State University—a series I myself had attended faithfully for many years. On the program that night were Barber's *Medea, Daphnis et Chloé*, Suite 2, and the *Fantastique*. I went to hear the *Fantastique* and returned smitten with *Daphnis*. That was on Sunday; on Wednesday in Richmond, Virginia, Munch was found dead by his valet, having succumbed to heart failure earlier that morning.

Munch was also a central figure and certainly one of the most intriguing characters in the history of the Paris Conservatory Orchestra, or the Société des Concerts du Conservatoire. The first major dossier I studied from that archive was titled "Affaire Munch," which dealt with the long saga of his departure. The next was labeled "Guerre, 1939–45." And when *The Société des Concerts du Con- servatoire, 1828–1967*, was done, I harbored, in the case of Munch, a strong sense of unfinished business—further, perhaps, of a debt as yet unpaid. I under- stood too little about Strasbourg and the Munch dynasty, virtually nothing about the Boston Symphony between the time of my own birth and when I began to be aware of the broadcasts of the late 1950s, and nothing at all of what had transpired in the life of Charles Munch between the great Berlioz recordings and that dramatic week in November 1968. Too, I thought I had learned from *The Société des Concerts* something about what concert programs and, slipperier still, audio and video artifacts can tell us—and what they cannot.

I also wanted to spend more time around Boston and its orchestra in order to understand the forces at work in a historic and advanced musical culture, a place teeming with institutions of higher learning in the arts—much as I had tried to understand the same kinds of things about the Paris Conservatory Orchestra. I would come to have the same curiosity about Strasbourg later on.

The sources for this book repose for the most part in three obvious collections: the archives of the Société des Concerts du Conservatoire and the Orchestre de Paris, those of the Boston Symphony, and the composer's estate. This latter—what had not already been given away—was left in its totality to his closest relatives and the companions of his old age, Jean-Jacques Schweitzer and his spouse, pianist Nicole Henriot-Schweitzer.

The Strasbourg archivist and scholar Geneviève Honegger, a natural sleuth (unrelated to the composer), had been accorded virtually free access to the Henriot/Schweitzer collection in the late 1980s, when both were still living. Fleshing this information out with documents from the Alsatian and Swiss families involved and from various public collections, she presented what remains the most useful published resource on the conductor, *Charles Munch: Un chef d'orchestre dans le siècle* (1992), as well as the remarkable exhibition "Charles Munch: Strasbourg, Bibliothèque Nationale et Universitaire, 23 November 1992–31 January 1993; Boston, Symphony Hall, 19 February–31 March 1993."

Honegger deposited photocopies of virtually all of her sources in the Bibliothèque Nationale et Universitaire in Strasbourg. (The building lies just beside the equally grand structure that housed the Strasbourg Conservatory in the Munch years.) Here Honegger's collection complements an impressive collection of source documents, photographs, and recordings that form part of the library's Alsatian patrimony division.

The vast majority of known letters *to* Charles Munch come from his own collection, notably the dossier he labeled "Compositeurs" and into which he would slip autographs of individuals he considered major composers at the time or, interestingly, those who he thought might someday reach that stature.[24] Those who made the list included Roussel, Ropartz, and Honegger, of course, as well as Poulenc and Milhaud, but also Tcherepnin, Martinu, and others of that generation who had become his intimates. Additionally, there is a large prewar correspondence with Wilhelm Furtwängler, important for what it shows of the maneuvers of both French and German artists leading up to the Occupation.

Also among the conductor's papers is a list of early concerts kept by his wife, Geneviève (Vivette) Munch, lovingly typed on octavo-sized notebook paper. There are perhaps a hundred letters from his mother to "Concertmeister Charles Münch" in Leipzig and a few from his father, in a dossier marked "Papa." The close relationship he enjoyed with his older brother, Fritz, is richly documented, especially in pictures. Finally, the Henriot/Schweitzer collection also includes leatherbound volumes of his Boston Symphony Orchestra programs, as well as a bound collection of mint copies of his recordings.

From his wife's side of the family there is precious documentation of her father's life and work and of the formidable musical life in Villefavard, stimulated by her younger sister, Juliette Maury Ebersolt (1889–1982). Of Geneviève in adulthood there is very little—a single photograph, accounts from nieces and nephews—and nothing at all of her considerable literary estate and what must have been a large correspondence with her husband. This is attributed by the family to the inadvertent disposal of an attic's worth of old property.

I describe the formidable archive of the Paris Conservatory Orchestra elsewhere.[25] In Boston there are the season programs and press clippings for every season, plus correspondence and contractual files, the trustee minutes, press releases, and many dozens of press photographs, as well as rather good collections of ephemera and memorabilia. Additionally, there are the Boston Symphony Transcription Trust master tapes, a copy of each RCA record, and some of the original films and videos. What appears to be Munch's presentation copy of the Société des Concerts lithograph of Beethoven has been hung over an employee's desk; the handsome bronze bust that used to sit beside the microfilm reader has been installed in the upstairs lobby.

I have also had the privilege of interviewing many who were close to Charles Munch, beginning with the great flutist Michel Debost and then Michael Steinberg and Margo Miller, two former journalists with the *Boston Globe*. Geneviève Honegger made all her work, published and unpublished, available to me from the start. Jean-Philippe Schweitzer and his wife (and two formidable German shepherds and a donkey) welcomed me to the breathtaking property in Louveciennes and introduced me to his fond memories of his uncle, whom he called Pia and with whom he "played cars" every morning. Likewise, Jérôme and Annie Kaltenbach graciously opened the Maury family estate in Villefavard for my study, and Agnès Schoeller, whose favorite aunt was Geneviève Munch, née Maury, shared memories of Munch and his wife in Paris, Villefavard, and Boston—including the concert in March 1937, when Munch conducted an all-Ravel program in the Salle Pleyel with Ravel in attendance: hunched over and feeble, he stood just behind her to take his bow.

Most precious of all, especially for a writer who has spent most of his career wondering what the nineteenth century actually sounded like, are the audio and video artifacts left by Munch and his players in the twentieth. Efforts to bring this wealth of material under control include Philippe Olivier's *Charles Munch: Une biographie par le disque* (1987) and, rather more usefully, Philippe Morin's "Discographie intégrale de Charles Munch" (in *Le monde de la musique,* 1988) and James H. North's impressive *Boston Symphony Orchestra: An Augmented Discography* (2008).

Electronic databases taking shape at the Boston Symphony Orchestra and elsewhere provide chapter and verse on recording sessions and publication history. In due course we will consider less formal ways in which the Munch performances circulate. Suffice it to say here that a good portion of what appeared on 78 RPM and LP discs is now widely available in digital formats.

NOTES ON ORTHOGRAPHY

Munch or Münch?

The diacritic in the family name is used in Europe without necessarily suggesting nationality. What is clear is that Charles Munch was born with his umlaut and that it was more or less officially dropped by common consent of conductor and constituencies on the occasion of his arrival in Boston. The first Munch recording published in the United States, a Columbia release of the Saint-Saëns Organ Symphony with the New York Philharmonic-Symphony (1948) gives "Muench" on the original jacket but "Munch" in its re-release.

The conventional explanation is that, owing to the absence of diacritics in American newspaper fonts, a decision was made in 1949, jointly with the Boston Symphony administration and its new conductor, to adopt what became the familiar Americanized orthography. ("He has dropped the umlaut," reported the *Christian Science Monitor* on September 8, 1949, just as he got to town.)

In France, on the other hand, the usual explanation is that he dropped the umlaut at the time of the Occupation, that is, beginning in 1940. (At the Gewandhaus he had been called Carl Münch.) In fact, he himself used both styles in the 1940s, gradually giving up the umlaut in his signature; he used it very clearly in 1946, well into the postwar period.

Many of his European correspondents never gave it up when addressing letters to him, and his wife always used it even when writing in English. But for all intents and purposes the new spelling became definitive in 1949. In the United States it is customary to pronounce Charles in the American fashion and the last name with a hint of umlaut so as not to rhyme with "crunch."

ABOUT THE COMPANION WEBSITE

www.oup.com/us/charlesmunch

Charles Munch continues in an online appendix titled "Charles Munch: The Recorded Legacy." The narrative, presented in e-book form, treats the audio and video artifacts left by Munch as conductor, from his first recording in 1935 to the first recordings of the new Orchestre de Paris in 1967 and 1968. Linked to the essay (signaled with Oxford's symbol ⏵) are more than 125 brief audio clips that illustrate particulars of Munch's artistic approach and achievement, as well as video clips from televised broadcasts in the United States, France, and Japan.

Additionally, the Companion Website offers the Munch discography in the form of lists of recordings by date and label, by composer, and by CD reissue; it also provides summaries of off-air CDs and DVDs.

Users may access the companion website with the username **Music1** and the password **Book5983**.

Charles Munch

CHAPTER 1

⌒◊⌒

Strasbourg, Paris, Leipzig

September 1891–October 1932

At fin de siècle, with all of its insatiable appetite for classical music, Strasbourg ruled proudly over the intersection of the French and German cultures at their most vibrant. There Charles Munch sprang from an Alsatian family of striking character, given to careers in the clergy, education, and the arts. Even without the strong lineages Charles's generation acquired by marriage, it was a family of extraordinary accomplishment in both music and religion—sober, simple, perhaps stern.

Both parents, Ernest Munch (1859–1928) and Célestine Munch (née Simon) (1861–1942), came from serious stock. Ernest and his brother Eugène (usually called "Munch of Mulhouse") were important organist-choirmasters who had studied Bach with Phillip Spitta in Berlin (1882–1884) and were accustomed to playing the organs built in Alsace by the Silbermann dynasty.

Célestine was by birth and inclination unreservedly French, daughter of the noted Protestant minister Frédéric Simon, who finished his career as pastor of the Oratoire du Louvre in Paris. Five of her six children—Emma, Louise, Geoffroy (Idy), Frédéric (Fritz), and Charles (Charry)—were born virtually one each year between 1886 and 1891; Hans (Hansi) was born in 1897. Another near-sibling was their cousin Ernest-Geoffroy, called Nesti, who at age ten moved in with the family after the death of his father, Eugène, in 1898. They were all conspicuous achievers, especially Fritz, by all measures but international celebrity as important a musician as Charles. Emma was an admired local teacher whose own two children figure prominently in the story to come; Hans became a physician.

Ernest Munch is a central figure in Alsatian Protestantism, having guided regional practice toward a sophisticated classical-music tradition, one that absorbed into its active repertoire the more-or-less complete Bach canon following its publication in the Bach-Gesellschaft Edition. Of his multiple appointments, his work as organist at the church of Saint-Guillaume, a small, plain building on the quais of the river Ill, constitutes his most lasting legacy. Here, in a sober "temple of peace where men of good will might congregate,"[1] he established the celebrated Chœur de Saint-Guillaume. Its performances of the sacred music of Bach were soon noted by the press and slowly but gradually won over the public. Tourist guides mentioned the concerts, calling Munch the "cantata man." Future clergymen and teachers began to seek membership in the choir as part of their university education. Every year on Good Friday there would be either the Saint Matthew or the Saint John Passion. The repertoire came to include more than sixty cantatas, the passions, the Christmas Oratorio, Magnificat, and B-Minor Mass.

Munch would gather his associates around to examine each new volume of the Bach Edition as it appeared. Cantatas would be chosen for performance, and often the parts were extracted by hand, since the published ones did not yet exist. The concerts would be offered with the choir and members of the municipal orchestra squeezed into the choir loft with its Silbermann organ. ("I have never heard such sonority!" said organist and musicologist André Pirro, a student of Widor.[2]) When the choirloft and organ were eventually rebuilt to accommodate the increased numbers, they were inaugurated with a gala performance of the B-Minor Mass in February 1898.

This advanced music program was financed by cajolery and politics ("St.-Guillaume should be proud of a church choir that undertakes such noble tasks. Where is there another church choir in Alsace of which the newspapers speak so frequently?"), also by a charge of one deutsche mark for preferred seating at the otherwise free concerts. Amateurs mingled with professional soloists and orchestral players drawn from Strasbourg's historic civic orchestra.[3]

"What marvelous musical ardor prevailed at these rehearsals! Munch did not have to pay any attention to the choir, for the choir knew its business; he was able to concentrate exclusively on the orchestra. He conducted the rehearsals with much care and sensitivity and never wearied the performers. It was evident that he had prepared these rehearsals down to the last detail. He never lost time with secondary matters but devoted all his efforts to the essential thing."[4] Any number of other particulars of this story evoke a kind of déjà vu, so similar is the Munch family of Alsace to the Bachs of Leipzig: Madame Munch, for instance, surrounded by her brood but at the same time attending to the choir's music library, then habitually inviting the soloists and distinguished guests to dinner after the concerts. "We, who had a chance to appreciate her activities close at hand, were filled with admiration for her gentle and distinguished manner in everything. Hers was a remarkable personality, with a great nobility of soul."[5] No relative escaped one manifestation or another of the Bach fever radiating from Strasbourg.

Munch and his company concerned themselves, too, with Schütz, Handel, and Mozart; requiems of Verdi, Brahms, and then Berlioz; the sacred music of Franck. Eventually there was a *Missa solemnis.*

Ernest Munch played and conducted at Saint-Guillaume for more than thirty years, seldom taking a vacation, always "edifying the faithful by his prestigious playing."[6] His reputation for fidelity to his post and to the repertoire he loved more than made up for his occasional outbursts of temper. And if Saint-Guillaume was on the whole a small enterprise, less official than the Strasbourg Conservatory and its Orchestre Municipal, it was nevertheless a formative influence on the French. Later, in 1928, Fritz Munch's version of the Saint Matthew Passion with the Paris Conservatoire orchestra and the Saint-Guillaume choir was the first Conservatoire concert to be broadcast on the radio.

His father's example at Saint-Guillaume encouraged Charles to master the great orchestra-and-chorus scores—a repertoire he took with him to Boston. He absorbed, rather than rebelled against, the family's spiritual rooting and moral compass, which went on to serve him well in a decidedly secular career. He was unwavering in his religious faith even though he did not outwardly practice it. Inwardly, he was a man of humility before a powerful God, in whom he found certain refuge from adversity, as promised to agents of peace and goodwill.

With Fritz Munch, older by only a year, the fraternal relationship was deep and lifelong. The cellist of the family, Fritz went on to have a major career as conductor and music administrator in Strasbourg. There must have been rivalry in their youth: Charles likely felt the need to find his own way into situations where he was something more than the younger of the Munch brothers. Meanwhile, Fritz was the serious one, purposeful, studious, given to sobriety of dress and the bespectacled look. This is not to say that family life was always tame. The spectacular quarrel was common, in one case involving broken furniture. There was the chaos of many children in the house at once, not to mention the ongoing cultural and linguistic tug-of-war. Nonetheless, there was always music and merriment. The country house in Niederbronn-les-Bains, in the Vosges, was affectionately called La Boîte à Musique: the Music Box.

The Munch family lived a comfortably bilingual life, at home speaking Alsatian to one another and French to their mother. (Fritz was sent to Paris for a year to perfect his French.) In primary and secondary public schools in Alsace-Lorraine of the period, classes were taught in German. German was the language of Martin Luther (and Bach), and Charles Munch always thought of and cited biblical quotations in German. Papa's preserved letters to his sons are in German; Maman's in French. German phrases pepper the French-language correspondence with Albert Schweitzer in the kind of insider patois that persons of bilingual culture enjoy: dialect, word plays, things that can be said better in one language than another. Posters and concert programs in Strasbourg were published in French. Charles Munch spoke correct, often beautiful German but thought in and preferred to use French. His manner of expression was throaty and guttural, often with bemused facial expressions. Everybody in both Paris and Boston did Munch imitations.

For some a bicultural identity strikes imbalances that must be resolved in favor of the one or the other. The Strasbourgeois, after all, witnessed firsthand the Franco-Prussian War and both world wars—to say nothing of Strasbourg (where Rouget de Lisle wrote the *Marseillaise*) in the aftermath of the French Revolution. For Charles, having two nationalities enhanced his access to the international stage he came to seek. It was also a fundamental factor in his tolerance and humility, since he had grown up accepting sharply opposing forces. He ended up remarkably free of pettiness.

The catalyst in the brew, the defining personality, was Uncle Eugène's favorite pupil, the young Albert Schweitzer, who came to town at age eighteen to study theology at the University of Strasbourg. Schweitzer already knew Ernest Munch by virtue of musical collaborations between Strasbourg and Mulhouse, so the Munch household received him *en famille* from the moment of his arrival, all addressing each other with the familiar *Du* and *tu*. Schweitzer, fresh from his organ studies with Widor in Paris, was put right to work in the Bach concerts and was soon second in command. (The other leading figure was Ernest's younger brother Geoffroy, or Gottfried, Munch, called Friedel, also a pastor.) Albert Schweitzer's loving essay "Ernest Munch, as I Remember Him" is a powerful account of the Strasbourg Bach revival.[7]

Charles Munch was a toddler when Albert Schweitzer became a member of his extended family. He thus grew to witness, as he himself was emerging with prodigious artistic gifts, the explosion of the Schweitzer phenomenon: Schweitzer's doctorate in philosophy in 1893, his licentiate in religion in 1900, his sermons as minister of the Saint Nicholas Church beginning in 1899, his epochal work, *The Quest for the Historical Jesus,* in 1906—when Munch would have been fifteen. At the same time came Schweitzer's pamphlet *The Art of Organ Building and Organ Playing in Germany and France* (1906) and *Johann Sebastian Bach* (1908).

It is no small thing to have one's worldview formed by the direct influence of a great thinker. At a minimum Charles Munch was a disciple. But Munch and Schweitzer were also mutual friends who nourished their affection for each other for six decades. In 1918 Schweitzer offered the counsel that allowed Munch to construe a simple but compelling personal code. Later Munch not only kept a watchful eye on Schweitzer and his hospital in Lambaréné, Gabon, but also followed his example by routinely associating himself with peace movements and humanitarian undertakings. Albert Schweitzer was quite simply the most potent intellectual force in his life.

The Munch family was closely identified with all three official institutions of musical life in Strasbourg: the conservatory, the subscription concerts of the Orchestre Municipal (now the Orchestre Philharmonique), and the regional musical festivals, which traced their roots to the mid-1880s and coalesced into the modern Strasbourg Festival. This last, to which both Fritz and Charles Munch lent their considerable prestige, was primarily the work of the reigning dynasty of serious music in Strasbourg, the house of Seligmann Wolf and his offspring, Lazare, Gustave, and Roger. The Maison de Musique S. Wolf à Strasbourg, just across the street from the presbytery that housed Ernest Munch and his family, was a music store, publishing house, subscription service, box office, and production agency for concert music in the whole of eastern France. It was a place of rendezvous and crossover for French and German artists: At the Magasin Wolf, for instance, Richard Strauss met Gustav and Alma Mahler to read *Salomé* to them in 1905.[8] The Wolfs were also important philanthropists and leaders in guarding the welfare of the Jewish community in the region.

The Strasbourg Conservatory, with its noble building and pervasive atmosphere of accomplishment, was also a place of political intrigue and not a little partisan struggle. In the aftermath of the Franco-Prussian War, Alsace-Lorraine had been proclaimed a Reichsland under the direct authority of the German emperor. While the state government focused its attention on establishing a Reichsuniversität and mandatory instruction in German, the largely French city council concentrated on reestablishing its municipal infrastructure, including its Conservatory of Music, which reported to the mayor. It was in this context that Franz Stockhausen (1839–1926) was appointed director, a position he held for nearly four decades. He was an Alsatian, with long family ties to the area.[9]

As the theater had its own orchestra, the professors and their students were free to run a municipal orchestra and concert series of their own. The net effect was that the Germans dealt with opera (and the opera house) and the French, with concert music. "*Nous ne devons laisser aux Allemands que ce que nous ne pouvons faire nous-mêmes,*" thought Stockhausen: "we must leave to the Germans only what we can't do ourselves."[10] The municipal concerts resumed in 1872, and by 1877 the conservatory was fully reorganized. Though based on German models from Leipzig, Cologne, Berlin, Munich, and Stuttgart, the charter was written in French. In the first decade of the twentieth century the Strasbourg Conservatory had twenty-six professors and some 400 students, including 181 in advanced classes: 147 French, 19 Germans, 15 foreigners. Ernest Munch was appointed professor of the Protestant organ class in 1885, simultaneous with his creation of the Chœur de Saint-Guillaume.

Stockhausen also conducted the subscription concerts, which soon became central to Strasbourg life. His repertoire was rooted in a mixture of German and French composers that, tellingly for Munch, emphasized Brahms, still unpopular in Paris. In 1905 the first festival of Alsace-Lorraine featured a remarkable concert in which Strauss and Mahler each conducted half the program; later in the week Mahler led Beethoven's Ninth. At the second festival, in 1907, Colonne came to conduct the complete *La damnation de Faust*—a work Munch later popularized in Boston. Otherwise, neither Berlioz nor the New French School—Fauré, Debussy, Ravel—was high on Stockhausen's list.

Stockhausen's illness and subsequent decline led to the appointment in 1908, after the failed candidacy of Ernest Munch, of Hans Pfitzner as director of the Strasbourg Conservatory. Pfitzner, a German, revamped the conservatory to focus on composition and rebuilt its connections to the theater/opera house, generally looking to the leading German institutions of music making for his personnel. On the whole he enjoyed his life in Strasbourg and at his nearby country house, where he was surrounded by good students who stimulated his work; in the end his Strasbourg years were among the most productive for his composition. He also enjoyed posing as an adversary of French music, famously remarking in front of the students *"Französische Musik? Das gibt's ja gar nicht!"* ("French music? No such thing!")[11] Yet not only did he conduct the Orchestre Municipal in its first performance of the Franck D-Minor Symphony, but he also led important performances of Berlioz, Bizet, Chausson, and Dukas.

Ernest Munch's career advanced during Pfitzner's tenure, since he was put in charge of the combined choirs of the conservatory and Saint-Guillaume—the festival chorus of nearly three hundred. He also conducted two of the ten concerts in each year's subscription series, the ones with full chorus.

Charles Munch's instruction in music and liberal studies took place primarily within the family circle, a chapter of his life he summarizes in less than two pages, so similar was it to the education of everybody named Munch. He mentions having been assigned to sing "Vom Himmel hoch" as a boy soprano in the choir and spending passionate hours at the organ, piano, violin, and even trumpet. There was chamber music *en famille*, with Idy and Charles at the violin desks, Emma and Louise with violas, and Fritz and Hans, cellos. His lessons in harmony and counterpoint came from Marie-Joseph Erb, and his first advanced violin lessons from concertmaster Anton Nast, who had come to Strasbourg in 1897 and remained until the end of the war. Munch succeeded him in that seat in 1919.

As close as we can tell, Munch began playing with the municipal orchestra, having been slipped into the last stands by his father, when he was fourteen or fifteen, possibly in 1905, more likely in 1907. (The incident he recounts of following Vincent d'Indy around Strasbourg, lugging his scores, must date from 1904, though d'Indy was in town not for a concert but a lecture.[12]) By this time Munch had become "a violinist first of all," allowed to put the instrument down only to study for his baccalaureate at the Gymnase Jean Sturm.[13] The first documentary evidence we have of Charles's playing is for a concert in Markirch, now Sainte-Marie-aux-Mines, near Ribeauvillé, south of Strasbourg, on December 9, 1911. Here Fritz and Charles, identified as violoncellist and violinist *aus Strassburg,* joined the local musical union and chorale for the seventy-ninth subscription concert, presumably in works by Bach.

In Strasbourg Charles Munch absorbed orchestral practice of unusual quantity, quality, commitment, and celebrity. Three near-contiguous passages in his autobiography—on the power of the pipe organist, the daily life of a musician, and his failed attempts at composition—also suggest an inborn understanding of the substance of being a conductor:

> The organ was my first orchestra. If you have never played the organ, you have never known the joy of feeling yourself music's master, sovereign of all the gamut of sounds and sonorities. Before those keyboards and pedals and the palette of stops, I felt almost like a demigod, holding in my hands the reins that controlled the musical universe.

> Walking [to work], opening the little door to the organ with a big old key, looking over the day's hymns lest I forget the repeats, finding a prelude in a good key in order to avoid a difficult modulation, choosing a gay piece for a wedding or a sad one for a funeral, not falling asleep during the sermon, sometimes improvising a little in the pastor's favorite style, not playing a long recessional because it would annoy the sexton—all this filled me with pride.

> I am forced to conclude that my mission as a composer was a delusion. I did learn something from my spatterings on music paper. I have an idea of the composer's compulsions. Knowing what difficulties he has had to overcome, I can admire his skill and his genius with fuller understanding.[14]

Hans Pfitzner, having become the director of the Strasbourg Theatre, was the benevolent monarch of all three musical institutions in town, assembling around him German assistants and associates with whom the young Charles Munch certainly interacted. Among these was Wilhelm Furtwängler, who spent a year in Strasbourg as apprentice conductor. Munch meanwhile earned his Gymnasium diploma on schedule at age twenty-one and set forth at once to Paris to study violin at the Conservatoire—and, in a striking parallel with Berlioz, medicine.

His Paris teacher was Lucien Capet, whose acquaintance Munch almost certainly made when the Capet Quartet played in Strasbourg. To no one's surprise the medical studies evaporated after a few weeks. He established himself in an attic apartment at 62, quai des Orfèvres and made frequent round-trips from home (as did Arthur Honegger from Zurich). The weekly lessons with Capet brought Munch in close contact with Honegger, who became an intimate, and Ivan Galamian, destined to become the most famous string pedagogue of his time. Capet, just turning forty, was approaching the peak of his fame as grand master of the Beethoven quartets: his third Capet Quartet (Capet, Maurice Hewitt, Henri Casadesus, Marcel Casadesus) had hit its stride. Munch would have thus mastered the Beethoven cycle (and the quartets of Debussy and Ravel) and, equally important, been conditioned in the bowing strategies that were at the core of Capet's technique—and of his book: *La Technique supérieure de l'archet* (Paris, 1916). The financial arrangements for this course of private study were not recorded. Presumably the family paid his living expenses, the lessons were offered at modest cost, and Charles earned a little spending money from his playing.

The difference between Charles Munch's student tenure in Paris and that of thousands of other promising musicians over the years, hundreds of them violinists, was how very short it was: the two academic years and concert seasons (1912–1913 and 1913–1914), what amounted to his freshman and sophomore years, at age twenty-two and twenty-three. Yet this was certainly enough time to have wandered into significant contact with musicians who were to become leaders of the profession, to have markedly broadened his exposure to the currents of contemporary metropolitan life, and to have developed an urbane outlook and a certain good-humored cynicism: "The more you know people, the more you like dogs," he quipped at the family table later on, quite captivating his mother.[15] There is evidence that he began to acquire his lifelong passion for art and art galleries in those two years. But two years was not long enough to bring him into circles of power and influence near the top of the French musical establishment. When, nearly two decades later, he returned to Paris with the firm determination to become a conductor and with formidable credentials as an orchestral musician, he was still, but for the familiarity of his family name, largely unknown. "Another Munch," the Parisians must have thought, in much the same way earlier generations elsewhere had greeted another Bach.

Fritz, meanwhile, matriculated in theology at the University of Leipzig, a development that subsequently yielded good connections for both his younger brothers. His cello teacher was Julius Klengel, principal of the Gewandhaus Orchestra, friend of Brahms and Nikisch, and teacher of Feuermann and Piatigorsky. He also profited from his father's close friendship with the cantor of the Thomaskirche and thus Bach's successor, Karl Straube.

In Paris, Charles naturally found his way into Protestant circles, including the salon of the retired pastor Édouard Maury—a foyer centered on literature, music, and art and architecture in an overall context of commitment to social equality and material progress. Here Munch encountered yet another astonishing dynasty of Protestant high society, wealth in quantities no Munch or Schweitzer could have known before then, and the gifted young woman who would much later become his wife and in due course stake him to his conducting career: Geneviève, the elder daughter.

The wealth was that of the Nestlé industries, located on the banks of Lake Geneva at Vevey, where in the late 1860s the German-Swiss chemist Henri Nestlé had invented and commercialized baby formula: Farine Lactée Henri Nestlé. In 1875, at the end of his career, he sold his business to a consortium of his partners, headed by Jules Monerrat. With the near-simultaneous invention of milk chocolate in Vevey, as well as Nestlé's subsequent merger with the Anglo-Swiss Condensed Milk Company, Nestlé secured its position among the fabulous success stories of European industry.

Monerrat, as proprietor of the *de luxe* Hôtel des Trois Couronnes and holder of mayoral offices, was already a significant figure in the region; the marriage of his daughter, Sophie, to the young clergyman, Maury, may thus have struck him as beneath her station—though his eventual satisfaction at the life she made for herself is abundantly clear. Sophie Monnerat brought to her marriage with Édouard Maury monetary comfort along with a first-class education and a certain taste for adventure. From their honeymoon they reported, in 1883, to Villefavard, a Protestant village in the French heartland north of Limoges, where Édouard had his first congregation. There, far from the family in Switzerland, Édouard and Sophie Maury established a life together based on the simple pleasures and personal associations to be found in that rustic environment—the place they would always consider their true home. There, too, the first of their two children was born, Geneviève, called Vivette, in 1886. Juliette, or Lili, followed in 1889.

Sophie kept a journal, later published by her granddaughter as *Du Léman au Limousin* ("From Lake Geneva to Limoges Country").[16] Her journal chronicles the wrenching story of Vivette's mysterious *maladie*, which she contracted at the age of ten, crippling her, to a greater or lesser degree, for life. The family had left

Villefavard at the end of 1886 for Saint-Gall in German-speaking Switzerland, where Édouard was the French pastor; from there they moved in 1890 to the Protestant church in Le Raincy, a suburb of Paris. In January 1896, with Sophie visiting her family in Switzerland, Vivette began to complain of pain in her right leg. By the time her mother got home, she was trailing a foot behind her and hardly able to stand. Rheumatism was at first suspected, then, as the pain and fever worsened, life-threatening influenza. After two weeks she stabilized, only to discover the aftereffect: one leg had drawn up to be shorter than the other.[17]

This was one effect of what was then called coxalgia ("painful hip"), now termed septic hip or septic arthritis: a bacterial infection within the joint. Vivette is lucky to have survived it at all in that pre-antibiotic era. In a few short weeks the Maurys saw what had thus far been an idyllic family life transformed into a nightmare of diagnoses and attempted cures, the certainty of braces and crutches for whatever time was left to their child, and inevitable psychological burdens on everybody involved. At one point Lili took to her bed for a time with the same symptoms and, wrote her mother, "It's not like she often acts out." When the primary physician prescribed a change of air, Édouard Maury resigned his ministry to be with his family in Biarritz—there buying and subsequently wrecking his first automobile, a three-wheeler, in an accident that left him unconscious for twenty hours and dazed for weeks. Nor did months at the seaside do much for Vivette's recovery.[18]

On the death of Sophie's father in late 1897, the Maurys inherited the bulk of his considerable estate. The unlimited resources made it possible for them to return to Paris in order to send the two girls to *lycée,* enhancing the school years with a healthy dose of European travel—in the old aristocratic fashion, with big hotels and a governess—during vacations. At home in the rue du Ranelagh and then a substantial private house in the rue de la Tour, the young women were given a patrician education in languages and the arts. Lili studied the violin with Pierre Monteux: "a small man, discreet, with a bass voice and a distinctive face with all the traits of a brown-eyed Israelite from the East." Saying "that's not how we play Haendel," Monteux and his new student rebuilt the piece at their first lesson, with "such precision that we knew right away our little girl was in good hands."[19] A few weeks later they all went off to hear the Joachim Quartet play the Beethoven cycle. Later Lili was a student of the great Édouard Nadaud, at the Conservatoire. In May 1904 her doting parents bought her the Guarneri del Gesù violin she owned for seventy years—now called the "Ebersolt" violin (1739).[20] By 1908 Lili was playing concerts with good orchestras, including a *Messiah* at the Trocadéro under the noted Baroque specialist Félix Raugel.

No less a figure than Romain Rolland took an interest in Vivette's writing and became in due course her mentor. Artists and artisans of similar quality—Paul Jouve, the art-deco masters François-Louis Schmied and Jean

Dunand—frequented the Maurys' Paris establishment. Though the Paris house is long gone, some of the artworks remain in the family.

Meanwhile, their hearts were still at Villefavard, and in June 1900 Édouard bought property overlooking the village pond and had a Swiss architect build his villa, La Solitude, using progressive materials such as reinforced concrete. In 1901 he funded and oversaw construction of a modest but lovely new Protestant church a few steps away; by 1907 there was a model utopian farm community to which several dozen children came for summer vacations. Papa's farm was thought by those around him to be eccentric, like his passion for photography and his Cavaillé-Coll chamber organ. Now that La Ferme de Villefavard is a successful venue for music study and performance, they think of him as a charmingly obsessive-compulsive patriarch.

Vivette earned her baccalaureate diploma, rare for a woman of that era, and wrote and published her first work in 1912. Her rustic short stories soon appeared as *L'Enfant à la charrue: Huit contes limousins du temps de guerre* ("The Plough-Boy: Eight Limoges-Country Tales from Wartime," 1918).[21] Lili married an architect, Jean Ebersolt (1879–1933), in 1913 and returned to Villefavard, establishing in turn a singing group, a concert series, and an artist colony that thrive today. After their parents were gone, La Solitude became Geneviève's house, and the chateau by the farm became Juliette's. It was Munch who thought the Cavaillé-Coll organ misplaced in the salon and convinced Mme. Ebersolt to have the instrument moved down the hill to the church, where it is still used for public concerts.

Geneviève was not cured: Rather, she learned to live gracefully with her physical condition and for the most part overcame its worst effects. She took the stairs unassisted for most of her life—her bedroom at La Solitude was on the second floor—but very slowly and as seldom as possible. By her twenty-ninth birthday, her mother observes, she had "grown stronger and can come and go in the house without her crutches. Her sweet face with the pensive eyes is as beautiful as ever."[22] But there is indescribable sadness in her story, too: When Lili becomes engaged and Geneviève and her mother are left to a life on their own, her eyes fill with tears. "It's not natural for a woman not to marry," she cries, obviously thinking of her own circumstances: "She must marry and have children."[23] And great poignance: On New Year's Eve in 1896, after the onset of Vivette's illness, her mother hugs her at evening prayer and says, "Won't you be happy to say goodbye to a year that's brought you all this suffering?"—to which Vivette, on the verge of turning eleven, responds: "It wasn't as bad as you might think, and if God sent this, it must have been for my own good."[24]

In all probability Geneviève Maury met Charles Munch in the spring of 1913, when she would have been twenty-eight and he twenty-two. She was already a free spirit, "not at all like anybody else in the family," according to her beloved niece Agnès Schoeller.[25] She became something of a secularist and an iconoclast—adopting a little boy at one point, then turning him over to other family members before she married. As for Charles Munch, with whom she was smitten from the beginning to the end, there rapidly developed a companion-ship that was to afford both of them paths to their fondest dreams and at least some degree of domestic contentment.

In a text released by the Boston Symphony at the time of Munch's appointment, the standard version of the Munch biography as regards World War I reads as follows: "When the clouds of war descended, in the summer of 1914, Charles Munch, the 'most French' of the family, with Paris residence, was unfortunately on vacation at Strasbourg. He was caught in the draft, for, together with his brothers, he was subject (by a circumstance of boundaries) to conscription in the Germany army. He was wounded at Verdun and discharged after the armi-stice at the age of twenty-six."[26]

The first part of this account, to the effect that Munch was vacationing in Strasbourg, is patently untrue. Madame Maury refers to him twice that summer in back-to-back journal entries written in Villefavard, both mentioning the impending war:

27 July [1914]. A pleasant day. Charles Munch spent his time at the piano, playing with that passion that young men of Germanic temperament often have. . . . The political news is bad. Austria has attacked Serbia; Germany will march with her for sure. What will happen next?

28 July. The papers are more and more alarming. Charles Munch is packing his bags to go home to Strasbourg. This he announced to us at 6:00 last evening, with the insouciance of his age and firing an imaginary pistol: bang, bang. It will be different when he has to put on the pointed helmet and fight against his French brothers.[27]

He was, by his own account, "on the last train to cross the blue ridge of the Vosges" before Germany declared war on France (August 3, 1914).[28] This seems altogether likely. Fritz, Charles, and Hans were all three conscripted and sent to the front by the end of the year.

Why he did this—go home to Strasbourg, given the near certainty of being drafted into the German army—can only be conjectured, though certainly he regretted it for the rest of his life. He may not have had a clear view of his options to begin with: It may have mattered only to be with, and not against, his brothers. Almost surely he had never thought much about nationality, and such ideas as he might have had were doubtless framed more by Schweitzerian altruism than any practical approach to the ethics and principles of citizenship. Strasbourg was home, after all, so natural a place to alight under these circumstances that he may not have given the implications of his last-minute train ride much consideration. Perhaps, in a clash of his two native cultures at that moment in his own life, there seemed no real choice but to side with the nation of Beethoven and Bach.

Perhaps the Maury family agenda was closing in, so leaving Villefavard for Strasbourg was a way not to spend the war years under their umbrella. The Maurys went on about their business: Geneviève made the Paris house into a way station for refugees and organized good works under the aegis of the Red Cross—much as she and her husband would do again during the Occupation. By several accounts she corresponded with Charles throughout the war, though this exchange does not survive. In Africa, Albert Schweitzer was detained by the French and later put into a concentration camp near Paris. In Strasbourg, Ernest Munch continued his responsibilities at Saint-Guillaume and the municipal concerts. People tried not to think about the aftermath.

The boys were at the front, thus in France, with Charles serving in the 51st Artillery. It appears that he was gassed during the battle of the Somme, near Péronne (July–November 1916), and wounded at Verdun, probably in late 1916. He was sent home, probably on medical leave, shortly afterward and was again in Strasbourg, by one account, in early 1917. However, he clearly went back into battle: A letter from his father to Charles, as late as June 1918, is grateful for news from the front and for the care Charles has taken to secure his brother Hans various contacts in Berlin: "Berlin is not an altogether harmless place for a young person."[29] The letter goes on to allude to Charles's agonies of personal makeup and to his career dilemmas:

> I am also blessed to think on you, dear Charri. May the time soon come when your inner being can find contentment and good fortune. Peace may be nearer than you can see. And our love is there to sustain you where and when it can, as your life takes a more favorable direction—already four years have passed since your career was waylaid. For now we look forward to your vacation; perhaps we can all meet at the country house. In the meantime farewell, and take heart in your music.[30]

The parents did not hide their concern with Charles's fragile emotional state during these months and with his nervous probing for career paths in the ensuing decade. It is clear that the war and its dénouement brought him to a crossroads he could no longer simply detour, then drove this impressionable young artist to personal and professional despair. We get the most direct wind of this from passages in the Munch-Schweitzer correspondence of many years later, which allude to a particular conversation they both saw as a turning point:

(Munch to Schweitzer, 1938.) To finish this letter, my dear Albert, let me repeat what I may have failed to acknowledge in so many words: the influence your being around had on my development when I was very young, the considerable stimulating role you exercised on the formation of my faculties. Never doubt the profound effect your powerful personality had on me. These are things we don't often talk about but which are nevertheless the most important things in life, and which stay engraved in our hearts forever.[31]

(Schweitzer to Munch, 1949.) I'm moved when you tell me of the place I occupy in your existence. I've not forgotten what you told me one day in Strasbourg after the first war: *Ich habe es im Herzen behalten.*[32]

He goes on to marvel that his ideas of *Ehrfurcht vor dem Leben,* commonly translated as "reverence for life," had gone on to win followers the world over. "I accept this as a gift of grace," he wrote Charles, "as I also am graced by your devoted friendship."[33]

A few months later, Munch's preface to a Schweitzer anthology in English confirms the moral compass he had found in Albert's philosophy during the painful days: a workable life code based on the simple ethics of human worth and the value of pardon. He pays particular homage to Schweitzer's *Out of My Life and Thought,* published in Leipzig in 1932 as *Aus meinem Leben und Denken.* "It was this book which kept alive my hope, my belief in victory. It inspired my work and helped me to fulfill my duty."[34]

Schweitzer's precepts afforded a spiritual path that freed Munch from denominational doctrine, at the same time reinforcing deeply held and irreversibly inculcated sentiments of his family upbringing. They had a role in knitting back together a worldview twice shattered by the Germans and in fostering his natural affection for his players and his publics as his various pursuits took their course. They may eventually have helped him establish a style of leadership that at once fulfilled family expectations and allowed him to discover his particular voice.

His postwar employment with the Compagnie Générale d'Assurances Rhin et Moselle, whose home office was in Strasbourg, lasted only a few months. With the arrival of French troops in Strasbourg and the consequently long-awaited return of Alsace to France came also the expulsions and recriminations leveled against representatives of the German governments and culture, as well as unimpeded opportunity for the French. Hans Pfitzner, the dominant figure in

Strasbourg music during wartime, left France permanently in 1918 to establish himself in Berlin and Munich, never to return.

The Schweitzers, now in-laws, suffered more consequences than the Munch family by virtue of their German name and language preference. Madame Munch notes in a letter to Fritz: "I opened the door and all the Schweitzers were there, thrown out of their home without a hearing! In two weeks they have to have emptied the house."[35]

Albert had quarreled with Ernest, probably about Bach, leading Madame Munch to write: "Albert is a Satan, the real thing: he'll be the death of Papa." Later Schweitzer was heard to say *"Dr. Münch isch a Simpel."*[36]

They had problems of their own: "They say our whole family is German. What do you do about that kind of accusation? . . . One day they're going to throw us out, too, and what Frenchwoman is more French than me?"[37]

Meanwhile, the new mayor and town council set out to ensure continuity at the conservatory, where Ernest Munch, was asked to be interim director. In a few weeks Guy Ropartz had been called to Strasbourg, commencing April 1, 1919, and Munch, as dean of the faculty, wrote to welcome him, looking forward to a warm and sincere collaboration, "all the more so as a Frenchman working under the banner of France for art in general and French art in particular."[38]

This masks what was in fact a bitter disappointment for the sixty-year-old Ernest Munch, inasmuch as this had been his last chance to assume the directorship of the conservatory himself. Nevertheless, Ropartz proved a capable, even visionary director and at length an icon of civic arts, not to mention the most significant artistic mentor to Charles Munch during what were probably the most critical of his formative years. In a poetic stroke Ropartz would come to be succeeded at the Strasbourg Conservatory in 1929 by none other than Charles's older brother, Fritz.

Guy Ropartz, of bushy beard and provincial inclination, so enjoyed emphasizing his Breton character that it masked his shrewd cosmopolitanism. In Paris he had studied with Théodore Dubois, Massenet, and Franck. During his two decades as director of the Nancy Conservatoire and orchestra concerts, some seventy-five miles to the south, he had overseen the creation of works of Chausson and Magnard (including the Chausson *Poème*) and had composed assiduously and with striking success. He came to Strasbourg with four symphonies, his opera *Le Pays* and not a few well-known works in other genres. Ropartz was comfortable financially and had acquired an estate at Lanloup on the Breton coast to the west of Saint-Malo.

In Strasbourg Charles Munch won the titles of second violin *solo* (principal violin II) and then concertmaster in legitimate *concours*, but there can be no denying the benevolent participation of Ropartz in a decision that surely pleased everyone. The results of his avuncular affection for Munch did not go unnoticed by his protégé: "He was to become my second father. Since then he has been my counselor and my guide. Without him, I would still be concertmaster of the Strasbourg orchestra."[39]

By the 1920–1921 season, Charles Munch's career as a professional orchestral musician was well under way. He describes his rehabilitation from wartime as a gradual return to the violin reached through playing the piano again using an old, rented piano: "Alone in my room I satisfied my hunger for music."[40] Now he led the "ardent life of the provincial musician whose fame is unlikely to cross any borders."[41] In addition to the orchestra concerts, he was entitled to a professoriat at the conservatory, where he gave lessons—focusing, said his successor and sometime student Alfred Grégoire, on bow technique (as Capet had done with him) and character and grandeur of sound. He also played in a string quartet and from time to time in the pit orchestra of the Strasbourg Opéra. The quartet was led by Théophile Soudant, with Munch as second violinist, Arthur Geurten, viola, and Émile Mawer, cello. The group would typically appear four times a year on the town subscription concerts, more often than not in musicales that involved a singer, pianist, and other visiting artists. At the opera he played under Paul Bastide, soon to become another mentor.

As a violin soloist Charles Munch was now, by virtue of his abilities and his position at the head of the orchestra, in considerable demand. He frequently appeared as soloist in the *concerts populaires* led by E.-G. Munch, playing the Saint-Saëns Third Concerto (April 6, 1921), the Mozart A-Major, K. 219 (June 7, 1922), the solo works in a memorial concert for Saint-Saëns (July 19, 1922), and double concertos of Corelli and Bach together with the noted virtuoso Marcel Reynal (July 26, 1922). He was in Paris for Saint-Saëns's funeral in December 1921, where he heard Philippe Gaubert and the Société des Concerts.

However, his best press resulted from a family event in April 1922: a Bach concert in the Church of Saint-Guillaume, featuring the A-minor and E-major concertos, with his father conducting. The press coverage mentions that he had recently played one of these with "the orchestra of Paris" and quotes the reviewer for *Le Monde musical,* who praised his "impeccable technique, breadth of phrase, and perfect intonation"; the *Courrier musical* mentioned the "sustained, pure expression in the Andante [of the A-Minor], and a lack of reticence that allows him to express at will the thoughts of the masters." Between the concertos, he played "one of those curious sonatas for unaccompanied violin, a work of noble inspiration where the composer arrives at true polyphony":[42]

He is at a stage of complete mastery of the pure classical style, acquired from his father, a specialist whose expertise is recognized everywhere. From his teacher Capet, he inherited a handsome, broad, delicious bowstroke. Its richness and beauty afford him supplemental charm and expressivity; his hard work has resulted in a solid technique—all of which allows him to render at will a master composer's thoughts.[43]

During the summer vacations, Charles Munch traveled to Berlin to study at the Berlin Hochschule with Carl Flesch, teacher of, among many others, Ivry Gitlis, Ida Haendel, Ginette Neveu, and Henryk Szeryng—all of whom were to figure in Munch's own biography. Flesch had an approach to violin playing that must have struck Munch as altogether different from what he had found in Paris with Capet: comprehensive violin playing, one might say, embracing a repertoire that went back to the beginnings of the violin itself, giving as much attention to the full corpus of chamber music as to quartets and concertos. His method book, *Die Kunst des Violin-Spiels* (1923, with its famous appendix, the Carl Flesch Scale System), was being recognized as the most influential since Baillot. So far as we know, Charles Munch's encounters with Carl Flesch represented the last of his lessons. There was little left to teach him, and the obvious lacuna in his education, metropolitan experience, he needed to fill for himself.

Strasbourg music making, however genteel, could not long succeed in sustaining the interest of a musician of Munch's talents and ambition. Already, he says, a new career goal was taking shape in the back of his mind as he felt himself observing Bastide and Ropartz "as an entomologist watches insects."[44] He learned scores as they came to his attention and studied the habits and needs of his fellow players as the weeks elapsed.

But it was an opportunity in violin, in Germany, that opened the next chapter in his career. For the 1924–1925 season he served as a principal player, probably the temporary concertmaster, in the historic Gürzenich-Orchester of Cologne, with a substitute engaged for the season of the Conservatoire Quartet back in Strasbourg.[45] Flesch sent him a warm letter of congratulation that September, in which he noted that Munch would be playing alongside the celebrated Bram Elderling, professor of violin at the Cologne Conservatory. Then, in early spring 1925, Karl Straube wrote from Leipzig that a front-desk position was open at the Leipzig Gewandhaus Orchestra, which Munch won by audition but hesitated to take—owing to the increased distance from Strasbourg and the need to extend his leaves of absence at home.

In a pair of letters dated March 1925, his parents argue strongly for Leipzig: "Your papa says that this is the kind of position you take without the slightest hesitation. If we'd thought that you were going to hesitate we would have telegraphed," wrote his mother. "And you can't come back to Strasbourg until something changes here: Soudant is trying to get his brother in your spot. . . . *Accept*, and the rest will work itself out."[46] In a subsequent letter she offered further arguments against Cologne: a workload that would compromise his health, the Catholicism there, the higher cost of living. The Gewandhaus was simply more important than the Gürzenich, and he already knew the three leading figures in Leipzig: Furtwängler, Straube, and Max Pauer, the director of the Leipzig Conservatory.

Ropartz did indeed grant him a second year of leave, and at length he yielded to the obvious arguments in favor of increasing his own professional prestige. He left Strasbourg definitively in June 1925 and was working in Leipzig by July. He was thirty-five. Strasbourg would be the locus of triumphant returns but never again his place of residence. His uncommon loyalty and devotion to the Strasbourgeois and their cherished institutions, on the other hand, he kept with him always.

Before he left France he acquired a 1734 Antonio and Ombono Stradivarius violin. Stolen from Ysaÿe in Saint Petersburg in 1908, it had resurfaced in Paris after World War I in the *lutherie* of Albert Caressa. We will encounter this instrument several more times before its arrival in Jerusalem, where it is now called the Kinor David (lyre of David).

In Leipzig he was called Carl and Karl, Münch and Muench, but seldom Charles Munch. The principal conductor of the great Leipzig Gewandhaus Orchestra was Wilhelm Furtwängler, successor (in 1920) to Arthur Nikisch and widely regarded in both Berlin and Leipzig as the heir to Richard Strauss. Furtwängler, for all his physical idiosyncrasies, was indisputably the master conductor of his era and in that respect very likely the most compelling one Munch ever came to know intimately. (Established conductors seldom enjoy the luxury of studying each other's work.) An articulate student of orchestras and conductors, Furtwängler was keenly aware of the tendency of the public and the critical establishment to worship instead of listen and was properly fearful of "a bored, hedonistic society that keeps orchestras as one keeps prize dogs: as a sport. . . . We have more compelling things to do than to take the old argument of which is better, the Boston or the Philadelphia Orchestra, more seriously than it deserves to be taken."[47]

Furtwängler was a stern disciplinarian though not a martinet, rehearsing for detail while allowing for spontaneity and for changing attitudes toward the canonic works. His understanding of music as anchored in Beethoven, Mozart, Haydn, and, because it was Leipzig, Bach was a matter of faith—long before the Nazi propagandists co-opted those composers. (At the Thomasschule this led to a certain rivalry with Straube over the "ownership" of Bach; Furtwängler was, on the whole, opposed to "period" practice.) He commanded a broad repertoire, a healthy portion of which was from his own time and place. Furtwängler and Munch got along well enough to have conceived an admiration for each other's work that demanded honoring before and after National Socialism.

Munch later credited Furtwängler with teaching him how to approach orchestral counterpoint. "But it was difficult to play with him. I often discussed with him his wavering beat that made things so hard for the orchestra. 'I do it because it sounds different,' he would say." Munch grew to dislike the Nikisch-Furtwängler tradition of delayed response to the baton: "When I conduct, I want an orchestra to play precisely on the beat."[48]

The Leipzig orchestra was, and had long been, at dead center of the German art-music establishment. Its activities and trends were scrutinized in multiple papers and magazines by the leading intellectuals of the day. Furtwängler's work was compared to Nikisch's, and traditions that went back to Mendelssohn were repeatedly referenced. How rapidly economic conditions were deteriorating and how the orchestra was being squeezed out by the galloping costs of basic living became clear only in retrospect.

The closer personal link was with Straube, who reported the following to the family:

> It's a great joy to have Charry here, but I fear he feels like a foreigner and is unhappy, despite my every effort to smooth his way. At the moment he's fulminating over the catastrophic performances at the Opera at the end of the season. He thinks he's in the nether boondocks. Tomorrow, Sunday [July 5, 1925], he'll play church music for the first time. I fear his critical judgment like a schoolboy would.
>
> On the whole his sensibility and spirit are too Latin for him to feel at home in Germany. France would have been more opportune for him but, better yet, Alsace. But let's wait and see. I'll do whatever I can for him myself: for me it's a joy to work with a Munch.[49]

They had argued the night before about the Brahms Requiem, which Fritz was conducting in Strasbourg a few weeks later: "I would have strongly counseled my brother against it: . . . it's flawed." Straube had retorted that, by that standard, nearly all of Berlioz's works would have fallen and yet Berlioz was still one of his favorites.[50]

Munch was second Konzertmeister to Edgar Wollgandt, who was also leader of the celebrated Gewandhaus Quartet; Julius Klengel, the cellist in the quartet, had been Fritz's teacher in Leipzig. The principal oboe player in the Gewandhaus was the young Rudolf Kempe, later a great conductor as well. The ensemble was populated with any number of musicians who had ties to Strasbourg, to the Munch family, or to Bach, and Munch probably found the work more congenial than he let on. He was to stay for six full concert seasons, 1925–1926 through 1931–1932.

Leipzig, a city central to music history from the early Baroque on, remained a major intellectual hub, located along the Vienna-Berlin axis and home to historic institutions of learning, publishing, and music both secular and sacred. Munch fell in naturally with the Baroque contingent, partly owing to his family associations, partly because he was the titular second violinist in any trio deployment. Within a few weeks of arriving he was featured with Wollgandt and Hans Munch-Holland in a Locatelli concerto grosso as edited by Arnold Schering, the distinguished musicologist who was a product of the university. The trio of Wollgandt, Munch, and Munch-Holland became a popular local commodity. It opened the 1929–1930 concert season, for instance, in which Handel's Concerto Grosso, op. 6, no. 6, was broadcast over the radio and, as it happens, was preserved as a disc transcription.

Meanwhile, he absorbed the Austro-German orchestral canon—cherishing the music of Schumann and Mendelssohn at its source, exporting Reger and Mahler, importing Bartók and Prokofiev—as a principal player in one of the world's major orchestras. He grew accustomed to the daily life of a full-season orchestra, resigned to its repetitiveness, intrigued by its capacity to reach into hearts and minds.

In June 1926 he tendered his resignation to the Strasbourg authorities. There had in fact been serious discussion of his returning, but his requirements had seemed to "the administration" too demanding, and no formal offer was extended. "It's regrettable for Strasbourg and its musical institutions, to which you bring such precious collaboration," wrote Ropartz. "It's regrettable also for you, whose career should naturally have developed in your native city. But you can still be of great use abroad as spokesman for an art that is too often unknown past the French border."[51]

Just afterward his mother wrote to sympathize with his case of *Heimweh*— homesickness. "But you know, dear child, that when you were here, you didn't pay much attention to us. . . . If you came back you'd just be unhappy again. . . . The main thing is to earn your livelihood and to do something that matters."[52] He was restless indeed—enough to look elsewhere: in April 1927 Otto Klemperer wrote to assure him that he had been offered the concertmastership of the Berlin Philharmonic, effective immediately.[53]

Over the next few seasons Munch led the ordinary life of a big-orchestra principal and became a familiar face to the Leipzig concertgoers. The German composer Kurt Hessenberg (1908–1994) writes in his autobiographical sketch that Munch was already a celebrity when he arrived in 1927; Hessenberg also had a particular memory of the premiere of his teacher Günter Raphael's Third String Quartet, where Munch, as a member of the Davisson Quartet, played the very difficult viola part.[54] He was frequently identified on the radio for his solo work, and his name crops up on the rosters of any number of outside concerts of the period.

In April 1928 his father's death from an abscess came during the brunt of the season, so he was unable to be in Strasbourg for the funeral. His mother soon focused her attention on getting a job for Fritz and a wife for Charles. In May 1929 she asks Charles:

How did things turn out? Married or not? Now that Fritz has been appointed, it's my biggest concern. I really want you to get engaged to Maury [i.e., Geneviève Maury, "Vivette"], but if afterward she wasn't happy with you, I'd never hear the end of it. I also wanted to say that it's not essential to be attracted to the body, my child: I've lived that. Papa loved me; our bodies were made one for another, but you know how our life was sometimes difficult. It seems to me that a companion who understands you, who loves you is a wonderful thing; furthermore she already has all the qualities necessary to your own *métier* and she already has affection for the family. But one thing I ask for sure: don't leave her in constant suspense. If you think you can marry her, tell her so, and quickly; if not, then tell her that too, so she knows where things stand: otherwise such a situation is doomed, and even though that would end her devotion. Such a love merits no less. Emma, who knows everything about her, says the same thing. If you don't marry her you'll need to stay in Leipzig until you find something else. You know, dear child, that if you don't marry her you'll certainly regret it some day, and if you do, you'll think you shouldn't have. You are like that. Stop worrying about it.[55]

Bruno Walter came to the Gewandhaus Orchestra in 1929–1930, at fifty-three, with every intention of finishing his career there. "To care for its continued mission and its enduring importance in the musical life of Europe seemed to me . . . a worthy task for the rest of my life. Like so many others, I expected to see Nazism decline . . . and, with the Gewandhaus as the center of my work, looked forward to a flourishing activity in a progressively musical and decreasingly political world."[56] Finding the city ugly and uninviting, he maintained his Berlin residence and commuted to Leipzig by car. Walter's arrival in Leipzig coincided with the stock market crash in New York and the collapse of the German economy.

Walter's first concert featured Munch as soloist, and there is some indication that they reasonably survived the difficult process whereby principals and new conductor grow accustomed to each other. Before the season was far advanced, Munch fell ill with a bladder infection that led to his hospitalization. "I'm living in a barracks room where the doctors mistreat me. They poke electric lights in there to see what's going on. . . . But on the whole I can't say that I'm suffering much, and I'm in good humor." The doctors, "crazy about their injections," told him he could go back to work in a few days.

During the 1930–1931 season the sinister truths enveloping Leipzig were becoming clear even to Munch, who would rather have paid no attention. The elections of September 1930 brought the National Socialist party within sight of controlling the country. Hostility was brought to bear on Walter as a Jew.

Nevertheless the 1931–1932 season of the Leipzig Gewandhaus Orchestra was its 150th anniversary, celebrated with a concert tour that took the orchestra to Strasbourg and beyond. For the Strasbourg concert on June 1, 1931, in the Palais des Fêtes, Charles Munch was the featured soloist in Mozart's Fourth Violin Concerto in an all-Germanic program that also included the *Eroica,* the *Unfinished,* and the *Meistersinger* Prelude. Of Munch in the "adorable" D-Major Concerto, the critic wrote:

> He occupies the brilliant but redoubtable post of *violon-solo* with the Gewandhaus orchestra. The excellent musician gave us the most intelligent, the most musical, the most exquisite performance of the concerto. The nobility and purity of his tone quality, the perfection of his style, showed the qualities of a master. He was warmly called back many times.[57]

After Bruno Walter's "thunderous" performance of the *Meistersinger* Prelude, the orchestra offered encores of the "Danse des sylphes" and "Marche hongroise" from Berlioz's *La damnation de Faust*—as though cultivating the French.

This was more than just another tour appearance by just another German orchestra, for it confirmed to the leaders of the Strasbourg musical establishment— Fritz Munch, Paul Bastide, the Wolf brothers—that gala concerts out of season could attract a viable public. They had long wished to assemble such events into a summer festival to complement the subscription concerts and theater performances of the main season. The umbrella organization, L'Association des Amis de la Musique de Strasbourg, reasoned that their undertaking had been baptized. The first Strasbourg Festival came into being the next year—in June 1932.[58]

Munch played solos twice in late 1931: a Handel concerto grosso on October 29, Bruno Walter conducting, and the violin solos in the B-Minor Mass on December 3, with Karl Straube. When Straube sprained his ankle, apparently sometime that fall, he asked Munch to stand in as conductor of a Sunday morning service—not so different from situations that must often have transpired at Saint-Guillaume in Strasbourg, but this one in Bach's own Thomaskirche and coinciding with Munch's growing lust for a conductor's career. It was a dramatic save that left his colleagues "wide-eyed."[59] It may also have led to his next appointment—to lead the Gewandhaus forces in their annual end-of-year *concert historique,* conducting from his seat "as [Mendelssohn's concertmaster] Ferdinand David had done about a hundred years before." His semiofficial conducting debut was thus on December 28, 1931, in the orchestra's smaller hall, where he led and played Spohr's Eighth Violin Concerto and works of Dittersdorf and C. P. E. Bach. A poster advertised *Leitung Konzertmeister Carl Münch*. "This concert was the decisive event for me," he recalled two decades later. "I decided to give up the violin and try my luck as a conductor."[60]

That he bragged about these successes directly to Furtwängler suggests that they were, at this point in their lives, rather closer than later accounts acknowledged. Munch regretted Furtwängler's departure and thought Bruno Walter the lesser talent. Furtwängler, though pleased to hear from Munch, was scarcely happy with conditions at the Gewandhaus: "Your message afforded a little consolation. I've sometimes thought that everything I built was reduced to rubble, that the things I did had been forgotten before they took hold. It's as though my six years of activity in Leipzig—six long years—counted for nothing."[61]

This is the first of some three dozen preserved letters from Furtwängler to Munch, beginning on the eve of Nazism in Germany and continuing through any number of failed and then purposefully diverted plans for Paris appearances by the elder conductor. The correspondence concludes with a get-well note on the occasion of Munch's first heart attack in 1952—where Furtwängler writes wistfully of passing his days in studied seclusion from the outside world. Agnès Schoeller, the favorite niece, says that Munch tried repeatedly to talk Furtwängler into leaving Berlin and relocating to Paris while there was still time and that Furtwängler's refusal to leave Berlin caused Munch real personal anguish and eventually a feeling of betrayal. Their one personal encounter after the war was brief and correct but hardly warm.

Walter returned to Leipzig in the spring of 1932 after a concert tour, only to be turned away from his concert and hall. During his absence Mendelssohn's statue had been removed.

The Boston Symphony press—and accounts based on it, including the most recent edition of the encyclopedia *Die Musik in Geschichte und Gegenwart*—suggests that as early as 1929 Munch was forced to decide between his positions in Leipzig and his French citizenship. That does not appear to be the case. Instead, it was at the very close of 1931, if even then, that he began seriously to consider relocating to Paris.

What is certain is that just as the summer reached its end and rehearsals for the 1932–1933 season began to loom, Munch suddenly notified his employers—the Leipzig town council, the conservatory, and the Gewandhaus Orchestra—of his irrevocable decision to leave at the end of the month. The orchestra and conservatory accepted with keen and clearly authentic regret, mentioning the great kindness, enthusiasm, and energy he had brought to his work in Leipzig. Bruno Walter sent warm thanks for his "precious work as Konzertmeister, soloist, and [in English] *last not least*—as conductor." They asked him back for the next season to conduct the *concert historique* in December: "You mustn't just steal away from our Gewandhaus."[62]

The key component in breaking the status quo in his life was neither politics nor dilemmas of race and nationality but rather his decision to take Geneviève Maury as his wife. That news reached Strasbourg, to his mother's delight, in June 1932, prompting an avalanche of letters.

Learning from Charles that marriage was at last a possibility, his mother went to Goetzenbruck to meet Geneviève Maury at the home of her own daughter and son-in-law, Emma and Paul Schweitzer. (Geneviève, a family friend, had been kind to their older son, Pierre-Paul, during his visits to Paris; her sister Juliette Ebersolt maintained the family connection with Pierre-Paul Schweitzer until her death in 1982.) Early on the morning of May 16, she sat on Emma's porch and, before the household awoke, tried to organize her thoughts about Mlle. Maury:

> I'm perfectly happy with the idea that you want to marry her and I'm persuaded that you can't find a better match. She was here nearly a week and spent a whole day with me. Now that she's not afraid of losing you and that a certain embarrassment of one sort or another has disappeared, I can only say that she's the person for you and for the whole family. Of course she isn't some little thing you can do with as you like, now embracing her, now sending her off according to your whim of the moment. Her character is already shaped, but we love her greatly. Emma says they will be fast friends, and when Emma makes a judgment you can take it seriously. And since she works, she's never bored. She's helped Emma with her fashion, and is a good deal more sensitive to that sort of thing than I am. She's tranquil, never *chi-chi*, never embarrassing, though she says what she thinks. She knows when to be quiet and listen. Her manners are exquisite, as are her opinions, and at 60 she'll have the same figure she has now. . . .
>
> And you, dear child, you'll pass over her bodily fault, which she can do nothing about; after all she's obliged to overlook plenty of faults you have and have had. I assure you that you will not be able to find better and I will gladly share with her the affection you have for me. That's not easy for a mother. What would you do with a wife who wanted to be entertained and admired? Mlle. Maury has qualities of the heart, and those last. She and I talked a good deal of the marriage. That was difficult, but we both got through it. I would have been happier if you had already married her before or just at the beginning of the summer vacations, so you would not have come to Strasbourg an unmarried man, but she tells me that you don't want it known in Leipzig that you're marrying a French woman. So the moment you've left, you'll publish the banns, which will take four weeks, and then you'll get married in the quietest way possible.[63]

On August 11, 1932, we encounter our only direct evidence that a *mariage blanc*—an unconsummated marriage—was planned in advance:

Since you left I've thought only of you and your future. Happily I had an opportunity to talk to Fritz, to whom I expressed my disquietude, and was astonished to learn from him that Maury knows exactly what to expect from you—or rather what not to expect.

If she really knows this and if she marries you anyway, then everything is fine: she's no longer a child. She knows what this is all about and, *alors,* I can only say that I would be happy if she does marry you and I hope further that you will be, if not entirely happy, at least at peace with her. It's because of her that I wanted to object, because it seems to me that it's shameful if you make her your wife without her really being one; but if she knows your intentions, then I won't object. With a person that one respects one can just ignore that part, and we all respect and love her; she's already part of our family. Your departure was so sad, even without my going with you to the station. I will be happy if you find a home life with her, on condition that you can be kind to her and good for her. As far as your job is concerned I can't be mixed up in it, since I don't see that part clearly. I understand that you want to leave Leipzig, but will you have the wherewithal to find an equivalent one or one better? Will your health permit you to live the life of an artist? If you want me to write Maury about this I'll do it, even though it would be delicate and difficult to do. . . .

(If you reach a decision, let me know, even if you don't want her to know: I know how to keep a secret.)[64]

We cannot know precisely what to make of this other than that something goes unsaid. Given their ages, there were unlikely to be offspring in any case; according to one source, there was a prenuptial contract designed to keep La Solitude in the Maury family. Geneviève would certainly have been embarrassed by the notion of coping with her handicap in intimate circumstances; Charles's mother alludes to the colorful romantic history Charles had had—and would continue to have. News of her son's move from Leipzig to Paris nevertheless came as a shock to Mme. Munch: "I'm afraid to think more about it," she writes in September 1932.[65]

Munch's most significant character traits had long been molded by the time he reached Paris at age forty. For all intents and purposes his worldview had been established by his experiences in World War I and the conscious moral principles he adopted in the immediate aftermath, when he would have been in his twenties. Of these the most obvious was his personal commitment to music making as a path to spiritual equilibrium. That was a simple tenet: "I believe that next to religion music is the most important spiritual influence in our lives."[66] Another was his rigorous pacifism; another, his warm generosity (though so far he lacked the means to give much away). From the beginning an unusual self-effacement in his style of leadership is evident.

Some of these attributes left him vulnerable: It seemed to him obvious that the things men hold in common are more important than the ones that separate them. He could also be impetuous and overcome by brooding and melancholy; both parents allude to these traits. He has a pattern established already of keeping his distance from loved ones, sudden onsets of great sadness, also of finding an antidote to those episodes in bursts of travel and occasional dramatic relocations. He is not yet surrounded by the trappings of luxury he later so enjoyed; these were acquired with Vivette's money, then with the profits of his own stardom.

Still, his professional promise seemed all but unlimited as he set out by train that September for Paris, gripped by "a burning desire to make it known *urbi et orbi* [to the city and to the world] that my destiny as a conductor was written in the stars."[67]

CHAPTER 2

༾

Paris

November 1932–May 1938

However dark the gathering clouds of economic and political collapse, orchestral life in Paris, when Charles Munch first encountered and then won over the city, seems not so different from an impressionist's view of the sea: vast, constant in its change, seductive in its light and in its shadows. Four philharmonic societies gave concerts every Sunday afternoon, each nourished by its own traditions along with healthy doses of newly composed music and a parade of first-quality soloists. Records and radio afforded new diversions every day.

Paris, like London and Vienna, remained a crossroads of art music, where robust intellectual currents collided and commingled. Here, also, maestros both established and aspiring came to extend their hegemony. Between the Russian Revolution and his departure for Boston in 1924, Serge Koussevitzky organized and led concerts said to be consistently the best in town.[1] Pierre Monteux, who had launched *Le sacre du printemps* in 1913, returned after his Boston and Amsterdam engagements to establish his Orchestre Symphonique de Paris (1929–1935); both the man and his orchestra were to serve Charles Munch as career models. Toscanini appeared in Paris with some frequency in the 1930s, and the two counted their professional acquaintance from that period. In 1928 Bruno Walter came to lead an ambitious Mozart festival with recordings; then— after Munch had played for him in Leipzig—came back a decade later as a refugee, guest-conducting the Société des Concerts du Conservatoire on more than one occasion. There were capable French conductors as well, but it was on the careers of these traveling virtuosi that Munch meant to model his own.

The annual concert statistics given by the *Courrier musical* counted 1,300 events for 1933–1934, including 384 orchestra concerts. New music was *de rigueur*, with one or two premieres to be heard every Sunday, sometimes four or five. The *Courrier's* Maurice Imbert was given to complaining if there were *aucune œuvre nouvelle* in a week's offerings to attract his attention. First performances got mixed, sometimes overtly grudging public response, but they were expected as the natural course of things in so forward-looking a place as Paris.

Among the progressive alternatives to the Conservatoire concerts were d'Indy's Schola Cantorum, from 1891; the École Normale de Musique, established just after the First World War by Alfred Cortot and Auguste Mangeot; and Nadia Boulanger's American Conservatory in Fontainebleau, established in 1921. All manner of modernist movements, schools, and affinity groups presented concert fare that went above and beyond that of the now venerable Société Nationale de Musique, founded by Fauré and others a generation before. There was the famous "Groupe des Six," so identified and pictured together (often with Jean Cocteau) from the early 1920s. In 1924 a saucier "École d'Arcueil," centering on Henri Sauguet and conductor Roger Désormière, took its name from Satie's dwelling place outside Paris.

Munch was especially close with the group of *émigré* composers sometimes called the École de Paris: (in rough order of the closeness of their friendships) Bohuslav Martinu, Alexander Tcherepnin, Conrad Beck, Tibor Harsányi, Marcel Mihalovici, and Alexandre Tansman. His personal and professional experience with these composers was substantial, and his fundamental idea of interesting new music was likely rooted more in their idioms than in those of, say, Bartók and Stravinsky. After the war he was pleased to reestablish contact, when he came to Boston, with the ones who had sought refuge in the United States.

Just as Munch arrived in Paris, the Triton chamber music society, organized by Pierre-Octave Ferroud in 1932, aimed to promote the best new music regardless of its affinities and was quick to recognize the new conductor's value to their interests. The governing committee included several of the composers mentioned earlier, as well as Henry Barraud (later to claim Munch for the Orchestre National), Prokofiev, Jean Françaix, and Jacques Ibert. Munch, who frequented their weekly encounters, became an important agent for their music—that, for instance, of Ibert, whose last works he both fostered and premiered. He also interacted there with the French composer-conductors whose career paths were to parallel his own: Henri Tomasi, Roger Désormière, and Jean Martinon, the last of whom amounted to a protégé. Finally, the group that coalesced around Yves Baudrier in 1936, calling itself Jeune France, included two composers who came to figure significantly in the Munch repertoire of the 1940s and '50s: André Jolivet and Olivier Messiaen. The Parisian bill of fare was a far cry from that preferred in Strasbourg or even Leipzig. A formidable upbringing in Bach and the Viennese masters was now counterbalanced by the idea that a living orchestra was obliged to breathe the air of the present.

Munch's Paris debut, on November 1, 1932, in the Théâtre des Champs-Élysées, was purchased for him by Geneviève Maury, as she had wished, and announced with a poster proudly noting the "Premier Concert d'Orchestre Dirigé par Charles Münch." The ensemble was the Orchestre des Concerts Walther Straram—that is, Straram's usual contracted players, the same used by Ida Rubinstein for Ravel's *Boléro* and by Stravinsky to record the Symphony of Psalms. The program consisted of the Dittersdorf symphony, which he had conducted in Leipzig the previous season (though in Paris it was a premiere), Bach's E-Major Violin Concerto with the *débutant* as soloist-conductor, Ravel's *Pavane pour une infante défunte,* and the Brahms First Symphony. Noted music journalist Suzanne Demarquez wrote the following:

> This was, if I'm not mistaken, the first appearance of M. Charles Munch on the podium of a Parisian orchestra, and a more promising debut than usual. It goes without saying that M. Charles Munch is a musician. He's also born to the profession, endowed with a fiery spirit and able to communicate to his orchestral force the flame that burns within him.[2]

Demarquez thought the Dittersdorf flat and without the interest of a Haydn or Mozart symphony. She also suspected Munch had introduced "awfully Romantic" tendencies in the Ravel. Yet:

> How well suited he is to the C-Minor Symphony of Brahms! How intense the life he breathed into it, enough to win over a typically stubborn public where it comes to Brahms! Inspired with his exalted mission, the *chef* built his themes and colored them, his right hand freed of the baton—which, in his left for a moment, seemed to be there only to keep the flow from spilling over. It was a spellbinding account, made possible, too, by the supple and disciplined artists of the Straram Orchestra.

Munch was mostly dazed: "I cannot honestly say that I conducted the orchestra for I was fully occupied with allaying the fear that paralyzed me. . . . I conducted like an automaton. My sympathetic audience mistook my panic for inspiration."[3]

Straram died later in the season, and the Munch debut, along with Toscanini's 1934 concerts given in Straram's memory, amounts to the last stand of this prestigious ensemble. The niche was filled by concerts organized by Pierre Monteux and Robert Siohan and soon enough by Munch himself.

He had not yet married Geneviève Maury. When, at the beginning of 1933, he briefly considered taking a firm job offer back in Germany, his mother could not hide her consternation:

> I see you so rarely that I don't want to address subjects I already know you won't want to talk about—among them your future. But mustn't a mother bring up the things that are the most important to her child? I hope you've entirely given up the idea of going back to Germany. If they want you now, they'll surely want you just as much in March. Stay in Paris, where I hope you'll find a way to occupy yourself doing what you want, because it seems to me you're in good hands. And marry Maury. That's the only just thing for you to do. I know how afraid you are of making this decision, but once it's done you will be tranquil and happy and so will I. Don't wait too long, and don't look for another excuse to delay. Do it for me. We all love Maury for your wife with all our hearts. She makes absolutely everything possible for you. I can't understand how you can in good conscience accept her generosity without wanting to give back anything in exchange, unless you have reasons that you don't want to tell me. But then stop accepting. . . .
>
> Think of your old age, when you will want to look back on this new life without blushing from embarrassment. I'll stop asking God to direct and guide you, but at least let yourself be protected by Him. And finally, dear child, think of your father: . . . you knew his principles, for he wrote you on the subject several times. I'm certain that if you marry Maury, he would approve.[4]

This is to cite only the most relevant extract from a winding letter that goes on and on in its maternal admonishing—to check up, for instance, on her nephews Pierre-Paul and Jean-Jacques Schweitzer, by then students in Paris. The latter had grown pale, she thought: "Can't you get him to go to bed earlier?"

So Munch came around to the family's way of thinking, and the marriage was at last set for January 31, 1933. The Strasbourgeois did not make the trip, owing to a cold spell that saw the temperature reach −10° C. Célestine Munch wrote her last words on the subject on January 29, two days before the quiet ceremony:

> *Mon Charrikind:*
>
> You know I'm thinking of you all the time when I'm alone, which is always, and my thoughts are with you and Mlle. Maury. I would be so happy over your forthcoming marriage if I weren't still a little afraid that you will flinch at the last moment—or get the flu. When you want something so badly, obviously you're always afraid of whatever will keep it from happening. Your aunts and I talk of little else. *No weiss doch des Charri wo er ane ghert!* [And now I know which country Charlie comes from!]
>
> I know Papa approves from Eternity: he always said of Maury: "she has a pure heart"—which these days is a rare thing; and if her past life is pure also and she truly

loves you, that is the essential thing. Won't you always be good to her? A woman needs so little to be happy: tenderness, and the feeling of being something to some-body. That is all that is asked.

We love her with all our hearts and are pleased to welcome her into our family. . . .
Now I can greet death with open arms: Maury will love you in my place.[5]

We know little indeed about Geneviève Maury as Madame Munch other than that their most elevated acquaintances always took care to be remembered to her, as though recognizing her considerable social stature. Others who met her, especially Americans who would not have been able to converse with ease, remembered only her reserve and her infirmity. By the 1930s and '40s she was nevertheless a figure of substance in the literary world. After the publication of her early tales of the Limoges, she gradually found a niche as translator from the German: Her French-language texts of Thomas Mann's *Tonio Kröger* (1923) and Hermann Hesse's *Knulp* (1949)—and other stories by each—are still in print, and she also translated popular children's books.[6]

In the years between their marriage and the war, she appears to have devoted herself largely to advancing her husband's career, as she had been expecting: keeping accounts and tracking his repertoire, contributing financially to organi-zations that employed her husband. Of course, she had brought the full extent of her material wealth to the marriage, not only her generous annuities but the family estates and the servants that tended to them as well. Though she owned a stylish apartment building on the quai des Orfèvres at the Pont Neuf, the couple established themselves at 11 *bis*, avenue du Maréchal Manoury in the XVIe *ar-rondissement* (moving a few blocks to 8, rue Alfred Dehodencq, a quieter street, in 1943).

From the outside one cannot help seeing their marriage largely as a shrewd business solution to the problem of advancing in the arts in a sometimes harsh metropolitan environment. Their relationship typically reads as kind and solici-tous but lacking the elements one would associate with romance or desire—a kind of marriage common enough in European aristocracy. Those who knew them the best concur that she adored him and that he was never insensitive to the depth and length of their relationship and ever grateful for the role she had played in his career.

For all his experience as an orchestral player, section leader, and armchair con-ductor, Munch had to work hard to keep up with the repertoire demanded by the concerts for which he was now routinely contracted. He tells us that from about 1933 he studied conducting with Alfred Szendrei or Sendrey (1884–1976), the distinguished Hungarian conductor/composer/musicologist whom he had known in Leipzig as conductor of radio broadcasts and of the oratorio society and as the recent author of a conducting treatise[7]—and a fresh PhD in musicology from the University of Leipzig.

Sendrey, a Jew, left Leipzig as the political situation worsened and arrived in Paris just after Munch did. The conducting lessons were thus a welcome transaction in both directions: Munch badly needed the coaching, and Sendrey needed to support himself, his wife, Eugenie (who had sung for Mahler), and two children. He found work as director of programming for RDF, the national radio service; in 1940 he and the family were brought to the United States by the New York–based Emergency Rescue Committee and settled in Los Angeles.[8]

Paul Bastide (1879–1962) had come to Strasbourg in 1929 to assume direction of the municipal concerts at the same time Fritz Munch became director of the conservatory. In this period he also conducted at the Opéra-Comique and Opéra in Paris (1932–1935) and at the summer casino concerts in Vichy. Munch naturally regarded Bastide as an important mentor:

> I visited Paul Bastide often during this time and profited greatly from his advice. I told him my troubles, let him know my doubts, and discussed countless problems with him. He came to my concerts and then with extraordinary perception took up one by one and measure by measure the mistakes I had made. It was still a time of working and learning.[9]

In the summer of 1939 Munch, by then a mature conductor whose Legion of Honor had just been announced, appeared in Vichy. Bastide, pleased as only a teacher can be, wrote to congratulate him:

> Accept, then, a ritual accolade from a patriarch all too happy to welcome you into the bosom of this great family. It's only the beginning: it's hardly over.
>
> Dear Charry, you don't have to apologize for not spending more time with me. I know all about professional commitments. But however great my joy at seeing you on the podium in Vichy, it was even greater when I got your fine letter, which proved to me beyond the shadow of a doubt that despite the honors now showering down on you, you've kept a pure heart, still able to grasp so noble a sentiment as gratitude. I'm awfully proud of what you remember of the years we passed together.
>
> And if my basic beliefs have become part of you, the recompense is in the feeling you have expressed so sincerely, so nobly. Always keep your naturally fond predisposition toward your musicians, your worker-bees. Keep making them love you. They are the ones who will support you best in life and who will most often return the real performances.
>
> *Make yourself love, and you will be loved.* And with this lever of affection, you will be able to accomplish great things.

As for me, I'm ever yours from afar. My thoughts are with you. You've made *immense progress*. Your arm is much more *flexible*. And your explanations to the musicians are clear.

The memory you've left here is excellent. And I'm sure you'll come back a *star*.[10]

The third of his prominent coaches in the apprentice-and-journeyman period was the legendary accompanist and *répétitrice* Irène Aïtoff (1905–2006), famous for her ability to teach any singer anything and to play *Pelléas et Mélisande* from memory. Munch would conduct an imaginary orchestra, as she played, "like he were already in the middle of a concert." They challenged each other to memory contests, where he would sing the individual parts one by one. She cites specifically the Franck Symphony and the Brahms Violin Concerto, works that entered his repertoire in 1933 and 1934.[11]

Someone, too, taught him to reduce the phrase count of movements to a graph on a half sheet of paper; we find several of these in a notebook from his early years. In addition, his collection of souvenir programs suggests that he attended many concerts of the groups he would later conduct—as though scouting.

He had started late—but near the top. There were few if any wrong turns, and his career now follows an essentially uninterrupted trajectory toward the pinnacle of the profession. He was already forty-two; his conducting career was to last thirty-five more years.

The Straram debut was followed by an engagement for three concerts with the Lamoureux Orchestra: January 22 and March 13 and 15, 1933. Among the programmed works that went on to become staples of his repertoire were the suite from Rameau's *Dardanus,* as arranged by Vincent d'Indy; the Handel A-Minor Concerto Grosso, op. 6, no. 4; and Mozart's *Prague* Symphony. In January he accompanied the great violinist Jacques Thibaud; in March, Lotte Lehman, singing Wagner. The Lamoureux renewed him for the following season, and Munch went on to conceive a lasting affection and loyalty toward an orchestra that was not always competitive with the others but was unfailingly appreciative of his gifts. Toward the end of his career he made important recordings with the Lamoureux and agreed to serve as its *président d'honneur.*

A critical advance in his new career came later in the first season, when Munch conducted a Sunday concert of Monteux's Orchestre Symphonique de Paris (OSP) on April 2, 1933. Pierre Monteux (1875–1964), of singular appearance and personality and a near-legendary past, is the next artist of international note to exert a shaping influence on Munch. Geneviève Maury would have remembered Monteux as her sister's violin teacher. Munch certainly followed the fortunes of the new orchestra with interest and envy; given his Leipzig experience as soloist in the Prokofiev Violin Concerto, he would have been naturally drawn to the OSP's premiere of Prokofiev's Third Symphony in the first of its six seasons of activity. Over the decades, Munch and Monteux settled into a comfortable, simple collegiality based on shared musical interests, language, and admiration for each other's accomplishments. Each can be said to have prolonged the other's career.

Virgil Thomson was among the many observers who came to see Monteux and Munch as a pair that, together, embodied the French orchestral style. He thought their work, for instance, more detailed and nuanced than Toscanini's "oversimplified" style. (He held, with some justification, that Toscanini had, so far at least, little or no influence on European orchestral practice.) Certainly Munch and Monteux, along perhaps with Ansermet, became the foremost exponents of a national repertoire—Fauré, Debussy, Ravel—that was to be embraced in the 1940s and '50s as canonic the world over. Monteux was a full generation older than Munch, however, and already nearly twenty-five years into a major international career. In 1933 he would have held enormous sway over Munch in his signature programming and his accounts of the allures and dangers of the American symphony orchestra. He also gave Charles Munch his first repertoire niche, Roussel's *Bacchus et Ariane* suites.

Bacchus et Ariane, descending so obviously from *Daphnis et Chloé,* demanded similar editing into concert suites: excising the extraneous theater-specific bars and leaving as much as possible exactly as in the ballet. That much had been clear since the 1931 ballet premiere, conducted by Philippe Gaubert, its only performance to date. Monteux moved forward with the idea and secured Roussel's participation in refashioning the score, then offered Munch one of the two suites to perfect and premiere. Hence, it was Munch who gave the first performance of Suite 1 in April 1933; Monteux then introduced Suite 2 the next season, in February 1934. According to Dutilleux, Suite 2 owes "some of its success to Munch's cuts. It was Munch who gave the suite its shape by making cuts that Roussel, I'm sure, never envisaged." Munch, who had "an inborn sense of proportion," went on to suggest similar cuts to many composers, not least of whom was Dutilleux himself.[12]

Albert Roussel (1869–1937), enigmatic and elusive, practiced the better part of his composing career from his seaside estate at Varengeville in Normandy. His health, always fragile, was by the time of our narrative in decline, but his life story had been nonetheless intriguing, from naval service to sojourning in India to his single voyage to Boston for the premiere of his Third (and best) Symphony by Koussevitzky and the BSO in 1930. A trip to Belgrade for a festival of French music had kept him from attending *Bacchus et Ariane,* but his wife and friends reported a "perfect performance," and on April 12 he penned a note of hearty thanks that suggests that he and Munch had met in the course of preparing the suite.[13] They kept in touch thereafter and grew close enough that at one point Munch is to be found revising Roussel's bowings for him.

If prior allegiances meant that the remaining works—the Sinfonietta, Fourth Symphony, and *Rapsodie flamande*—were to be premiered by others, Munch nevertheless promoted all of them and in due course became their chief agent. When Roussel was appointed president of the sixteenth festival of the International Society for Contemporary Music, to be held in Paris in 1937, he chose Munch to prepare the orchestral music. After his death a few months later, Munch wrote of an adorable, simple, good man: "I have lost a great friend."[14]

Roussel's work had figured importantly in Strasbourg while Munch was living there. In 1928 his cousin Ernest-Geoffroy Munch, called Nesti by the family, had premiered *Le bardit des Francs* [The Battle Cry of the Franks], a work Charles later programmed several times during the Occupation for its political overtones: A men's chorus with brass and percussion evokes a mythical rallying cry of forty thousand Franks before a bloody battle with the Gallo-Romans in the fifth century. It may have been in the Strasbourg milieu that he learned Roussel's only sacred work, the great Psalm 80; most probably he also knew *Le festin de l'araignée* [The Spider's Banquet] before he came to Paris.

After *Bacchus et Ariane* Munch cultivated Roussel and his music methodically and had much of it in his grasp while the composer was still alive. He featured Psalm 80 in his second Paris season (January 1934, repeated in June), with results that Roussel found "truly magnificent: . . . the care you took with the chorus and orchestra rehearsals let[s] you communicate to the performers the spirit and conviction that drive you, and to breathe into them the enthusiastic warmth so clearly to be sensed in the work."[15] In 1934–1935 he took Roussel's Third Symphony to Prague, Vienna, and Budapest; the next season he began to conduct *Le festin de l'araignée*. In November 1936, with Yvonne Gouverné's chorus, he led a *Bacchus et Ariane* billed as the second complete performance ever. Roussel heard that it, too, was magnificent: "That doesn't surprise me, because Munch has always understood and conducted my works admirably."[16] In January 1937, a few weeks after the Brussels premiere with Erich Kleiber, Munch introduced the *Rapsodie flamande* to Parisian audiences. Again Roussel was there, writing Munch of "the joy and emotion" occasioned by the performance and the way the conductor had discovered the true character of the themes and color of the score. He found the orchestra, under Munch's "energetic impulsion," supple and understanding.[17]

For Munch, not the least of the dividends of *Bacchus et Ariane* was the occasion to encounter and then befriend Yvonne Gouverné. On one occasion, for instance, Charles and Geneviève Munch joined her for a drive to Brussels to hear *Aeneas,* op. 54, Roussel's new ballet with orchestra and chorus. She went on to provide the chorus for Munch's later great triumphs with Debussy and

Honegger: "The years that I was privileged to prepare the choruses for Charles Munch's concerts in Paris," she recalled, "are among the most beautiful memories of my life." It had all begun with Roussel: "For more than three decades, these works, so palpitating with life, seemed almost effortlessly to be reborn whenever Charles Munch was on the podium, in the end radiating them throughout the world."[18]

Yet another concert society active in Paris during those years was that of the indefatigable conductor and intellectual Robert Siohan (1894–1985), later an important biographer of Stravinsky. The Concerts Siohan were devoted specifically to programming new music (alongside standard fare), notably Messiaen's, so it was a mark of Munch's rising prestige that he was given a half-dozen engagements in the new season December 1933–February 1934. The first, on December 2, was reported as "a remarkable reading under the energetic direction of M. Charles Munch of three works of the highest interest": Schubert's Fifth Symphony, the Bach *St. Anne* Prelude and Fugue in an orchestration by Arnold Schoenberg, and Ropartz's *La chasse du Prince Arthur.* In January the featured work was Roussel's Psalm 80, which again attracted critical notice for the "lively and communicative leadership of M. Charles Munch."[19] Beethoven's *Emperor* Concerto with Emil von Sauer was not so successful.

Three successive Saturdays in February 1934 were notable as much for the caliber of the soloists as for the repertoire: Robert Casadesus in the Brahms Second Piano Concerto and d'Indy's *Symphony on a French Mountain Air* (February 10); Stravinsky in his Capriccio for Piano and Orchestra (February 17); and Jacques Thibaud in both the Bach E-major and the Brahms violin concertos (February 24). "What sonority! What rhythm! What accent!" wrote Charles Bouvet of the Stravinsky: "a huge, fully warranted success."[20]

On February 24 the novelty was the pairing of Wladimir Vogel's new *Ritmica ostinata* with another ostinato, Ravel's *Boléro*—too much for one concert, the review remarked. Nevertheless, "the whole program was well conducted by M. Charles Munch and well played by the orchestra to a hall stuffed to the bursting point and torrid in temperature."[21]

Munch's Siohan concerts continued on March 24 with another impressive soloist, Zino Francescatti. One critic noted how much more interesting these appearances had been than the Lamoureux engagements earlier in the season:

> M. Charles Munch led the orchestra, and with this young, ardent phalanx of artists his sensibility, his precision, his good sense from multiple perspectives and complexities, his gift of recognizing the essential character of works, comes across better here, perhaps, than at the Salle Gaveau during a Lamoureux concert.

A remarkable performance of the Brahms First. . . . But what crowned the evening was the profound and powerful, airy and bright performance of the Beethoven Violin Concerto with M. Zino Francescatti. Never have we heard so brilliant an account of these pages.[22]

On June 21, 1934, Munch split the last concert of 1933–1934 with Siohan, leading Roussel's Psalm 80 in the first half while his senior colleague conducted Honegger's *Le Roi David* in the second. This was to have been the arrangement for 1934–1935, when Munch was announced in the press as an official co-conductor of the Concerts Robert Siohan. By autumn, however, circumstances had changed, and Munch moved on to other pursuits while Siohan merged his series with that of Gaston Poulet.

Not all of the press from the first seasons was positive, and there are more than a few suggestions that impetuosity at any price was a Munch trademark from the start. Of the *Emperor* Concerto in January 1934 we read:

The divorce between M. Emil Sauer's conception and that of M. Munch was obvious on multiple occasions. Munch submitted to and let himself be carried away by violent impulses. The performance was fatally harmed by this lack of accord between soloist and conductor. Even the players were bothered.[23]

In January 1935 the complaint was similar:

Chez Lamoureux the traveling baton passed into the hands of M. Charles Munch. We've written about him before. We know that he's gifted with a volcanic temperament. But he has yet to succeed at mastering the tempest when you'd like him to. This subtle lack of control extends to matters of tiny detail and does little to establish the basic logic, leading to the lack of clarity in the basic tempo of a movement, floating attacks, and so on. In the Finale of [Beethoven's] Seventh, the orchestra players had to rely on all their skill to avoid catastrophe. So exaggerated was the fast tempo that even the nimblest would have been prevented from observing the essential nuances of their parts.[24]

Respighi's setting of the Bach Passacaglia and Fugue in C Minor (December 2, 1933) suffered from a lack of dynamic restraint as well, as did the Roussel Psalm. "He had the brasses thunder loud enough to crack the wall. This abuse of force is awfully disagreeable to the listeners."[25]

On the whole, though, Munch got few negative reviews, at least until after he was a known quantity in Boston and the metropolitan critics had sharpened their pencil points. So steadfast a supporter as Arthur Honegger acknowledged in 1941 that people were known to use the word "amateur" to describe Munch:

> We can only smile at this calumny. Think about the programs of Charles Munch and the number of new works, both classical and modern, he has conducted, mostly from memory. Think about not just this season's concerts but also those he has conducted for the last six or eight years. Compare them to those of certain other professionals of the baton and it will be easy to see who has best served the art of music. Let's hope there are many more "amateurs" of this ilk.[26]

That fall, toward the beginning of the new 1934–1935 season, Toscanini was in Paris to conduct Walther Straram's orchestra in his memory. Munch was fond of recounting how he took his violin and a borrowed part for Debussy's *Ibéria* to a rehearsal and quietly found a place at the end of the first violin rank, only to discover that the bowings in his music were out of synchronization with the rest. Every effort he made to correct soon failed. There was an explosion, explanation, and reconciliation that both Toscanini and Munch remembered for the rest of their careers. Thereafter, Munch always kept a photograph of Toscanini on his worktable. Their paths would cross again in New York, and Munch never abandoned the notion that Toscanini might eventually be persuaded to come conduct in Boston.

Likewise, Richard Strauss came to Paris the following season to conduct the Orchestre Philharmonique in a first French performance of *Die schweigsame Frau / La femme silencieuse,* along with *Till Eulenspiegel* before intermission and the *Sinfonia domestica* afterward (April 3, 1936). Munch collected the composer's autograph on his printed program and kept it with a lithograph portrait of Strauss from the same period. Almost surely they conversed, probably remembering encounters in Leipzig and even Strasbourg. Munch had been conducting the Strauss orchestral works since 1933 and by the time he got to Boston had most of them in his active repertoire.

Like the other Paris conductors, Munch accrued a good deal of his podium time leading the provincial *concerts classiques,* which brought art music to a swath of cities extending to the farthest reaches of the country. Between 1934 and 1938 he covered a portion of the seasons in both Cannes and Marseille, some fifteen or sixteen engagements in all. In Brest, with the orchestra of the "Friends of Colonne," he led eleven concerts over three seasons (1935–1936, 1936–1937, 1937–1938), nearly all of them cited approvingly in the Paris press. These were not insubstantial services: In Cannes he shared the series with first-rank conductors such as Philippe Gaubert, Pierre Monteux, Paul Paray, and

Rhené-Baton. In Marseille the cohort included Georges Sebastian, Louis Fourestier, and Henri Tomasi. The soloists, too, were of the first quality: Thibaud, Stravinsky, Rubinstein, Wanda Landowska, Cortot, Marian Anderson. An equally significant indication of his value is that during 1934 and 1935 he was twice called to the Budapest Philharmonic Orchestra to cover for the ailing Ernst von Dohnányi, putting him in an august company that also included Weingartner, Carl Schuricht, and Edwin Fischer. He left a favorable enough impression to be invited back for the 1936–1937 season.

Munch found these peregrinations altogether natural. Although he loved Paris and when he was away complained endlessly of missing the artists of whom he was fondest, he also thought it a conductor's obligation to travel widely with his own personal repertoire. He was thus an early partisan of guest-conductor arrangements—happy to accept such engagements, happy to leave his own orchestras in the hands of guests of his caliber. This was radical thinking in circles, including both the Paris Conservatoire and the Boston Symphony Orchestra, bound to the tradition that the house conductor should remain in residence from the beginning of the season to the end.

If there was a single turning point in the early conducting career of Charles Munch, it came when Alfred Cortot proposed putting him in charge of a new orchestra organized from what was left of the progressive concert series of Straram and Monteux. This was the Orchestre de la Société Philharmonique de Paris, often abbreviated OSPP and OPP and generally called the Orchestre Philharmonique. Geneviève Munch appears to have provided the capital for this venture, too, though its inaugural concerts in December 1934 and January 1935 had been led by Nadia Boulanger (Bach, Monteverdi, Schütz) and Roger Désormière (Stravinsky). Munch earned the podium as the result of a highly acclaimed concert on June 12, 1935, commemorating the one-hundredth birthday of Camille Saint-Saëns, where Cortot joined him in the Fourth Piano Concerto. On the same concert was a work he later programmed frequently and recorded twice, the Japanese-flavored overture La princesse jaune.

He went on to plan and conduct three brilliant seasons of the Société Philharmonique (1935–1936, 1936–1937, and 1937–1938) as his primary employment. "Not quite a new orchestra," remarked Suzanne Demarquez in the Courrier musical, but rather "some dissidents organized by M. Alfred Cortot."[27] They had the very good idea not to give their concerts on Sundays at 5:00, as the unwritten laws of classical music seemed to demand, but rather on Thursday nights at 9:00 p.m. in the Salle Pleyel.

Charles Munch, still only three seasons out from his professional début, now found himself at the head of his own orchestra, with full responsibility for programming and for the engagement of guest artists and orchestra personnel.

Artistically, the new orchestra provided an opportunity for him to undertake new music suited to his particular tastes and to build his repertoire at his own pace. Politically, the engagement positioned Munch toward the top of the Paris establishment, a real career leap, and showed the public at large what partisans already knew: his unlimited potential, the promise that he might join the ranks of the great conductors.

By chance Munch's first concert with the Philharmonique, on October 19, 1935, was offered jointly with former colleagues: the boychoir of the Thomasschule, Leipzig, and its conductor, Karl Straube. Straube led the choral portion (Bach's Cantata 67, the motet *Singet dem Herrn,* and three Mozart choruses), while Munch offered the D-Major Suite of Bach and the *Prague* Symphony of Mozart. Munch was henceforth a lifelong partisan of such joint ventures, arranging, for instance, London-Paris and Amsterdam-Paris swaps in the years to come.

On December 8, 1935, there was recent music extending from Ravel to the first performance of a new symphony by Robert Casadesus and an early performance of Roussel's Fourth: "A greatly talented conductor, he lent his marvelously certain beat to the service of new music, conducting Roussel's Symphony, an impetuous music served admirably by his generous ardor, to triumph."[28]

"Powerfully communicative ardor" was held to be the secret of a Bach Christmas Oratorio later in December, resulting in warmth and spirit. "Bravo, M. Munch!"[29]

What drew the attention of leading intellectuals to the Orchestre Philharmonique was its bracing association with the Triton chamber music society. This, too, had been Cortot's idea, with Munch's enthusiastic endorsement: There was unmet need for a first-rate chamber orchestra in town. The Triton concert in the Salle Chopin on December 11, 1935, played by an ensemble drawn directly from the Philharmonique, is typical of the kind of programming for which Munch felt a natural affection: first performances of Poulenc's *Suite française* (in its smaller orchestration) and Hindemith's chamber opera *Hin und Zurück.*

In January patrons of the Orchestre Philharmonique saw two hundred performers assembled for Florent Schmitt's *Salambô,* new works of Ferroud and Tcherepnin, and Prokofiev's Second Violin Concerto—which Munch had played in Leipzig. The season closed in May with two other novelties: a new oratorio by Igor Markevitch, with three hundred performers, and the inestimably historic first Paris performance of Bizet's C-Major Symphony on May 29, 1936.

Munch's multiple recordings of the Bizet Symphony come to occupy a significant place in his legacy. Here it is important to note his crucial role in establishing the work in the repertoire to begin with. Jean Chantavoine had identified the manuscript at the Paris Conservatoire, and Felix Weingartner played it shortly afterward in Basel. Walter Goehr and the London Philharmonic made the first recording in 1935, attracting conductors interested in the French repertoire, including both Munch and Beecham. In 1947 Balanchine's ballet *Symphony in C* gave the score an influential new audience, perhaps ensuring its permanence in the repertoire. It was certainly Munch, however, who sold the work in Paris by putting it squarely at the top of his first season with the Société des Concerts and discovering in its sometimes problematic and juvenile outpourings a merry, convincing vehicle for virtuoso orchestra.

In March 1936 Munch gave one of his last performances as violinist, in a Strasbourg recital with the distinguished pianist Lazare Lévy. The review suggests a "mitigated" success: "Perhaps we expected too much." This was attributed directly to his emergence as a conductor. "Last year we were talking with a Parisian acquaintance about the violinist Charles Munch. Our interlocutor immediately riposted: 'You mean to say, the orchestra conductor Charles Munch.' It's true. We forget that our excellent co-citizen carries a baton now more often than a bow."[30] What was also true was that he no longer had time to play. He declined a Bach concert with Schweitzer that summer,[31] and nobody remembers him even holding a violin for any length of time after that.

The 1936–1937 season, too, centered on the Orchestre Philharmonique de Paris, with six major concerts in the new Salle Pleyel between October and March. It was to conclude with the International Society for Contemporary Music ("ISCM") festival in Paris, where Roussel chaired the organizing committee and Munch was to arrange for the orchestral readings and conduct the orchestra concert. The Philharmonique opened in October with a Bach-Mozart concert very like the one a year before, again with Karl Straube and the Thomanerchor; the November concert started with new works by Milhaud, Lazar, and Ferroud, then introduced Louis Krasner in the Paris premiere of the Berg Violin Concerto and the complete *Bacchus et Ariane* with Yvonne Gouverné's singers. In January 1937 there were Bruckner's Seventh, new works by Bondeville, Reisserová, and Françaix, and the French premiere of Roussel's *Rapsodie flamande,* another work championed by Munch for the rest of his career. In February came Florent Schmitt's *Oriane la sans égale;* in March, an all-Ravel program with Ravel in the house, featuring the first French performance of the Concerto for the Left Hand (Jacques Février, piano) and a complete *Daphnis et Chloé* with Gouverné's singers—meaning that within a brief period Munch had led full performances with chorus of *Bacchus et Ariane* and *Daphnis et Chloé* in the presence of their composers, neither of whom would survive the year.

Charles Munch's central role in piloting so central a work as *Daphnis et Chloé* to popularity should not be overlooked. Honegger reminds us that what keeps the public away from a modern work is not its modernism but its unfamiliarity:

Here is a case in point. Ravel cannot be regarded as a "classic" in the ordinary sense of the word. He wrote *Daphnis et Chloé* in 1912. For some 30 years it was seldom performed. Then, after a particularly brilliant rendering by Charles Munch and the Société des Concerts du Conservatoire de Paris, it was suddenly "launched." Since then, this Second Suite has been constantly played at concerts and over the wireless. (I have seen it announced nine times in a single week.) It has as great a success and draws as large audiences as Beethoven's *Pastoral Symphony*. And quite rightly.[32]

Poulenc had the same idea, writing of Munch's treatment of Ravel: "To be sure, Ravel's knowledge and technique are prodigious, but let's be clear: if an ardent heart and infallible hand were not guiding it, this music would not have grown as it has from year to year nor carried the stamp of indisputable permanence."[33]

Fred Goldbeck, a critic of consistently insightful commentary on new music in Paris of that era, had much the same to say of Schmitt's *Oriane la sans égale:*

The performance was altogether beautiful and merits a gold star in the annals of first performances. . . . Among the great Kapellmeisters who are his peers I see only a few who might be at equal ease with an orchestra like his. I see fewer still who would be equally at ease—by "at ease" I mean aflame, boiling—with a concerto grosso of Corelli, a Schumann symphony, and *Oriane.* Fewer still who know how, in the soberest fashion, to find, like Munch, the wingspan, the trembling, as Goethe says, which is the best part of a score. And *not one* who confects such seasons, without needing virtuosi, without the *Meistersinger* prelude, and in so dedicating himself, sees questions of personal interest abandoned by all the participants in favor of the work of art.[34]

Alfred Cortot continued to exert a formative influence on Munch and his programming. Cortot grasped his colleague's unlimited potential as a much-needed figurehead for French achievement in classical music, while Munch was happy to profit from Cortot's unlimited access to power and influence at the highest levels of the profession. Munch effectively became Cortot's *dauphin.* Cortot saw to his appointment in several capacities, including as professor at his École Normale and as conductor of the Concerts Privés de l'École Normale for the next several seasons.[35] Cortot himself appeared as soloist with Munch in these concerts, playing Chopin, Liszt, Franck, and Ravel. Among the intellectuals in Cortot's circle, soon to be found in Munch's, was Nadia Boulanger, who also taught at the École Normale. Moreover, Cortot was an important lecturer with the Université des Annales, the symposia series spun off in 1907 from *Les annales politiques et littéraires* by the remarkable journalist Yvonne Sarcey. The Université des Annales, at the peak of its influence between the wars, sponsored concerts organized by Cortot and conducted on several occasions by Munch.

In July 1935 Cortot had taken Munch with him to England, where they recorded the Saint-Saëns Fourth Piano Concerto, capitalizing on their success with the work at the Saint-Saëns centennial concert. Thus, Munch was brought face to face with the classical-music recording industry just exactly as the seriously recorded 78-rpm set was beginning to control the economics of classical music on an international scale.

Our narrative approaches wartime, when Cortot, in his sixties, pursued artistic and political beliefs that resulted in his ostracism from the mainstream of French art. For the 1930s, however, it is difficult to imagine a more capable mentor, and Cortot thus needs to be added to the already strong cast of formidable musicians who helped orient Charles Munch and negotiate his inborn gifts into a unique career: his father and uncle and older brother, Albert Schweitzer, Lucien Capet, Hans Pfitzner, Guy Ropartz, Paul Bastide, Karl Straube, Wilhelm Furtwängler, and Pierre Monteux.

One of the several reasons for locating the ISCM festival concerts in Paris that June was the 1937 Exposition Internationale then under way—occasion for the replacement of the old Trocadéro palace by the dubious Palais de Chaillot, directly across the river from the Eiffel Tower. Munch would have been interested in at least the art, featuring as it did Picasso's *Guernica* and Dufy's fresco *La fée électricité*, said to be the largest painting in the world. His primary contributions to the festival programming that summer took place at Royaumont Abbey near Asnières. Here the placid remains of a thirteenth-century monastic retreat housed foundation-supported activities in music, poetry, and architecture. Here the *Revue musicale* funded a series of more or less spiritual concerts, where Munch led Yvonne Gouverné's chorus and the chamber orchestra of the Philharmonique in works by Monteverdi, Rameau, Delannoy, two Bachs, Mozart, Clementi, and, from the present, Milhaud and Schmitt. There followed the orchestral concert for the ISCM on June 25, 1937, the fourth of the long festival events, lasting until after midnight: seven new compositions, of which the best were held to be by Conrad Beck and Hanns Eisler.

Munch had summer engagements in the vacation resorts of Aix-les-Bains and Biarritz, then probably took his first real vacation in five years. He was on the Riviera when he learned of Roussel's death on August 23, 1937.

It was thus fitting to open the Orchestre Philharmonique's 1937–1938 season at the Théâtre des Champs-Élysées with an all-Roussel concert in the composer's memory (October 13, 1937): the Suite in F, Piano Concerto, and *Rapsodie flamande;* then the Fourth Symphony and *Bacchus et Ariane,* Suite 2. "The audience left trembling with emotion and joy," said the reviewer, "thinking Roussel isn't dead; Roussel lives."[36] Cortot and Munch later honored Roussel's memory at a smaller concert at the École Normale, presenting the Sinfonietta and Cello Concertino.

Two weeks later Fritz Munch brought his now-celebrated Chœur de Saint-Guillaume from Strasbourg to Paris to share two concerts with the Philharmonique. Charles conducted the Brahms Requiem on November 1; the next day Fritz led a complete Saint John Passion. In December Charles conducted Berlioz's *Harold en Italie* for the first time, as well as an important premiere by Louis Aubert, *Les Saisons.*

His London debut, on December 17, 1937, consisted of a contemporary program with the BBC Orchestra, drawn from the summer's Paris ISCM concerts. Also, there was Riéti's Second Piano Concerto, premiered the previous summer at the Venice Festival, to be played by Marcelle Meyer, said to be Ravel's favorite pianist.

Célestine Munch, in Strasbourg, fretted that it was a bad time of year to travel and scolded him for not taking his wife ("Is it because you don't speak English?"), insisting he be home by Christmas. Still, the artistic result was successful enough to prompt discussion of a return visit, and Munch came home with his first London press. The notice in the *Musical Times* termed the Riéti disappointing: "One could not help feeling that Poulenc would have done the whole thing so much better." The concerto by the Catalan composer Joseph Vals intrigued audiences as it had in Paris, confirming that it had been "one of the few worthwhile 'discoveries' of the Paris Festival." Most inflammatory was Alois Häba's *Nova Zeme* overture, wherein, "combatting a great deal of noisy twelve-tone theorizing, the trombones blared forth the tune of the *Internationale,* thus exhibiting for the second time in one week the 'Bolshevist' tendencies of the BBC! The orchestra throughout the concert seemed somewhat unresponsive to the keen but at times over-violent conducting of M. Charles Munch."[37]

In Paris the Orchestre Philharmonique's season continued with its customary commingling of the classics (Schubert's Fifth, the Brahms Haydn Variations) with the moderns, now including Martinu, Harsányi, Malipiero, Grovlez, and Manuel Rosenthal. By the beginning of 1938 it was clear that Munch was for all intents and purposes unstoppable. Fred Goldbeck now finds him "one of the most universal performers of our time. Concert after concert he touches up his panorama of every trend of contemporary music, snooping into the last nook of every score, lending to the least of these his musician's enthusiasm and all his craft as an animator."[38]

The number of works he managed to master in five years is substantial even for a conductor in the ascendant. In 1937 he introduced more than fifty new works to his list; in 1938, more than seventy—from Mozart's G-Minor Symphony,

Mendelssohn's *Italian* Symphony, and the Berlioz Requiem to Ibert's *Escales* and Bartók's Music for Strings, Percussion, and Celesta.

Scrutiny of the early repertoire, its order of acquisition, and its omissions raises a number of questions: Why was the *Pastoral* the last of Beethoven's symphonies to attract his attention? What did he have against the Brahms Third, when, in every other way, he was the high priest of Brahms in unwilling France? When and under what circumstances did his commitment to Berlioz coalesce? We can also spot trends that go on to become hallmarks of his style, like his fondness for centenary retrospective and his interest in novelties such as Monteverdi, on the one hand, and the *ondes Martenot* on the other: contagious music, one might say, for it invites the public to take an ongoing interest in the bigger picture.

This was also the period of his short tenure as a professor of conducting at the École Normale (1937–1939). A photograph from the estate of the Czech composer-conductor Vitezslava Kapralova (1915–1940) shows the class on January 13, 1938, five women and three men.[39] He arrived at his first class and asked the students, "What am I to teach you?" He then went on to develop, according to his book, a curriculum based on analysis of phrase structure and harmonic content, followed by live conducting while another student realized scores at the piano. His recollections reveal three pedagogical principles:

> I did not permit conducting without a baton, which has unhappily become fashionable. It is a bad habit.
>
> I did not require my pupils to learn their scores by heart. . . . I have seen some of the greatest memory-acrobats make catastrophically sad mistakes. It is especially dangerous to conduct [concerto] accompaniments by heart.
>
> It is not wise to send young conductors out to do battle without preparation by an acute observer whose principal purpose has been to correct their every motion, suppress their every superfluous gesture, refine their styles.[40]

On March 6 and 13, 1938, Munch guest-conducted the Société des Concerts du Conservatoire in a program of Schumann and Brahms one week and a concert built around the work of the *claveciniste* Marguerite Roesgen-Champion the next. His "fiery conducting" attracted an important new admirer, the venerable music biographer Henri de Curzon (1861–1942), reviewer of the Conservatoire concerts for *Le Ménestrel*: "His gestures are thoroughly pliable and seem to evoke all the nuances in the music, and freer still since he moreover conducts without score."[41] When Philippe Gaubert's long-expected (and, by some, long-sought) retirement from the Société des Concerts was announced, the name leading the list of candidates was that of Charles Munch. By April it was widely assumed he would become the new principal conductor; he filed the mandatory letter of application during the first week of May. The election took place on May 10, 1938, with Munch elected vice president/conductor, the title held by all of his predecessors. On May 27, 1938, Charles Munch, though he had never attended the Conservatoire, was named the 754th *sociétaire* in the orchestra's history.

CHAPTER 3

cᐰɔ

The Société des Concerts

June 1938–May 1945

The Société des Concerts du Conservatoire was established in 1828 for the express purpose of presenting the Beethoven symphonies to the Paris public. What began as an orchestra-and-chorus consisting of the Conservatoire professors and their students past and present soon evolved into a full-fledged philharmonic society comprised almost exclusively of *1r prix* from the Conservatoire, with a recognized virtuoso in nearly every seat. For well more than a century it had weathered artistic, political, and economic vicissitudes—not to mention a healthy competition bred from its own descendents—to reemerge, generation after generation, as the pride of the nation. If, since 1918, it had become even more than usually set in its ways, it nevertheless wore its emblems—the Franck Symphony, the Saint-Saëns Organ Symphony, *Afternoon of a Faun,* and, still, Beethoven—with real pride. One of its particular treasures, a chorus, had disappeared in the 1920s. Otherwise, its traditions remained largely intact: government by a committee of the musicians, an elected conductor expected to appear for all the concerts, payment by equal shares of the season's net proceeds, and association of every member with the Conservatoire as faculty member or alumnus. The president of the Société was, by statute, the director of the Conservatoire; its most powerful member was the secretary, soon to be called the secretary-general.

Henri Rabaud, as director of the Conservatoire, flatly opposed Munch's nomination on the grounds that he had not been a student at that august institution. His position was valid and unsurprising, given his own lineage: His father had been an important cellist and officer of the orchestra, and two found-ing members were among his grandparents. Jacques Chailley, then holding a position at the Conservatoire, says that it was he who smoothed the way.[1]

Munch was undeniably qualified for the new post, but he was certain to face challenges beyond the relatively minor question of his Conservatoire pedigree. For one thing, the repertoire, like the institution, was notoriously tradition-bound, while Munch had for three seasons been located well toward the pro-gressive end of the spectrum. There were concerts every Sunday without a break. He had very little experience in the daily-life governance of an orchestra—its hirings and firings, its budget, its patrons—and, as it soon became obvious, very little interest in these matters. He had no experience at all with the expecta-tion that his entire conducting career be focused exclusively on a single orches-tral society. One might venture to suggest that from the start he had little or no intention of being the only conductor of the Société des Concerts or that it would be his only orchestra.

For a time it appeared that he would be successful at conducting both his orchestras, the Orchestre Philharmonique de Paris and the Société des Con-certs du Conservatoire, at once. He liked that kind of stretch as a matter of course, even if his handlers did not, and, at a farewell banquet eventually given by the Philharmonique, went on to say so in so many words:

> Dear colleagues: I think we've all done our best to show ourselves worthy of the confidence that's been placed in us. We've already fought mightily for music and for the good name of France. The reputation of the Orchestre Philharmonique continues to grow both here and abroad. And if, now, a society older than ours, the illustrious Société des Concerts, has just honored me by calling me to its podium, I owe that to you. And I would be less than gracious and well contrary to my own best interests if I agreed now to leave you altogether. My eminent friend [Jean Gabriel-Marie, *fils*, the *président-fondateur*] can testify to the hesitations I passed through when I learned that the Société des Concerts was thinking of me. Today, thanks to the broadminded view of M. Marie and M. Savoye, the two activities don't seem incompatible. Our goal at the Philharmonique was to introduce works of every kind of inspiration, of different genres, shimmering from the variety of their spiritual foundations, apt to provoke discussion—in a word, to create a movement. The goal of the Société des Concerts is completely different, as you know. It's a sort of Louvre, where one displays the most consecrated works under perfect conditions.[2]

This comparison of the Conservatoire concerts to the Louvre has its roots in an incident a hundred years before, when the empress Eugénie, wife of Napoléon III, asked the conductor Narcisse Girard, "And do you play only compositions by dead people in your lovely Conservatoire concerts?" "Madame," replied Girard with a bow, "the repertoire of our society is the Louvre of musical art."[3]

On June 16, 1938, Munch gathered both his orchestras, the Orchestre Philharmonique de Paris and the Société des Concerts, additional ensembles of military brass, and several choruses—six hundred in all—in the *cour d'honneur* of the Invalides, for a centenary performance of the Berlioz Requiem, his first public encounter with the work. In all it was a problematic performance. Despite "magnificent" conducting, the constituent ensembles, with the four brass choirs relegated to the indoor galleries overlooking the square, separated frequently. "Nevertheless," wrote Paul Bertrand, "the work retained its prestige. Munch lent it incomparable fire and emotional intensity, despite unexpected *accelerandi* where the opposite seemed merited." It was "too bad that for the same reason— the [large outdoor] venue taken out of an error in principle—one could not make out the individual sonorities in the *Amen,* and that someone had had the unfortunate idea of adding a triumphal march at the end."[4]

Three and a half decades later, in a bar, the conductor Paul Paray was still taking pleasure in recounting Munch's discomfiture. His version has Cortot, the "thoroughly rattled" producer, telephoning Paray after a difficult general rehearsal: "Come quickly, dear maestro!" The brass, initially placed at the four corners of the large exterior courtyard, were unable to synchronize with the main group. "Come get us out of this bad situation."

Paray's purported response—"What are you thinking? I couldn't do that to a colleague"—seems unlikely on the face of it. The anecdote, coming so long after the fact, may be a result of the bitter enmity that later arose between Munch and Paray over their wartime activities.[5] In any case the performing force was redeployed between the rehearsal and the performance, with mixed result. Munch survived the experience and went on to program the Berlioz Requiem on a half dozen other occasions in his career, including in the semioutdoor Tanglewood Shed (August 1954); he recorded it twice.

Only a few weeks later, still in the summer before their first official season together, the Société des Concerts was summoned to provide the music for a state dinner honoring George VI and Elizabeth of England. (This was the occasion on which the queen captivated the fashion industry by always appearing in white, a symbol of mourning for her mother.) During the seven-course meal for the new king and queen—from clear tortoise broth to *foie gras aux truffes de Périgord,* with seven fine wines ending in a Grande Fine Champagne 1848—the nation's most prestigious orchestra serenaded Their Britannic Majesties with more than a dozen movements carefully chosen to show the best of modern France. There was music by Saint-Saëns, Fauré, Rabaud, Debussy, and Ravel, as well as works of composers by then closely associated with Munch himself: Roussel, Ibert, and Milhaud.[6] The choice of repertoire and performers was, like the food and wine, a statement about quality of life, emphasizing, as the orchestra and its supporters often did, the perfection of French taste, along with the suggestion that such a lifestyle demanded to be retained, whatever was to happen next in the international political arena.

From Lambaréné Albert Schweitzer wrote in July 1938 to congratulate Charles for the life he had begun to carve out for himself. Paris was, he believed, a difficult place to succeed on one's merit alone:

> I don't imagine your flock is as easy to lead as it was in times past when I knew it. But you will carry before them the torch of the Ideal and they will follow. . . . If only your father could have known that one day you would be conducting the orchestra of the Conservatory! Your way of conducting resembles his most of all the Munch family. I'll never forget how he conducted Brahms: never did I understand Brahms better than from his interpretation.[7]

Munch responded, philosophically, that the task, though formidable, did not frighten him: "For the moment my sheep are yet to be over-excited . . . at least it looks that way."[8]

The long season opened, as was the custom at the Société des Concerts, with Beethoven: the Seventh Symphony and the *Emperor* Concerto with Marguerite Long. Munch left his personal stamp by premiering a *Nocturne* of Guy Ropartz, followed by *Daphnis et Chloé,* Suite 2. The second week was equally personal, with centenary performances of Bizet (*Patrie* overture, the symphony, and the suite from *La jolie fille de Perth*), Poulenc's insouciant *Concert champêtre,* and *La Valse.* Before Christmas the soloists had included the cellist André Navarra, Rubinstein, Francescatti, Alfredo Casella, and Magda Tagliaferro. As if to demonstrate how he meant to run things, he yielded the podium to Walter, Monteux, and Boulanger and in November took the opportunity to travel to Athens, where he appeared with the American artist Nathan Milstein.

The Orchestre Philharmonique went on largely as before. Straube and the Thomanerchor again appeared, this time in a Saint Matthew Passion at the church of Saint-Eustache, October 27–29; Furtwängler conducted the orchestra in December: Beethoven and Brahms, Pfitzner and Richard Strauss, also Berlioz and Debussy. In a string of letters that autumn, Furtwängler asked for Munch's advice, a correspondence that suggests how much the two conductors valued each other's artistic opinion. It also gives a good glimpse of the practical considerations of the trade, as Furtwängler seeks to find a copy of the Shostakovich Fifth Symphony in Paris and leaves documentation of his very high fee, four thousand francs. Yet Munch was in Strasbourg on his vacation by the time the German conductor arrived in Paris, as though purposely avoiding the encounter.

Philippe Gaubert's departure from the Société des Concerts, after a brilliant career but too long after he had lost interest in the game, was not especially lamented. The players in their youth and early middle age were hungry to rebuild their orchestra into an exciting, modern ensemble, whose traditional Sunday concerts were only the beginning of a full-time, year-long schedule with guest conductors and star soloists, broadcasts, recordings, nighttime concerts, student events, and a chamber orchestra ("to put butter on the spinach," said one member). Munch was already identified with many of these efforts, and to the *sociétaires* he seemed the obvious key to a brilliant future.

His chief collaborator in reshaping the Société des Concerts was violinist Jean Savoye, who had been elected secretary of the governing committee. Savoye was capable and shrewd, a considerably more agile administrator than Munch himself, and the resurrection of the society as a powerhouse in Parisian music was as much his doing as anyone else's. He did not object to the Munch initiatives that fall—the conductors, soloists, leaves of absence, even the contemporary music—but rather welcomed the progress all these represented.

The press welcomed the overall freshening of the atmosphere. "The ardor of M. Munch is not to be resisted, an effect emphasized by the absence of music, music-stand, and podium. Sometimes with him you have the feeling that he adds value to every work he leads through the color he controls beneath quivering hands."[9] The public found him irresistible, too, especially women, and to what would be called the bobby-sox set, the *munchettes,* he was nothing less than a cult figure. Women soloists (and they were plentiful in the Paris of those years) became welcome on the stage of the Société des Concerts (but not as members of the orchestra), where before all but the *divas* had been merely tolerated. Everyone enjoyed the spectacle of Munch and his Muses: Monique de La Bruchollerie, Magda Tagliaferro, Ina Marinka, Geneviève Joy (later Mme. Dutilleux), and more than a dozen like them.

With at least two of these artists, the relationship grew into personal intimacy. The violinist Ginette Neveu (1919–1949), winner of the *1r prix* at the Conservatoire at age eleven, then winner of the Wieniawski Competition in 1935, was slightly ahead of Munch in international allure, having managed to reach Poland, Germany, the United States, and Canada before the war. They appeared together for the first time in February 1942, when she was twenty-three, then as frequently after that as it could be arranged. He took her to England on his first visit after the war, then to Vienna and Prague. Their performances in New York and Strasbourg in 1949 have been preserved on record. Backstage talk at the Conservatoire linked them romantically, the inevitable by-product of frequent joint engagements. (In fact, her predilections tended, it was said, toward the sapphic.)

Nicole Henriot (1925–2001) was a student of Marguerite Long at the Paris Conservatoire, where she took the *1r prix* (thus ending her course of instruction) in 1938, at the age of twelve. In 1939 she won the Fauré Competition in Luxembourg. Munch encountered her for the first time when conducting for the Marguerite Long Competition—a task he particularly disliked, owing to its necessity of working with children and their parents. The work was the Brahms Second Piano Concerto. By all accounts he was rushing nonchalantly through the dress rehearsal, taking the second-movement scherzo so fast that the child simply stopped playing. When Munch turned inquisitively in her direction, she said, "You're taking it too fast, *maître*. I can play it that fast, but it would not be correct." Munch stormed out of the rehearsal.

That night at midnight, Madame Henriot answered the door to find the subdued conductor and his score, desiring to review the work with her daughter at once. "But she's sleeping, *maître*." Cajolery proved unsuccessful, and it was arranged that they would go over the work together once again the next morning before the concert. The Brahms went on to be featured prominently in their joint repertoire.

We encounter Nicole Henriot at the Société des Concerts for the first time in March 1941, in a Saturday-morning public dress rehearsal conducted by Gustave Cloëz. Her first official appearance with the orchestra under Munch appears to have been when she was seventeen: on April 12, 1942, in the Liszt E-flat Concerto—another work they frequently did together for twenty-five more years. Her appearances with the Société des Concerts became, like Neveu's, routine; he took Henriot to London in 1944, Strasbourg in 1945, then to Israel, Vienna, and The Hague before introducing her in New York in January 1948. By this time, their careers were inextricable. After Ginette Neveu's untimely death, she became his unrivaled favorite protégée—traveling most often with her formidable mother, who approved of Munch wholeheartedly. Altogether Nicole Henriot and Charles Munch appeared together roughly two hundred times and formally recorded together a half dozen works, the centerpieces of the French concerto repertoire.

The precise details of their relationship make little difference to our story, though in many quarters—especially to Americans amused by European stereotypes—the implications seemed obvious. Whatever the case, Henriot is to emerge as the single most important figure in his personal life after Geneviève Maury. She was key to whatever contentment he found in old age. Her strikingly dignified presence in professional and family photographs is a theme of the Munch iconography. In addition, almost everything we know of the private life of Charles Munch comes down to us through Nicole Henriot, the primary agent of his legacy until her death in 2001.

The 1938–1939 season was altogether triumphant, twenty Saturday-Sunday pairs between the beginning of October and the end of March, with a twenty-first concert to benefit the pension fund—this was pretty much in the manner things had always been done. The last three concerts (March 12, 19, and 26, 1939) were those of an orchestra fully restored to health: an all-Fauré concert under the patronage of the Fauré Society, with Marguerite Long playing the Ballade; a concert with Szigeti in the Ernest Bloch Violin Concerto, recorded for French Columbia the following week; *Rapsodie flamande* by Roussel; and a concluding Ninth Symphony. As though reluctant to yield the first-season thrill, Munch and the orchestra set out for Strasbourg, Saint-Etienne, Lausanne, and Geneva with the *Rapsodie flamande, Eroica, La Mer,* and *L'apprenti sorcier.*

The Strasbourg establishment was ecstatic, as it was always reliably to be. Jacques Feschotte wrote in the program that the locals, "with joy and fully understandable pride . . . welcomed Charles Munch back to his birthplace, at the head of the most glorious orchestral phalanx in France. Son of the unforgettable Ernest, brother of Fritz, he fights courageously for his contemporaries and for the young, though is still faithful to the masters."[10] He had, the article noted, earned constant and magnificent ovations since his appointment in October, and it was recalled with pleasure that he had put Ropartz, Fritz's predecessor as director of the Strasbourg conservatory, on his first Paris program.

Early June took him on to Brussels and then to Brest. When he returned to Paris, he learned he had been awarded the Legion of Honor on August 5, 1939. Another tradition of the venerable Société des Concerts was to secure that distinction at the start of each new conductor's tenure.

When France officially declared war on Germany on September 3, 1939, the evacuation of Strasbourg was well under way. From a communication originating at the Strasbourg recruiting office, we learn that Charles Munch volunteered for military service that week, and "note was taken" of his willingness to serve. It was never seriously expected that people his age (forty-eight) would bear arms; his younger brother Hans was called up, but his older brother Fritz was not. An entire generation of Paris musicians was soon mobilized, including Savoye (b. 1902), Jolivet (b. 1905), Messiaen (b. 1908), and Martinon (b. 1910), all of whom went to the front and were captured. Something on the order of two dozen members of the Société des Concerts became prisoners of war.

As the *drôle de guerre,* the "phony war," played out during the winter of 1939–1940, no effort was made to have a formal concert season, though on December 10 and 17 Munch drew together enough personnel to offer the Ropartz Requiem and the Franck Symphony on one concert and, at the other, the *Eroica,* alongside works by Dukas, Ravel, and Roussel. The proceeds were sent to provide Christmas trees for the troops.

Munch had had every intention of considerably expanding his guest-conducting career after his first season with the Conservatoire. He was thus in Lisbon when war was declared and hurried back to France out of general principle (not, as some accounts suggest, because he feared being locked out otherwise). His American debut had been fixed for Saint Louis during the holiday season. The *New York Times* mentioned the booking in a summary of the seasons announced by the major American orchestras and, as late as Christmas eve 1939, looked forward to the Munch concerts the following week. Ropartz's letter of December 12 bids him farewell, as though the trip were imminent; in those weeks, too, a flyer was prepared in English summarizing his biography through the Legion of Honor in late summer 1939. The Saint Louis patrons first learned of the cancellation from the printed program for December 29–30, 1939—which attributed it not to political events but to the weather:

> It is with a feeling of extreme regret that the Saint Louis Symphony Society finds it necessary to announce the inability of Charles Muench, who was to have been guest conductor at this week's concerts, to appear with the orchestra. Certain commitments for concerts in Paris made it imperative for Mr. Muench to stay in France until a few days before the time for his first rehearsals with our orchestra.
>
> Planning to travel to the United States by air, Mr. Muench encountered an unprecedented period of unfavorable flying weather over the Atlantic. When it became problematical for even two or three rehearsals for his program, there was no choice but to cancel the projected visit, which was to have been Mr. Muench's American debut.[11]

Vladimir Golschmann, the resident conductor, covered for the absence.

Charles and Vivette Munch took refuge at La Solitude in Villefavard, meaning to wait out the events and give shelter to refugees from Alsace. Juliette Ebersolt came, too, choosing as her most prized possession to bring from Paris her volumes of the Bach-Gesellschaft Edition. Bohuslav Martinu and his wife could not be accommodated in the villa as planned, owing to the Alsatians. Munch went about the region until he found a house for rent in the village of Le Clops, close by, and acquired it as a way station for the Martinus. The same sort of things quietly went on all over that area, far from railroads, highways, and, it was hoped, soldiers. (Yet the massacre of Oradour-sur-Glane on June 10, 1944, would take place just a few miles from Villefavard.)

They were back in Paris in the spring of 1940, leaving the avenue Manoury for the rue Dehodencq in order to distance themselves from the artillery batteries surrounding the city. They also spent considerable time in Yvonne Gouverné's country house at Grosrouvre, in the forest a few dozen miles southwest of Versailles, where Munch and Honegger are pictured playing *boules* toward the beginning of the Occupation; they subsequently bought the property. Munch appeared twice in April to premiere contemporary music (Honegger's *Nocturne*, Tcherepnin's *Suite géorgienne*, Harsányi's *Histoire du petit tailleur*) at small concerts, but that was all. The Germans entered Paris on June 14, 1940, and the "armistice" was signed on June 22. Hitler came to Paris for a few hours the next day, famously beginning his tour with a visit to the Opéra, illuminated as though for a performance.

In early September Munch was induced to return permanently from the country to Paris to organize the concert season. Otherwise, he had been threatened, the occupying authorities would place a German conductor at the head of the Société des Concerts—a similar threat, that otherwise Karajan would conduct, was later used to sway him to undertake the Orchestre de Paris. He writes Martinu that his *rentrée* is eminent: "Farewell to the chickens and rabbits, the horses and cows; farewell Christiane (my most recent acquisition—a mule)."[12] He convened the orchestra in the third week of September with prepared remarks:

> I don't need to remind you of the great sadness we all feel in coming together under circumstances so different from those we had hoped for when we separated at the end of last season.
>
> Now we are united by the suffering of our country and overcome with woes both general and particular. But a ray of joy: with us again, safe and sound, are many who were away last year. We welcome them cordially. Alas, sixteen of us are still held in captivity. We remember them with ardent sympathy and share the concerns of their families.
>
> My friends, in the dark days we've just lived through, you have all certainly sensed the precious things no force can defeat, especially deep affections, real friendships, the joy of working together toward a shared ideal. The enemy can ruin us materially, but it cannot take away our artistic gifts or patrimony, if we remember to defend them. On that field of battle we are not beaten. On that field we will continue the fight. And in the difficult future opening before us, only that which is worthy to live will continue to live. Our Société must, at all costs, survive. May we be united; may we spare no effort to sustain the reputation of the Société des Concerts. Think of all this next Sunday.[13]

And on September 29 the Société des Concerts reopened with a program designed on the one hand to ensure a sense of business as usual and on the other to proffer a significant juxtaposition of names: Beethoven's *Egmont* overture and Seventh Symphony, Ravel's *Pavane pour une infante défunte* and *La Valse*. Not many of the occupying troops are likely to have been able to secure admission to the Salle des Concerts, and in any event it was hardly a natural place for their agenda to play out. Orchestras and orchestral music figured importantly in the German nationalism, to be sure: Bach, Mozart, and Beethoven were considered prima facie evidence of the superiority of German culture. That argument would be made in grander and more modern venues than the threadbare Salle des Concerts, like the Palais de Chaillot, as well as over the radio. Given the magnitude of the underlying issues, the 1940–1941 season looks surprisingly ordinary, with thirty Sunday concerts and a summer festival in June. The clashes of principle and propaganda grew strident in 1941–1942. Meanwhile, the orchestra tried to carry on, Munch arriving for rehearsals on his bicycle, his *employé* Roger Toureau sometimes seen behind him carrying baguettes for the players' families.

"Anyone who was not there," thought Simone de Beauvoir, "is not privileged to criticize those who were."[14] Few who stayed in Paris had the time or the willingness, let alone the knowledge, to formulate a considered code of response to what might happen next. Principles of conduct were discovered one decision at a time, one reaction after another, to problems ranging from inconvenient—the lack of butter or of Brahms—to mortal. The urge for normal daily life was so strong among the occupied, and the need to seem to provide it so strong among the occupiers, at least with regard to the citified upper class, that boundaries between surviving the enemy and contributing to its purposes were anything but clear. Was there really a difference between Beethoven's Ninth in Paris and the same work in Berlin? What if Goebbels were in the front row? What did *Le martyre de St.-Sébastien* mean when swastikas flew outside and German officers were found within?

The Germans packed off to Paris whichever musical personalities were interested in making the trip: Wilhelm Kempff and Walter Gieseking, the conductors Abendroth, Knappertsbusch, and Mengelberg. The recommended fare was by Richard Strauss, Franz Lehár (a personal friend of Hitler), Pfitzner, and Werner Egk. The Beethoven cycle was encouraged, then expected. Paris wind players, whom all the conductors coveted, were offered inducements usual and unusual to carry on their careers across the Rhine.

In truth, Bach and Mozart and Beethoven—but seldom Wagner and Strauss—paid the bills during the Occupation. They kept French musicians in France and away from the obligatory work program in Germany, since what musicians did was recognized as essential to the proper functioning of metropolitan life. Classical music fed and clothed and warmed musicians and their families, and it gave a surprisingly numerous public some solace and strength. That a good deal of the music was by German-speaking composers was, for most people most of the time, irrelevant except to the Germans.

Collaboration is the very essence of live performance, and in that respect painters and writers and even composers—artists who make their art alone and can bide their time until external conditions improve—had it better than those whose livelihood meant appearing in public. Collaboration with the German occupants of France and of Paris in particular was so easy a charge to level after the fact and so difficult to carry much further than the charge itself that the word alone becomes highly charged, like "sympathize" and "Vichy." The suggestion that Munch collaborated with the enemy was made publicly and dramatically just after the war and continues to surface from time to time in gossipy asides in the press.[15]

So it is crucial to dismiss, categorically and near the outset, any question as to Munch's loyalty to France—and, most especially, any and every suggestion that he ever acted other than in the best interests of his musicians, all of whom were, by statute, French. Sympathy for the occupying force was simply never at issue: Munch was incredulous that Germany might seek to own France. For every day of the remaining twenty-five years left to him, he felt betrayed by a civilization he had once admired, even claimed as his own. His embarrassment over his association with the German forces in World War I was thoroughgoing by the time he left Leipzig. It is almost surely responsible for his vigorous ethic of good works, usually unseen—atoning, that is, for something he could scarce have controlled.

By not one of the standard measures is his loyalty as a French citizen even remotely suspect. He declined to appear in Germany from well before the war until May 1952, when he brought the Boston Symphony Orchestra to postwar Germany under Allied Occupation. He would neither be photographed with anyone in uniform nor broadcast over the collaborationist Radio Paris. There is not a shadow of anti-Semitism to be found in his life or work. He betrayed no one, protected the institutions for which he was responsible, his employees, and their families at considerable risk to his person and his properties, and took more than one publicly courageous stance. Privately he cared for others in every conceivable way before, during, and after the war. "He was the breath of our life," said his niece. "His music was our balm."[16]

For Charles Munch was by birth, spiritual inclination, and family connection first and foremost a pacifist and thus found the very notion of armed conflict abhorrent. His closest intimates paid the terrible prices of war—Nicole Henriot and Pierre-Paul Schweitzer were tortured by the Gestapo, and most of one brother's family was killed in the bombing of Strasbourg. Munch himself spent more than one night in custody for refusing to comply with official demands for his services as conductor for undisguised political purpose. From 1940 to 1944 he gave material aid in the form of food and money to poets, peasants, and passersby, shelter at the family properties in central and southern

France to refugees trying to reach Spain and Portugal, and hiding places in and around Paris for musicians in danger of being deported to the camps. His joy at the liberation was all consuming—even more in private than in his conspicuous public outpourings. He had virtually nothing else to do with Germany for the rest of his life.

He was for all intents and purposes untouched by prejudices of religious belief, nationality, or race. His misery over the inhumanity Germany visited on the world during the 1930s and '40s became more pronounced as he grew older: This is the standard explanation for the loneliness and melancholy that plagued his private life. Sometimes a quiet moment would come in a conversation, and he would begin to cry. His household staff would occasionally greet visitors with the warning: "He is sad."

His friend Marcelle Margot-Noblemaire, née Rateau, attached to an immense fortune—the Wagons-Lits company and Thomas Cook tours from her husband, René; royalties on turbine engines from her father, Auguste Rateau[17]— owned a 285-acre monastery in Grasse, fifteen miles due north of Cannes. This she used, along with her husband's railroad cars, to help children escape from Germany. Groups would be trained in Paris to move by flashlight and to give Christian French names if questioned; they would be taken by wagons-lits to stations near Grasse, then housed in the monastery until boat passage could be arranged from nearby Nice to England. Munch used these connections to aid his friends, as well. The beautiful Madame Margot-Noblemaire, who, early on, conceived a lifelong passion for the dashing conductor, is a major figure in his professional and personal life, and her several activities in his behalf will form a part of our narrative to come.

Outwardly, Munch meant to be seen as tending his sheep, as the French are inclined to put it: taking care of his musicians but not stirring up trouble. He and Savoye hoped to deliver concert seasons that seemed, to the public at large, ordinary. This would be difficult, given pressures real and implied on the repertoire. English, Russian, and American music was forbidden outright, as were works by Mendelssohn and Dukas. Ravel was frowned upon. Jewish employees of any sort were forbidden to work, so protection had to be arranged for those orchestral players who were in harm's way. (Since Colonne was a Jew, the Concerts Colonne were renamed the Concerts Gabriel Pierné. These were watched more closely than the Conservatoire concerts.) The soloists, of course, were limited to those staying in Paris or, more controversially, those whom the authorities allowed to make the trip.

Given these conditions, it is instructive to watch Munch and sometimes his entire orchestra outflank the propaganda service. Most often this was a matter of nuances of repertoire and of being "out of town" when Berlin officials and high-ranking conductors like Abendroth passed through. Seen in this light, the three festival concerts in the Palais de Chaillot in spring 1941—Debussy, Ravel, and Beethoven (with Marguerite Long as piano soloist)—have a particular patriotic thrust. The several Joan of Arc oratorios in 1941, 1942, and 1943 have nuanced and multiple meanings, and the movies for which the Société des Concerts quietly recorded soundtracks—*Les enfants du paradis,* for instance—were outright subversive. So, too, was the routine programming of works by composers whose compositional daring or personal lifestyles placed them counter to German ideals: Poulenc, Stravinsky, and probably Honegger as well.

It is certainly true that Charles Munch willingly continued his personal and professional relationships with two figures whose activities in Germany and on behalf of German music were later—and widely—deemed impure: Wilhelm Furtwängler and Alfred Cortot. Both were mentors to whom Munch knew he owed his success. Furtwängler had turned to Munch again and again in 1938 and 1939 as his most trusted Paris contact, struggling to keep his opportunities there open when in London and elsewhere he and the Berlin Philharmonic found empty halls and demonstrations:

> Like I told you, I rather fear the emigrants [i.e., refugees] and the Jews, now grown quite influential in musical life. Besides, I'd like to conduct in Paris because one must sidestep Austria, Italy, etc., and I don't much want to go to London, that obtuse city. That is to say: I love Paris and feel close to it intellectually, not to mention my delight that you are there.[18]

In April 1940, "I wait ardently for the end of these circumstances, so abnormal for us artists, but it's impossible to see a way out."[19] Munch invited Furtwängler to Paris in both the 1941–1942 and 1942–1943 seasons, to judge from Furtwängler's eventual response: "Ordinarily I wouldn't have any interest whatever in going to Paris [under the changed circumstances], but I would have gladly accepted your invitation."[20] Furtwängler did take care to note his desire to stay on the list of potential guests "if that's really what you and your orchestra want."[21] Similarly, Cortot remained a friend and colleague, a powerful artist, and a central agent of interaction with the governments in power.

If any single musical event can be said to characterize the artistic climate of these uncertain times, it was the sensational Paris premiere of Arthur Honegger's *La danse des morts* in January 1941—strongly evocative of what Ravel meant by *La Valse,* yet so hollow, so stark as to constitute an even more frightening commentary on the end of a civilization. The text, by Paul Claudel, was declaimed by Jean-Louis Barrault. The singers and chorus (Odette Turba-Rabier, soprano; Eliette Schenneberg, contralto; Charles Panzéra, baritone; Yvonne Gouverné's famous choir) were the best in town. La Voix de Son Maître records provided a *de luxe* presentation that included full-color souvenir programs and posters. These same designs were used for the recording, made on March 27–28, after a repeat performance in February and a gala at the Palais de Chaillot on March 23.

What the public made of this dialogue between the Claudelian narrator and God, with its message of comfort in the cross and of death as a means of achieving inner life, is difficult to know, given the circumstances outside the hall. What is clear is that *La danse des morts* sealed the lifetime association of Honegger and Munch. Honegger was among those who had chosen to stay in Paris with his wife, Andrée Vaurabourg (Vaura), and daughter, Pascale, and not far from Claire Croiza, the famous singer, with whom he had a son. The Honeggers socialized with the Munches, including the *boules* at Grosrouvre. Honegger was working at the time on his Second Symphony, always intended for Munch and soon to be at the core of his repertoire. His earlier mixed-media composition with Paul Claudel, *Jeanne d'Arc au bûcher,* would be the feature of Munch's second season in the United States.

Honegger, like Munch, was later said to have had too easy a time of it in occupied Paris and was sharply criticized for having traveled to Vienna in 1941 for the 150th anniversary of Mozart's death, a notoriously politicized event. He was also attacked for writing criticism for *Comœdia,* which in those years showed obvious leanings toward appeasement. (He had already been affiliated with the publication for more than a decade.) In 1941 Honegger's work was read as an act of resistance—not so offensive as to result in censure but obvious in message.

In the case of Poulenc, composer and conductor developed a certain artistic admiration for each other's work, but Munch exhibits little of the personal mission he showed toward Roussel and Honegger. Mostly this is a matter of opposing personality types: Neither Munch nor Poulenc found the other especially attractive. Yet, after the cantata *Sécheresses* had failed in its premiere with the Colonne and Paul Paray in 1939, Poulenc sought out Munch to reintroduce the revised version. This negotiation led to the concert of February 14, 1941, in which the cantata was presented by the Gouverné singers, as Poulenc himself appeared in the *Concert champêtre.* He also appeared as one of the pianists in Stravinsky's *Les Noces* later in the spring. Munch offered Poulenc's Organ Concerto (with Duruflé) in December 1941, and in due course their long association and to a certain degree their joint audience appeal led to two important Boston premieres.

The 1940–1941 season was otherwise on the whole a relatively tame mixture of safe drawing cards—Bach's Christmas Oratorio and Saint John Passion, a good deal of Beethoven, some Mozart—and noncontroversial French works, with a Duruflé première and the Ibert Concertino for saxophone with Marcel Mule. (There was Wagner, too, most of it brought in by guest conductors.) Increasingly the concerts took place at the Palais de Chaillot, where, despite the cold, large audiences, including soldiers in German uniform, could assemble. The single-composer concerts there in June (June 13, 20, and 27: Debussy, Ravel, Beethoven, respectively), sponsored by La Voix de Son Maître, took on the character of a summer festival, anticipated annually.

To Paris musicians, especially the celebrities, the 1941–1942 concert season posed the most difficult questions of wartime. Occupation policies and propaganda were firmly in place, while resistance, on the part of urban intellectuals, became more organized by the week. In September 1941 Parisian artist-musicians, partly responding to Hitler's campaign against the USSR, organized themselves into a Front National de la Musique, gathered around the leftists Roland Manuel, Roger Désormière, and Elsa Barraine, with the stated aim of combating the German repertoire. Auric, Poulenc, Rosenthal, and Munch were remembered to have joined the central committee in 1942, then Honegger ("a misled collaborator to *Comœdia*," noted one internal document)—"literally all the composers and conductors who matter."[22]

December 1941, then, marked the 150th anniversary of Mozart's death. In October the German authorities ordered a full-scale festival for the first week of December, prompting the membership of the Société des Concerts, in a sequence of events I have chronicled elsewhere, to meet and conditionally assent to the directive: all recorded in their minutes under the bold rubric "Concerts de Collaboration."[23] Munch could not avoid conducting the first of these, a regularly scheduled Sunday concert on November 30, 1941, in their venerable old hall, with a program headed "Orchester der Konservatoriums-Gesellschaft." Jacques Thibaud appeared as violin soloist. Munch then went to Brussels to conduct the Philharmonic Society there, making himself unavailable as his forces presented the Mozart Requiem at the Palais de Chaillot, then a closing concert (the Franck Symphonic Variations, strangely paired with a Mozart Piano Concerto and Max Reger's Mozart-Variations) with the Leipzig pianist Hans Belz and the Gewandhaus conductor, Hermann Abendroth.

Increasingly he sought to escape the fraught politics of programming by playing new music of French composers, his own niche anyway and unlikely to be forbidden a hearing by the occupying authorities. December 1941, then, saw Duruflé in Poulenc's Organ Concerto, which became a favorite title on his list, and *Le sacre du printemps*, which did not. In January a free concert offered all contemporary music, including Jean Martinon's *Stalag IX*, Messiaen's *Offrandes oubliées*, Thiriet's *Oedipe-Roi*, and Roussel's Third Symphony, now well known. Honegger's fiftieth birthday was celebrated in February with a program of his established works and, more significantly, during the June festival at the Chaillot, with a gala that included the first Paris performance of the Second Symphony and a full-scale revival of *Jeanne d'Arc au bûcher*.

Munch also took a pronounced interest in Pierre Capdevielle (1906–1969), premiering a revised version of the *Incantation* on the death of a young Spartan. A few weeks later, discovering that Capdevielle was on the verge of giving up his career, an ailing Munch telephoned with the offer of money to keep him in the business. His callow, earnest response typifies the kind of reaction such unexpected generosity would usually earn in exchange: "It's important, Munch, that you sense the depth of my gratitude, that you know exactly of the rehabilitation, the redress of my existence that your simple goodness has afforded me.... Thank you, Munch, thank you. It's *chic*, what you did. Get well soon, and may your first trip out [of the sickroom] be to come here and see what your generous, fraternal gesture kept intact."[24]

The end of the season brought ever more delicate solutions to political dilemmas. The twenty-third concert offered the Brahms Third, an excerpt from *Lohengrin* in a version associated with Furtwängler, Nicole Henriot in the Liszt E-flat Piano Concerto, and Alfred Bachelet's *Surya*, for tenor, chorus, and orchestra after a text by Leconte de Lisle. Bachelet (1864–1944) was a grand old man from Nancy, at the border with Germany, and his work had been commissioned by the interim government in 1940 and refashioned from a youthful sketch. The rapturous critical response to this kind of recovered Romanticism was all but unanimous; nonetheless, the multiple implications of the text, with its references to "men of pure blood" and "the peaceful races" had their sinister overtones.

Similarly, *Jeanne d'Arc*, the multiauthored oratorio in seven parts (April 28, 1942), sends mixed messages. Joan is manifestly a symbol of French heroism against an intractable enemy, but that enemy was the English; moreover, both the Vichystes and the Free French relied on her to reach the citizenry. The work in question had been commissioned by the Association Jeune-France for the national Joan of Arc holiday week in 1941 and was composed by Louis Beydts, Georges Dandelot, Raymond Loucheur, Tony Aubin, Jacques Chailley, Capdevielle, and Jolivet. The results in 1941, not involving Munch, had been unsatisfactory, and the 1942 revival appears to have been his way of lending support to a group of composers in whom he believed.

Immediately following the close of the season, the orchestra proceeded to Bordeaux, Nantes, Rennes, and Le Mans, again to suggest all was well. They returned to the June galas at the Palais de Chaillot in repertoire that sent more confusing messages still: a Debussy-Fauré program with Marguerite Long and *Le martyre de Saint Sébastien*, a Bach-Françaix program, featuring the premiere of *L'apocalypse de Saint Jean* by Françaix; and three Beethoven concertos with Wilhelm Kempff, dispatched directly from Berlin—anchors of the modern French repertoire, music of martyrdom and Christian faith, and Beethoven from Berlin. What was being said—and to whom?

One of the more curious musical projects of the Occupation was the journey by Marguerite Long, Munch, and the Société des Concerts to Vichy for a concert on October 22, 1942, in overt *hommage au Maréchal Pétain.* The program consisted of Mozart and Beethoven, Ravel and Roussel. Breathless promotional material by violinist Dany Brunschwig (sometime sonata partner with another well-known journalist of the epoch, Suzanne Demarquez), noted "a hall full to overflowing, where one could recognize Marshal and Mme. Petain, [Louis] Hautecœur, the director of Fine Arts, and the most eminent personalities of the diplomatic world from all the countries of Europe, plus all the noteworthies of the provisional capital—who gave a grandiose ovation, at the end of the concert, to the great conductor and distinguished musician Charles Munch." She closed her remarks by touching on the orchestra's long-held and most precious desire: "It's high time the Société des Concerts du Conservatoire became the national orchestra of this great country, so that it can tour the world as ambassador of French musical thought."[25] This, precisely, was the first reason advanced decades later, under the government of de Gaulle and his minister André Malraux, for creating a new Orchestre de Paris.

Any number of programs that fall suggest intricate maneuvering behind the scenes: an all-Strauss concert at the Palais de Chaillot, for instance; a Ravel-Debussy program in the rail yards and an all-Beethoven program, both mysteriously canceled at the last minute. In December there was another "gala of works by prisoners, organized by the Office of Fine Arts of the City of Paris and the Société des Concerts, with, acting as presidents, M. Georges Scapini, ambassador, and M. Maurice Pinot, commissioner-general for prisoners"—both of them high-ranking officials from Vichy. But Munch left the conducting of this event to an associate.

In late 1942 Munch at last succeeded in scheduling an all-Ropartz concert, with a premiere of Psalm 129, *De Profundis,* along with the prelude to *Le Pays, La chasse du Prince Arthur,* the D-Major Fantasy, and Ropartz's Requiem. The composer later remembered his Festival Guy Ropartz (January 24, 1943) as the red-letter day in his long career; it was of this concert that Honegger wrote of "that fervor, that dynamism, that profound understanding of the substance of music that make [Munch] the best conductor of our time."[26]

Twice that winter (January 10 and February 21, 1942) Munch and the Société des Concerts revisited Honegger's String Symphony; on February 14 he let Georges Dandelot lead the premiere of a new Symphony in D, later published with a dedication to him. On February 28, 1943, came the important premiere of the *Trois complaintes du soldat,* composed by André Jolivet and sung by Pierre Bernac. (Later in the year the Jolivet was recorded, a haunting artifact of the industry in wartime.) During the same concert Honegger was captivated, against his better judgment, by the Franck Symphony, a work he was prone to think of as diffuse and simpleminded. This performance he found "quite simply overwhelming":

> When [Munch] has gotten to the kernel of a work, he leads it with such spirit, such passion, such a powerful will to express its greatness that it's positively irresistible. [It's not a matter of analytical details:] You're carried away, convinced it can't be any other way, and at the last chord, you erupt and join the unanimous expression of enthusiasm surging through the room. The person who can do this is not just a great conductor but a man possessed by Music.[27]

In May 1943 Munch led the Prix de Paris award concert, which presented the first performance of Jean Martinon's Psalm 136, or *Chant des captifs* (King James Psalm 137: "By the rivers of Babylon, / there we sat down, yea, we wept, / when we remembered Zion"). Composed during Martinon's two years as a prisoner in the deadly Stalag IX at Bad Orb, near Frankfurt, the work was placed comfortably between Roussel's Fourth and *Daphnis et Chloé* for the Sunday concert. Martinon's letter of thanks to Munch is quite similar to Capdevielle's of the previous spring, attributing the success of the work as much to the conducting as to the composition:

> I know you to be so solicited, so surrounded, so flattered that I'm thoroughly amazed at the affection and interest you've shown me with such spirit. I feel that I owe it all to you, since nearly everything about the beginning of my success is your work. . . . How did this little violinist so interest his conductor? Who else would have drawn an unknown musician thus from the shadows? You alone knew how to accomplish this miracle. You alone could get me taken seriously by this famously snobbish public, linking your name with mine, your glory with my obscurity. The single thing I worry about is whether or not I really merit your affection.[28]

Jean Martinon (1910–1976), already a protégé, later claimed to have been one of Munch's conducting pupils. He was soon to be a leading candidate for the podium of the Société des Concerts—Munch thought him the only viable one.

Concert life did survive. The authorities in Vichy and in Paris, from local committee member to the ministry—republicans, socialists, and communists—saw to it. This was a long-proved strength of the French bureaucracy: powering its cultural infrastructure, come what may. By 1942–1943 and 1943–1944 Munch and the Société des Concerts were presenting not only the traditional thirty-odd Sunday concerts but also ancillary events that amounted to full employment for most of the players. All told during those two seasons there were something like 175 individual services for concerts, broadcasts, records, and films—not counting rehearsals. The orchestra was not merely surviving: It was thriving.

Like the rest of the government, the radio orchestra, commonly called the Orchestre National, had left Paris in the evacuation, wandering first to Rennes in Brittany, then to Marseille. In 1943 what was left of the orchestra reassembled in Paris, where one of its first undertakings was the Berlioz Requiem. Emmanuel Bondeville oversaw an immense performance at the Opéra on November 27, 1943, the proceeds of which were to benefit the Red Cross. The cover photograph of L'illustration on December 4, 1943, shows the more than six hundred musicians and the public packing the house, another indication of the solidarity that kept good music soldiering on.

The Conservatoire orchestra had in effect become its own master. It navigated successfully through, for instance, the national Journées de la Musique (March 12–26, 1944) as overseen by the Propaganda-Staffel, without incident. The recording and film studios began ramping up to full production. Musical life achieved an eerie status quo as everyone marked time toward the liberation they knew was coming.

Munch continued to map a career that extended far beyond Paris. He was already traveling, as circumstances allowed, with a freedom others envied. When Honegger could not get permission to go home to Switzerland for a pair of first performances, a well-placed patron asked, "What's the reason he has to stay in Paris when Charles Münch is free to leave it at any time and come and conduct concerts in Switzerland?"[29]

This is not to overlook the mortal danger that still lurked everywhere. For Parisians it was the cruelest winter for cold and famine, and the roundups and deportations were unrelenting. Shortly after D-day Nicole Henriot's apartment in Paris was ransacked by Gestapo agents looking for papers in her brother's custody that might have identified other Resistance workers. Reaching home by bicycle and surprising the squad at their work, she was struck with a rifle butt to the extent that one of her kidneys was destroyed. When they learned that she was a pianist, they purposely broke her left hand. The hand healed sufficiently for her to begin reappearing in November of the following 1944–1945 season, but for the rest of her career it caused her trouble and eventually led to severe arthritis.

In a radio interview in 1967, Munch's attention was drawn to the customary explanation of Honegger's Second Symphony, composed in 1940–1941, as a reflection on the war and, with the trumpet chorale at the end, the promise of victory. His voice falls dramatically in nuance as he responds: "It's the expression of this terrible time," then, rising in excitement, "and the end is just the liberation, when come the American soldiers in Paris, and then this big revolt, big tumult, and finally start[s] the chorale. The victory." The interviewer, drawing a parallel with the movie *Is Paris Burning?* asks, "You remember those days, of course?"

"Oh, yes," replies Munch. "I was in the street at the time."[30]

Quite possibly this is true, and any number of accounts confirm how elated he was with each new Allied advance toward the Rhine. It took another three months to liberate Strasbourg, and during the course of the campaign, on September 25, 1944, came the family's worst tragedy. That night the Strasbourg Conservatoire was destroyed by Allied bombs. The director of the conservatory, Charles's brother Fritz, had sent his family and a number of the music students to take shelter in the concert room, thinking it the sturdiest place in the *quartier*. Most of them were killed, including Fritz's wife, Elisabeth, and two of their three children: Marie-Louise, seventeen, and Marc, twelve.

As would be the case at other family turning points during his career, Munch had little choice but to mourn in private while fulfilling in public the demands of a packed calendar. He and the Société des Concerts played an important role in celebrating the liberation of Paris and helping reestablish a buoyant, unfettered concert life. Yehudi Menuhin's account of reopening the Opéra with the Mendelssohn Concerto backed by Munch and his orchestra on October 7, 1944— cobwebs swept away, marble washed, ushers assembled in the nick of time, and tickets sold out in two hours—captures the excitement of the *rentrée*.[31] For the opening of the 118th season of the Société des Concerts on October 22, Munch programmed a cerebral, personal expression of the moment: Ibert's *Ouverture pour une fête*, Roussel's *Le bardit des Francs*, Honegger's new *Chant de libération* (since lost), and Debussy's *Le martyre de St.-Sébastien*, a work of which he was especially fond and which he later recorded with the BSO.

As early as October 29, after a seemingly innocuous program featuring Jacques Thibaud in a Mozart violin concerto and works of the French moderns, it was clear that the period of recrimination was at hand. Munch was "hissed as a German," and Milhaud was booed for having spent the war years in the United States. Munch had neither the time nor the inclination to worry about such matters, expected as he was to lead the London Philharmonic in a tour of northern England. He traveled in a military aircraft and as a representative of liberated France.

He reached England on Tuesday, November 5, 1944, for a ten-day visit of four or five concerts with the London Philharmonic in Albert Hall and at least one broadcast with the BBC. He was guest of honor at a reception given by the orchestra as "the French conductor who carried on an anti-collaborationist campaign during the German Occupation of Paris." "M. Munch," the *London Times* reported, "had many offers to play in Germany during the Occupation, but consistently refused and under difficult conditions kept his own orchestra going."[32]

The review, though welcoming the "fresh air of international exchange," deplored "a program consisting mostly of hackneyed things," by which was meant the Liszt E-flat Piano Concerto with Nicole Henriot and Tchaikovsky's Sixth. (Also on the program were Ibert's *Ouverture pour une fête* and Benjamin Britten's *Variations on a Theme of Frank Bridge*.) It was noted that Munch conducted the Britten, as well as the *Pathétique*, from memory. In the scherzo of the Tchaikovsky he "pulled the fundamental pulse about too much. Even so he made it plain that he had the plan of the symphony in his head."[33]

For more than a year the art scene in Paris was giddy, out of control—and above all gossipy. Maurice Chevalier was rumored to have been shot as a Nazi sympathizer. Casals, not to be found, was said to be in a concentration camp: Both an American GI and Jacques Thibaud found it necessary to assure readers of the *New York Times* that he was alive and well.[34] The most famous artists under suspicion as sympathizers were Serge Lifar and the Wagnerian soprano Germaine Lubin, both of whom had catered to Hitler at the Opéra, and Alfred Cortot, who had played in Berlin and signed decrees prohibiting Jewish musicians from working. (Lifar, after being released from house arrest, went to live at the Ritz with Coco Chanel, "who is very sad that her SS lover has left."[35]) Other noted musicians under scrutiny were the singer Claire Croiza, the composers Marcel Delannoy, Max d'Ollone, and Florent Schmitt, and the critic Émile Vuillermoz.

Lincoln Kirstein was at the time an interpreter attached to General Patton's Third Army and in that capacity traveled with a typewriter. In a series of letters written to Virgil Thomson that fall he attempts to make sense of bewildering stimuli, including the concert where both Munch and Milhaud were booed:

> Truly, the atmosphere of Paris was electric when I was first there some ten days after the Liberation. But *hélas*, before I left on all sides could be seen familiar signs of new scandals, *épurations*, fractions, frictions, horror, denunciation, as if in spite of four years of hell nothing had changed. . . . Such carrying on you have never heard, as to who had really collaborated and who had protected their friends and families, who were real French and who were the *salauds*.

His next letter recognizes that "The *épuration* game is very nasty. The worst are let off and the in-betweens get it in the neck."[36]

Inevitably Munch was drawn into the fray—and by a colleague, Paul Paray. While Munch was conducting in England, Paray had engineered a flamboyant *rentrée* of his own to the Colonne at the Châtelet. Always adroit at managing his own press—considerably better at it than Munch—he had circulated promotional texts meant to establish himself as the iconic Resistance hero from classical music circles, "for the entire Occupation, first in the northern sector and then, after November 1942, in the southern sector, refusing all compromise [with the Germans]" and declining to conduct his own orchestra because its Jewish musicians had been dismissed.[37]

The concert consisted of Mendelssohn and Dukas, composers not heard in France for four years. The violin soloist was Jacques Thibaud, now cast as a hero himself for having continued to teach his Jewish students (and having lost a son in the war). At the close of the concert Paray was called back to the stage four times and finally addressed the public: "By the warmth of the welcome you have extended me, and which deeply touches me, our first concert takes on the character of a concert of liberation and reparation. You thus erase the injury that Germany, which I hate, visited on our founder, Édouard Colonne, and, by consequence, on our dear Gabriel Pierné"—Colonne's son-in-law. "I feel stronger because of your unanimous support and motivated by it to raise my voice high to combat certain last-minute Resisters, who for four years at the Palais de Chaillot and elsewhere shamelessly played the German propaganda and served German musicians and artists."[38] Paray's target was certainly Munch.

The aftermath of his offensive was not long in coming. Returning from London in the last week of November 1944, Munch discovered from reading a kiosk poster that he and his orchestra had been replaced by Paray and the Colonne for a ceremony commemorating the *grand résistant* Fred Scamaroni (1914–1943) because he had conducted concerts in the occupied zone in rooms where Germans were present.

This was undeniably true: There are, for instance, news photographs of uniformed German officers at Conservatoire concerts in the Palais de Chaillot. That alone proved nothing at all. It was Paray, Munch went on to write in a prepared statement, who had taken the easier path "since he was the one who didn't come back to Paris, after the exodus [of 1940], to confront the Germans. And he nevertheless continued to give concerts in the Southern Sector when it was still occupied, notably in a Marseille hall as frequented by Germans as any in Paris."[39]

Another complaint was that Munch had given a concert with the German pianist Wilhelm Kempff. This, too, was true: Kempff, Munch, and the Société had offered three Beethoven concertos together in June 1942:

> The demand was made by the chief of German propaganda, Dr. Piersig [i.e., Fritz Piersig, the Bremen musicologist, 1900–1978]; I flatly refused. I went to conduct concerts in Brussels, and when I returned I saw posted all over Paris the announcements of Kempff's recital, accompanied by the Société des Concerts under my direction. I went immediately to the administrative office of the Propaganda service and was told that my orchestra and I were requisitioned and that the sanction for my refusal would be the deportation of the young musicians in the orchestra.[40]

Maurice Schumann, one of Charles de Gaulle's most trusted lieutenants and the voice of Free France broadcasting from England, was reluctant to be seen with Munch. "Go ahead and have the concert, if you like, and I'll even speak," he told the organizers. "But I won't shake his hand." Schumann later denied that version of the story.

It was also noted that Munch had conducted one of the 150th-anniversary concerts for Mozart, but this essentially peripheral event had been swept into the Mozart week by the Germans "because of its date alone" (November 30, 1941; the festival ran from November 30 to December 7):

> They say that someone has proffered photographs where I was standing with the Germans, but I never let myself be photographed with Germans. They said I spent the weekend with Dr. Piersig, which is an odious and scandalous calumny.
>
> Then they said that I was in the German army in World War I. Exactly. That was what happened to every Alsatian in 1914. I had never had any military training, having been excused from it. I was mobilized in 1915 and discharged in 1918 as a second-lieutenant, a rank I was given for my academic degrees alone. My younger brother, who also left as a second lieutenant, became a captain in the French army and served in the campaign of 1939–40.[41]

Munch was sufficiently alarmed about his situation to have dictated the statement from which this account is drawn, presumably made to his attorney. The document may have made its way through the various purging commissions, but there is little indication that they were much interested. On the contrary, Munch was free enough of wartime baggage to have been designated an *officier* in the Legion of Honor just afterward. Given his innate distaste for confrontation, he preferred to let matters melt away on their own. We hear little more than whispered gossip after that, gossip that, had it been stated openly, could just as openly have been refuted.

Yet Paray continued his campaign to defame Munch and advance his own identity as a *grand résistant*. The thrust of his advance press for a visit to the United States in late 1945 was to this effect. In New York, an interview in the *New York Times* led with a portrait of "a fearless leader of resistance among French artists to the enemy during the war, [whose] reputation has long preceded him."[42]

Ropartz, sending Munch and his wife New Year's greetings from his estate at Lanloup, acknowledged that the innuendo of the last weeks of 1944 must have proved a sore test. "May the new year be clement, may it see the end of the drama, may it see as well the end of antagonism and quarreling among Frenchmen."[43] Honegger, writing a Portuguese friend a few months later, was less optimistic:

I don't envy you the visit of Paul Paray, a virtuoso conductor but a professional defamer. He returned here with the reputation of a *grand résistant* and immediately began his attacks and public pronouncements—first of all against Munch, whose success he could not stomach and whom he couldn't forgive for having been called to London before he was. What resulted was a lawsuit for defamation of character, where he was made to retract his statements and apologize. As a result, Munch is more acclaimed than ever and Paray booed by the conservatory and university students when he played his Second Symphony. He was the same toward me in Toulouse (and will certainly be again in Lisbon), where, at the end of a chorus rehearsal, he said, among other elegant inventions, that I had got money from the Germans.[44]

In the end it was clear that Paray's motivation was that of simple jealousy. He had begun ahead of Munch and fallen well behind. One British journalist described the Colonne under Paray in Edinburgh as "small beer."[45]

Munch, meanwhile, reveled in the string of celebratory concerts that carried on through the rest of 1944 and into 1945. Before going to England, he had led a brilliant commemorative concert, with Marguerite Long, on the twentieth anniversary of Fauré's death. Just after his return to Paris, on his way to the Saturday morning open rehearsal of the Société des Concerts on November 25, he learned of the liberation of Strasbourg. The young Michel Debost, in the audience with his mother, remembers Munch taking the stage and announcing "*Strasbourg est libérée!*" and launching into the *Marseillaise.*

Concerts in 1945 honored the liberation of Alsace-Lorraine, commandos, Stravinsky, the Red Army, the U.S. Army—whatever group of Allied warriors had yet to be acknowledged. There were memorials for the dead and salutes to the victorious. Victory in Europe came on May 8, 1945. On May 9 Munch led the Société des Concerts in a more or less official *concert de victoire* on the terrace in front of Notre Dame.

Ernest Munch at the organ, circa 1895

Collection E. Munch, BNUS

Célestine Munch with her son Charles, circa 1894

Collection E. Munch, BNUS

Charles and Fritz Munch, circa 1912

Collection E. Munch, BNUS

Charles Munch, circa 1918

Collection E. Munch, BNUS

Geneviève and Juliette Maury, circa 1920

Collection E. Munch, BNUS

"Karl Münch, concertmaster of the Gewandhaus Orchestra," from a 1931 concert program

BNUS

Charles Munch as violin soloist, circa 1931

Boston University Library

Alfred Cortot and
Wilhelm Furtwängler,
Paris, Roger Hauert,
1947

Roger Hauert heirs

Inaugural portrait for the Société des
Concerts, Boris Lipnitzki, 1938

Getty Images

Conducting the Société des Concerts in the Salle du Conservatoire, circa 1940

Press clipping, origin unknown

Playing *boules* with Arthur Honegger and his family, Grosrouvre, spring 1941

Collection Pascale Honegger

Bronze bust by Irène Codreano (1897–1985) of the "Paris school" of immigrant modernists, 1939

Boston Symphony Orchestra

Nicole Henriot, circa 1945

*Collection Jean-Jacques and
Nicole Schweitzer*

Promotional portrait for foreign appearances,
Studio 56, Neuilly-sur-Seine, circa 1946

BSO

Arriving in New York, October 1950

Enell, Inc. BSO

Inaugural portrait for Boston Symphony
Orchestra, Fabian Bachrach, autumn 1949

Getty Images

Monteux, Koussevitzky, and Munch
following a performance by the Israel
Philharmonic conducted by
Koussevitzky, Boston Symphony Hall,
January 21, 1951

Associated Press, BSO

With Mark Antony DeWolfe Howe before a
radio appearance on WGBH, October 1951

Bernard H. Lewis, BSO

Signing autographs
after an open rehearsal,
circa 1951

John Brook, BSO

Practicing his golf swing at home in
Milton, circa 1951

John Brook, BSO

Geneviève Munch and Pompey
at home in Milton, fall 1949

Yale Joel

Last recording sessions, with Nicole Henriot-Schweitzer, late September 1968

attrib. Sabine Weiss. Collection Schweitzer

CHAPTER 4

Leaving France

June 1945–September 1949

Altogether between the liberation of Paris in August 1944 and the end of World War II in May 1945, Munch conducted some thirty concerts in England over the course of five separate visits, including appearances in Manchester, Liverpool, and Birmingham. London and the London lifestyle considerably broadened his horizons. He met Thomas Beecham, Adrian Boult, Benjamin Britten, Peter Pears, and William Walton, developing a real affection for Walton—and for Boult, who gave him his early edition of the Berlioz Requiem. He learned music that would go on to occupy a sturdy place in his repertoire, notably Handel's *Water Music* in the now famous arrangement by Hamilton Harty, as well as the idea of playing the Scherzo from the Mendelssohn Octet as a work for full orchestra. In March 1945 he welcomed Britten and Pears in Paris for the Serenade for Tenor, Horn, and Strings and the Sinfonia da Requiem. That same spring the Société des Concerts premiered Arthur Bliss's *The Phoenix*, a six-minute march for orchestra composed "in homage to France, August 1944."[1] Ralph Vaughan Williams and Frederick Delius were soon to be featured in his programs, and a regular Franco-Britannic interaction for both Munch and his orchestra—exchange concerts, recordings in London with both Decca and EMI, visits to the Edinburgh Festival—was soon under way.

In November 1945 Munch and Beecham swapped both venues and orchestras, with Munch taking the London Philharmonic Orchestra (LPO) as far as Nottingham, then conducting the Société des Concerts at the Stoll Theatre in London on November 4 and the Philharmonic in Paris on November 11.

Roussel's Third Symphony in London was "quite unknown here," as was the Conservatoire orchestra itself, readers of the *London Times* were told. "The tone quality of the orchestra in a tutti has a certain bright acuity due to the number and bore of the brass instruments and to the keen edge of the strings. The flutes, on the other hand, have a mellowness characteristic of French manufacture." The notice complained that the speed of the finale in Mozart's *Haffner* Symphony had gathered as it went along; it noted that *La Mer* "conjured up wind and salt water," where typically in London *La Mer* paled in comparison to the *Daphnis et Chloé* suite, also heard that night. Roussel seemed to the reviewer descended from Berlioz, though without the extravagance and with a certain "acid tang" to the harmony.[2] The Paris concert with the LPO saw Munch conduct the second performance of Walton's First Symphony. It seems certain that, but for the lure of Boston and New York, an important home would have been found for Munch in London. As it was, a major string of recordings with Munch and the LPO was soon readied, and much later four of the great recordings of the 1960s were with London ensembles.

For Munch the deepest personal signal of victory and peacetime must have been his triumphant return to Strasbourg, where he led the municipal orchestra on November 28, 1945, in a long program with a Vivaldi concerto, Mozart symphony, and, in the second half, the Tchaikovsky Piano Concerto, Ropartz's *Chasse du Prince Arthur,* and *La Valse.* The *Dernières Nouvelles d'Alsace* praised the "dizzying" account of the Tchaikovsky "by a stunning young pianist, Mlle. Nicole Henriot, of fantastic fingers, the aura of a veteran, in a masterly interpretation where everyone was drawn into the spirit of the piece." Concerning the Ropartz, the reviewer thought that "the old Breton master should be happy with his reception in Strasbourg: it's certainly true that the Munch brothers have always been *très chic* toward him."[3]

He continued his expedition with a concert pair in December 1945 for Ansermet's Orchestre de la Suisse Romande, Paris appearances until year's end, seven concerts with the Concertgebouw in January 1946, and Paris again in early February.

Charles Munch was now well along on a fast track to the very top of the profession. His affairs were managed in Europe by Charles Kiesgen, and it appears to have been through the Valmalète dynasty of concert impresarios that he was turned over to Arthur Judson and the nascent Columbia Artists' Management, Inc. (CAMI) to arrange his first American appearances for the 1946–1947 season. The time when he could be satisfied by the conditions of his appointment with the Conservatoire orchestra was long gone. Neither could the orchestra, by following its century-old statutes, tolerate a drop-in conductor as its chief steward. The practice of a single conductor's remaining in residence for thirty-six weeks of rehearsals and concerts was all but dead (though precisely that expectation remained the case in Boston as well). By early 1946 Munch was actively seeking a way out of his presidency of the Société des Concerts, while the orchestra was looking hard to find a replacement for him. The candidates Munch preferred were Martinon and Jean Witkowski, the former of whom was about to be appointed to a good job in Bordeaux, while the latter had been found "notoriously incompetent" by the players.[4] The Société des Concerts was inclined toward the Franco-Belgian conductor André Cluytens, who had enjoyed success in Paris since 1945.

Munch was hotly opposed to Cluytens, for reasons that until recently seemed inexplicable. We now understand that Munch had been fed copies of the eyebrow-raising case concerning Cluytens's wartime activities. The accusations were damning indeed: free lodging in the notorious Hôtel Splendide (subject of the film *Bon Voyage*), where he and his wife kept up an open, intimate relationship with M. and Mme. Verhum, later shown to be enemy agents; a larger-than-life portrait of a uniformed German officer in his living room; his habit of saluting a friend *à la hitlérienne;* German officers routinely in the conductor's box at the theater. He had overruled a musicians' union strike called from London by de Gaulle and the FFI (Forces Françaises de l'Intérieur). Eventually Cluytens was dismissed from the musicians' union of Bordeaux, the accusations of his *sentiments germanophiles* and desire to see German victory having been proved to the satisfaction of the local authorities.[5] Cluytens survived the inquiry and went on to become a top-quality conductor of the Société des Concerts, its last, with a discography equivalent in substance to Munch's with the BSO. The prestige of the position in Paris did not prevent public incidents during his early tenure there, which were uglier than any Munch ever experienced. Cluytens's appointment and subsequent success with the Conservatoire orchestra did little to soothe Munch's feelings about his own rupture with the ensemble or enhance the possibility of his eventual return to that podium.

Munch fell ill enough in February 1946 to cancel several Paris concerts and check into a hospital. Martinon took the concerts of February 17 and 24, and those of March 3 and 10 were postponed for two weeks. Madame Munch told Cortot in late February that her husband was much improved, but Munch himself later wrote of several more difficult weeks and the expectation of a long recovery. He was nevertheless back on the podium at the end of March and spent most of April on the road. The nature of the complaint is not clear, but documentation of his subsequent major illness—a fistula infection in 1948—includes the remarks that a previous episode "had been poorly attended to in Paris some time ago."[6] Agnès Schoeller, his niece, had been trained in nursing at the American Hospital during the war, and he summoned her in 1946 to take care of him and give him his injections—embarrassed, however, for her to be "familiar" with his hindquarters. ("They were like anybody else's," she said.) Schoeller was too polite to inquire as to the nature of his condition, but she had the impression that he had just undergone intestinal surgery.[7]

Meanwhile, the membership of the Société des Concerts convened in emergency session to consider "a *malaise* at the heart of our society," that is, the friction between Munch and their secretary-general, Jean Savoye. This was in large and telling measure about repertoire: how to reconcile free-market expectations of the ticket buyers with their conductor's predilection for programs Savoye found uninviting. Roussel and Messiaen were cited as cases in point. It was also about management style—Savoye had for some time run the organization as a director-general, and there was a good deal of the scoundrel in him—and about the need for an exit strategy. Munch was present at a second general assembly, on June 30, 1946, to press for his own release: "You must choose between M. Savoye and me. If you name another secretary-general, I'll stay as your president-conductor and do the next season." But that was not his preference. "I'm no longer young. Give me a leave of absence. You did it for others, for Gaubert."

When someone shouted "Never!" he begged, "Don't deny me that. . . . Choose, vote, decide. Let me know the outcome." The meeting, transcribed in its entirety, veered out of control. One member tried to inject calm by observing that "Everybody in the orchestra knows that M. Munch is irreplaceable" ("Not at all," Munch replied: "No one is irreplaceable.") Challenged on whether the Société des Concerts was still first in his allegiance, Munch crossly answered: "I've always put it in first place. . . . Have you had anything to complain about monetarily since I've been at the helm?" Personal insults began to fly, and the stenographer gave up, writing simply *brouhaha*.[8]

Munch's intentions were clear. He must by that time have already accepted engagements to conduct in Boston and New York in December 1946 and January 1947, signed contracts, and provided the publicity materials the public would soon read in the international press. This, the Société des Concerts believed with some justification, was a clear violation of a contract held to be in effect through the 1947–1948 season. And it was only the most obvious of his violations. As early as April 1946 he and Nicole Henriot had traveled to Israel for nine concerts with Bronislaw Huberman's Israel Philharmonic. In May he and Ginette Neveu went to Vienna for the first Prague Spring Festival—a three-week annual event that came to play a major role in easing the new socialist state into the modern world. It was also the fiftieth anniversary of the Czech Philharmonic.

He looks tired and overweight in the photographs taken in Prague, but his presence was noted and appreciated by writers who understood the symbolism of Rafael Kubelik playing Smetana, Leonard Bernstein with the American repertoire, Boult with the British, Mravinsky with the Soviet, and Munch with the European moderns.[9]

Before the standoff of June 30 he had conducted the Société des Concerts in their Grande Saison Internationale—the June festival concerts—then taken his orchestra to Nancy and Strasbourg to inaugurate the postwar Strasbourg Festival. Savoye objected strenuously to having Messiaen's *Offrandes oubliées,* a Milhaud premiere, and a large chunk of Monteverdi's *Orfeo* on a program with Francescatti, let alone having two violin virtuosi, Francescatti and Szigeti, in ten days. He thought Beethoven's Eighth and *Bacchus et Ariane* a poor choice for Strasbourg. The public came anyway, leaving the situation at the Conservatoire all the more uncomfortable. Munch then left with Magda Tagliaferro for concerts in Rio de Janeiro with the Orquestra Sinfônica Brasileira, July 27 and 30, 1946. The repertoire of Debussy, Ravel, Roussel, and Honegger was the same he would take to the United States in the fall. On August 17, 1946, he led the premiere of Honegger's Third Symphony (*Liturgique*) in Zurich.

Munch was adamant about not conducting in Paris in 1946–1947 (in order to pursue his international career), agreeing only to recording sessions at Decca and public concerts in England that October with the Société des Concerts. On September 29 the musicians were read an apologetic letter to this effect; a lawsuit for breach of contract was filed just afterward, leading to a mediation on October 25 in the government's office of fine arts. The administrator, Jacques Jaujard, outlined commonly held desires for Munch to stay on as president-conductor of the society, to cancel planned appearances with the rival Orchestre National except for UNESCO benefit concerts in November and December, and to conduct two-week engagements with the Conservatoire through the end of his contract in 1948. A gentlemen's agreement was thought to have been reached, though Munch immediately wrote his brother that the so-called gentlemen were in effect common gangsters, who, by calling (again) on his patriotism, had forced him to yield for yet another season.

Both the concerts and the recordings in England that October went well. The reviewer in the *Musical Times* found the playing "remarkable" and quintessentially French. "Such fine voicing, throughout the dynamic range, is rare, and one seldom feels the presence of such understanding within the ranks. It showed how in technique and ideals, French playing could differ from English, and surpass it in at least French music."[10] The eight new titles recorded by London Decca in the Walthamstow Town Hall with the Société des Concerts, seventeen individual discs, are themselves artifacts of the orchestra's transition into the international market. The sound, in Decca's new "ffrr" system (full frequency range response), was inviting, and the works on deck, from Berlioz to the Franck Symphony to a highly prized first recording of both suites from *Daphnis et Chloé,* gave Munch a convincing claim to that corner of the repertoire in an exploding market.

The 1946–1947 season also brought the French premiere of Honegger's Third Symphony, offered by the Orchestre National in Paris on November 14.

The concert was meant to celebrate the establishment of UNESCO's head-quarters in Paris and the first UNESCO Month, November 1946, but since it was widely understood that Munch was leaving momentarily "to conduct Toscanini's orchestra" in New York, the program became something of a fare-well. It consisted of the Ropartz Fifth Symphony, its first performance in France; the Honegger, always intended for Munch (though the score did not reach him until November 1); and Prokofiev's *Le Joueur*. Ropartz was de-lighted, though on the whole disapproved of Munch's plans: "I hope you find satisfaction and all the success you merit during your travels of the next few months, and that in returning to Paris recharged with more glories, you will again take up, at the head of the magnificent orchestra of the Paris Conserva-toire, your Paris duty, so productive and *so indispensable* to musical life here in France."[11]

He proceeded to an engagement with the Amsterdam Concertgebouw in late November and then, at last, departed on his concert tour of the United States, arriving on December 19, 1946, at La Guardia airport on a Pan Ameri-can clipper aircraft.[12] The three-month tour was to include a concert pair in Bos-ton on December 27–28, 1946, eight concerts over two weeks with the New York Philharmonic, then appearances in Chicago, Los Angeles, and Montreal. He brought with him the *Water Music*, Honegger, *Bacchus et Ariane*, Rabaud for the Bostonians (since Rabaud had been a conductor of the BSO), and the Saint-Saëns Organ Symphony for New York (since there was an organ in Carnegie Hall). In his two weeks in New York he played nine compositions by six French composers.

Munch was by this point in his career exceptionally well traveled and had for all intents and purposes already encountered every vicissitude his profession had to offer. But America was yet to be won over: American audiences and critics, the musicians, and perhaps most of all American business practices and management. Curiosity about the new maestro ran high, and Munch's photo-graph appeared prominently in the *New York Times*. *Time* magazine, under the headline "Le Beau Charles," gave details of his first encounter with the New York players:

> "Gentlemen, gentlemen! Please play lightly." When the orchestra finally caught on, Charles Munch threw the men a kiss and shouted "Bravo!" In the musicians' locker room afterward, there was a buzz of enthusiasm: a good many of the Philharmonic players had caught some of the Munch spirit that is proverbial in Paris.[13]

The thorough seduction of Boston and New York in so short a time, not to mention the dramatic turn of events in New York while he was there, must have struck both the conductor and his agents as dizzying. Boston was "a hit," and insiders were certain they had seen Koussevitzky's successor. Olin Downes led his piece with the excited language of a New York toast of the town:

> The instant that Charles Muench raised his baton as guest conductor of the Philhar-
> monic-Symphony Orchestra last night in Carnegie Hall it was evident that we had
> with us a superb musician and orchestra leader to boot. The beat, the gestures,
> sometimes very economical, sometimes high, wide, and handsome, brought imme-
> diate results. No motion was superfluous or insincere.

Downes captures, first time out, the essence of the matter: "Mr. Muench knew that it was the orchestra that was performing the symphony and not him-self. . . . Mr. Muench, a great French musician, a magnetic leader, is no egocentric or sensationalist, but a full-blooded and thoroughly equipped performer."[14]

On Munch's departure the *Times* noted an "unprecedented tribute" paid to him by the musicians in the form of a surprise cocktail party in their ready room. "Persons with long memories had to go back to the farewell party the orchestra gave for Arturo Toscanini to match the occasion." Munch saluted their work and promised to sing their praises to his musicians back in Paris, then lifted his glass "To America, which helped save France."[15]

That was on February 2, 1947, following his last concert in Carnegie Hall. The next day's headlines concerned the Philharmonic, too, for at the board meeting on February 3, Arthur Rodzinski, the resident conductor, resigned, using his state-of-the-orchestra report to level a seething attack on the manager, Arthur Judson, and the essential monopoly exerted by Columbia Artists. This was not just a local squabble, either, since the implications extended not only to Chicago, where Rodzinski landed, but also to all of the cities where Columbia placed its conductors. Nor was it simply a matter of who gets to choose the music, as had been the case in Paris during the dispute between Savoye and Munch. Rodzinski had put his finger on what was widely considered to be, in the end, the principal issue facing big orchestras after the war: the genuinely exorbitant cost of the star system.

One day later, on February 4, the board of the New York Philharmonic responded by terminating Rodzinski. Stokowski was rumored to be in line to finish the season with as many concerts as he could arrange, and "it was thought possible that Charles Muench . . . would be invited back if his other engagements would permit."[16] Musical circles "buzzed" with gossip about the permanent succession, with Stokowski and Munch leading the pack. Sto-kowski was already known to want to come to New York permanently, and "if he should be invited to take the post, Mr. Muench, French conductor who made his American debut this season with considerable success, would prob-ably be asked to serve as guest leader for an extended stay."[17] Given all we now know of Judson as a king maker (*Time* called him "music's Mr. Big"), it seems possible that the sequence of events unfolding in New York that January and February was less than coincidental—that Columbia had already targeted Munch as its next big money maker, but not for New York. His name now figured routinely alongside those of Toscanini, Walter, Stokowski, Szell, Mitropoulos, and Ormandy in the list of the era's leading conductors. His triumph in New York showed he had all it took—box office appeal, the respect of the professionals, and important things to say musically—to be an American star, a maestro.

The concerts in Chicago (February 20–28, 1947) were an equivalent success, to judge from the limited but positive press. The *Los Angeles Times* subtitled its advance piece on his visit (March 6–7) "Alsatian Who Has Aroused East Will Conduct This Week" and went on to speak of the "veritable furor" his work had prompted. "Reports from local music lovers who have heard his concerts while on recent visits to New York, Boston, and Chicago have unanimously praised his effectiveness in virtually all styles of music and the penetration and command he has exercised in his direction."[18] Edwin Schallert's review described the "Rodinesque power" of the Munch style in the "oft-cumbersome" *Fantastique* and reported enthusiastic cheers constituting a "summit among ovations." It also hit on an important detail: how these performances were a "brand-new adventure" for American listeners.[19]

He spent April 1947 exactly as he had spent April 1946, with the Palestine Orchestra–Israel Philharmonic, some fifteen concerts in four weeks—another relationship that would surely have continued had crisis in the Middle East and the job in Boston not intervened. In June he conducted Bach at the Strasbourg Festival, including a Magnificat in the nostalgic setting of the church of Saint-Guillaume. He concluded his summer and his first international season with Milstein at The Hague, then the Lucerne and Salzburg Festivals. The *contretemps* in Paris was fast receding into dossiers of unread paperwork.

The 1947–1948 season was anchored in New York with a first American performance of Honegger's seventy-five-minute *Jeanne d'Arc au bûcher,* never before heard in the United States and in some circles long awaited. The title role was played by the Norwegian dancer Vera Zorina (1917–2003), recently divorced from Balanchine and remarried to Goddard Lieberson, an executive with Columbia Records. The young Belgian actor Raymond Gérôme (1920–2002), later a major figure in French film, had created the narrator's role in France.[20] The subject matter now belonged to popular American culture through Ingrid Bergman, who played the part on stage in 1946 and in the 1948 film—and later in a 1954 film of the Honegger/Claudel work made by her husband Roberto Rossellini: *Giovanna d'Arco al rogo.*

The crossing of genres in Carnegie Hall attracted enormous preconcert coverage, including picture spreads in the weekly news magazines. Virgil Thomson
was greatly taken with the idea, if not, in the end, by the music:

> The performance itself was perfection. . . . A work of some musical and literary pre-
> tentions, *Joan at the Stake* aims to please all, save possibly the Marxian Left, by
> exploiting religious and patriotic sentiments without doctrinal precision. It appeals
> to the theater instinct in us all by the realistic evocation of horror scenes. It appeases
> the lover of modern music with bits of polytonal composition. It impresses all by its
> elaborate mobilization of musical effects. . . . It is picturesque at all moments, varied,
> and vastly detailed; but it lacks the monumentality that its oratorio layout would
> seem to impose. It is all in close-ups. At no point do we get a panoramic view, an
> epic breadth in the narrative. . . . [It] remains somewhat trivial.[21]

Before he left New York that November, Munch made his first American
recording, the Saint-Saëns Organ Symphony with Édouard Nies-Berger and the
New York Philharmonic, on the Columbia label.

There was provocative critique of his work in New York that year: the sharp
distinction between the "classical" style of the Handel concerto and the other
works; the "unduly neglected" Franck Symphony; how and why the Saint-Saëns
Organ Symphony remained "controversial." The two Honegger symphonies and
the Roussel suite were considered with respect, then genuine enthusiasm. Both
featured soloists, Ginette Neveu and Joseph Szigeti, were warmly praised—as
was Nies-Berger, the Philharmonic's Alsatian organist, who was enjoying a
reunion with an old friend. By the second New York set, even an afternoon concert featuring two young Americans, the Texas pianist Jacques Abram and the
Wisconsin composer Earl George, drew a full house.[22]

Both *Times* reviewers spotted downsides to the Munch approach: "His ideas
of Ravel's 'La Valse' differed violently with that of other conductors who have
given the piece hereabouts. The tempi were exceedingly speedy, and no sensu-
ousness, or firm patterning was feasible, at such a headlong pace" (Noel Straus).[23]
"[The Franck Symphony] had unforgettable moments, and enough temperament to supply a dozen conductors with that commodity. But why such fury?
The symphony was hurried and over-emphasized, the orchestra whipped to frenetic climaxes. Where were the grandeurs and the secret communings of César
Franck? It was given an extrovert accent" (Olin Downes).[24]

Certain influential figures in New York had already focused on Munch as a
leading contender for the Philharmonic, which was sorely in need of a charis-
matic, vigorous chief who could turn things around at the box office. One of the
trustees later wrote to congratulate a Boston counterpart for their successful

recruit: "It was my private conviction that he would have been ideal to lead our own orchestra, as I firmly believe that he is a great conductor, a superb musician, and a man of powerful and winning personality. . . . I know of no conductor who was so completely admired and beloved by the musicians of the orchestra."[25] It seems unlikely that this opinion was shared by Arthur Judson and Bruno Zirato of Columbia Artists Management, who had other ideas for New York. The board in New York dawdled, while Munch proceeded to earn in the United States an ever-growing level of critical acclaim.

Civic leaders in Boston had had Munch in their sights since early 1945. Henry B. Cabot, president of the orchestra, and George M. Judd, its general manager, sensed that peacetime would bring massive changes to classical music in general and to Boston in particular. With that in mind, and from the conviction that the trustees, and not the outgoing conductor, needed to control the orchestra's destiny, they solicited well-placed informants in Europe and the United States for news of the leading conductors and orchestras. One of these was the critic Frank Perkins, on active duty "somewhere in Luxembourg," who wrote to Judd that winter of the Conservatoire concerts he had attended in Paris on October 29 and November 26, 1944. Concerning Munch, he reported a thorough technique, good control of the orchestra, and the Franck Symphony led "with notable elegance." He liked the Tchaikovsky *Pathétique* rather less but thought Munch had done "a very neat job with Benjamin Britten's variations of a theme by Bridge. . . . His advocates are vigorous and positive and at times sweeping."[26] From Europe the Bostonians also acquired a list of the Munch recordings to date (and at least some of the discs), suggesting that retaining a leading position for the BSO in the record industry was an important priority of the evolving new financial regime.[27]

Speculation that the seventy-five-year-old Koussevitzky and the Boston Symphony were soon to part had become commonplace by the time Munch first visited in late 1946; in January 1947 *Variety* reported that Koussevitzky had personally chosen Leonard Bernstein to succeed him.[28] This grossly oversimplified the state of play in a nuanced transition, closely watched but in essence secret. Henry Cabot, convinced that the BSO needed a thorough break with the Koussevitzky style, quietly but firmly exerted his quite considerable personal will to ensure that very outcome. In February 1947, sensing his recruit's fast-rising market value, he dispatched Judd to New York to secure from Munch a verbal assurance not to make ongoing commitments elsewhere.

Koussevitzky, meanwhile, began promoting the 1947–1948 season as a co-production with his two favorites, Bernstein and Eleazar de Carvalho. It is true that the phenomenal accomplishments of the young Bernstein were exciting acclaim with the very same orchestras Munch was now conducting, including the Israel Philharmonic. Perhaps even more, his youth, looks, multiplicity of accomplishments, and ethnicity seemed to represent, in the Boston–New York corridor, America bringing out the best in itself. However, it was the urbane, seasoned Frenchman who brought with him, in his personification of traditional Europe, something many Bostonians wanted even more.

Then Judd's son, William, employed—in a fine example of how the empire actually functioned—by Judson at Columbia Artists in New York, telephoned to tip his father off that the Los Angeles Philharmonic was expected to approach Munch with an offer during his concerts there in late January 1948. This prompted the BSO Board of Trustees to take decisive action: On January 21, a straw vote on the question of Koussevitzky's succession showed consensus for Munch, and Cabot and Judd were authorized to pursue his engagement as conductor beginning with the 1949–1950 season. Now working frantically, the Bostonians dispatched no less venerable a figure than Mark Antony DeWolfe Howe (1864–1960) from his retreat in Phoenix to the Biltmore Hotel in Los Angeles, there to divert Munch toward the Boston point of view before their plan could be undone by the Angelenos (or, for that matter, by anybody else). In Chicago, after Rodzinski was fired during his first season, Munch was one of six (with Walter, Ormandy, Szell, Monteux, and Busch) who agreed to come to the rescue and thus became de facto candidates for the position.[29]

Munch replied serenely to Howe that he was under contract to Judson and CAMI for another season, 1948–1949 and was committed to leading the Orchestre National on an American tour in the fall. As for Koussevitzky, Judd wrote to Howe, in Los Angeles, "I have gathered . . . that he is not pressing for Leonard, though he might still prefer him." Yet as late as the March meeting of the board of trustees, where the outcome was already certain, Koussevitzky was still vigorously advocating "a young American." Eventually he was gracious enough to yield to the inevitable, admitting that "if the Trustees were not going to take one of his bright young men"—Bernstein, Carvalho, Thor Johnson— "Mr. Munch was the best candidate."[30]

Meanwhile, a flurry of telegrams resulted in a conference in New York on February 4, 1948, attended by Munch, Cabot, and Judd and the lawyers. Here the principles of the appointment were agreed to, though many concerns remained to be worked out. The trustees voted formally—given the state of play, retroactively—on March 15, 1948, "to authorize the President and the Manager to enter into negotiation with Mr. Charles Munch with a view to engaging him as conductor and Music Director for a period of up to three years beginning with the symphony season 1949–1950." Munch officially accepted in a written note addressed from the Concerts Symphoniques de Montréal on March 17, 1948. He was introduced to the trustees at a reception and dinner at the Somerset Club in Boston on March 25. The draft contract for two seasons was initialed on April 7, 1948, though word of the appointment—still not officially announced—had already spread through the corridors of musical power in the United States and abroad. The news made the Boston and New York papers on April 9, the day of the official press release, and the *Los Angeles Times* on April 18, 1948.

Though the patrons and press could not have known much about what was happening in the board room, the general situation was widely understood. Munch was thus watched closely during his Boston concerts in March and April 1948, both for his attitudes toward music and musicians—especially beyond the French school—and for whether or not he might eventually be convinced to reverse his initial position of disinterest in the summer programs at Tanglewood. After one concert a patron wrote to suggest that the new conductor stick to the canon: "People are apt to write about the concerts they do not like and take for granted the ones they find pleasant. I do not like Stravinsky's music and have felt that I have had an overdose in the last few years. [While there is] no one quite like Mr. Koussevitzky, I felt that Mr. Munch would be a worthy successor."[31] Cyrus Durgin, the Boston critic, posed in his headline a question everybody was asking, "What Sort of Man Is Charles Munch?" and then answered it in the subhead: "Kind, Amiable, Sheds Shyness Making Music."[32]

Cabot wrote to Geneviève Munch in Paris to express his great satisfaction in the decision that had been reached and to cover for the apparent gaffe of not knowing there *was* a Mme. Munch. "I and the other trustees feel confident that the great traditions of the Orchestra are in good hands and that the preeminent position of the Orchestra will be continued under the direction of your husband. It has been a great pleasure dealing with him and in every way satisfactory." Cabot promised to help the couple find a comfortable place to live—and proved as good as his word.[33]

Leonard Bernstein, of course, was less satisfied. "Everyone in Europe is amazed and upset about Munch coming to Boston," he wrote Koussevitzky from Budapest. "Klemperer yesterday was sure it must be a joke!"[34]

By late May 1948 Munch was in Paris again, where between May 24 and May 27 he and the Société des Concerts made their last recordings together: Berlioz's concert overture *Le Corsaire* and a very important recording of Tchaikovsky's *Pathétique*—his first (and last) six-disc set. In September, with the Concertgebouw, he recorded the Brahms Violin Concerto and *Danse macabre* with Ossy Renardy (1920–1953), the Viennese violin virtuoso who, as a member of the U.S. Army, had spent the war years entertaining American troops. (He died tragically, in a car accident near Santa Fe, New Mexico.)

In March the musicians of the Société des Concerts circulated a petition signed by the majority of the players, wishing to make known their desire "to have invited back to their head, as president-conductor, *maître* Charles Munch, beginning with the next season, 1948–49, and that everything be done in order that their desire might become fact."[35] This noble but futile gesture was typical of how little they grasped of what was happening in the conducting world at large and of how committed Munch now was to concerts with their rival, the Orchestre National.

Among these was a Berlioz Requiem in the Strasbourg Cathedral in June 1948, where Fritz had prepared the singers—the first time they had worked actively together since before the war. After the closing concert by the Orchestre National, Munch wrote in their *livre d'or*:

> *Avec ma profonde reconnaissance en souvenir du concert de Strasbourg du 20 Juin 48. /*
> *et* vivat sequentes —*New York etc.*
> > *De tout cœur*
> > *Charles Munch*

—the fractured Latin expressing a good wish for the forthcoming American tour. The leading figures of the Strasbourg Festival expressed their great satisfaction at having brought the Orchestre National to Strasbourg, "here in Alsace recovered, on the banks of the Rhine, the frontier of civilizations and cultures, where it so magnificently serves the cause of French music."[36]

From Strasbourg Munch continued with the orchestra on its summer circuit, with concerts at the Lucerne and Edinburgh Festivals. In Lucerne, before the Mendelssohn concerto with Isaac Stern, a well-wisher presented himself backstage: "tall, cadaverous, with deep eyes, high cheekbones, thinning gray hair." This was Wilhelm Furtwängler, with whom Stern had refused to play in the United States since the war. They greeted one another politely, and when Munch said something funny, everybody laughed, and a flashbulb went off. The subsequent frenzy in the American press—why does Stern continue to refuse to play with him in the United States, yet enjoy his backstage company in Europe?—was in part the result of everyone else in the room having been cropped from the photograph.[37]

The farewell gesture from Charles Munch to French musicians was to lead a flamboyant, in the end overly ambitious, American tour of the Orchestre National: thirty-nine concerts in seven weeks, the first by a major foreign orchestra in two decades. Some ninety-six players made the trip, including sixteen women. Published materials explained that the tour was "through the courtesy of Radiodiffusion Française" and "under the patronage of Monsieur Henri Bonnet, French Ambassador to the US." It lasted from the middle of October to the beginning of December 1948.

The repertoire was what was now understood to be the French stock in trade: Berlioz's *Corsaire* overture and *Fantastique*, *L'apprenti sorcier*, the central works of Debussy and Ravel, *Bacchus et Ariane,* and Honegger's *Symphonie litur-gique* (no. 3). The novelty was Walter Piston's Toccata for Orchestra, "written especially for Charles Munch and played for the first time anywhere in the world on this Goodwill Tour of the Orchestre National."[38] Its inclusion rather contra-dicts the positions Munch later took against playing Prokofiev to the Russians and Sibelius to the Finns, but Piston had after all composed the Toccata for Munch, and they appear to have met one another in Paris in the 1930s.

The BSO took care to telegraph a welcome to Munch and his musicians on board the *SS Nieuw Amsterdam* as it approached New York harbor. Cabot in-vited Munch to tea on October 20, preceding the first New York concert that evening, and all of the musicians to supper with the BSO afterward.

For many Americans this was the first opportunity to see and hear the work of a conductor on his way to the podium of what most people considered the best orchestra in the country. (The Big Five had yet to coalesce: Cleveland and Chi-cago were "out there," as one Bostonian remarked; New York had problems both administrative and financial. Only Philadelphia, at the time, was so well heeled.) The degree of the positive reception accorded the French in the professional press is remarkable and a little surprising—"The Orchestre National is as good as our top-flight orchestras" and "comparable to our best American orchestras."[39]

Munch's gestures and "beautiful coordination in every part of his body" were praised. "The silver-thatched Munch, who will succeed Koussevitzky as con-ductor of the Boston Symphony next season, is a sensitive and expressive musi-cian, a thorough master of orchestral technique, a leader whose interpretations are precise and logical without sacrifice of a liveliness," said the *Indianapolis Star* of the concerts at Indiana University in Bloomington. Inevitably the heartland reviewers were struck by the conductor's courtesy and elegance, as well as his deferential charm toward the public, the musicians under his command, and the music he had chosen. "It's civilized, and cosmopolitan, and likable."[40]

A pair of important essays by Virgil Thomson (an established Francophile) tried to get to the bottom of the Munch phenomenon. In "French Loveliness," October 18, 1948, he writes of the concert the night before in Carnegie Hall:

> From beginning [Berlioz's *Le Corsaire*] to end the concert was both electrifying and delicious. In certain ways [it was] better work than we are accustomed to hear. The clean unanimity of its string playing, the exactitude of its string and woodwind bal-ances, the shading and stability of its percussion section and, of course, the match-less phrasing and other tonal refinements of the French woodwind soloists are standards of comparison. . . . The French thinner brasses, which operate as wood-winds in soft passages and in loud ones as a stronger counterpart to the nasal timbre of strings, oboes, and bassoons, are consciously avoided in this country, even in the performance of French music.

How brilliant, how tender, and how poetic French music can sound when played in the French way is a rare experience for us. The French orchestral style is one of equiliberation, of clear balances and clean colors, of poetic luminosity rather than of animal warmth. And the whole repertoire of French music composed since Berlioz has been designed to profit by this delicate performing style. When French orchestras are not in form or well led, which is all too often, they are without vitality. When they are playing well under a good leader, and playing French music, they offer orchestral sound at its maximum of sophistication.[41]

In "France at Its Best," he begins with the memorable line: "Any French orchestra will play beautifully for Charles Munch, whom all musicians genuinely like and respect. This is not Munch's orchestra. . . . It is a compliment both to Mr. Munch and to the prestige of New York's musical judgment that last Sunday the National played as I have rarely heard any such group playing in France or anywhere else." He gives his reasons: the single school of thought, the blend and the balance, the transparency of the fabric—a "trite" thing for American tastes but an important aspect of the sound. In sum, the "French sound" was about clarity and true balance and very fine tuning. The rhythm was correct in every bar. The orchestra itself was the star, not the individual players.[42] Much of this assessment seems trenchant: The French orchestras often did find a clarity not even sought by the Germans or the Americans, and the pitch was considerably tighter than the ordinary sound of the NBC or the BSO.

In Los Angeles, Munch signed his official contract with the Boston Symphony Orchestra. Among the Californian admirers who sought him out were Stravinsky, Milhaud, and Charlie Chaplin,[43] also William Grant Still and his wife, Verna Arvey. Insiders sensed a certain disappointment that Los Angeles had not been able to attract Munch to follow in the footsteps of Rodzinski and Klemperer and sojourn with their philharmonic, but Munch did like Los Angeles and in the 1960s visited annually, sometimes on his way to the Far East. By contrast, he went to San Francisco only once with the BSO and once on his own.

The sheer number of miles traveled on the old highway system had taken their toll by the time the caravan reached California in mid-November 1948, and the tour itinerary announced the previous summer had to be adjusted as they went along. The Portland–Seattle–Vancouver run was annulled as being too ambitious. There was ongoing disagreement with the American tour representatives about the arduous conditions of the trip. This was altogether similar to the experiences of the Société des Concerts during its American tour of 1918; as though the lesson of traveling musicians—how common it is to overcharge the itinerary and underbudget the daily expense—is somehow not easily learned, the conditions faced by the Orchestre National when it returned in

1962 were still primitive. Eventually the orchestra sought $2,500 from the tour manager, Jack Adams, for unreimbursed laundry expenses, while Adams contended that he had lost $28,000 "due to the temperamental members of his orchestra" who had refused to play a concert in Minneapolis as a protest against the conditions of travel. Among the grievances later adjudicated were that in La Crosse, Wisconsin, fifty beds had been provided for a hundred musicians after a nineteen-hour bus ride from Ann Arbor, and the musicians, rather than accept these accommodations, had sat up all night in the lobby. The three buses assigned to the orchestra were held to be old and inadequate; when one of them broke down while crossing the Rockies from Denver to Provo, its occupants had had to stand in the aisles of the other two. At an arbitration hearing, Munch himself testified that the musicians had played properly and to his satisfaction despite "such arduous bus trips."[44] He later wrote sympathetically and at some length about the trials and tribulations of musicians during long tours.

The story made the *New York Times* under the naughty headline "Dirty Linen Is Aired in Orchestra Dispute." Eventually judicial proceedings were launched, and the ministry opened an investigation; Munch was said to have put up half the funds necessary to reimburse the players for the cancelled concert in Minneapolis.[45] After a last concert in Teaneck, New Jersey, he left his musicians aboard the *Queen Elizabeth* for their return journey, orchestra and conductor now sensing to each other a firm allegiance. In due course this would come to complicate the metamorphosis of the old Société des Concerts into the Orchestre de Paris.

The plan had been for Munch to go on conducting a variety of orchestras after sending the National home, first in New York for the rest of December 1948 and the first two weekends of January 1949, then Havana in February, then back to New York, Rochester, Pittsburgh, and Montreal before a series in Chicago in April. (Two broadcast recordings from the New York set now circulate: the concert of December 19, 1948, with Robert Casadesus, and that of January 2, 1949, with Ginette Neveu.[46])

In early February 1949 the office of the BSO had received word that Munch had been taken ill in Havana and undergone a surgical intervention. Dispatching the Havana representative of the First National Bank of Boston to look into matters, they were informed that Munch was not allowed visitors. Their emissary, W. W. Caswell Jr. had, met his entourage, which consisted of a Miss Robinson from Tanglewood (probably Gertrude Robinson Smith, who spoke excellent French), Nicole Henriot, and her mother:

> These ladies told me that Mr. Munch arrived in Cuba in poor physical condition and that he had had a serious recurrence of a fistula infection which had been poorly attended to in Paris some time ago. Due to this, his Sunday and Monday concerts

with the Havana Philharmonic Orchestra were cancelled and he was operated on on Monday by Dr. Jorge Muniz, who is a first class surgeon and I believe a specialist in this type of operation. . . . Mme Henriot informed me that she will stay in Cuba and that the Philharmonic Society are arranging to have him give his concerts some time in March when he is fully recovered.[47]

The operation had taken place in the posh new Miramar Clinic (now the Cira García International Clinic), where Munch "lacked not for attention."

Caswell did succeed in visiting him on February 16, reporting satisfactory recovery but that the patient was in considerable pain due to the nature of the operation. The doctors predicted he could leave the hospital within the week, though for four weeks the wound would have to be dressed daily. The Bostonians never did believe that Munch could receive proper medical care anywhere but in Boston. Henry Cabot wanted him back in the United States right away: "We here in Boston are very proud of our doctors and medical services and if you feel like it, it would be very pleasant to have you here for a period during your recuperation." On February 23 Munch felt up to attending to business, writing Judd on clinic stationery:

Dear Mr. Judd,
    Please excuse the pencil, but I must write in the bed.
    Thank you very much for your letter.
    I will come with great pleasure to Boston for my reconvalescence. The doctor said that in 4 weeks the blessure [wound] is closed.
    [Three matters of business on the upcoming season.]
    Je pense retourner à l'Hôtel Presidente la semaine prochaine.
    Excusez-moi la tournure enfantine de ce mot. Rappelez-moi au bon souvenir de Mons. Cabot—et à bientôt, cher ami,
    Charles Munch[48]

He proceeded, before he should have, to Chicago, where he was booked to conduct all four weekends in April. His physical condition worsened: Cabot again urged him to seek treatment in Boston and even arranged an appointment with a specialist for May 4. On April 27 the manager of the Chicago Symphony Orchestra telephoned with disconcerting news: "I talked again with Mr. Munch after our telephone conversation. He is determined to have the Cuban physician do [a second surgical] operation, but promises to get to Boston as soon as he leaves the hospital. I'm sorry you have this trouble. I've been much concerned about his condition ever since he first arrived here."[49] In mid-May he was back in Havana, where he wrote Judd that he had been unable to get to New York because the wound had yet to heal completely.

He ended up returning directly to Paris in order to make his last three appearances with the Société des Concerts: May 27 and June 3 and 10, 1949. These featured his favorites—Nicole Henriot and Ginette Neveu—as soloists, as well as much of his central repertoire. With that his long and illustrious history with the Société des Concerts du Conservatoire was summarily and definitively over. His only other appearance was at the Strasbourg Festival in June, where the program included what was to be his last concerto with Ginette Neveu.

Meanwhile, the pace of preparing for the Boston season and the need to achieve a good working relationship grew into a frenzy over the summer, the very period of the year Munch himself was least willing to focus on such matters. Already there were misunderstandings about his contractual arrangements, with the BSO opposing his plans to appear in Montreal and Havana during the season. The Boston management, though disapproving of a number of their new conductor's expectations, consistently yielded to him out of determination to make his first months comfortable on every account. They even went so far as to engage "the juvenile"—Leonard Bernstein—to cover for Munch so that he could go to Montreal. They pressured him to think about the personnel he would need, notably a new principal oboist, a bassoonist, and eight or more section players. Richard Burgin, the concertmaster and assistant conductor, was to hear the preliminary auditions, then discuss matters in person in Paris. Frantic letters were dispatched to Burgin at American Express in Paris to ascertain Munch's medical condition and his final repertoire choices, but Burgin failed to pick them up. Only in July did the programs for October begin to take shape. There must have been moments in Boston when the management doubted the wisdom of their choice, wondering to anyone who would listen whether Munch would ever actually arrive.

In one of those extraordinary coincidences that make the world seem smaller, Albert Schweitzer was in the United States that summer to speak at the Goethe bicentennial celebrations in Aspen and receive an honorary doctorate from the University of Chicago. Several weeks before Munch arrived to take up residence in Boston, Schweitzer made a much-heralded visit on July 19–20, 1949, to examine the new Aeolian-Skinner organ being built for the fiftieth anniversary of Symphony Hall. It was a superb public relations opportunity,[50] and the photographs taken as Schweitzer signed the organ case could not have made a better fanfare for the arriving conductor.

In early September Munch recorded the *Fantastique* with the Orchestre National as they had played it on the road, then set forth to begin his life in the New World.

CHAPTER 5

⌀

Winning Boston

October 1949–June 1951

For thirteen seasons and then some, the confluence of Charles Munch, the Boston Symphony Orchestra, and the Bostonians offered serious music a steady stream of wonders, hungrily consumed by listeners on every continent. It was a natural affinity that brought together from all of the constituents a rare urbanity and sophistication of outlook as to the things that matter in orchestral art. Boston, accustomed as it was to dealing with aristocrats, recognized the prestige of Munch at once.

From the beginning the BSO had had strong links with the European continent, especially with France. Henri Rabaud, director of the Paris Conservatoire and for all intents and purposes a co-conductor of the Société des Concerts, led the BSO briefly beginning in 1918 (after Karl Muck had been arrested at the podium, interned, and subsequently deported). He was succeeded by Pierre Monteux (1919–1924), fresh from the Ballets Russes and the Metropolitan Opera. Koussevitzky (1924–1949) had been engaged in Boston on the strength of his Paris concerts in the early 1920s.

The Boston Symphony Orchestra had virtually the same expectations of its conductor as had the Société des Concerts orchestra: all the concerts, all the time, including the summer festival, and no appearances anywhere else. Munch had quit the Conservatoire concerts in part over precisely these conditions, and, in Boston, all sides would consequently have to do some yielding. Still, the brutal workload implied by all of those concerts, the sometimes stultifying routine, the need for wizardry in the confection of programs—these were already second nature to him.

Boston of the postwar era may have surpassed Paris in its commitment to art music. Both were historic seats of arts and letters. The cast of brilliant, internationally important figures who frequented the orchestra concerts was similar in the two cities. (Boston was the source or refuge of a good portion of the politicians who ran the country.) The Sorbonne and Harvard spoke with roughly equal authority, but beyond Harvard Yard New England could boast another dozen colleges and universities in the uppermost echelons of the American academic establishment. G. Wallace Woodworth and his Harvard Glee Club–Radcliffe Choral Society made possible the very works that most interested Munch; soon the New England Conservatory Chorus under Lorna Cooke de Varon would offer Munch and the BSO attractive alternatives for the chorus-and-orchestra repertoire. In 1957 a third ensemble, Alfred Nash Patterson's Chorus pro Musica, was added to the mix.

In Paris Munch had been a partisan of the mass media, both broadcasts and (rather more warily) recordings, and even before that, in Leipzig, he had logged considerable airtime. By the time he left the Conservatoire orchestra he had accrued a significant discography with Decca, marketed in the United States as London Records. In England Munch was an established presence on BBC radio.

But on this score, too, Boston was equally innovative. The RCA Victor Company had recorded the BSO in Symphony Hall since November 1928 (and, in Camden, New Jersey, well before that). Broadcasts of the BSO extended back to 1926, and if America's national passions had been focused on Toscanini and the NBC Symphony since 1937, it was also the case that the Boston had, through its established connections with RCA, direct access to NBC. Moreover, the city was on the verge of becoming a national leader in public radio, and its educational broadcasting services coalesced almost immediately as WGBH-Boston. The Massachusetts Institute of Technology pioneered the mechanics of television, and the BSO was soon experimentally, then successfully, and then routinely telecast. Virtually every program of the Munch era was broadcast on the radio.

Both the Paris and Boston orchestras had already seen their public dress rehearsals grow into phenomenally successful concert seasons aimed toward the nonworking public, especially unaccompanied women ("the Friday-afternoon ladies" in Boston, famous for the clicking of their metal knitting-needles; les samedi-matinistes in Paris). Paris had much the more historic youth-in-music movement, but Munch soon saw to it that student concerts became an important opportunity for a broad swath of Massachusetts young people. The student concerts, too, were soon oversubscribed.

In all its manifestations the BSO, or "Symphony" as the locals usually said, was by 1950 a tradition that catered to its publics in a way that only long-standing institutions, imbued with good taste and good breeding—and not a little plain good luck—can muster. Writers like Lucius Beebe and Willa Cather describe the concerts as central to understanding Boston; for Cleveland Amory, in *The Proper Bostonians*, "The day of days for the Proper Boston woman comes twenty-six times a year—every Friday all winter—at Symphony. Here she blossoms in all her glory."[1] Symphony Hall was itself a treasure, constant in its appearance and welcome. The concert bulletin was mailed weekly to subscribers who actually studied the programmed works in advance—marvels of documentation and commentary, a superb overview of concert culture at the time. (Most of its contents were written by John N. Burk, who annotated the RCA recordings as well.) Scores for each week's repertoire were always available at the Music Room of the Boston Public Library, the nation's oldest, a few blocks away.

For the musicians in both cities, the concert season consisted of full-time, nearly round-the-clock work. In Paris there were for-hire concerts and movie soundtracks, plus the live-theater jobs from which the players had traditionally made most of their income: In the 1950s a Parisian musician's day began at 10:00 a.m. and went on until midnight. In Boston, on the scaffold of weekly rehearsals and two dozen concert pairs, from the first week in October until the last week in May, were built ancillary enterprises—in addition to the recordings and broadcasts—extending to the most complex (then and now) of all runout schedules, with routine college appearances, an annual domestic tour, and since the 1890s a series in New York city.

The Boston Symphony Orchestra, as Munch inherited it, was thus a virtuoso, old-blood ensemble. Since Monteux it was said to have played with a "French" sound, by which was meant strong presence of the principal winds, technically superb strings dominated by the first violins, and a crisp, clipped manner that lent clean detail and overall good humor to its performances. The orchestra's fiftieth-anniversary season in 1930–1931 had famously yielded Roussel's Third Symphony, Honegger's First, and Stravinsky's *Symphony of Psalms;* more recently the Bartók Concerto for Orchestra (1944) had confirmed the BSO's reputation for being capable of the most demanding new commissions.

The memorable BSO characters will emerge as our narrative unfolds. For now it is important to meet the concertmaster and assistant conductor, Richard Burgin (1891–1982), Polish-born violinist—the only member of the orchestra with whom Munch routinely spoke German. Burgin was comfortably ensconced in an authoritative position when Munch arrived; he was consequently aloof and unapproachable, especially to the younger players. Nor does one sense much personal warmth between the conductor and his concertmaster: Burgin was sometimes dismissive of his superior, and it is certain that Munch, in the early 1960s, helped in the orchestra-wide effort to lead the unwilling Burgin into retirement. Burgin was nevertheless exceptionally useful as a conductor of repertoire Munch disliked or did not wish to learn—Mahler, Bartók, Shostakovich—and was capable of standing in for rehearsals and concerts on little or no notice. He was married to the noted violin soloist Ruth Posselt, a virtuoso in her own right who had given the first Boston performance of the Samuel Barber Violin Concerto.

The personnel manager, who helped Munch with the vexed and vexing matter of appointments, was the popular bass clarinetist Rosario Mazzeo. The office staff were fond of Munch from the first, and for some this grew into genuine familial affection as the seasons passed: "Salut, Sally," he would trill each morning to the secretary, Sally Hempel, as he merrily (and as quickly as possible) passed through the administrative office. To the younger employees, he styled himself Uncle Charles. He was invariably addressed as Mr. Munch and, out of earshot, "the Boss." No American ever called him Charry or Charlie.

We have already met Henry Cabot and George Judd, with whom Munch comfortably shared executive power. It was Cabot, recalled one of the musicians, "who set such a marvelous tone. The relationship the orchestra had with management in those days was famous for its compatibility, for its pleasantness, and for being able to get along. That didn't exist in any other orchestra." All of the executives, following Cabot's lead and Bostonian tradition, called each other, as well as every employee, "Mr.," and the musicians followed suit.[2] Cabot would have been a persuasive advocate even without his Brahmin family name ("the Lowells talk only to Cabots / and the Cabots talk only to God"). At every major decision, every crisis, every turning point, Cabot's trusted counsel guided Munch into ever closer ties with Boston—from which locus his repertoire and budget, personal tax matters, medical care, legal representation, and immigration status were soon thoroughly controlled. Cabot's operatives included the cardiologist Paul Dudley White; Conrad Oberdorfer, dean of Harvard Law; Ambassador David Bruce in Paris; members of the presidential cabinet; and both Presidents Eisenhower and Kennedy. No other trustee of the BSO expressed himself with quite the same eloquence or quite the authoritative blend of family name and sheer longevity.

The work of Charles Munch and the Boston Symphony Orchestra was covered in the press by Cyrus Durgin of the *Globe,* Rudolph Elie of the *Herald,* and Harold Rogers of the *Christian Science Monitor,* all based in Boston. Owing to its New York seasons, the orchestra was well covered there, too, notably by Olin Downes and Harold Taubman, later Harold C. Schonberg, for the *New York Times.* Munch was *Time* magazine's cover story on December 19, 1949 ("The Cabots Keep Their Eyes Open"). Durgin and Elie did most of the work, however, and they are the two critics who accompanied the BSO on its international tours in 1952 and 1956. (Durgin also went to Japan in 1960; Elie died in 1958.)

Though fastidiously regal about it, Koussevitzky did not go quietly. He complained directly to the orchestra on learning the name of his successor. ("When I see you," Judd had written to Cabot the previous April, "I will acquaint you with the unhappy speech which he made to the Orchestra yesterday."[3]) He expected two or three weeks of engagements each season and the upper hand at Tanglewood. One of the reasons Munch was initially so uncomfortable at Tanglewood was Olga Koussevitzky's insistence on what "the Master" would have done or how "They" had done it. Then, when most of the desired courtesies had been extended to Koussevitzky, he cabled that he would accept no appointment in Boston in 1949–1950—and in fact conducted the orchestra again in Tanglewood only that summer (1950) and for two sets in November and December 1950.

None of these maneuvers mattered, as Koussevitzky must have sensed. Munch was a man of considerable stature and quiet self-assurance. Approaching sixty, he was certainly old enough. He was very nearly as multinational as his predecessor and had at least as good a professional formation. In New England, both politically and socially, there were inestimable advantages to an Alsatian at the helm—much as there had been in Paris in 1938: a pan-European, comfortably allied with both victory in Europe and with Beethoven and Brahms.

Charles Munch took up his duties in Boston on September 20, 1949, with the traditional ceremony—one he loathed from the beginning until the end—of unveiling the season to the press, then joining the trustees and invited guests at tea. First noting the deaths that summer of Richard Strauss and their former conductor, Henri Rabaud, he proceeded to outline a season that would unveil the new Aeolian-Skinner organ and recognize the Bach bicentennial year, 1950, with performances of the Brandenburg Concertos, the orchestral suites, and the Saint John Passion. In November there would be a benefit for Albert Schweitzer's hospital in Lambaréné, again centered on Bach. New music was to begin right away, with André Jolivet's concerto for *ondes Martenot* at the fourth pair, November 4–5, 1949.

He told the press he expected only one change in orchestral personnel and that—for the moment—there would be no change in seating plan or pitch standard (A = 444).[4] Above all, Munch said in a touching observation picked up by *Time* magazine, "There will be joy." This was to gloss over, in halting English, matters already known to be flashpoints. Actually the orchestra was redeployed almost immediately, and experiments with raised platforms began within the season. An assault on the abnormally high pitch standard (favored mostly, it would appear, by Mr. Burgin and Koussevitzky himself) began during the third season.

Munch attended his first meeting of the board of trustees the next day, September 21, 1949. This look at American business practice, so different from the governance by administrative committee of the Société des Concerts, must have been a central revelation of his first weeks. He would later take care to mention the trustees whenever he talked of the orchestra's structure, and his handwritten drafts were peppered with the indication "P&T," for "president and trustees."

In a daring stroke, his first rehearsal, on Monday morning, October 3, 1949, was broadcast. By the concert that Friday afternoon, the musicians were said to be delighted by the change of pace: "freedom from anxiety" soon became the much-referenced code for the end of Koussevitzky's autocracy. Munch later summarized the changeover more diplomatically: "It is not funny when you are told like a schoolboy to repeat over and over again the same passage."[5] Small but significant marks of self-effacement and community with the working players were widely noted, as when Munch would stay at the players' level for his bows rather than retaking the podium. Within weeks, it was being reported that "the musicians love him to a man."[6]

Geneviève Munch had meanwhile arrived in New York by ship and was received dockside by a delegation of three staff members from Boston. It took four hours to find the suitcases of music and complete the necessary formalities—and a $35 tip to "the big boss on the pier."[7] By opening night the couple and their household had only begun to settle into their lodgings in suburban Milton, Massachusetts.

On behalf of the citizens of Boston and the subscribers assembled before him at the concerts on October 7 and 8, Cabot publicly and officially greeted their new conductor:

> I am strongly opposed to speaking at Symphony concerts. However, today is ex-ceptional. We are welcoming our very distinguished new conductor, and it is the 50th season of Symphony Hall. Mr. Munch—I must tell you of our delight that our orchestra is in your strong and capable hands. Relatively speaking, we are a young country, and yet we have traditions and institutions which we cherish. Your program for today shows that you recognize this. We are grateful. And now let's listen to the music. I hope it is twenty-five years before another speaker interferes with a concert.[8]

After a memorial reading of Rabaud's *Procession nocturne,* the program dupli-cated the opening concert in Symphony Hall forty-nine seasons earlier, with Weber's *Euryanthe* overture, the ballet music from *Rosamunde,* Handel's Fourth Organ Concerto, and Beethoven's Fifth Symphony. E. Power Biggs played the new organ, which was not quite finished; he reinaugurated it the following sea-son in a series of concerts and recitals. Byron Janis was welcomed to Boston for the second pair, playing the Rachmaninov Second Concerto; Piston's Second Orchestral Suite and the Strauss *Domestic Symphony* completed that concert, and a combination of the two programs gave the orchestra its repertoire for the annual "western swing"—to Ann Arbor and Toledo—over the next two weeks. Aside from the Rabaud work, this was not an especially personal opening for Munch in Boston but rather inherited programming.

Any doubts as to the new conductor's predilections were answered with the next three programs, each of which bears his particular stamp: *The Art of Fugue* in its arrangement by Ernest Munch, with Beethoven's Seventh; the *Prague* Symphony of Mozart and first performance of Jolivet's new Concerto for Ondes Martenot and Orchestra; and a Munch signature program: Fauré's *Pelléas et Mélisande,* Roussel's Fourth, *Daphnis et Chloé*—and an unknown work, Copland's *Statements.* The arrival of André Jolivet and his soloist, Ginette Martenot, along with their curious instrument, was closely tracked by the press. Audience and critics received the strange composition politely, perhaps more out of enthusiasm for the foreign celebrities than anything else. Ginette Neveu was to have visited as well, but Munch had been in the United States just over a month when the news reached Boston of her death and that of her brother, Jean, in a plane crash in the Azores.

On Tuesday, November 14, 1949, between the fourth and fifth pairs, Munch led E. Power Biggs and the orchestra in their Schweitzer benefit, which featured the Poulenc Concerto for Organ, Strings, and Timpani as premiered in Boston by Biggs in 1941—in Paris by Munch the same year. (The famous Munch/ BSO/RCA recording, featuring Berj Zamkochian and Vic Firth, was not made until 1960.) The net receipts were $4,179.47, which Munch rounded off with a personal gift to yield $4,500 for the hospital in Africa. It was a princely amount for the time, the more welcome in that it was unexpected. Schweitzer wrote from Lambaréné:

> I have been profoundly moved by what you and the Boston Orchestra have done for my work and myself. When I came back here on November 18th, I was obliged to face a series of unavoidable expenses which I had not expected. I was depressed, overwhelmed by the prospect. And behold, you in Boston, a few days before, without my knowing it, had already relieved me of many material cares. Nobody knows what a burden of responsibility this hospital, grown so big, represents to me. It is terrible not to belong to oneself. But you have helped me to carry this responsibility at one of the critical moments of my life, at a time when I was really wandering in a dark valley.[9]

This comes from a moving letter that goes on to evoke their tender moments in Strasbourg after World War I, as noted earlier. The repeating intersection of their careers and interests in 1948 and '49 was important to them both, and each took familial pleasure in the other's accomplishments. Shortly after, Munch wrote an affectionate preface for Charles H. Joy's *Music in the Life of Albert Schweitzer, with Selections from His Writings* (1951). It says as much about Charles Munch as about Albert Schweitzer: "His simple philosophy of reverence for life is the expression of a great man's faith in God and of his own humility. His work is an example of self-sacrifice and dedication to humanity."[10]

After the Schweitzer benefit Munch took his first leave of the BSO in order to conduct in Montreal. The opening salvo of the Munch tenure had left few Boston heads unturned. Naysayers had so far kept to themselves. On the whole it was as exciting a two months as any orchestra could want. This continued during his absence from town, when Leonard Bernstein programmed still another pathbreaking work, Messiaen's *Turangalîla-Symphonie*. At the time, this was the longest single composition the BSO had ever performed. The press reported a "huge public flight" from the hall. Durgin called it, memorably if not quite fairly, "the longest and most pointless music in recent memory."[11]

The Munch household was established on Brush Hill Road in suburban Milton, Massachusetts, in a property rented from the widow of the Episcopal bishop William Lawrence. A comfortable though simple two-story dwelling a half hour's drive south of Boston, the home offered vistas of the nearby Blue Hills, where Munch loved to walk. He employed a personal staff of three: his chauffeur and factotum Roger Toureau, Toureau's wife, Cécile, who managed the household, and Alice Latorre, Mme. Munch's companion and caregiver, who gradually took over the cooking. Secretarial support was provided in both Paris and Massachusetts by Henriette Hirschmann, the Franco-Russian beauty painted by both Valentin Serov and Zinaida Serebriakova. Madame Hirschmann appears to have drafted the English versions of Munch's public addresses,[12] and Dutilleux recounts how she tried to amuse him, on his first visit to the United States, with trips to the Boston museums.[13] Another frequent companion was Marcelle Margot-Noblemaire, wealthy in her own right and married to railroad money accrued since the very beginnings of the industry. Women of her stature often occupied themselves by supporting good works: She was, by virtue of her wartime activities, honorary secretary of the International Federation of Settlements (IFS). She thought it her particular mission to oversee the best interests of Charles Munch, with whom she was deeply in love, across the whole spectrum of his activities.

Madame Noblemaire is remembered as an imposing beauty, "*impressionante, in the English fashion*": tall, conservatively but glamorously turned out, elegantly coiffed, and almost without exception the best-dressed woman in the room. "She was adorable, in her time," said a member of the family. She was engaged by Munch to arrange his journeys—purchase the tickets, find the proper hotels and restaurants, and in general facilitate his peregrinations: something between a manager and a traveling companion.[14] As was typical of this sort of arrangement between Munch and his women associates, it evolved into romance where she was at first the suitor and then the protectress. She also played golf, an important requirement of his intimates.

Marcelle Noblemaire was universally disliked by the other women in Munch's life for her controlling ways, overbearing manner, and narrow-mindedness. There was particular friction between Mme. Noblemaire and Nicole Henriot, in part because she liked to claim responsibility for having arranged Nicole's marriage to Jean-Jacques Schweitzer. For his part Munch, by all accounts, enjoyed watching his lady friends jockey for position. The competition intrigued him, and so long as he was surrounded by handsome women, their hierarchy did not much concern him.

Roger Toureau was, by a certain distance, Munch's closest male confidant. His primary duty was to spirit the *maître* quickly away from rehearsals and performances to any place that did not require small talk in English. Additionally, he oversaw such tasks as attending to the music cases and altering his employer's extensive business and formal wardrobe. He kept a well-stocked bar in the trunk of the automobile, and he was handy in the kitchen. He was the only witness to numerous romantic trysts, some of which he arranged. Unlike Mme. Munch, he was well known to the musicians and the BSO's inner circle and liked by them all.

Geneviève Munch came to Boston only the first year and, despite a considerably better command of English than her husband, kept a low profile. In one of her few public forays she gave a lecture on Thomas Mann at the Boston Academy of Arts and Sciences. Bostonians remember her only for her occasional appearances in the conductor's seats at Symphony Hall. One of the musicians' wives took tea with her at the house in Milton and recalled a charming and well-expressed invalid. The only known photograph of her is in the *Time* magazine story, where she is seen behind an open door with the dog, an Airedale named Pompey. Portraying her as a docile housewife, *Time* describes their daily routine as beginning with a breakfast of bacon and eggs with tea, complaining that "in Boston we have not yet found good bread"—nor, she goes on, proper Alsatian wines. She says her husband liked New England clam chowder well enough but remained partial to *pot-au-feu* and kidneys cooked with Chablis. The interviewer might just as profitably have posed these questions to the cook, while the observations Mme. Munch might have offered on literature, the arts, and society went unsolicited.

Whether from disinclination to continue in this unaccustomed role or for reasons of her rapidly declining health, Vivette's decision to remain thereafter in

France was not entirely unwelcome by her husband. She was sensitive about the women houseguests in Milton and, on one occasion, speaking sharply to him from her wheelchair, refused to accompany a woman friend to Symphony Hall. Presumably the "Madame Munch" mentioned as his companion in coverage of the BSO's 1951 appearance in Washington, before President and Mrs. Truman and President and Mme. Vincent Auriol of France, was in fact Nicole Henriot; moreover, which woman was meant as the Madame Munch invited to John F. Kennedy's inaugural ball in 1961, after Geneviève's death, is anybody's guess.

Munch's closest friend among the musicians was the Franco-American trumpet player Roger Voisin, along with his vivacious wife, Martha, a North Carolinian. Fond of Martha's cooking and the comfortably bicultural life Voisin had established, Munch spent many evenings at their house. He enjoyed the one-table Chez Voisin, a bistro operated by Voisin's mother. Voisin was Munch's chief opponent in his favorite card game, *belote.*

There are enough Munch-and-*belote* stories to sidetrack our narrative for pages. Their common points are two: He would make up the rules as he went along in order to win, and he was a bad loser. For doubles Mr. Burgin would engage and secretly bankroll his young French colleague Roger Shermont as partner, mostly to enjoy watching Munch's outrage when he lost. "Give him a dollar," Munch told Roger-the-chauffeur, "but Canadian, not American." (A dollar was also at stake when he lost a golf match to Martha Voisin in Tanglewood; he autographed the bill but would never play with her again.) One musician learned *belote* from a book in order to gain access to the inner circle; others knew enough to stay away. "You always cheat," reproved Mme. Noblemaire, who refused to join him at cards.

Naturally Munch identified, too, with the *émigrés,* especially those he had helped escape from Europe in the 1940s. The Martinus had been in the country since 1941 and were living in New York. Alexander Tcherepnin and his second wife, Ming (Lee Hsien Ming), arrived in the United States shortly before Munch and had teaching appointments at DePaul in Chicago.

Munch was always happy in New York, where he typically stayed at the Drake Hotel on Park Avenue. There, for instance, he met Edgard Varèse. One disadvantage of New York was that persons of high Boston lineage who lived there would seek to disrupt his solitude: Gertrude Robinson Smith, especially, and Olga Koussevitzky. For true *repos* he preferred to go to Montreal, where he could speak his own language and where, over the years, he also developed close ties.

For all the goodwill expressed both publicly and privately in the inaugural season, there were areas of considerable discord over the simple first contract, which had been negotiated in New York between George Judd of the BSO and

Munch and his Franco-American attorney, Lucien R. Le Lievre, with Munch's Columbia Artist Management agents, Arthur Judson and Bruno Zirato, also providing counsel. The document initialed on April 7, 1948, in New York preceded a more detailed contract signed later on.

This first contract was in effect for two seasons, from September 1949 through August 1951, with an option for a third year to be instigated by either party in January 1951. The proposed starting salary was $30,000 for a season of thirty weeks not to exceed 120 performances, with increments to $45,000 by the third season and travel expenses for Munch and his wife to and from Paris; these were eventually negotiated upward to $35-, $45-, and $50,000 for the first three seasons. Munch's presence was required at the Berkshire Festival, Tanglewood, in July and August under separate financial arrangements, noting that it was "understood that the concerts shall be grouped in such a manner as reasonably to require from the Conductor the least possible time in the United States."[15]

Boston demanded exclusivity of his services in the United States and Canada, counting recordings and broadcasts by radio and the new medium of television: He was, in short, forbidden from entering into any other contract that would interfere with his availability to the BSO for a period of nearly forty-six weeks each year. The orchestra assigned to him total control of programming, rehearsals, concerts, broadcasts, recording sessions, and personnel. He had full powers of discipline over the members of the orchestra and the power to suspend or discharge players for cause. No soloist or guest conductor was to be engaged without his direct approval. It was understood that Richard Burgin or a similar figure would provide necessary assistance and that Dr. Koussevitzky "shall be requested to conduct a substantial number of concerts at the Berkshire Music Center."[16]

Munch was from the beginning genuinely uncomfortable, given his lack of experience in the area, with the notion of bearing sole responsibility for the orchestra personnel. He was unhappy, too, about the exclusivity clauses, especially considering the brevity of the single vacation offered. His "sentiments on this subject" were conveyed to the trustee meeting of February 1949, and by the meeting in May he was insisting that other conductors be found for periods long enough to allow him to guest-conduct elsewhere.

On April 20, 1948, Cabot wrote to Munch's lawyer that the orchestra would be "very reluctant" to grant him permission to appear as guest conductor in Canada or elsewhere in the United States. "It has been and remains our policy not to have a regular conductor of the BSO appear as guest with other orchestras." As for the summer: "I do not see how it is possible for Mr. Munch to avoid being in the United States for the full three weeks of the Berkshire Festival"—that is, the big concerts in the Shed.[17] A week later management yielded slightly to Munch's most pressing desires: "It is our present intention to do all we reasonably can to arrange for appearances of Mr. Munch with the Boston Symphony Orchestra in Canada during the period of his contract."[18] This satisfied, for the moment, all of the parties, and three copies of the contract were forwarded for signature.

Cooperating at least in spirit with the notion of an exclusive conductor, Munch returned from Montreal to lead the BSO runout to Washington, D.C., in early December and made his first recording for RCA—Beethoven's Seventh—on December 19–20, when he had originally hoped to be away. As early as the December 1949 board meeting the trustees decided to exercise their option for a third season with Munch, 1951–1952, and in their satisfaction offered him an extra week off, effectively releasing him from five of the twenty-four pairs each season. In early 1950 they signaled their desire that Munch remain indefinitely, and he replied—as always, through Henry Cabot—that this was his desire as well.

Given the linguistic and cultural distinctions and the rapidly evolving United States tax code and immigration laws, it was a major accomplishment that Munch and Boston survived the first contract. His primary attorney for salary matters, Guido R. Perera, worked to establish his status as a nonresident alien engaged in a trade or business, trying thereby to reduce the tax liability on his $55,000 total income to something below $26,845. (He got that down to $21,000 by successfully arguing that the 15-percent commission Munch owed the Judson agency was deductible.)

Meanwhile, Lucien Le Lievre tried to sort out the matter of the recording contracts, a negotiation that went on all summer. It was out of the question, he believed, for his client to be forbidden to complete the Orchestre National recordings already contracted for September 1950; furthermore, the ten-year prohibition against recording the same works with a different orchestra would need to be altered to five. Munch could not be bound by a prior contract between RCA and the BSO, one he had never read before signing. (This last was not quite true.) "Situations such as the present one," Le Lievre admonished, "which are embarrassing to all concerned, could be avoided if contracts on which the signature of Mr Munch is required were submitted to him in advance so that he could have them translated in French and reviewed by counsel."[19]

Finally, Munch and his retinue needed to attend to their immigration status. Munch himself meant to become a resident alien, for obvious tax purposes. The French quota for 1949–1950 having been exhausted, he was advised to return to the United States as soon as possible after July 1, 1950, to ensure being counted in the 1950–1951 quota. In proper Boston fashion it was directly arranged with David Bruce, U.S. ambassador to France, for him to call at the embassy in June 1950 to get his papers, though, as it turned out, he was "unable to arrange" to go.

In both April and May 1951, management urgently reminded Munch of the necessity of paying a courtesy visit to Ambassador and Mrs. Bruce before coming back to the Berkshire Festival.[20]

Through it all Cabot maintained his patrician equanimity:

> I like to think of our relations as those of partners where, although there is a written agreement, the relationship is fundamentally based on good will, friendly feeling and a common purpose.... Have a good rest this summer! I would like to think that you and your brothers were having some of those days of music, wine and golf which you told me about.[21]

In January 1950 Francis Poulenc came to play his controversial Piano Concerto, composed, insouciantly, after an informal suggestion from Munch. The concluding *rondeau à la française* sets a classical French eighteenth-century tune to Creole rhythms and scoring—"*un shakehand,*" Poulenc called it, with a country that had proved "by far, my most loyal public . . . a kind of souvenir of Paris from the pianist-composer."[22] Others thought it the work of a *boulevardier* who had lost touch with serious music. The Boston reception was guarded but satisfactory: "Thank you, thank you for the Concerto," Poulenc wrote Munch. "I would have liked to bring you an unclouded success, for that would have been a better measure of the admiring affection I have for you."[23]

The first season continued to unfold with a jaw-dropping list of first performances that affords a sharp reminder of how recently new pieces for big orchestra had become an ordinary part of concertgoing: Honegger's *Joan of Arc,* Pfitzner, Walton (the only British composer who seems to have particularly interested Munch so far), William Schuman, and Lukas Foss.

To promote the spring events, which would include the Saint John Passion and Saint-Saëns Organ Symphony, Munch agreed to a live radio interview with Martin Bookspan, which took place at WBMS on February 1, 1950, just after his first *Pathétique* in Boston. Even though it was still difficult for him to speak in public, he recognized his responsibility to do so and was willing to give it a try so long as he could work out his responses in advance. The typescript he took to the radio station shows his penciled notes for pronunciation—canceling, for instance, the "t" in "listener"; moving the accent from the francophone last syllable to the previous one for "tradition" and "performance." (Later handwritten pages show that he was eventually able to draft public remarks in English with relative facility.) The idiom is his alone. He reiterates the concept of joy, his theme for the year, as he had found it with the Boston players and with the repertoire, and promotes the upcoming Saint John Passion and *Missa solemnis.* As to the summer, "I intend to give concerts all over France and keep busy until August, when I hope to have a good rest before my return to Boston."[24]

Just afterward it was learned in Boston that the Orchestre National's September 1949 recording of the *Symphonie fantastique* had won a Grand Prix du Disque. Bookspan, thinking this mark of prestige needed explaining in America, devoted another program to Munch shortly afterward, reading letters of audience response to the earlier live interview and playing, for the first time over the air, the new recording of Beethoven's Seventh, which had been made in December and just released by RCA (LM 1034).

Under Munch, BSO seasons typically began to peak with Easter-week chorus-and-orchestra works along the lines of the Parisian *concert spirituel,* then built toward the final pair, often another major choral work—in this case Beethoven's *Missa solemnis*—with proceeds to benefit the BSO's pension fund. That April the listeners heartily approved of the Saint John Passion, still relatively unfamiliar at the BSO, and its success led management to promise the Saint Matthew for 1950–1951. By season close the public was cheering a splendid first year.

As was the press. Virtually everyone concurred that Munch had achieved the impossible: He had eclipsed Koussevitzky in a single season. Rudolph Elie, in the *Boston Sunday Herald,* expressed his admiration:

> He has filled a gap that few of us really believed could be filled in so brief a time, if, indeed, it could be filled at all. . . . For 25 years [the BSO] had been dominated body and soul by a man of immense complexity, a man of iron will, of passionate temperament, of imperious authority, and a musical genius of the first rank.[25]

And Munch had proved his equal. Every seat for the entire season had been sold. If there had been friction in converting to a new mode of work—and there was probably very little—it went unnoticed by the public. Munch won over the musicians, Elie suggested, by "his immense technical command, his uncanny ear, his extraordinary memory, and his profound musicianship." Winning over the Bostonians took only a few weeks longer. "It seemed to me—tuning in on this wave—that the audience recognized his musicianship from the very start, but it was not until the ninth concert, when he did Tchaikovsky's Sixth, that I began to feel that the audience really took him to its heart."[26]

Munch himself was fully aware—more humbled than proud—that he had arrived in the uppermost echelons of international orchestral practice. There was much to enjoy in this circumstance and certainly a moral and financial comfort to be savored. The issue of the moment, however, was for him to reclaim a little of the French lifestyle and, most of all, to get some rest. When Munch took the Boston job, he agreed to conduct a season of twenty-four pairs in the twenty-eight weeks from October 1 to April 30—not fully grasping that the ancillary events boiled down to something every night. By the end of 1950–1951, after Tanglewood, he had worked thirty-one weeks embracing 135 concerts. In 1955–1956, during the BSO's seventy-fifth anniversary year, there were more than 80 concerts in the Boston season alone, plus the regional tours and New York seasons and, with increased frequency owing to Munch's own enthusiasm, national and international expeditions. To be sure, Munch did not have to conduct every one of these, and numerous clauses in his contracts promised *repos* and other forms of relief. But whatever was written down, it was in fact expected that he not be away for long, ever.

In Paris, of course, the demand for his professional services was pent up: The senior French conductor had not been seen for months. He took the first concert of the fourth citywide Paris Festival that summer, on July 11, 1950, to lead a program in memory of Ginette Neveu and her brother: the Mozart Funeral Music, Beethoven's Fourth Piano Concerto with Nicole Henriot, and the Brahms Fourth Symphony. A substantial net revenue was rounded by Henriot and Munch to 520,000 francs and forwarded to the Neveus' mother. A festival concert at Aix-en-Provence, on July 24, 1950, was also dedicated to their memory—the only time Charles Munch ever conducted there. On the program was the French premiere of Poulenc's new concerto, on which occasion Claude Rostand characterized Poulenc as half bad boy, half monk. Clarendon, too, panned the Poulenc, and a proper brouhaha was on the verge of breaking out when the writers found themselves diverted by the next evening's French premiere of the *Turangalîla-Symphonie,* under Roger Désormière.[27]

In August and September Munch eked out his few weeks of rest by successfully remaining incommunicado. Boston was alarmed to discover how completely he could make himself unavailable by the simple expedient of not responding to letters and telegrams and how little interest he was inclined to take, during his repose, in personnel matters or the launch of the new season. It was in this context that a new figure came to prominence in the Munch household: Leonard Burkat (1919–1992). Burkat, whom Koussevitzky had engaged as Tanglewood librarian, became something like a personal artistic assistant to Munch by virtue of his acceptable French and his overall familiarity with the repertoire of art music and the mechanics of producing it. That summer the BSO management paid him essentially to catch up with their elusive conductor and wrest from him the decisions necessary to proceed with the next season. Burkat was not especially popular with the Bostonians; the French mocked his French; many resented a non-musician's advising Munch. It is not even clear that Munch was particularly fond of him. Nevertheless, Burkat was able to accomplish what others were not, and he was very smart. It was thus often he who actually came up with the season programming. One BSO regular recalls that he was the first person she ever saw using a three-year calendar. He also served as factotum in assembling the many original scores and parts Munch went through each year, and later it was widely but incorrectly assumed that he had ghost-written Munch's book *Je suis chef d'orchestre / I Am a Conductor.* In point of fact, he translated the text from the French and wrote a good, detailed introduction.

In the summer of 1950 Burkat reported to Boston on the Munch household:

> One of the most impressive things I took away from my first visit with Munch is the intensely human quality. . . . It seems clear to me . . . that he wants to make his pro-grams and to conduct and to bear no other burdens. Personal contacts mean a great deal to him but business formalities do not. There was on his desk a letter from [RCA] Victor, single-spaced, at least three pages long that I am sure he cannot have read. The idea of recording the four works mentioned . . . was completely new, as though no one had ever mentioned them to him before. One hour of conversation seems to be worth many letters, even though he retains the right to change his mind. . . . He seems interested in other people as human beings and not as tools. . . .
>
> He was very proud for having achieved a genuine vacation, without a single item of business intruding. Everyone deserves a complete rest from his work, he said, and there is almost nothing in the world that can't wait two weeks. What a happy conviction![28]

By September 1950, interesting Munch in a true commitment to Tangle-wood had become the trustees' top priority. He quietly concluded that he would not be able to escape Tanglewood, so he proposed that Koussevitzky conduct the Bach and Mozart concerts in the first two weeks, while he would rotate the nine full concerts among Bernstein, Carvalho, and himself. This would cost him two, possibly three, of his summer weeks. A later plan showed just the reverse: He would do the Bach-Mozart concerts, a repertoire he loved anyway, and Koussevitzky would take over thereafter—leaving Munch free to go back home to France after only two weeks in the Berkshires. The trustees responded by adding a $2,000 fee for each Shed concert and, more significantly, relaxing the provisions of his exclusivity clause: "All we ask is that you consult with us first. We have two reasons why we don't like your acting as a guest conductor. First, we want to keep you to ourselves, and, secondly, we want you to get a real rest."[29]

The second season, as every artist and impresario knows, is the defining one: a time to be bold about changes that need making, a time to assert one's own personality. From the conductor's point of view it needs to be about estab-lishing idiomatic repertoires old and new and finding solutions to problems identified in the first months. These, Munch concluded, were a righting of the BSO's soured relationship with Pierre Monteux and redeploying the orchestra in its historic hall, the better to improve an acoustic he had found damp and uninteresting. The trustees, though still troubled by his ambivalence toward

Tanglewood, were otherwise well pleased and eager to affirm to the public what it already knew: that the orchestra had found its man. They greeted his return to Boston on September 21, 1950, with the announcement that Charles Munch had officially been named music director of the Boston Symphony Orchestra.

The season launch, including the traditional press conference and patron tea, assured those assembled that there would be no repeats from the previous season. New works by American composers—Lukas Foss, Peter Mennin, and David Diamond—would dominate the bill of first performances, alongside new-for-Boston works of Martinu and Tcherepnin and the premiere of Honegger's Fifth. Munch and his musicians would continue to flesh out their canon of Bach's great orchestra-and-chorus works with a Christmas Oratorio in December and the Saint Matthew Passion as soon as the daunting technical arrangements could be agreed on. He would continue to emphasize the French repertoire, with the Franck Symphony, the suite from *Pelléas et Mélisande, Rapsodie espagnole,* Ibert's *Escales,* and possibly Debussy's *Nocturnes* with chorus. As for Berlioz, the first season had offered only the symphonic movements from *Roméo et Juliette;* now there were to be both the *Fantastique* and a season-concluding Requiem, with talk of *La damnation de Faust* in the near future.

Munch confirmed his plans to introduce gentle risers on the stage of Symphony Hall, leaving only the violins at left and violas at right at floor level, an arrangement soon diagrammed in the program book.[30] Experiments went on for two seasons, with Munch roaming the hall to listen as Burgin conducted; members of the press and public were invited to give their reactions. He also recognized the successful establishment, for the previous season's *Jeanne d'Arc au bûcher,* of a full-fledged symphony chorus, so far without a name, organized and prepared by Arthur Fiedler. "Its *raison d'être,*" said the press, "is to assist Mr. Munch in bringing important choral works to performance in Boston. The chorus is a volunteer group held together by enthusiasm and satisfaction in its mission. The ranks contain professional singers, as well as amateurs."[31] This arrangement for providing a chorus proved temporary, but it did signal the primacy of that division of the repertoire.

At the press conference there appears to have been little or no mention of a wholesome addition to Boston musical life, the annual hosting in Symphony Hall of a visiting orchestra and its celebrity conductor. When Munch had brought the Orchestre National in October 1948, it had been noted that this was the first such visit in the modern era. Now Sir Thomas Beecham and the Royal Philharmonic came to call; soon there were the Chicago Symphony Orchestra under Rafael Kubelik (1953), the Amsterdam Concertgebouw with Eduard van Beinum (1954), and the Berlin Philharmonic with Herbert von Karajan (1955).

Those who attended the presentation noted the *maître's* great progress in English and his obvious pleasure in the New England autumn: "So beautiful it is! Already the color of the leaves is *extraordinaire!*"[32] Munch was determined not to become too fluent: His limited English was a convenient excuse, and he did not try to correct the general impression that it was halting. By the mid-1950s he could move in and out of his third language without thinking much about it, understanding virtually everything in due course and able to get what he wanted however it came out.

In the long run, the signal advance of the new season, however, was the Thursday night student "open rehearsals" at $8 for the series (federal tax included), $2 for a single event, unreserved seating. The Friday afternoon rehearsal, originally opened "to all who paid a coin at the door," had long since turned into its own subscription season with its particular profile. The Harvard series, begun in the orchestra's second year—Higginson's idea, again: to "make music available to students"—had been overtaken by townsfolk and faculty and had grown too expensive for students anyway. Opening a few rehearsals to all, with preferential purchase for students and special-interest groups such as the employees of Filene's department store (this particular program following on several precedents of utopian living, including that of the Bon Marché department store in Paris[33]), was good for all concerned, especially for those who thought in terms of the higher mission of art music.

The program bulletin attributed this initiative to Harvard students, who had complained to George Judd of being marginalized from symphony activities. Munch drew the obvious parallel with European practice and added his hearty endorsement. The musicians were quickly brought around by the time-honored device of donating the proceeds to their pension fund.

Nothing was staged: Munch felt free to talk to the musicians and occasionally to stop and go back, even when they were on the air—though Thursday nights were usually given to final runs. At the first open rehearsal, on November 9, 1950, Yehudi Menuhin appeared for his Mozart concerto in an untucked plaid shirt and Munch in "a khaki jacket, a pair of tweeds and crepe rubber soled sport shoes." The students were equally informal, "some of them in their shirt-sleeves, too, and all as gay and informal as a bunch of students can be."[34] Symphony Hall was packed.

Five days later, at the second open rehearsal:

> He went right to work on a Haydn symphony [no. 103], stopping the orchestra in full cry to give musical instructions in his lightly accented English, singing along with the orchestra in a husky baritone, jumping off the platform among the players to illustrate how softly he wanted the passage to go, crying "Sing!" at the top of his voice to achieve a more expressive tone quality, and leaping off his rehearsal stool like a lion with his mane in his eyes to get a more dramatic attack on a loud passage.

Munch, of course, paid the audience little or no attention in circumstances like these, but "the listeners caught the significance of his repetitions of various passages and seemed to find the process of starting and stopping highly enjoyable as well as instructive." In sharp contrast to his post-concert attitude toward adult well-wishers, he affably received young people in the Green Room afterward. But nobody tried to speak French. "I was going to," said a student to his girlfriend, "but I got cold feet. What do you say to a guy like that, anyway?"[35]

By the measures of strong new initiatives or of audience satisfaction or of artistic merit, the Munch years had begun in triumph. What was more difficult to assess at the start of 1950–1951 was the orchestra's financial stability. The postwar, post-Koussevitzky era was characterized by inflation, sharp market swings in sectors that affected the orchestra, and frequent adjustments in the tax codes. An orchestra's annual deficits before contributions typically accrue in direct proportion to its artistic success: Every concert costs more than the ticket income brings in. This was the trend at the BSO, and by 1950 the trustees were aware that they were past the point where they and the Friends of the Boston Symphony Orchestra could simply divide up the shortfall.

In very round figures, a BSO season in that era cost about $1 million and brought in perhaps $800,000 in ticket sales. The other two revenue streams were royalties on records sold and fees for broadcasts, figures that fluctuated with that volatile marketplace. The long-playing record war (and the loss of income from Koussevitzky's 78s) had cost the BSO dearly. Once that shortfall was met, income from radio sponsors plummeted, from more than $65,000 in 1951 to about $10,000 in 1952. Since the house was essentially sold out every day, increased sales could come only from price increases—with little promise that they would much narrow the gap.

It is instructive to follow Cabot's orations as he annually reminds the Friends of their centrality, then launches the orchestra on each step of a modern infrastructure. At the Friends meeting of March 19, 1951, he lectured those assembled on the many ways an orchestra is distinct from a business. Ticket prices high enough to pay the full price of the orchestra were out of the question: "We conceive it to be our duty to reach a happy mean so that great numbers of our fellow citizens may share with us the thrill and deep satisfaction of listening to great music." He sounded an appeal that resonates well even today:

> You are our reserves. Every prudently managed business has reserves. . . . We have never been able to build up reserves sufficient to cover more than relatively small miscalculations. . . . So you see you serve two absolutely essential functions: You give us each year the sums needed to keep us going, and your existence gives us courage to venture forth upon financial seas full of uncharted rocks, for we know

that you will rescue us if we are shipwrecked. . . . (Parenthetically, those of you who are tax conscious will recognize that as a gift to the Orchestra is tax deductible, it is cheaper to give us money than to pay more for tickets.)[36]

On January 22, 1953, for the first time, the trustees invited 120 businessmen to Symphony Hall to hear a rehearsal (Schubert's *Rosamunde*, Samazeuilh's *Nuit*, and an excerpt from *Die Meistersinger*), followed by New England clam chowder and appeals from Cabot and from the week's soloist, Isaac Stern. Stern noted that two years had gone by without raises for the musicians:

> Orchestras the world over are compared to the Boston Symphony. There's no other orchestra like it. It has created a standard; it has an *esprit de corps*, a pride in itself. The concerts in Europe by the Boston Symphony last spring did more to help Europeans understand Americans than all the diplomats have been able to do. Our orchestra can be our greatest ambassador. The Boston Symphony should not ask for your support. You should ask to be able to give your support to the Boston Symphony.[37]

The businessmen were good humored about the pitch ("the first time I've heard it set to music," one remarked), but a reader of the *Boston Herald* suggested that such appeals might not be necessary if the orchestra were more efficiently managed, perhaps with a shorter season or, failing that, multiple assistant conductors drawn from the ranks to reduce the costs of the guests. Cabot's vigorous reply noted, in closing, that during the Depression the trustees had urged the general manager to reduce the size of the orchestra in every aspect of its operation. "He replied briefly that it had not been his observation that a second-rate orchestra was easier to finance than a first-rate orchestra."[38]

What is clear in these episodes, with regard to Munch himself, is the certainty of his draw at the box office and then the enormous financial success, within only a few months, of his long-playing recordings. In fact, RCA considered the Haydn Symphony no. 104 and the Brahms Fourth, recorded in April 1950, "the finest musical results yet realized by Victor company."[39] The company was genuinely excited about its program of recordings with Munch and the BSO. Records were released once a month: *La Valse* in September 1950, the Brahms Fourth in October, Schubert's Second in December, French light classics in January 1951, and Haydn's 104th in February. The December 1950 and January 1951 recording sessions included the Hamilton-Harty *Water Music*, more French titles, and Haydn, Beethoven, and Schumann. The five-year exclusivity of the Decca recordings with the Société des Concerts and London Philharmonic orchestras would begin to lapse in 1951, leaving Munch free to rerecord a substantial portion of his favorite repertoire with his new ensemble.

The trustees were committed to achieving an amicable arrangement to such an end: "Recording represents one of the most promising methods of widening support for the Orchestra and its musical public. The value of the close association of your name with the Orchestra is incalculable."[40]

In hindsight it was neither the financial restructuring, the student concerts, the formation of the new chorus, nor even the RCA recordings and broadcasts that subscribers remembered about the early '50s but rather the rehabilitation of Monteux in Boston. (Monteux had left the orchestra in 1924 after a confrontation with the labor union; Koussevitzky, his successor, had not invited him back.) As early as January 1950, contemplating the 1950–1951 season, Munch wrote to Monteux and insisted on his returning to Boston for a concert pair. Monteux's response was at first salty, then, after a mollifying letter from the Cabots, enthusiastic.[41] He reckoned the gesture, he told the *Boston Globe,* to have come ten years too late, then added with his customary twinkle, "but 10 years ago Mr. Munch was not here to invite me."[42]

Pierre Monteux was thus booked for the thirteenth pair, in late January 1951, plus ancillary events. The centerpiece of his visit would naturally be *The Rite of Spring,* alongside works of Beethoven, Wagner, and Brahms. In the concert Monteux (conducting, as always, from memory) miscounted in the treacherous score, but the reviewers were ecstatic anyway. The *Christian Science Monitor* of January 26, 1951, spread a feature on his return across a full page, while the famous Associated Press photograph of Koussevitzky, Monteux, and Munch together in Symphony Hall ran on January 25. In the aftermath RCA taped what some believe is his best rendition of *The Rite* (RCA LM-1149).

Monteux wrote Munch shortly afterward with warm thanks for the opportunity, after their infrequent meetings to date, "to know you properly and to love you." Various gestures of quid pro quo were proffered: Nicole Henriot was invited to appear with the San Francisco orchestra; Monteux's twenty-one-year-old protégé, Anshel Brusilow, would come to Boston. The Boston and San Francisco orchestras were to exchange conductors in November 1951. Munch rightly characterized the return of Monteux as "the great event of the season."[43]

Thereafter, Monteux's thorough absorption into the fabric of the BSO was so effortless as to mask its substantial impact on the Munch regime and its legacy. The self-effacement Munch always showed with regard to his elder colleague is to be admired; it is as though the idea of their competing over the French repertoire had not occurred to either of them. The payback came immediately, when Monteux agreed to co-conduct the BSO in its first venture abroad, in 1952, thereby making possible a real turning point in orchestral history— rather, a series of them—otherwise in jeopardy owing to Munch's ill health that year. Monteux also appeared and taught at Tanglewood, co-conducted the long

American tour in the spring of 1953 and the 1956 tour to Scandinavia and the Soviet Union, shared the podium with Munch and Bruno Walter for Toscanini's memorial concert, and celebrated both his eightieth and eighty-fifth birthdays with the orchestra. "I have known two conductors who were masters," Munch was fond of saying: "Toscanini and Monteux."

As the 1950–1951 season took shape, the nature and degree of Munch's commitment to new music by American composers and foreign ones living in America became clearer still. David Diamond wrote in the program note for the first performance of his Symphony no. 3 (November 3, 1950) that it had been composed in 1945 and intended for Rodzinski and the Chicago Symphony Orchestra but gone unplayed. Munch had taken a look at the score in Paris and said: "But this is ridiculous—we must have it performed. I will do it next season."[44] For some, the performance sealed Diamond's growing reputation as a leading symphonist, though what the composer remembered was how Princeton composer Milton Babbitt "snickered through most of Munch's performance of my Third Symphony."[45] In the same season Samuel Barber conducted his own Second Symphony; Schoenberg's Chamber Symphony was heard in its scoring for full orchestra; likewise, Peter Mennin's Fifth Symphony. By foreigners there were Honegger's Fifth and Prokofiev's Sixth, new piano concertos by both Tcherepnin and Martinu, and a Concerto for Orchestra by G. F. Ghedini. The world premiere of Nicholas Nabokov's *La vita nuova* established a relationship soon to have very far-reaching implications.

Munch also introduced Boston to works that soon became BSO favorites: Saint-Saëns's *La princesse jaune* overture and a suite from Rameau's *Dardanus* arranged for orchestra by Vincent d'Indy. For the Christmas Oratorio in December and a Schubert Mass in March, Fiedler's amateur chorus was used; for the Saint Matthew Passion and Berlioz Requiem in the spring, the Harvard-Radcliffe singers under G. Wallace Woodworth were back on the billing. The reasons for this, though not recorded, seem obvious: Fiedler did not much like the job, and Munch did not much like the results. We know that Professor Woodworth, a proponent of the strict, metronomic style when it came to Bach, found the Munch renditions excruciatingly slack, but there was little doubt from either side as to the mutual benefits of the arrangement.

In February Nicole Henriot came for a Brahms concerto and apparently stayed in the United States through a state visit from Vincent Auriol, president of France. The orchestra rearranged its schedule to travel to Constitution Hall in Washington, D.C., for a gala concert on Saturday, March 31, 1951. Among the dignitaries were President and Mrs. Truman, Secretary of State and Mrs. Dean Acheson, Justice and Mrs. Felix Frankfurter, and, of course, the French diplomatic mission to Washington, including its financial attaché,

Pierre-Paul Schweitzer. The program, characteristic of the flair Munch and the BSO always showed under such circumstances, began with the two national anthems, then Samuel Barber's *School for Scandal* overture, Copland's *Quiet City* with two recognizably French soloists—Roger Voisin, trumpet, and Louis Speyer, English horn—the Ravel G-Major Concerto with Nicole Henriot, and finally the *Fantastique*. Afterward, the distinguished guests, led by the Trumans, were received at the French embassy.

Only three weeks later, Munch led the BSO and multiple associates in the first Boston performance of the Berlioz Requiem—a work he had last led at the Strasbourg Festival in 1948. The runaway success in Boston prompted several reprises in the following months, launched the Berlioz cycle, which was in full swing by 1952–1953, and in due course led to the great recording of 1959 that proved the work to the world at large.

Munch now found himself effectively at the end of his probationary period. Cabot wrote:

> A year ago I told you we wanted you to stay. Intervening time has made us more anxious than ever that you remain. Let me add a personal word of admiration. After every concert I come away with the feeling that I had never before fully realized the beauty of the works just played. Somehow or other you add a freshness and a something, I know not what, which reveals new beauties. I sincerely trust that Boston is now your home and the Boston Symphony Orchestra your orchestra for keeps.

Concessions were the order of the day, and the trustees were in a conciliatory frame of mind: "We also join your wife in wanting you to have more rest during the season. . . . In fact what we want is to do everything in our power to make your job here with the Boston Symphony Orchestra fruitful, satisfactory, and pleasant. You are the greatest single asset of the B.S.O. We want you to be happy."[46]

Nonetheless, since there were obvious soft spots in Munch's approach and technique, the honeymoon with the press could not last forever. In April Warren Storey Smith wrote in the *Boston Post*:

> In the Symphony of Brahms [April 27–28, 1951] he revealed again his tendency to go to extremes, to whip music up to an unwarranted degree, to distort it and thus transform the composer's personality. It happened earlier in the season with the Symphony of Franck [April 17, a Tuesday concert]. And it must be said that in both instances the audience went for this misinterpretation in a big way. . . . For American listeners, one fears, nothing can ever be too loud or too fast.[47]

The previous February 1951 Olin Downes wrote of an unfortunate performance of Richard Strauss's *Don Juan,* in which Munch "ran away with himself. There was a loss of distinctness and even of the most effective articulation of the themes. The final climax lost its grandeur and the full measure of dramatic affirmation because it was hurried." Still, Downes found the A-minor chord at the end, pierced by the F natural "as by a sword thrust . . . the true interpretation of Strauss's thought—life turned to ashes and emptiness. . . . Here was a distinctive touch in an imperfect performance."[48] There were downsides, that is, to the Munchian spontaneity.

The BSO's premiere of Honegger's Symphony no. 5 on March 9, 1951, was the first of numerous performances that spring and summer. Subtitled "*di tre re,*" that is, "of the three Ds" with which each movement concludes, *pianissimo,* in the timpani, the symphony amounts to the composer's squaring of accounts with himself as he contemplates a life being brought to a close by cardiac disease. He called the first movement a "march of human folly"; the last movement is about life slipping away. It is the new work perhaps most directly associated with Munch between *Bacchus et Ariane* and Dutilleux's Second Symphony, emblematic for both composer and dedicatee of their shared tribulations.

On the evening of March 10 Munch wrote Honegger to report the birth, wondering:

> how to thank you, how to convey my emotion and my gratitude. Once again, thanks to you, all the pain and suffering, all the effort and sacrifices of a difficult existence, find a reward that consoles and explains all this. I can't find the words, and it's impertinent of me even to write you, but I sense your music and the mystery surrounding it, and my throat tightens and the tears fall.[49]

Munch thought it a tragic score: "the confession of a man without hope."

He played it then in Hartford, New Haven, Brooklyn, and twice in New York. Olin Downes, though he said it was "cryptic" and "enigmatical," got the point just fine: "This music, sombre and self-questioning, speaks of a world of lost faiths, inner strife; a girding of the loins for a supreme struggle, and issues fought indomitably by the spirit of man—the quest for 'the answer,' though it be as remote and undecipherable as the Sphinx."[50] At the performance in Strasbourg that June Munch was still haunted by the music, still "fervent as a disciple," conducting "by heart and with all his heart."[51] He would record a stunning rendition with the BSO in October 1952; much later there would be a live broadcast with the Orchestra National, eventually released on disc.

Full of anticipation at playing the Honegger in France, he hurried home from Boston the minute the season was over. The Paris premiere was with the

Orchestre National at the Théâtre des Champs-Élysées on May 7, Honegger attending. Subsequently he took the orchestra and work to Bordeaux (May 28, 1951) and to the closing concert of the Strasbourg Festival on June 25. In July, August, and September he meant to rest.

After the Boston performance of his Chamber Symphony, Schoenberg had inquired of Munch: "I wonder how the audience will accept this work this time? After all, it is 42 years since the first performance in 1908."[52] It was a legitimate question in and of itself, all the more interesting in what it asks about the Boston public. It remains a thing of wonder that the Bostonians absorbed Jolivet and Messiaen and Haieff and the like, week after week, with as little complaining as there was—and with not a seat unsold. Certainly for many it was, as it is today, the price an audience member pays for citizenship in a dissonant world: One sat politely through the work just before intermission in order to get to the show-piece at the end. Yet Symphony Hall audiences had also been sensitized to modern idioms through decades of experience.

We have any number of clues as to how Munch thought about "new" music. In his autobiography he writes:

> The music of our own century interprets the preoccupations and the concerns of the world we live in. We must play it and listen to it, learn about advanced aesthetic positions, new theories of harmony, and new principles of construction. . . . There is only one proper attitude to take toward the music of our own time: be patient, open our hearts, listen without prejudice and without snobbery. . . .
>
> A conductor must be a treasure hunter. This is a duty he too often neglects but one that may gain him the greatest recognition in his own time. I for one have had the good fortune to live among such musicians as Roussel, Honegger, Schmitt, Messiaen, Martinu, when they still needed to be played. In twenty years the list will be much longer, for the history of music has no end.[53]

In his 1954 address inaugurating the Tanglewood season, Munch said this to the students:

> You have a right to criticize, to find a music tiresome. You have the right to say that a work seems incomprehensible to you. Who knows? When you know the work better, the day may come that you take it into your heart. Because contemporary music reflects all the passions and pressures, all the nervousness, of modern life. We have to consider it as a part of a continuous process of art history. In the past, music grew naturally like flowers; like trees. Now it must be looked after.[54]

In 1957 he took on a complainer in print:

You reproach me for playing too much contemporary music, and I understand your point of view since you come to concerts for amusement or distraction or perhaps for consolation—surely for pleasure. But we are asking you to do something, to participate actively in an exchange between performer and public when we want you to listen to something new, something difficult to understand, even difficult to listen to, especially at first encounter.

I consider it our duty to devote, let us say, one-quarter of a concert—which is truly the minimum—to the music written in our time. It is our duty to make live again not just the masterpieces of the past dear to our hearts. We must also make heard the music that represents the artistic expression of the time we live in, music that may at the same time prepare for the future.

It is our duty to the young to give them the opportunity to be heard. Music written on paper must be realized and considered. The painter's work or the sculptor's work, when completed, exists for all to see. Music to exist must be played—and who is to play it if we do not? I tell you frankly that it would be easier for us to play only older music just as it would be easier for you as a listener, but if we imposed this restriction on ourselves, we should be abandoning our obligation to history.[55]

It is worth noting here what has perhaps been obvious all along: The works to which Munch was spontaneously drawn, the ones he programmed, do not often fall into the category of the most "difficult" music to listen to. Generally they tend toward near-classical formal arrangements: multi-movement symphonies and concertos, calling for the big post-Romantic orchestra with piccolo, English horn, bass clarinet, contrabassoon, and full percussion—plenty of hardware to divert the wandering mind. Usually there are enough references to classical orchestral tradition, say, fugal passages or cyclical elements, to anchor the attentive and reasonably experienced listener. Some connection with the past was especially important to Munch himself. He needed to sense the lineage from Bach and Beethoven.

CHAPTER 6

oso

Boston after Koussevitzky

July 1951–July 1956

It was as difficult to contact Munch abroad, the second summer, as it had been the year before. Already notorious for not answering letters, he now refused to take telephone calls. Having tried various options, the Bostonians hit again on the idea of positioning a third party on location. This was the harpist Bernard Zighera, who each year would also hurry home to France for his vacation and who, along with his brothers, had been in Munch's intimate circle since the Société des Concerts.

One of Zighera's first tasks was to find Munch and let him know just how alarming Koussevitzky's health had become. As early as the third week of May 1951 it was known that Koussevitzky would miss Tanglewood. "Dr. Koussevitzky will not be able to conduct at all," Judd told Zighera in the course of a transatlantic telephone call. "They have tried to keep this from him because they are afraid it will affect his immediate condition." That was also the reason the Tanglewood schedule had yet to be announced to the public. "Please acquaint Mr. Munch with the fact that his predecessor is not in good health." There were some options for the school: It appeared that the assistant director, Aaron Copland, could take charge. "In other words we do not expect to be obliged to involve Mr. Munch this summer in school matters except to the extent he may wish to take an interest in all activities at Tanglewood. . . . I am sure that the situation affecting Dr. Koussevitzky will remain completely confidential."[1]

On June 3 management cabled Munch, who was conducting in Turin, that hope had been abandoned for Koussevitzky. He died the next day from the effects of an ongoing cerebral hemorrhage. That news was dispatched in a second telegram from Judd to Munch; Cabot, meanwhile, drafted conversation points for what appears to have been an extended transatlantic telephone call the next day.

This began with a review of the situation. As Koussevitzky began fading away, his wife had sent for Leonard Bernstein, who arrived in time to spend the last hours with the master. Plans so far in place for Tanglewood were that Richard Burgin and Eleazar de Carvalho would take the student orchestra and Bernstein, the conducting classes. Bernstein preferred to conduct only the Tanglewood memorial, a *Missa solemnis* on August 9, 1951; the Berlioz Requiem would be postponed. Meanwhile, flowers had been sent on behalf of Munch and the orchestra, and the necessary press releases readied. "Our thoughts now must turn to the completion of all plans for the summer, and we have in mind to make public announcements of the Festival and the School next week," Cabot jotted. "Our great desire is that you will be there."[2]

Munch agreed to return at once, pausing to conduct the last Strasbourg Festival concert on June 25 (Honegger's Fifth Symphony, along with Zino Francescatti in a Saint-Saëns concerto and Roussel's Third). His arrival at Logan Airport in Boston was covered in the press, with a photograph of Munch on the tarmac, carrying (in July) his usual briefcase, overcoat, and hat.[3] He proceeded immediately to the traditional opening ceremony, where Bernstein did most of the talking.

It was under this unusual circumstance that Charles Munch, diplomatically playing out his part in a nuanced scenario, became director of one of the most American of all institutions of classical music: Tanglewood.

The distinguishing features of the Boston Symphony Orchestra were Symphony Hall, the Pops (in which Munch took no interest at all), and the summer program at Tanglewood, properly the Berkshire Symphonic Festival, and its teaching arm, the Berkshire Music Center. More than a decade older than the French summer festivals in Aix-en-Provence and Besançon, the BSO summer concerts had gathered particular momentum when Mary Aspenwall Tappan signed the family estate, Tanglewood, over to the BSO. (The name comes from Nathaniel Hawthorne's *Tanglewood Tales*.) As early as 1881, Henry L. Higginson had hoped for "a good honest school for musicians,"[4] and that was also one of Koussevitzky's fondest notions: famous composers, conductors, and instrumentalists forging successive generations of American artists.

The formula was to have two weeks of small-orchestra repertoire in July, thought of as the Bach-and-Mozart concerts, in the smaller indoor Concert Hall, while the Pops concerts were taking place in Boston. Then a full orchestra's worth of musicians would arrive for a month of concerts in the Shed, which had opened in August 1938 in conjunction with the fifth Berkshire Festival.

For Munch Tanglewood was problematic from the start, as he meant to spend his summers at the Strasbourg Festival and then in the surrounding countryside—as did Geneviève. He would count the weeks until he could return home: "How good it will be to rediscover the country, to walk in the Strasbourg streets, to hear the cathedral bells, to look out over the harmonious contours of our mountains."[5] Tanglewood was Koussevitzky's particular plaything: "my blood, my tears—and my greatest joy."[6] He had kept Tanglewood alive with personal funds during the war. Just recently, with Bernstein and Boris Goldovsky, he had added an opera program, which survived until 1961. (Goldovsky was to be on leave during the summer of 1950, when he would be replaced by Jan Popper and Sarah Caldwell.)

Munch, with bookings in Europe for the summer of 1950, probably never intended to come to Tanglewood that first summer. When Koussevitzky also declined to appear pleading an overbooked calendar, the BSO invited Victor de Sabata, chief conductor at La Scala, to substitute. Koussevitzky had assumed that, after a full season of keeping his distance from Munch and Boston, Tanglewood would be, if not for him, then for his protégés Carvalho and Bernstein. He was particularly annoyed at press accounts to the effect that it had been his idea to invite de Sabata. He had fired off a sharp letter to Munch in Paris about the "confused and equivocal circumstances in the Berkshires. . . . The faculty, the general public, and Sabata himself have the impression that he came to Tanglewood at my invitation. Questioned about this by the press, I broke silence and revealed the truth."[7] While not overtly hostile—Koussevitzky addresses Munch as *cher maître* and extends the customary niceties to Madame Munch— the letter could not have altered Munch's preference to remain outside the Koussevitzky circle and as far as possible from its Bernstein-Copland-Olga axis.

But at another level Munch implicitly understood Tanglewood's significance. For one thing, there was its balm, its sense of retreat from the harsh realities of the epoch: "In this troubled world of ours, it seems to me that here, surrounded by this beautiful nature, in wonderful conditions offered us for work, we can do our best and benefit from living together, trying to attain, each one in his own way, the aim of our lives."[8]

This point, made in July 1954, needs emphasizing. The world situation— Korea, Israel and Palestine, the Russians, fallout shelters—frightened even the jaded. Munch, having lived through more than one epoch of fear and deprivation, took music's capacity to ease tensions as an article of faith. He did not often mention his pacifism, but at Tanglewood it emerged naturally:

Music is, among all the arts, the most international means of communication between peoples because of its limitless way of expression. And thus our young generation can realize through experiences that the world is "one" and that the things which all men hold in common are more important and more productive than the things which separate them. This feeling must be our inspiration here and also our unifying aim.[9]

He was also able to grasp the essentially American aspect of the place. Tanglewood was not like Strasbourg, Besançon, or Montreux:

> It is rewarding and significant for America to observe the growth of the interest for Music among young people in public schools; the great popularity of summer schools that has immeasurably increased the general musical development in this country and has undoubtedly had a profound influence upon American cultural life. Of course we have to admit that phonograph, radio, and television have made music available to everyone, and though very often they have made *poor* music popular—still the interest for music has grown immensely through these channels. Our cultural pursuits strive to develop the taste and quality in our cultural life. We can really observe a continued advance of American music for the future and an improved position and appreciation of the American composers.[10]

Munch conducted the six Bach-and-Mozart concerts that summer of 1951 and seven of the nine Shed concerts. He ended up accepting the title of music director of the Berkshire Music Center and Festival. His actual duties in Tanglewood, as well as the length of them, remained roughly the same for the rest of his tenure in Boston. The students did not see a great deal of him or learn much from him one on one. He kept himself informed, however by sometimes wandering into a rehearsal and listening from the back row. One photograph shows him sitting behind the student orchestra, smoking and concentrating. Attendance during his first season was down only slightly; his last Tanglewood concert as music director, on August 26, 1962, broke all records for attendance. He continued to accept engagements at Tanglewood until the end and appeared there for the last time in August 1968.

Koussevitzky's memory naturally imbued the 1951–1952 season, which began with a sentimental but apt program of Mozart's Masonic Funeral Music, *Death and Transfiguration,* and the Tchaikovsky *Pathétique.* He would be remembered again at every runout and tour concert; Leonard Bernstein, arguably the most bereaved of his heirs, saw to dozens of other memorial details. Elegies were soon composed, and henceforth virtually every work commissioned by the Koussevitzky Foundation would be "dedicated to the memory of Serge and Natalie Koussevitzky," the second Mrs. Koussevitzky of three.

The 1951–1952 season was also a turning point in radio broadcasting of classical music. The FM station WGBH took its name from Great Blue Hill in Milton, where a transmitter had been built at the Harvard Observatory, broadcasting from the highest spot in the area to a sixty-seven-mile radius at twenty kilowatts on FM 89.7. The main studio, linked to Great Blue Hill by microwave, was carved out of Symphony Hall, and broadcasts of daily programming from 3:00 to 10:30 p.m. began on October 6, 1951. Both the Friday and Saturday concerts were broadcast live, and additional content was supplied by six participating colleges of greater Boston: Boston College, Boston University, Harvard, MIT, Northeastern, and Tufts, a consortium calling itself the Lowell Institute Cooperative Broadcasting Council. Other programming came from the Canadian, British, and French national radio services: the BBC's *Hamlet* with John Gielgud, for instance. Professor Woodworth had a series introducing "Tomorrow's Symphony." Rosario Mazzeo, a birder as well as BSO clarinetist, offered "Weekend Trails" on Saturday afternoons. There were courses on drama from Tufts, psychology from Harvard, geology from Boston University, and Greek politics from Boston College. On weekends when the orchestra was not occupying Symphony Hall there would be taped programs called "The Symphony Away." Within a few weeks additional broadcast concerts included offerings from the Museum of Fine Arts, Cambridge Collegium Musicum, and New England Conservatory Orchestra.

Munch certainly approved of Boston's leadership in establishing a viable alternative to the commercial networks. Aaron Copland remarked during the inaugural broadcast on WGBH that "the record of our own commercial radio is a poor one, and it is common knowledge that it is getting progressively worse rather than better." It was a major step for the fortunes of new-music premieres, since both the Friday afternoon and Saturday evening concerts would be heard. "We contemporary composers like that idea, for the second hearing often tells more about a work than the first. One's second impression of a new work may be more or less favorable than the first, but it is seldom exactly the same." Copland went on, as composers do, to advocate a world where listeners became "as familiar with the music of their own composers as they are with the classics." He salutes Koussevitzky (but not Munch) and pronounces it "a good omen that tonight's opening concert by the Boston Symphony Orchestra should connect his name with this bright new hope among radio stations."[11] In fact, and unusually for both Koussevitzky and Munch, there was no contemporary music on the program that night.

Television, too, with all its aspirations for educating the public at large, was seeking alliances with the orchestra. It was announced that following a full Friday afternoon performance on November 2, the musicians would travel to the Opera House, off the Boston Common, for a thirty-minute televised concert at

8:30 p.m. on NBC's affiliate WBA, Channel 4. The Pops, under Arthur Fiedler, would appear a week later. The BSO had been televised only once before, for a United Nations concert in New York on December 10, 1949.

In the first indication that the unremitting schedule might be compromising his health, Munch failed to appear for the fourth pair of programs, November 2–3, 1951, when he was to have led the premiere of Lukas Foss's Second Piano Concerto, followed by Debussy's *Printemps* and *Ibéria*. A flyer distributed with the printed program announced simply that illness prevented him from conducting and that Richard Burgin would lead the Foss, followed by the Brahms Fourth Symphony. The television broadcast was delayed for a week, until November 9. A notice released to the press on November 7 reported that "Mr. Munch is under medical advice to rest for a substantial period because of a circulatory disturbance which has developed after a recent virus infection."[12] For the half-hour television broadcast on November 9, viewers were told that, while he had been unable to undertake rehearsals and performances that week, Munch would conduct the *Rapsodie espagnole* after Burgin led Beethoven's *Egmont* overture. His appearance in the kinescope is a study in poise and control, and the performance very fine, without a hint of compromised physical condition.

Ignoring medical advice, as conductors in the thick of things usually do, Munch then went on to take the scheduled runout concerts in Washington and New York, then, sometime in the third week of November 1951, suffered a heart attack and was confined to his New York hotel. Monteux, who was to have exchanged orchestras with Munch anyway, agreed to cover two weeks (November 23–24 and November 30–December 1) while emergency solutions were sought for the next three months. Munch's San Francisco debut was canceled, as was, initially, a BSO trip to Europe being organized for spring 1952.

Word of his condition circulated quickly through the upper echelons of conducting and composition, and warm wishes for a fast recovery were dispatched to New York by Monteux, Martinu, Toscanini, Honegger (himself an invalid), Ibert, Claude Delvincourt at the Conservatoire, Milhaud, and the like—the French uncomfortably reminded of the unhappy decline from neurological disorder of the conductor Roger Désormière, still in his early fifties. Walter Piston wrote to encourage postponing the Boston premiere of his Fourth Symphony until the following season. Tibor Harsányi's Symphony was also delayed. "Nothing will keep me from presenting your lovely symphony—next year, however," wrote Munch.[13]

Reconfiguring the season became simpler when Ernest Ansermet agreed to a residence of two months. Thomas Beecham was to come at the end of January, and Bernstein would return early from his vacation in Mexico for concerts in March. Richard Burgin and G. Wallace Woodworth could manage the rest. The

European tour was restored when, in short succession, Monteux indicated his willingness to take half the concerts abroad, and Munch agreed that, if his recovery were slower than predicted, he would accept either Bernstein or Guido Cantelli as his substitute.

Munch stayed in New York through the end of January, then left for Havana, spending three nights in Miami en route—and was made to pay nearly $7,000 in federal taxes before being allowed to leave the country. Pierre and Doris Monteux joined him in Cuba, and Judd flew to Havana for a business lunch on Monday, February 18, presumably to clear the arrangements for the tour to Europe. The *Christian Science Monitor* reported Munch as resting comfortably and expected back for a Saint John Passion at Easter. Cabot and the Bostonian handlers continued to disapprove of Havana as a medical retreat and urged Munch to become a patient of Paul Dudley White, the famous cardiologist at the Massachusetts General Hospital.

Ernest Ansermet, of scholarly bent and nonconforming manner, left an important mark on the BSO. Some eight years older than Munch, the Swiss conductor shared with his Alsatian colleague a number of affinities with regard to the repertoire, as well as the same general approach to modernism. Ansermet and Fritz Munch, Charles's older brother, were closer still. The Boston musicians were familiar with Ansermet's recordings but knew only vaguely of the Orchestre de la Suisse Romande and had played for him only once before, in January 1949. His cerebral approach and idiosyncratic dextral technique— some said no technique at all—were well removed from what had become their customary working habit with Munch. Ansermet's program of February 1–2 1952 featured Honegger's *Monopartita* in a first American performance and *Pacific 231;* Honegger was, after all, a Genevan, his music as much Ansermet's turf as anyone else's. He closed his Boston series (February 8–9) with his own orchestration of Debussy's *Six épigraphes antiques,* then the Bartók Concerto for Orchestra, a work so closely associated with Koussevitzky that Munch did not conduct it. There had been Mozart and Beethoven in abundance, of course, but it was the revelation of a half dozen modern works that left the players so enchanted by Ansermet—more, one gathers, than by Monteux. Informed observers suggested that the orchestra played better under Munch after Ansermet had left. Henry Cabot's letter of appreciation to him said the following:

> When this orchestra in the course of the season suddenly found itself without Mr. Munch, it was in a serious predicament. I do not know what we would have done if, hearing of our conductor's illness, you had not generously given up your winter's plans and come to us in Boston. Your visit has been a personal pleasure and your series of concerts a rare experience for us all.[14]

At the end of February Munch's physicians authorized him to conduct again, though his handwriting was still shaky and he complained that he could manage stairs only with great difficulty. A program insert dated March 7 announced with pleasure that he would attend the annual meeting of the Friends of the Boston Symphony Orchestra on March 19. Seeing him enter the room after an absence of nearly five months, the supporters rose spontaneously in applause. Munch, touched, responded with an improvised encomium on friendship, then proceeded to conduct *Bacchus et Ariane,* Suite 2. The photographs that day show him looking, unusually, somewhat frail—a cigarette nevertheless dangling from his right hand.

He formally returned to the stage on March 28–29 with Franck's *Rédemption,* the Roussel, and the *Fantastique,* welcomed, during the WGBH intermission feature, as a breath of spring: "The sight of him is heart-warming and the sound of the orchestra as he resumes it is blood-warming." Lucien Price, the commentator, concluded his remarks with reference to the prayers of thanksgiving in the Lutheran prayerbook: "For a Recovery from Sickness," "For a Safe Return from a Journey," and "General Thanksgiving."[15]

Business, it seemed, was as usual. Still, in the aftermath his managers wondered whether his legendary stamina might be permanently compromised. Madame Munch interceded from Paris with her own concerns:

> Dear Mr. Judd:
>
> I think it *absolutely necessary* that Roger Toureau goes with his master to the Berkshires this summer. Please do not pay attention if Mr. Münch tells he wants him not. Do not speak of the question before the last moment! More diplomatic!
>
> Sincerely yours,
>
> Geneviève Münch[16]

Judd slipped suggestive remarks about having Roger come along "for your comfort" into letters of those weeks and in June wrote simply, "Please bring Roger at our expense."[17]

Negotiating a new contract to begin in May 1952 and to last through April 1955 was thus even more nuanced than before. The trustees offered an annual salary of $75,000 for a thirty-week main season with seven or eight weeks off but also to include six Bach-Mozart and six full concerts at Tanglewood. Any additional concerts would be paid at a per-event fee. Munch was urged, even warned, to use his vacation weeks solely for rest and recuperation. "Guest conducting during that period will take from your strength and add very little to your income because of taxes."[18] His concerns with the exclusivity clauses in his recording contract—notably his desire to record the new Honegger symphony for Pathé-Marconi with the Orchestre National—were formally noted, and it was promised that, when the umbrella contract with RCA expired in 1955, these matters would be addressed. The notion that the RCA recordings had little impact in France, on the face of it valid enough, was given a real setback when the new Brahms Fourth (LM 1086) won a Grand Prix of the Académie du Disque Français.

To reduce the tax burden, it was suggested that the cash salary be $21,250, while the BSO would pay medical expenses up to $12,000 and hold the rest on account. The matter of his American tax liability and his agent fees to Bruno Zirato at CAMI had become central issues in his financial life, and in the end neither was the responsibility of the BSO. Conrad Oberdorfer, noted attorney and professor of law, set out to establish a valid tax declaration with the authorities at both the federal and the state levels and to reconcile Munch's contractual arrangements with the BSO, CAMI, and RCA.

Cabot complained to Oberdorfer:

> In typical fashion Mr. Munch this morning handed your bill [for $1,544.67] to Mr. Judd with some remark that he understood Mr. Judd has said at some point that the Symphony would be paying it. . . . I do not think it is desirable for the Symphony to be paying the lawyer employed by Mr. Munch. Furthermore, if we pay it, it just adds that much to Mr. Munch's income and increases his tax. . . . Have you any objection to letting it ride until July when Mr. Munch returns, and I hope in not such a tense state of mind as he is in now just prior to the European trip?[19]

Munch did, in fact, return in July with a signed contract. Nothing would have kept him away from the chapter at hand.

The motivating stimulus for the Boston Symphony Orchestra's 1952 concert tour of western Europe came from Nicolas Nabokov, secretary general of an organization calling itself the Congress for Cultural Freedom. Nabokov wanted the BSO to anchor a huge Paris music festival, Masterpieces of the Twentieth Century / L'Oeuvre du Vingtième Siècle—specifically to open the festival with a replay of *Le sacre du printemps,* conducted by Pierre Monteux at the Théâtre des Champs-Élysées. The idea was personally conveyed to Munch in the summer of 1951, following the March premiere of Nabokov's concerto for soprano, tenor, and orchestra, *La vita nuova.* Munch, a born adventurer when it came to this sort of scheme, needed little persuading. It was later noted fondly that he enjoyed, "above everything else, a good trip—especially with the orchestra. Every four years, the spirit moved him, and the road called."[20] Accustomed as it was to runouts and regional tours, the BSO had never been abroad.

The pieces fell quickly into place. Munch took the project to the trustees, who were guarded at first owing to the conflict with Tanglewood and the need for a guarantor against financial loss. Limitations of the bankbook were over-come when—for reasons not fully understood at the time—$130,000 in sub-vention quietly materialized. The itinerary was arranged to display the power of American culture in the critical European theater of the Cold War: West Berlin, something in Frankfurt for the U.S. troops stationed there, a triumphant entry into Strasbourg with the city's favorite son at the head of capitalism's most successful orchestra.

Preliminary plans for the tour were announced to the patrons in the last program book for 1950–1951 and in simultaneous press releases by Nicolas Nabokov and George Judd. A group of 104 players would give at least three concerts in Paris in May (that is, between the twenty-fourth pair of BSO con-certs and the beginning of the Pops concerts) for an exposition "aimed at fo-cusing attention upon the vitality of the cultural achievements by free men of the world during the first half of the 20th century." Lest the political point be missed, it was reiterated that the Congress for Cultural Freedom had been "con-ceived by intellectuals and financed by philanthropic interests, to assert that there exists a vital culture in the free world, and to demonstrate the value of freedom of work and expression." Other participants included the Vienna Stats-oper in *Wozzeck,* the Vienna Philharmonic, and the major orchestras of Rome, West Berlin, Geneva, and Paris. Balanchine's New York City Ballet would pre-sent an "all-Negro company" in *Four Saints in Three Acts.* Munch was quoted as saying: "It has been my dearest hope to bring my American Orchestra to Europe."[21]

At the end of January, Rudolph Elie published more details in the *Boston Herald* and the BSO program book, reporting on a press conference held by George Judd, who had just returned to Boston from two weeks of planning in Paris. "Uncross your fingers," he said: "The Boston Symphony *is* to tour Europe." The concert schedule in Boston had been successfully adjusted to allow the orchestra to depart for Le Havre on a French Line vessel on April 28. After *Le Sacre,* the orchestra would "entrain" for The Hague; the details for several days in Germany were as yet unclear, but these would be followed by Brussels, Stras-bourg, southern France, and London's Festival Hall on May 26. The orchestra would return from Southampton on May 27, just in time to do the Pops. This really was big news: "It promises," said Elie, "to be, all in all, the most historic milestone in the cultural life of the city in our times."[22] Munch had not been seen for two months, and the nature of his illness had never been disclosed, but by then his recovery was being described in such optimistic terms as to make these seem insignificant details.

Another point glossed over in Rudolph Elie's account of the press conference was the matter of finances:

While [Judd] could not estimate the total expenses of such a tour, he explained that they are formidable. By far the largest percentage of the expenses are being met by the agency that invited the Orchestra, the Congress of Cultural Freedom. . . . Supported by civic and culturally minded people of the free nations, the Congress is completely non-commercial. Any proceeds of the concerts go to meet the Congress' immense deficits in guaranteeing the visit of the Orchestra. There are, however, Mr. Judd said, certain individuals who are also contributing to the expenses of the tour—American philanthropists, he indicated. But he didn't know who they were. "I don't think they're Bostonians, though," he added.[23]

He need not have avoided the question: The point men were already listed as Julius Fleischmann (Jr., heir to the yeast and liquor fortune and one of the nation's foremost patrons of the arts) of Cincinnati, "who represents the philanthropic organization and individuals who have made the exposition possible"; and NYU philosopher Sidney Hook, chairman of the American Committee for Cultural Freedom.[24] The funding, we now know, came more or less directly from the Central Intelligence Agency through its web of innocently named foundations. "'We couldn't spend it all,' one former agent said of the cash at the CIA's disposal for grants, conferences, exhibitions, and publishing subsidies. 'There were no limits, and nobody had to account for it. It was amazing.'"[25]

In the case of the BSO tour, then, the finest art from one of the most historic cities anywhere and one with solid ties to American brain power and the political establishment was presented to the public before an unseen backdrop of political propaganda, clandestine activity, and some outright espionage. The project was thus established on much the same footing as the touring production of *Porgy and Bess,* which launched Leontyne Price and was covered famously by Truman Capote in *The Muses Are Heard* just before Boston went to Russia in 1956.

The mapped itinerary consisted of a big circle (Paris-Amsterdam-Brussels-Frankfurt-Berlin, then Strasbourg-Metz-Lyon-Bordeaux-Paris), followed by a crossing of the English Channel for concerts in Birmingham and London. "Free Europe" was still showing the ravages of war, with Berlin freshly divided and access to the city uncertain at best. Cyrus Durgin called that leg "tough and tempestuous." The Strasbourg performance would be at the Free Europe University in Exile and broadcast over Radio Free Europe and the Voice of America to Russia and its satellites.[26] The concerts in Germany were to be presented under the auspices of the U.S. High Commissioner for Germany; the orchestra was to be flown on military planes from Brussels to Frankfurt and on to the Titania Palast in Berlin. The details changed[27]—Metz was substituted for Turin on the itinerary, for instance—but not the sometimes tiresome metaphor of an army on campaign led by its conquering hero, a son of France. *Paris Match* titled its account of the BSO in Paris "Charles Munch: *Lendemain de Victoire*"—the morrow of victory.

The Boston Symphony Orchestra's first European tour opened triumphantly at the Paris Opéra on May 6, 1952, a concert attended by President and Mme. Auriol, their retinue, and a military escort. Munch conducted a big program of the Barber *School for Scandal* overture and Piston's Toccata from the American repertoire, along with his own favorites by Honegger, Roussel, Debussy, and Ravel. Two days later, under Monteux at the Théâtre des Champs-Élysées, the "homecoming" of *Le sacre du printemps* quite overshadowed the first concert in public anticipation, "and was all that was talked about later." When it was over, Stravinsky, a "bald, bespectacled little man of seventy," acknowledged the applause long enough to have it captured in a photograph ("he bowed once, kissed Monteux affectionately, and walked off"), only to be gathered up by Munch and Monteux on either side and escorted back into the public view. Stravinsky, not given to excess, held that it was the finest performance he had heard.[28] *Le Monde* and *Le Figaro* took a chauvinistic but probably merited satisfaction in the idea of French masterworks as expressions of American high culture. Reception of the American repertoire was polite but on the whole tepid, with the William Schuman work gaining the lion's share of attention, perhaps because it was the longest.

Cyrus Durgin did not like the Paris Opéra for acoustics or audience comfort and a few days later was feeling the same way about the Concertgebouw, an "impossible place with a high stage toward which one had to crane a neck to see. . . . And an encompassing audience who tended to soak up resonance with their clothing. The ceiling, slightly domed, and the auditorium, level as a Kansas wheat field, were also negative factors."

Otherwise, the two concerts in the Netherlands were remembered as a social highpoint of the trip. Queen Juliana came to the performance on May 10 at The Hague and afterward summoned not just Munch and Burgin but also her subject Jacobus Langendoen of the BSO's cello section to receive her thanks. The next day in Amsterdam, where Monteux had been a popular conductor of the Concertgebouw Orchestra, a mayoral greeting was followed with a visit by boat caravan through the canals and harbor and a city hall reception with gin. (When the Concertgebouw Orchestra visited Boston in 1954, the courtesy was returned, with entertainment in the lobby of Symphony Hall and official proclamations and greetings—but no gin—extended to the conductor, Eduard van Beinum, and his players.)

Another face of touring showed itself when an oil strike in the United States resulted in the cancellation of all "nonessential" military flights. A train trip from Brussels to Frankfurt was arranged at the last minute and ended up taking eight hours, leaving the sleep-deprived musicians little touring time before two full concerts in the ruined city, one in the newly reopened civic playhouse and another for U.S. armed forces at a military base. At one of these the bürgermeister of Oberstaufenbach presented a testimonial volume to be carried back to Boston for the city's native son, ninety-two-year-old violinist Daniel Kuntz (1860–1959), a founding member of the BSO in 1881. The Frankfurt-Berlin journey was made in sealed carriages attached to U.S. and French military trains. The players were told to keep their shades drawn between 4:30 and 5 a.m., when they would be crossing the border. The news carried regular reports of passengers turned back at Soviet checkpoints, and there was some threat that the rails through East Germany to Berlin might at any moment be removed altogether.

The Boston Symphony Orchestra made its London debut on May 26, 1952, in a long program of *La Mer, Daphnis et Chloé,* Honegger's Fifth, and *Bacchus et Ariane*—plus the Barber and the Piston. Here again there had been drama. The players reached London on schedule that morning, but the trucks carrying the instruments, music, and formal wear had been stuck behind a bicycle race. British Railways arranged to transport all these items to London by 7:30 p.m., so the concert was delayed from 8:00 until 9:00 p.m. What resulted, according to a London critic, was:

> a dazzling exhibition of orchestral virtuosity and tonal splendor such as the Festival Hall has not known in the thirteen months of its existence. . . . During the last few years we have heard such bodies as the Vienna Philharmonic, Concertgebouw, La Scala, New York Philharmonic-Symphony, and Philadelphia Orchestra in this country (not forgetting our own Royal Philharmonic and Philharmonia), but not one of these surpassed the overall splendor of the Boston Symphony.[29]

The first portion of the tour served as the cover story of the *Saturday Review* on May 31, 1952, with photographs of Munch and Monteux, left and right, and behind them the Arc de Triomphe, through which can be seen Lord Nelson's column in Trafalgar Square. Cyrus Durgin's series "With the Boston Symphony in Europe" was closely followed at home, both in the *Boston Globe* and in excerpts published in major papers across the country.

Tanglewood that summer was thus, more than ever, for unwinding. Consensus was that the tour had been a thoroughgoing artistic success, precedent setting, and altogether modern. It had brought out the best in Munch, who, once the formula of the co-conductor had been found, was irrepressible in his determination to set out again.

Another of the permanent stamps Munch left on the BSO—and on American orchestral practice in general—developed as he came to consider appointments for the new season, 1952–1953. The retirement of principal flutist Georges Laurent left a plum position vacant, and the candidate to fill it would, as long as Munch was there, have to have the characteristics of a true star: There were, after all, the *Faun* and *Daphnis* and Fauré's *Pelléas,* along with the many other flute-centric works composed in France for the long line of flute virtuosi—Paul Taffanel, Philippe Gaubert, and Marcel Moyse. Munch had recommended Aurèle Nicolet, the famous Paris flutist then playing principal in Berlin. That was an unlikely gambit at best and would certainly take at least a season to work out. "Because of this situation," wrote George Judd, "I asked Mr. Mazzeo to enquire if Miss Anthony, the Los Angeles flute player, could secure a year's leave of absence. She believes she could do so and would like to have a year with the Boston Symphony."[30]

Doriot Anthony (soon universally known as Doriot Anthony Dwyer) had herself mobilized impressive advocates for her engagement in Boston, including Bruno Walter, who first hired her for the Hollywood Bowl orchestra, and Isaac Stern, a family friend. Misunderstanding a well-intentioned trick played on her by Walter and his daughters, she assumed for years that he did not write the letter she had asked him for; in fact, the letter from Walter had convinced Munch to take her candidacy seriously—that and the fact that Georges Laurent's favored candidate was also a woman made it possible to have what she called a "ladies' day" in the flute tryouts.[31]

The press remarked that "perky, dimpled Doriot Anthony, 30," had heard of Laurent's retirement in early summer 1952, traveled to Tanglewood, where she played for Munch on three audition rounds (Mozart, Debussy, Ravel), and then returned to Los Angeles with no indication of what might happen next. She was offered a one-year contract in late September for the season opening on October 3, 1952—when Munch nodded approvingly at her solos in Beethoven's Fourth and the *Boston Globe* pronounced her "a true find." By the third pair, October 17–18, she was being featured in the Bach Orchestral Suite no. 2.

The matching up of Doriot Anthony Dwyer, the BSO, and Munch was a good thing for all concerned. Her position at dead center of the orchestra, as well as the conspicuousness of her being, for some years, the only female principal in the nation, one who was seen weekly on television, does as much to characterize the look of the Boston Symphony during the Munch era as any other feature. Her playing in the core works was a real component of his success. Dwyer and Munch got along well enough personally: She tolerated his flirtations, and he eventually focused his advances elsewhere. "We were both pixies," she remarked. "I sensed what he wanted from the podium and knew how to provide it." The obvious pleasure he took in inviting her solo bows after works such as *Daphnis* was matched by her obvious pleasure in taking them. She was the next in the long list of his attractive, accomplished protégées. Women musicians of the next two generations regarded her as their priestess.

The only naysayer was Rudolph Elie at the *Boston Herald,* who thought this "a very serious matter. I am not a little dismayed by it. I find it difficult to accept the notion that any lady flute player could ever succeed Georges Laurent either as an artist or as an object of such veneration among men."[32]

A second new member that season, another American, was percussionist Everett Firth, called Vic, who also became by virtue of his homegrown pedigrees, good looks, professional acumen, and exceptional talent one of the BSO's stars. Later he acquired further note as proprietor of Vic's Sticks, the leading American purveyor of percussion ware. He had more or less pestered Munch into a job he later wondered whether he really deserved. Single at the time, he was inclined to run into Munch and his women companions at one of the few Tanglewood nightspots—long after Munch had told others he was retiring for the night. Tod Perry quoted Munch as saying that "My best decision in Boston was to hire Vic Firth."[33]

Munch preferred behind-screen auditions, at least for the early rounds. Gino Cioffi's successful clarinet audition, on the other hand, took place on stage at Carnegie Hall with Munch and the first-chair players. When Munch asked him what he had prepared, Cioffi responded, "Anything you want to hear." When he was done with the Mozart Clarinet Concerto, he remarked, "Pretty good, huh?" Munch gave him the job on the spot.[34] Joseph Silverstein's violin audition in Symphony Hall included the summoning of the BSO librarian to bring a Honegger manuscript since there was nothing in the audition materials Silverstein had not already played.

Having sole control over the orchestral personnel was the part of the job Munch found least natural. Relishing the power, Koussevitzky promised jobs and Tanglewood performances to impressionable young musicians, never to deliver. Munch was just the opposite and went out of his way not to promise and later disappoint. Likewise, he was not much interested in forcing change in the ranks and thus fired almost no one. The results were much debated as Munch aged with the orchestra, but as to job security in his era there was very little doubt. In the case of the legendary English horn player Louis Speyer (1890–1980), for instance, Munch ignored the pressure to ease Speyer into retirement and so incurred the inevitable charge of cronyism. Speyer stayed on past his lovely performance in the last concert of the Munch tenure and held on well into Leinsdorf's.

Munch was drawn to the francophone members of the orchestra for obvious reasons. He took a paternal interest in the fortunes of violinist Roger Shermont, who as a French Jew had spent much of the war in hiding and without his violin. After a solo appearance in New York he went to Boston at his own expense to play for Munch and ended up in the last stand of the first violins ("up against the wall: we couldn't see, we couldn't hear, but we learned the music"). When Shermont was called back to France to be present for his mother's last days, Munch not only granted him immediate leave of absence but inquired, as the young man was departing, "*as-tu besoin d'argent?*" In 1961, after Shermont had lost the auditions for concertmaster to Joseph Silverstein, Munch invited him to play the Brahms Concerto on a Tuesday night concert, then showed up at the rehearsal with his Stradivarius in hand. This is the instrument heard on the broadcast tape.[35]

The seventy-second season of the Boston Symphony Orchestra in 1952–1953, the fourth with Munch, was on the whole a tame, business-as-usual year as the institution enjoyed the reverberations of its success in Europe, a second year of broadcasts over WGBH, and visits from Monteux and Guido Cantelli, the latter well embarked on what seemed an unstoppable advance to succeed Toscanini— or Munch. It was anchored by Berlioz's long-awaited *Roméo et Juliette,* complete, in February (and its recording just afterward). Munch had opened the season with the Royal Hunt and Storm ballet from *Les Troyens,* not heard in Boston since 1928, and a complete *Faust* was known to be awaiting its turn. The list of other first performances in Boston—Haieff's Second Piano Concerto, Toch's Second Symphony, the symphony by Tibor Harsányi, Samazeuilh's *Nuit*—is strongly specific to the conductor's personal taste, as was the Boston premiere of Gabriel Fauré's *Dolly* Suite in its orchestration by Rabaud. There was good American music as well, notably including the postponed Fourth Symphony of Walter Piston and Samuel Barber's Adagio for Strings, the latter soon an audience favorite.

What better defined the season was the month-long concert tour of the United States and Canada, a North American counterpart of the European venture almost exactly a year earlier, the time slot having proved convenient. This was the orchestra's first coast-to-coast tour since a 1915 journey with Karl Muck. Now, between April 21 and May 22, 1953, Monteux and Munch led the orchestra in some twenty concerts in thirteen states and two Canadian provinces. The orchestra—"100 men and one lone woman (the flutist)"—traveled in a special train that comprised five sleeping cars, a dining car, and a baggage car. The advance publicity promised that representatives of the orchestra would hear auditions at each stop.

Each conductor had chosen signature repertoire (table 6.1), with Munch typically confecting his programs by opening with either the *Water Music* Suite or the *School for Scandal* overture and closing with Beethoven's Seventh or the Brahms Fourth, filled in with French works.

The evidence suggests a substantial and ongoing public triumph as the orchestra swung through the South, then west to Los Angeles, north to San Francisco, and back home via Chicago, receiving standing ovations nearly every night. "They just seem to explode with the music, here in the West," Vic Firth

Table 6.1. AMERICAN TOUR REPWERTOIRE, 1953

Barber: *School for Scandal* Overture	Munch
Beethoven: Symphony no. 2	Monteux
Beethoven: Symphony no. 7	Munch
Berlioz: *Roman Carnival* Overture	Monteux
Berlioz: Royal Hunt and Storm, fr. *Les Troyens*	Munch
Brahms: Symphony no. 1	Monteux
Brahms: Symphony no. 2	not played
Brahms: Symphony no. 4	Munch
Creston: Symphony no. 2	Monteux
Debussy: Prelude to "The Afternoon of a Faun"	Munch
Franck: Symphony in D Minor	Monteux
Handel/Harty: *Water Music* Suite	Munch
Honegger: Symphony no. 2	Munch
Ravel: *Rapsodie espagnole*	Munch
Ravel: *La Valse*	Munch
Roussel: *Bacchus et Ariane*, Suite 2	Munch
Schubert: Symphony no. 8 ("Unfinished")	Monteux
Sibelius: Symphony no. 2	Monteux
Strauss: *Don Juan*	Monteux
Strauss: *Der Rosenkavalier* Suite	not played
Stravinsky: *The Firebird* Suite	Monteux
Wagner: "Siegfried's Rhine Journey"	Monteux
Wagner: excerpts fr. *Die Meistersinger*, act III	Munch

told *Time* magazine after a concert in Provo.[36] The arrival in Los Angeles was nostalgic not only for Doriot Anthony and solo hornist James Stagliano, both of whom had come to Boston from the LA Philharmonic, but also for Munch, who had been there when he had decided to cast his lot with the BSO. Monteux's return to San Francisco was greeted with general civic euphoria and, on his entry, an unprecedented ovation.

The players remember this trip with special pleasure owing to the luxury of the private train: sleeping in roomette cars parked on a siding instead of the endless checking in and out of hotels. "That was a great thing. When you came to a new city you could do what you wanted: put your bed down and sleep or go sightseeing. We came home rested—for a change."[37] There were the usual Wild-West shenanigans incumbent on such a journey: a famous photograph of Monteux and his wife draped in Mexican serapes at the border near El Paso, a mock train robbery and conductorial hanging in Tucson. Hundreds of rolls of Kodak Brownie film came back to Boston for processing.

The trustees expected the tour to lose around $30,000 but considered the deficit as an investment in new friends for the orchestra and, in turn, new customers for their RCA recordings—thus, new income from afar. Their reasoning was impeccable even if the outcome is hard to measure. Chicago's *DownBeat* magazine, extending its annual reader survey to classical music for the first time, showed the Boston Symphony placing second (after the Philadelphia Orchestra) in its subscribers' preferences and Munch placing third among conductors (after Toscanini and Mitropoulos).[38]

Munch slipped back to France for concerts at the Strasbourg Festival and at Radio France, including the first performance, with Nicole Henriot, of Milhaud's *Suite concertante* for piano and orchestra, introduced to the Boston public in December. One senses Munch now developing a certain rapport with the music of Milhaud, who led a half concert of the BSO in January 1953. *La création du monde* figured at Tanglewood in July and was later made into a splendid recording (LD/LDS 2625, 1961). Also at Tanglewood that summer Munch recognized that he had the players in place to return Bach to a preeminent position at the Berkshire Festival—Dwyer, Gomberg, Voisin, and Burgin for the Brandenburgs; Burgin and Silverstein for the Bach Double, and so on.

By the beginning of his fifth Boston season, Charles Munch was widely held to be a civic treasure, his goings and comings reported in the press as routinely as those of the Kennedys or the Red Sox. He would be photographed stepping from chauffeured cars and escorted from airplanes by uniformed flight attendants. Airlines were proud to claim him as a client in their advertising. He was called on to endorse products from the Baldwin piano (the official instrument of Symphony Hall) to automobiles and life insurance. At the dreaded start-of-year press conference he seemed unmistakably pleased to be back in what Elie called "the world's most arduous and difficult musical post." He was also becoming easier to understand. Elie went on to observe that:

> Koussevitzky was essentially a man with an insatiable appetite for public and private adulations. . . . Munch is essentially a man of immense humility. . . . There are other fundamental differences. . . . Koussevitzky was a superb, if difficult, executive to whom no matter of detail, of management, of red tape was too insignificant. . . . Mr. Munch, on the contrary, is appalled by such details; he cannot accept, or rather happily accept, the singularly American concept that the conductor of a symphony orchestra is also its chief executive.[39]

Only Bruckner and Mahler fell outside the repertoire at his immediate beck and call, Elie noted.

In 1953–1954 the name that was on every lip when it came to Munch and his repertoire was Berlioz. He had systematically led his audiences through the wonders of the *Fantastique,* Requiem, *Roméo et Juliette,* and *Les nuits d'été;* this was the year of *L'enfance du Christ, Harold en Italie,* and the widely anticipated *La damnation de Faust*—thus completing a cycle of Berlioz masterpieces now considered standard. It was also the sesquicentenary of Berlioz's birth, when the influence of Jacques Barzun's two-volume biography of 1950 was first being felt in intellectual circles, when *Les Troyens* was beginning to reemerge in London and Paris, and when the American Berlioz Society was born, with Munch as president. ("Berlioz is the kind of composer," sniffed MIT's David Epstein, "who needs a revival every fifty years.")

But players and listeners seemed enchanted by every newfound work. *L'enfance du Christ* at Christmas went on to become eagerly anticipated for the holidays. *Harold en Italie,* the only multi-movement Berlioz composition firmly ensconced in Boston (owing to the pedigrees of its viola players), was once again revealed in what was assumed to be a more authentically French performance, first with the BSO's own Joseph de Pasquale as viola soloist in April 1954, then with William Primrose. The deliberate, systematic way Charles Munch learned and then sold the works is a cornerstone of what came next: a full-scale movement (carried out, it must be said, mostly in England) to solidify Berlioz's place as one of the foremost voices of Romanticism. Munch was not immune to the pandemic Berlioz myths—the "bad bass lines," to which he refers more than once, for instance—but he shared Berlioz's wonder at the orchestra's power as a teller of tales and found in the music precisely the bridge from Bach, Mozart, and Beethoven to his own world that he himself had long been seeking.

The recording of *Faust,* on February 21–22, 1954, in Symphony Hall was soon recognized as the most sensational recording venture of the year, its combination of long-sought revelation of major work, brilliant performance, and technical perfection positively seductive to customers with even a grain of curiosity. *Time* magazine counted it among the season's best recordings: "the smoldering romantic score excitingly fanned by Berlioz Specialist Munch."[40] In Paris, the Académie du Disque Français awarded the record its Grand Prix on December 19, 1955.

Tucked around the Berlioz elsewhere in the season were Honegger's First Symphony, the U.S. premiere of Dutilleux's First Symphony, and a new work of Pittsburgh *émigré* and composer Nicolai Lopatnikov, along with an entire program of Prokofiev. Ernest Bloch's new Concerto Grosso attracted considerable interest in Boston and New York as an example of a septuagenarian "writing music that is living and important" and that at last eschewed, said Downes, "the Hebraic idiom." The BSO's performance earned the New York Music Critics Award for best symphonic composition of 1953.[41]

He ended his fifth anniversary season without particular ceremony and returned home to conduct the Orchestre National at the Bordeaux and Strasbourg Festivals and to premiere Jolivet's First Symphony over the radio. At the Bordeaux Festival in late May there were two performances of *L'enfance du Christ,* as though echoes of the Berlioz year would carry on into the new season. He had gone to Strasbourg with Nicole Henriot, carrying an important program of his own, but on arrival was first pressed into service to cover for Evgeny Mravinsky, conductor of the Leningrad Philharmonic, who had been denied his exit visa from the Soviet Union. The concert featured nineteen-year-old soloist Annie Jodry in Khachaturian's Violin Concerto, which Munch learned in a day. On June 20, 1954, the closing concert of the Strasbourg Festival honored Guy Ropartz, just turning ninety, with his Fanfare for *Oedipe à Colonne.* It continued with the love scene from *Roméo et Juliette,* the premiere of J.-M. Damase's First Symphony, the Liszt First Piano Concerto with Henriot, and the Brahms Second Symphony. A photograph shows Munch and Albert Schweitzer together at the concert—probably the last time they met. The overaroused public had to be sent home by Munch, who waved them and the orchestra away with an archepiscopal "*Ite, missa est.*"

Charles Munch and Tanglewood had become inseparable after all. He liked the golf, whiffs of romance, and the repertoire; he did not mind the enormous crowds; and from time to time he actually enjoyed the students. Quite apart from the ongoing Berlioz fever, this was the season during which many BSO listeners first heard five of the six Brandenburg Concertos played in one concert: Twenty-eight hundred people crammed into the smaller of the performance venues and "stormily applauded the result."[42] The Brandenburg evenings became a staple and in due course an interesting two-record release (LM 2182 and 2198, summer 1957). The reviews of these "little" concerts remind us that even professional critics found the cycles novel, as they did Haydn, too, to judge from a headline reference to the "Little Known 'Nelson' Mass."[43]

Tanglewood had changed from the old formula of two weeks of chamber concerts (while the Pops played in Boston) followed by four weeks for full orchestra; now there were chamber concerts on Friday nights and the symphonic concerts on Saturdays and Sundays. This effectively quadrupled demand for the Bach-and-Mozart concerts, and the public flocked to the big concerts in ever more impressive numbers: 10,000 for the Saint-Saëns Third Symphony with E. Power Biggs; 135,000 altogether for summer 1954. Only reverses in the weather would keep the crowds away, and even then 9,000 were estimated in the audience for the Berlioz Requiem (August 15, 1954) and 9,715 for an all-Beethoven program (August 7, 1955), both in the rain. "Many of those who listened from the lawns were drenched, but it did not seem to dampen their enthusiasm and good spirits."[44] Nor did the heat wave of July 1955: A Beethoven Violin Concerto with Munch and Isaac Stern was said to drive away memories of "an overheated day's discomforts."[45]

On his retirement at the end of the 1953–1954 season, George M. Judd was succeeded as general manager of the BSO by Thomas D. Perry Jr., called Tod. (Leonard Burkat became administrator of the Berkshire Festival.) This was the high noon of the musical amateur as orchestra manager. Social background helped, and Tod Perry and his wife, Helen (Yale and Vassar), moved easily among the heavily Harvard trustees. Perry had come up through the administrative ranks and was properly positioned to undertake the job. Still, he was sufficiently younger than Cabot and Judd as to seem to represent a new generation, one brought up with record players, plane travel, and new understandings of music's place in one's leisure time—a generation understandably skittish about the implications of international politics and perhaps even more prone to look to art music as a commodity for brokering global understanding. Munch thought more highly of Perry than did some of the musicians, who found him inept in the face of organizational crisis (notably when something went wrong with the transportation of musicians or instruments on the tours). In their written exchanges Munch adopted a personal, avuncular manner he did not often use with others.

Nearing sixty-five, Munch had little aspiration to any other particular post in his profession. Nevertheless, he must have enjoyed the new intersection of his career with Toscanini's. His March 1954 stint with the NBC Symphony—he was recommended by Toscanini's protégé Guido Cantelli, even though Toscanini found Munch's *Fantastique* distasteful—was highly regarded. It gave him an opportunity to dine with the maestro for his eighty-seventh birthday. The NBC Symphony was nearing its end. Toscanini had conducted on February 29 and March 21, but on that day he announced that Munch would conduct on March 28. Toscanini's last concert, the all-Wagner program during which he suffered memory lapses, was on April 4.

The Munch concert consisted of *Ibéria, Le tombeau de Couperin,* and *Bacchus et Ariane.* Its 2007 release on CD gives us a precious record of the difficult Ravel work.[46] Munch skips many of the repeats but obviously relishes the virtuosity of the NBCSO, especially the solo players. The Rigaudon shows him at his most genial. *Ibéria* is profitably to be compared with the great BSO recording of 1957: not as elegantly shaped but in certain ways more exacting. In the Roussel, savor his guttural launch of the Bacchanale—the sort of detail trimmed out of the studio sessions.

Cantelli, meanwhile, was in Boston for his first visit. Munch was intrigued enough by all he had heard to delay his December vacation and stay on in

Boston for Cantelli's second visit, with *The Pines of Rome* and the Verdi Requiem (December 1954). Cantelli wrote Toscanini in Milan that he had found Munch "much better physically and of unbounded kindness." There was general euphoria when NBC announced its intention to replace the broadcasts of the defunct NBC Symphony with those of the BSO.

I Am a Conductor was released in French for the 1954 Christmas season and in English shortly thereafter in New York, and by January excerpts from Leonard Burkat's translation were circulating widely. Extensive passages were quoted in the leading periodicals, including the *Boston Globe* and the BSO program book. This affectionate, understated glimpse into the profession—there are no pictures—was for most readers a first. To newspaper reporters and program annotators it offered up a new trove of insightful quotations: conducting, for instance, as a "priesthood and often even a disease—a disease from which the only escape is death." Mark Schubart, then dean at Juilliard and later one of the visionaries of Lincoln Center, took issue in the *New York Times* with Munch's "somewhat platitudinous remarks" about "young musicians, [who] want to create a movement at any cost . . . with the expectation of freeing themselves from a past they scorn and disdain, and without the smallest concern for the masters who also sought, struggled and suffered."[47] This is missing the forest for a random tree: It was a pillar of the book and of the author's career that new music belongs in every concert, to say nothing of what Munch's Tanglewood meant to American youth. Schubart does, however, understand that what Munch meant by "new" and "modern" was not necessarily the kind of music young American composers wanted to write.

The advances to the French repertoire that season were Boston's first complete *Daphnis et Chloé* and an appearance of Victoria de los Angeles in *Les nuits d'été* and Debussy's *La damoiselle élue*. Both concerts mutated into RCA recordings (LM/LSC 1893, LM 1907). The chorus in *Daphnis* was that of the New England Conservatory (NEC) and its alumni, prepared by Lorna Cooke de Varon. De Varon had been G. Wallace Woodworth's assistant conductor with the Harvard-Radcliffe singers and thus had already helped prepare choruses for both Koussevitzky and Munch. Her work with the New England Conservatory Chorus—smaller than Harvard-Radcliffe but consisting almost entirely of singers preparing for professional careers—had earned favorable reviews in the Boston press. With Woodworth's consent ("Why not?") she successfully proposed her singers as an alternative to the overtaxed Harvard-Radcliffe program. Their ongoing relationship began with *Daphnis,* Suite 2, and the Honegger *Danse des morts* in 1952; it was gradually understood in most quarters that the NEC, with sopranos and tenors who could not be equaled, was preferred for the French repertoire. Harvard-Radcliffe retained its sinecure for Bach—and, owing to its inexhaustible numbers of Harvard men for the two male choruses, *La damnation de Faust.*

De Varon, embarrassed by her spoken French, saw Munch socially only once or twice, but she and her singers found their work with him and the BSO the central pleasure of those years. The music, from Berlioz through Debussy's *Le martyre de St-Sébastien* and the Honegger, was consistently intriguing, as were the conductor's antics in rehearsal: "Have you never *mourned?*" he cried during the *Danse des morts,* clutching at his heart. The women, like their Radcliffe counterparts, returned to campus as though under a spell. Lorna Cooke de Varon impressed Munch and Burkat enough that she was appointed to a teaching position at Tanglewood, where she stayed until Erich Leinsdorf reorganized the faculty.

The fifteenth pair, in mid-February 1955, honored Albert Schweitzer on the occasion of his eightieth birthday with Bach (of course) and the Symphony no. 2 of Ernst Toch (1952), dedicated:

> To the man who kindled this work in me
> To the lonely seer in a time of darkness
> To the only victor in a world of victims
> ALBERT SCHWEITZER

An eight-page excerpt of Schweitzer's Nobel Prize address, "The Path to Peace" (November 1954), was published in the program book, along with a poem from the pen of no less a Boston patriarch than M. A. DeWolfe Howe, taking as its point of departure the gift Schweitzer said he most desired: "a Sèvres vase, filled with time."[48]

Of the Boston premieres, Mario Peragallo's Violin Concerto got good play, and Carlos Chávez and Randall Thompson had symphonies introduced. Leonard Bernstein's Serenade for Violin and Orchestra was programmed as a vehicle for Isaac Stern. "Of course, drive the car up to Boston for the Serenade," Bernstein told his secretary, Helen Coates. "I'm anxious to know how it goes. Munch cabled me asking to make an enormous cut in the last movement (about half the movement!) And I said no."[49]

The more significant premieres were Samuel Barber's new *Prayers of Kierkegaard,* for soloists including Leontyne Price, chorus, and orchestra, as well as the premiere of a new work by Bohuslav Martinu, commissioned by and dedicated to Munch, variously called Symphony no. 6 and *Fantaisies symphoniques.* Of these the notion that "The Boston Symphony Brings New Barber Work to Town" got the more coverage in the papers, but the Martinu was far closer to Munch's heart. Olin Downes, taking his intermission after a Pfitzner overture and Schumann's Fourth, was surprised to hear the Martinu begin behind his back and missed the first few minutes; he returned to consider it at length when it was played again a few days later. Haunted by its Czechness, he liked the orchestration, the overall sound, and what he identified as an earnest and fearless return "in memory and emotion, to his homeland."[50]

The annual pension fund concert that year, on April 4, 1955, was an all-Beethoven program conducted by Pierre Monteux and celebrating his eightieth birthday. The decorations included wreaths and garlands with "PM" and "80" spelled out in white flowers, and all the musicians wore boutonnières. Thirteen players from Monteux's period as conductor of the BSO, 1919–1924, joined the concert, including Arthur Fiedler, who took his old seat in the viola section.[51] Monteux's gesture of donating his services for the pension fund was significant, since he was associated, for better or for worse depending on one's point of view, with the bitter strike of 1920.

At the close of the *Eroica*, Munch appeared from offstage with a large volume, typed remarks, and the mischievous grin he wore for such occasions:

> Pierre Monteux,
>
> I am not going to make a speech.
>
> I only want to thank you for the beautiful concert and to deliver the birthday greetings of your admirers all over the world. In this book are their letters and telegrams.
>
> Two composers have sent you musical birthday cards. Please permit us to play for you *Pensée amicale* by Darius Milhaud and *Greeting Prelude* by Igor Stravinsky.[52]

Both were settings of the "Happy Birthday" song, Stravinsky's a fanfare delivered in *Klangfarbenmelodie*, thus gently mocking the serialists. The musical salutes were not unexpected, having been announced in the printed program; Monteux, in an amusing radio interview the week before, suggested he knew a little something about it, too. Improvised greetings continued into the night at a reception at the Fensgate Hotel, presided over by the irrepressible Doris Monteux.[53]

Monteux's vitality was undiminished at eighty, and he would return in similar form for his eighty-fifth, where it would be noted that he had never missed a scheduled rehearsal or concert. The *New York Times* observed that over an eleven-day period in February 1955, the octogenarian had conducted the Boston Symphony nine times and the Metropolitan Opera once.

For his part Munch became a doctor of music, *honoris causa*, that June at Boston University—the first in a string of honorary degrees—in a class that also included John Fitzgerald Kennedy, Harvard president Nathan Pusey, and Israeli ambassador Abba Eban. The honorific title mattered in the Boston of those days: His predecessor was still always called Dr. Koussevitzky. From 1955 on nearly everyone in the United States took care to address him as Dr. Munch. This was probably the occasion for the conversation during which Kennedy indicated his interest in American composers and solicited from Munch a promise—easily enough made since that was his habit anyway—to play them on the road. The particular composer under discussion was surely Walter Piston, whose Sixth Symphony had been premiered during the season, since Munch associated the work with Kennedy well into the 1960s.

At last he took a summer vacation, limiting his post-Tanglewood appearances to a memorial concert for Wilhelm Furtwängler at the Salzburg Festspielhaus on August 30, 1955, and an *Eroica* in Florence. During the summer it was announced first that the BSO had accepted an invitation to appear at the Edinburgh Festival in August 1956. This soon mutated into another major venture abroad, including a visit to the Soviet Union. On July 24 the BSO was reported to be "eager" to respond to President Eisenhower's plea, made the day before in Geneva, to lift the Iron Curtain; in early September the tour was officially announced. The Boston was thus the first major orchestra to confirm such a trip, edging out Philadelphia and New York, and thus at the head of the stampede of cultural exchanges that characterized the late 1950s.[54] (Koussevitzky had wanted to take the BSO to Russia just after the war, but the Russians were not interested; the first invitation had gone to Philadelphia, following recommendations from David Oistrakh and Emil Gilels, two artists the Soviets had allowed to appear in the United States.)

The seventy-fifth anniversary of the Boston Symphony Orchestra, 1955–1956, was to be celebrated with enhanced domestic tours, the big venture abroad, and, of course, anniversary commissions. In October 1955 the orchestra took to the road again on a long trek through the South. From Charlotte, North Carolina, the second stop on the tour, Perry reported home to Henry Cabot: "Good so far, number 2 tonight in a brand new auditorium [Ovens Auditorium, 1955] which we are practically opening. Had a very good talk with CM this morning—he in fine fettle and all over his recent indisposition." They talked of personnel, broaching for the first time the delicate question of easing Richard Burgin into retirement—"nothing in any way abrupt lest Richard be displeased." There was also concern over the size of Munch's taxable income and the suggestion that the orchestra buy him a car or a house. "He replied that he seeks nothing, bless his heart, but we ought to think of what we can do." They also talked of improvements to the Shed in Tanglewood, and Munch agreed to donate enough to the project to get the changes done "before he retires . . . but he shows no evidence of wanting to stop."[55]

The "southern" tour played fifteen cities, of which more than half (Norfolk, Charlotte, Birmingham, Shreveport, Jackson, Urbana, Lafayette, Fort Wayne, and Saginaw) were first-time visits. The players noted that Munch chose to live on the train instead of in the first-class hotels to which he was entitled; he explained that he was trying to limit his expense account, in a year of substantial need, so as not to "perturb" his musicians.

Between them, the Koussevitzky Music Foundation and Munch commissioned fifteen new scores for the seventy-fifth-anniversary year (table 6.2).

The official commissioning had been done by the Koussevitzky Foundation, starting with a list suggested by Munch and then reviewed by Aaron Copland and Olga Koussevitzky. Copland had written her in August 1954:

> My impression is that we shall have no difficulty with the European composer-com-missions. Martin [Frank Martin, as a misreading of Martinu?], Dallapiccola, Milhaud, Dutilleux, and Britten are indicated. I am not so sure about Blacher being the best representative from Germany. I would think that Orff or von Einem ought to be con-sidered. The American composers are more of a problem. I note that Munch has my name down on the list. This is not necessary, as I shall be doing a revision of the Sym-phonic Ode for the occasion. The rest of the names I think need general discussion.[56]

It was difficult for Copland, as for Bernstein, to avoid belittling Munch, the out-sider. He told Irving Fine that he found the New York performance of his Ode

Table 6.2. 75TH-ANNIVERSARY COMMISSIONS

	Premiered
Barber: *Die Natali*, Chorale Preludes for Orchestra, op. 37	Dec. 22, 1960
Bernstein: Symphony no. 3 (*Kaddish*)	Jan. 31, 1964
Britten: [never submitted]	
Copland: Symphonic Ode, version II	Feb. 3, 1956
Dutilleux: Symphony no. 2	Dec. 11, 1959
Hanson: *Elegy in Memory of Serge Koussevitzky*	Jan. 20, 1956
Ibert: *Bostoniana* (movt. of unfinished symphony; also called *Movt. symphonique*)	Jan. 25, 1963
Martinu: Symphony no. 6 (*Fantaisies symphoniques*)	Jan. 7, 1955
Milhaud: Symphony no. 6	Oct. 7, 1955
Petrassi: Concerto no. 5 for Orchestra	Dec. 2, 1955
Piston: Symphony no. 6	Nov. 25, 1955
Schuman: Symphony no. 7	Oct. 21, 1960
Sessions: Symphony no. 3	Dec. 6, 1957
Villa-Lobos: Symphony no. 11	Mar. 2, 1956
von Einem: Symphonic Scenes	Oct. 11, 1957

"sort of stiff and unconvincing. I guess Munch got self-conscious. . . . I sure do wish I could hear it conducted by an American."[57] Munch, on the other hand, liked the piece and put it directly into the tour programs.

Meanwhile, he naturally invited his particular friends to compose something for the occasion, with or without the Koussevitzky imprimatur—for instance, Martinu's Sixth Symphony and, later, *The Parables*, both billed as "personal commissions" of Charles Munch. By contrast he was not close with many of the composers on the official list. Piston excepted, where the acquaintance was of long standing, he was not especially admired by the composers of the American northeast, and he was no longer in France often enough to keep up with the compositional currents in Europe. The circle to which he belonged in Paris in the 1930s and '40s had dispersed.

Alexander Tcherepnin's account of the genesis of the Fourth Symphony— not a seventy-fifth-anniversary work but a project put in play at about that time—is worth quoting *in extenso* for what it shows of the manner and style with which Munch sought out new work. Munch had conducted Tcherepnin's Russian Dances, op. 50, in Paris in 1936, then given the premiere of the *Suite géorgienne* with the Société des Concerts in 1940. In 1950 Tcherepnin had come to Boston to play his Second Piano Concerto with Munch and the BSO and was from then on a frequent guest at the house in Milton:

> It was during one of such visits (in 1953), after an intimate supper, that he asked me whether I would be willing to accept his commission to compose a Symphony for him. When I gladly accepted, he went to his desk and wrote out a check for $1,000, tells me that there are no strings attached. He pointed out that it could be a Symphony or any other form of composition for Symphony Orchestra and that there would be no question of deadline, that, in every respect, I should feel free from any pressure. . . .
>
> Unforeseeable circumstances . . . delayed the fulfillment of this challenging task and I came to it only in 1957. It was just before Christmas of 1957 that I completed the score. I called Charles Munch long distance and when he heard that the composition was done, he told me to take the first plane and to bring him the score. This I did. He sent his chauffeur to meet me at the airport and when I rang the bell at his home, he himself opened the door and greeted me by saying with a friendly but slightly sarcastic smile: "Tell me, how many forte are there at the end?" [There was a *ppppp* at the end of a long *Requiescat in pace*.]
>
> When we finished, Munch went to his desk, was for a moment busy writing something and then handed me another check for $1,000. "Why?" I asked, "you have already paid the fee in advance, when you commissioned the Symphony." "Don't you think it is worth it?" he asked. My answer was "of course not." He shook his head and said: "*On est jamais assez généreux*" (You can never be too generous).[58]

Munch programmed the work for December 5–6, 1958, and took it on the run-outs to Washington, D.C., New York, and Brooklyn. He told the composer, just after the founding of the Orchestre de Paris in 1967, that he would perform and record it on his return from the United States.

For the most part the seventy-fifth anniversary of the Boston Symphony was recognized with a sober dignity typical of how the orchestra usually went about its aristocratic business: commissions, the tour, retrospectives, and commemorative programs and press releases adorned with a birthday logotype.

But there were more flamboyant indications, too: a huge billboard placed in the parking lot behind Symphony Hall, with cartoons of the major players. For ninety-eight cents you could buy RCA's commemorative album, *75th Anniversary: A Musical History of the Boston Symphony and Boston Pops*, with selections led by Muck, Koussevitzky, Munch, and Arthur Fiedler, narrated by Milton Cross. At the end is a multi-conductor performance of Berlioz's *Marche hongroise* spliced together from performances by Muck, Koussevitzky, and Munch.

Munch was lionized as never before and widely considered music's man of the year for 1956. In June 1956 he made a special trip from France to Boston to collect not one but three more honorary degrees in five days. At Tufts on June 10 the doctor of humane letters degree had this citation: "To a long and highly-prized Boston musical tradition you have brought added honor and new accomplishments." At Boston College on June 13 direct reference was made to the orchestra's anniversary: The degree of doctor of music was a

> means to assert our gratitude and warm felicitations on the seventy-fifty anniversary of the founding of the Boston Symphony Orchestra. For we were mindful of the measure in which the Boston Symphony Orchestra has deepened and enriched the experience of beauty of all our people. We noted with pride and appreciation that in Boston a standard of orchestral performance has been raised which is the envy of all other great cities.
>
> We saw these values, so vital a part of the spiritual patrimony of our people, perpetuated and enlarged in the conductorship of Charles Munch. Coming to Boston in 1949, as the best conductor in France to the first orchestra in the world, he asserted from the first his right to leadership in the musical life of our city. We have been charmed and edified by his boundless capacity for work, his respect for his musicians and for his audience, his self-effacement on the podium, his humanistic predilection for the great spiritual themes expressed in the oratorio and the Mass.

At Harvard he was one of a crowd of luminaries assembled for hooding at the 305th commencement, which included Senator John F. Kennedy, Justice Felix Frankfurter, and Secretary of the Treasury George Humphrey. The press photographs that day suggest that Munch was less than comfortable in this atmosphere of toothy political grins and backslapping: He is the only one not to have a top hat in the parade and seems vacant and distracted at the end of the clot of dignitaries. A Cabot, Godfrey, was, at ninety-five, the oldest member of the procession of alumni.

In June Munch was in Paris for two weeks, officially on vacation but in fact leading the Orchestre National in its contribution to the nationwide jubilee for Marguerite Long—in this case an old-fashioned, multiauthored extravaganza along the lines of Paris in the 1930s and '40s. The *Variations sur le nom de Marguerite Long* included movements by Françaix, Sauget, Milhaud ("La couronne de Marguerites" [The Crown of Daisies]), Rivier, Daniel-Lesur, Poulenc, and Auric. He visited his wife, who was gravely ill, then was off again to Tanglewood and the necessary last-minute arrangements for the European journey. In one of his rare ventures into opera, he led a concert performance of act I of *Die Walküre* at Tanglewood, with Margaret Harshaw as Sieglinde and the young Albert da Costa as Siegmund. At the conclusion of the Berkshire Festival on August 12, 104 members of the Boston Symphony Orchestra, accompanied by staff, spouses, and the impressive baggage of musicians on tour, set off to play some twenty-eight concerts in thirteen countries in five weeks. Forty-five musicians and their wives traveled to Ireland on the liner *Nieuw Amsterdam,* as did Monteux and Henry B. Cabot. Another 78 flew from Boston to Shannon on August 15. The remaining 59 flew on August 23, just in time for the first concert in Cork on August 24. Along for the ride were Cyrus Durgin for the *Boston Globe,* Rudolph Elie for the *Boston Herald,* UP photographer Edward Fitzgerald, and Margo Miller of the *Berkshire Eagle.*[59]

CHAPTER 7

◆◇◆

The Iron Curtain and Beyond

August 1956–August 1958

Munch left the Berkshires on August 15, 1956, and flew to Paris for what was said to be "a week of rest prior to the tour."[1] He was still, after all, at risk for cardiac complications. Since his visit home the previous June it had been clear that his wife, Geneviève, was in irreversible decline; now she was under the care of her niece Anne-Rose Ebersolt and nephew Jean-Jacques Schweitzer. After conducting a concert at Chartres Cathedral on August 19, Munch went on to join his orchestra in Ireland, sending Vivette a telegram to assure her of his safe arrival. Ebersolt found her lifeless the next morning, August 21, holding the unopened envelope. Munch appears to have flown to France for the funeral on Thursday, August 23—then was back in Ireland for the concert on August 24.

Michael T. Kelleher, Irish-born trustee of the BSO, made a brief announcement to the orchestra before the opening concert in Cork; Kelleher broke down in sobs—"I am sorry, my friends, I am overcome," he said and left the stage.[2] Munch stood quietly with his head bowed, then carried resolutely on. The *Boston Globe* published a front-page notice the next day (August 25), which was picked up by the wire services. Vivette was laid to rest with her parents, Édouard and Sophie Maury, in Villefavard, after remarks delivered by Fritz, Charles's brother. Munch is remembered to have visited Villefavard one last time to pay his respects at the grave. In the village he continues to be regarded as a sort of deity.

The Boston Symphony Orchestra's tour, however, was of overriding significance, a true turning point in the Cold War. Munch had no option but to assume his public persona and leave the rest for later. Every photograph of that remarkable month, every eyewitness account, shows him in thorough command, at the peak of his abilities and style despite his personal loss. In the aftermath of his own crises of health and the death of his wife, we are left almost nothing by way of clues about his emotional state. These events were simultaneous with the ongoing euphoria of the anniversary season, the honorary degrees, and the conquest of the Soviet Union. However, in a letter to his niece Anne-Rose a week later, after playing the third movement of Schumann's Second in Edinburgh, he wrote of finding a moving soliloquy to Vivette in this

> music of nostalgia, tenderness, and sympathy with death. My darling, I am coming to be with you; but now I cannot find the words, because there are none, to express what I am feeling and what I owe to you. But that "inexpressible" will stay always in my heart, until He who has just delivered our loved one comes to deliver me also.[3]

To evoke the magnitude of the 1956 BSO tour, let alone evaluate its repercussions at home and abroad, is no trivial challenge. Even for Boston it was a stretch: Nothing like it—logistically, financially, politically—had ever been done before. The diplomacy alone was something remarkable, as was the cast of characters: heads of state, princes of music from Sibelius to Oistrakh to Martinu, with Munch always at the center. After the Dublin concert a leather-bound copy of Howard Hanson's *Elegy* to Koussevitzky was presented to the Irish president as the prime minister and lord mayor of Dublin, the archbishop, and U.S. ambassador William Howard Taft III looked on. At the Edinburgh Festival were the princess royal, Mary of York, and her son, the 7th Earl of Harewood, and his wife, Countess Marion Stein—noted pianist and daughter of music critic Erwin Stein. In Russia there was Shostakovich. "In the audience," wrote Kabalevsky of Moscow, "we could see almost all of our famous musicians."[4]

There remained, as there had been in 1952, abundant family connections between the musicians and old Europe. Michael Kelleher, the trustee, had emigrated from County Cork. There were four Russian-born or -trained musicians on the tour, including Richard Burgin, former concertmaster in Leningrad, whose brother flew from Warsaw to Russia to visit him. In Paris it was noted that sixteen of the 105 players were French.

Every program was sold out. In the Soviet Union the tickets were depleted weeks in advance, leading the government to plead for third concerts in both Moscow and Leningrad in order to slow the black market for seats. The scheduling was tight, and the transportation less reliable than had been promised. Though the musicians themselves flew the longest legs of the journey, the ships and trains bringing the cargo of instruments and evening clothes were delayed as often as not.

The programs in Cork, Dublin, and Edinburgh began, after the national anthems, with Haydn's Symphony no. 102, followed by Strauss's *Don Juan* and the Brahms Second, alternating with *The Sorcerer's Apprentice* and Schumann's Second Symphony. (In what was surely some sort of command performance, the audience in Cork also heard Leroy Anderson's *Irish Suite*—virtually the only intrusion of Pops literature into BSO programs during the Munch years.) The Edinburgh critic Stephen Williams, in a rather petulant note, found little to approve of in the programming but noted that "so magnificently agile is this orchestra, that I felt that if Munch had asked the players to jump through the roof of the Usher Hall they would have obeyed with the uttermost sangfroid." He thought Munch conducted the *Don Juan* "like a locomotive engineer making up for lost time."[5]

So much of the journalists' response, for the entire tour, was devoted to the excitement of the circumstances that it is difficult to judge what ordinary listeners went home thinking. The consensus was of having heard one of the best orchestras anywhere ("the best that will ever have been heard in Usher Hall," said *The Scotsman* of the Edinburgh Festival performance). The new works in the repertoire—Hanson's *Elegy in Memory of Serge Koussevitzky,* Copland's Symphonic Ode, Piston's Symphony no. 6, and later in the tour Honegger's Third— were largely unknown to critics. Since the French repertoire was being offered by its two acknowledged masters, Munch and Monteux, there could be little gainsaying that portion of the programs. But when it came to classical titles the critics knew, Haydn and Beethoven and Brahms, they had plenty to say. Moreover, they made interesting comparisons with the work of competing orchestras. Hugh Smith in Cork, for instance, compared the BSO favorably to the Vienna Philharmonic, which had appeared the previous May.[6]

The English critic Felix Aprahamian, a musician of substance, began his summary of the response from Scotland with a preemptive reference to "the world's most perfect orchestral instrument." As to the controversial offering of a Haydn symphony by the full orchestra to demonstrate the BSO's wares, he regretted the crafting of so obvious "a whip to flay Munch" and his players, suggesting greater attention to recent advances in the study of performance practice. The *London Times* found the "French-style trumpets" to be "indeed too shatteringly loud" and the Haydn "absurdly inflated. . . . Have French conductors no sense of style, and do they disregard the scholars' work done in the present century on the music of the eighteenth?" Aprahamian thought *The Sorcerer's Apprentice* dazzling; he did not much like the Piston or the Copland but rather preferred Monteux's rendition of Paul Creston's Second Symphony.[7] Sir Thomas Beecham, finishing his concerts in Edinburgh, scoffed that he did not expect the Americans to be up to British standards, but no sooner had he said it than Colin Mason wrote in the *Manchester Guardian* that the Boston Symphony was "better than the Scottish National, the BBC or the Hallé. Fortunately for our self esteem, it is also no less clearly better than the New York Philharmonic, the Concertgebouw, or the Berlin Philharmonic."[8]

From Edinburgh the orchestra traveled on to Copenhagen, Oslo, Stockholm, and Helsinki. In Finland thoughts naturally turned to Sibelius, and Mrs. Koussevitzky and the management visited the composer to present the orchestra's best wishes. Munch himself was disinclined to make pilgrimages—and was only just then adding the Seventh Symphony to his repertoire. (The only other Sibelius he knew especially well was the Violin Concerto, which he learned in the 1960s.) Richard Burgin and Roger Voisin also traveled to the house, and when Voisin asked the housekeeper for permission to take pictures, Sibelius, recognizing the labels on their bags, invited them in for an amiable chat.[9] These fleeting encounters with a composer whom many regarded as the greatest living symphonist were much in mind a year later, when the orchestra opened its season with concerts in his memory.

The orchestra flew from Helsinki to Leningrad on three 21-seat Aeroflot propeller planes shuttling back and forth, then boarded a special train from the airport to Leningrad Station, banked in welcoming flowers. Though the players arrived on schedule, their *matériel* did not, and the first concert was delayed for twenty-four hours, during which "found time" the Americans threw "longhair dignity to the winds."[10] Munch led a delegation to a pleasure garden to watch dancing girls, while Harold Farberman, on vibraphone, and two colleagues displaced a local band to jam at the roof garden of the Hotel Europe. The ensemble was housed by the government and given four "enormous" meals a day in private hotel dining rooms; there was sightseeing available during every free hour. Five interpreters worked for the group. (Others policed them: The critic Rudolph Elie was made to give back souvenirs he had pilfered from his room.)

By the time the Leningrad premiere finally took place, the excitement could be felt for blocks around Philharmonic Hall. The concert on September 6, 1956—the *Eroica*, Piston's Sixth, and *Daphnis et Chloé*, Suite 2—is certainly to be reckoned among the two or three greatest triumphs Charles Munch ever enjoyed. To relentless, ear-splitting acclaim, he returned again and again to the platform, then played *The Sorcerer's Apprentice* as an encore, motioning the players to leave the stage with him at the end. Still the audience refused to go home, chanting for him to take one more bow. Monteux found him in his dressing room, changing his clothes: *"Charles, Charles, on vous appelle!"*[11]

Following the second Leningrad performance the musicians took the Red-Arrow Express, an overnight sleeper to Moscow, where their train was welcomed by David Oistrakh and Sviatoslav Richter. Then they assembled in the Great Hall of the Moscow Conservatory for a concert on Saturday night and two on Sunday. A tamer response had been expected from the reportedly dour

Moscovites, but again there were ten-minute ovations at every opportunity. Taking Monday off for supervised tourism in Moscow, the company flew Aeroflot to Prague that night. This time six planes took the musicians, and an additional three brought the eight and a half tons of instruments and concert dress in their steamer trunks.

Americans, seeing in their newspapers the headlines, datelines, and photographs from a forbidden and demonized land, can only have been astonished. Among the images was a view outside the hall in Leningrad, where the Stars and Stripes hung alongside the Hammer and Sickle. The iconic photograph taken in the hall that night shows Munch at his most dashing, citizen-chief of his famous orchestra deployed beneath the fabulous crystal chandeliers of Leningrad Philharmonic Hall, packed to the bursting point with listeners craning around every column for a glimpse. From Moscow there were pictures of Bostonians in Red Square and of Munch and a female companion cutting cake during a farewell reception at the Hotel Metropole, as though there were no Cold War at all. The musicians, shown napping backstage and freely taking snapshots in Red Square and from their train cars, seem thoroughly at ease. If there were spies, they went unnoticed. Nor did the Russian public seem belligerent or enslaved but instead rather ordinary concertgoers enjoying an extraordinary turn of events. Crowds that numbered in the hundreds waited outside the theaters to cheer the orchestra as it came and went, and these, too, looked like typical Europeans. One would have had to be a born pessimist not to see in these vignettes some promise of a brighter state of things to come.

No Russian music was played in the Soviet Union since "we didn't want to look as though we were trying to come here and teach them their business"—a core principle of Munch's programming.[12] This was too bad: The *Pathétique* had long been one of his specialties, and he had been playing Prokofiev since his days as a violin soloist. Henry Cabot had felt that protocol demanded at least one Russian work, but Munch refused to talk about it even after Cabot conspired to telephone him at Roger Voisin's house after they had been drinking for awhile.

They were paid in rubles, which could not be taken out of the country. Tod Perry remembered "going to a room in our hotel to collect the money for the orchestra. There were three women with bushels and bushels of ruble notes wrapped in newspaper. Later, the ministry said they had overpaid us." Burkat recalled: "It's hard to believe, but *Daphnis and Chloé* was new music [to the Russians] and so was that Roussel suite." Young composers came backstage to ask about serial and electronic music.[13]

The desired person-to-person exchange was easily achieved. The recognized stars of Russian orchestral music—composers Kabalevsky, Shostakovich, and Khachaturian; violinists David Oistrakh, Igor Oistrakh, and Leonid Kogan;

conductor Kiril Kondrashin, and, of course, the young Rostropovich—were placed front and center in the photographs and toasts, and it was understood that they meant to return the visit. Kurt Sanderling, then a member of the Leningrad Philharmonic, was among the local players getting their first taste of music from outside of Russia. Many years later, as piano soloist with the BSO, Vladimir Ashkenazy recalled that hearing the orchestra was a high point of his conservatory studies. The young Leonid Gesin, later a member of the San Francisco Symphony, was taken aback by the informality of the rehearsal he was allowed to attend: the players in open shirts and slacks, even the conductor. "Mravinsky wore the same suit for twenty years." At the concerts the players came onstage as they liked and tuned and even conversed onstage.[14]

The American musicians met and compared notes with their counterparts—for instance, the entire orchestra of Tallinn, in Estonia, which had made the treacherous two-hundred-mile journey over primitive roads to Leningrad by bus—as time permitted. They were allowed unusual latitude in sightseeing. As a result, the musicians (but not so much Munch or Monteux) did encounter some measure of the poverty that lay just past the glittering *mise-en-scène,* and they left their spare mouthpieces, reeds, strings, and new-fangled sliding mutes behind in Russia. A year later the trombone section of the Moscow State Symphony Orchestra wrote Munch to express fond memories of the visit and to ask for a copy of *I Am a Conductor.*[15]

Kabalevsky's essay on the BSO in Moscow appeared in *Pravda* on September 15, 1956, with a familiar conclusion: "The ensemble has reached such a degree of mastery that technical problems no longer exist for them." Of Munch he said:

> Is it necessary to say what a tremendous part of this polished unanimity is due to the conductor? Charles Munch is a great artist whose mastery is as evident in old as in contemporary music. If I should try to define the mystery of Charles Munch I would say that it lies in his interpretative powers, combining breadth of conception with delicacy of detail. More important than his technical mastery is Charles Munch's human, sincere and deeply felt musical insight. He possesses the strong intellect of a wise man and the fresh approach of a young soul. . . . It requires a really commanding talent to bring out the original beauty [of the *Eroica* Symphony]. Charles Munch accomplishes this absolutely. We heard the real Beethoven—the great leader of humanitarian ideas—of beauty and freedom who leads us through difficult paths towards his ideals.[16]

Prague in the 1950s was as mysterious a place to most Americans as Moscow and Leningrad, so the front-page *Boston Globe* story picturing Munch signing autographs there was nearly as dramatic as the pictures from Russia. From Czechoslovakia the troupe proceeded by train to Vienna to open the fall season with the BSO's first appearance in the city of Mozart and Beethoven. (Both the Philadelphia Orchestra and the New York Philharmonic had visited Vienna since the end of the war.) Again the train bearing the musical instruments arrived late, and the public was kept waiting for more than an hour. The orchestra, with body language beginning to show the strain of their relentless schedule, stayed and played encores.

A perceptive review by the Viennese music historian Rudolf Klein gave the Honegger symphony the high marks of the evening. He compared the sounds of the Boston violins favorably to those of Vienna and praised a "precision and an exactness of fabulous dimensions. The virtuosity of the woodwinds and the brasses, in my opinion, has no equal in the world." He admired the French approach to *Daphnis et Chloé*, but for the Brahms he made the intriguing observation that the individual virtuosity of the principal woodwinds distracted from the wind choirs as a whole, limiting fusion and unity. He, too, thought that the trumpets stood out a "little too sharply"—a fair enough assessment of the Boston style. He then suggested that the difference between American and Viennese orchestras was, at heart, one of rhythm: The Viennese sense of measure was more elastic. He believed Vienna audiences would be willing to do with less of the Bostonian precision in order to sense more freedom in the melodies.[17] That this suggestion was made to so elastic a conductor as Munch is striking indeed.

Several months later the Mozart Society of Vienna presented the orchestra its medal, both in recognition of the BSO's Mozart cycle in the anniversary year 1956 and in fond commemoration of the Viennese visit. "In the opinion of the Vienna Philharmonic players, this orchestra, so idealistically disposed, should be the first foreign performing group to have the Mozart Medal."[18]

After Stuttgart, Munich, Zurich, and Bern—all first visits—the orchestra reached Paris and the Théâtre des Champs-Élysées, where in May 1952 it had achieved great success with Monteux and *Le sacre du printemps*. Munch opened a "tribute to Koussevitzky" with Hanson's *Elegy*—and with Olga Koussevitzky in the house. (Not everyone would have understood that this was a different Madame Koussevitzky from the one who had lived in Paris, and Olga herself might not have grasped all of the associations—the legacy of the Concerts Koussevitzky to French orchestral practice, for example—the evening brought into focus.) Martinu, too, was there to hear his Sixth Symphony. After *La Mer* came the Brahms Second Symphony, prompting the press to recall how recently Brahms had been accepted in France and what a significant role Munch had played in fostering the taste.

More memorable still was a concert in the Chartres Cathedral, where the orchestra, arrayed beneath the famous rose window at the west door, played Barber's Adagio, the Honegger liturgical symphony, and the *Eroica* to an audience of five thousand.[19] Émile Vuillermoz, at seventy-eight, was delighted at the simultaneous return of Munch and Monteux, whom he likened to a hot and cold shower: Munch vibrant, fiery, galvanizing; Monteux impassive, lucid, cool. "Nothing could have been more instructive than this astonishing contrast."[20]

Concerts in Leeds and London triggered the typically robust English criticism. The Piston had grown on the critics since Ireland and Scotland, and the French repertoire was agreed to be unrivaled in its refinement and crystalline transparency. As with the reception of the Brahms in Vienna, the most familiar work drew the strongest negatives. The *London Express* thought Beethoven's Fifth lacking in emotional depth; to the *Times* it was "noble but cold"; the *London Daily Mail* thought Munch had "staked too much on keeping it heroic, exciting, muscular."[21] The most perceptive essay was by Austrian émigré Erwin Stein, who praised the thoroughgoing range of the Bostonian virtuosity right down to the percussionists. "Where," asked Stein, "can finer be found—both players and instruments—than with the Boston Symphony?" He liked Munch's Beethoven considerably better than Monteux's Brahms (and regretted his programming of a Rossini overture and the *Rosenkavalier* Suite as too trivial for the occasion) and suggested that Munch's tenure in Leipzig had made him heir to "a Beethoven tradition which is almost lost today." Then, as was Stein's habit, he digressed to old Vienna: how he had stood next to Webern at the local premiere of *La Mer* and how Webern had gone away a convinced *debussiste*.[22]

After the last London concert, the twenty-eighth of the tour, the players went off sightseeing, then returned home on KLM Royal Dutch Airways. The second of two flights arrived in Boston on October 2, just in time to open the 1956–1957 season three days later. Two members did not survive the journey. Leslie J. Rogers, the venerable music librarian appointed during the tenure of Karl Muck, was sent to the military hospital when the orchestra reached Stuttgart on September 13 and died there a month later; cellist Leon Marjollet succumbed in Paris on September 20. The debilitating fatigue of such journeys was too often masked by the excitement, and the average age of the Boston players was not, after all, low. Both Monteux and Munch were constantly at risk of overextending.

It would be some time before a financial reckoning could determine the effect of so expensive an undertaking on the orchestra's fiscal situation. The governmental subvention, from a President's Fund for International Affairs overseen by the State Department and funneled through the American National Theatre and Academy (ANTA), had met only a portion of the costs. Still, the government was well pleased, and President Eisenhower's fulsome letter, made public as the orchestra opened its seventy-sixth season, observed that such expeditions advanced the cause of international understanding and applauded the exchange of artists as "one of the most effective methods of strengthening world friendship." With true Republican sentiment he added that "it is gratifying to observe that the Boston Symphony Orchestra has developed, in typical American fashion, with the sponsorship and devoted support of private citizens."[23]

The Boston City Council published its welcoming proclamation on October 1. At the Tuesday morning rehearsal on October 9 the players were greeted by the mayor of Boston, the president of the Chamber of Commerce, Massachusetts governor Christian Herter, and Chief Justice Raymond S. Wilkins, along with Henry B. Cabot. Munch responded with his customary remarks on the merits of friendship and cultural exchange, and Governor Herter closed the ceremonies by touching, as everyone else had done, on the wonder of crossing through the Iron Curtain:

> Obviously, you were the individuals under great leadership who have made a contribution for this country that statesmen, politicians, those of us who perhaps struggle in minor or major ways to help relationships between people, can't do at all. . . . The beauty that you contribute to all of our lives is something that will live with us during our entire existence and will go down to our children as one of the great heritages of this country."[24]

Among the other accolades was a congratulatory letter from the president of the American Federation of Musicians—the union—on behalf of its 252,000 members.

Television had now progressed to the point that the general expectation was for routine telecasts of the great orchestras. The BSO concert of October 30 was simulcast on FM radio and television from MIT's Kresge Auditorium, just adjacent to WGBH-TV. The idea was to tune a high-quality FM set to the radio broadcast and watch the images on television. Two cameras were used, one placed in the projection booth facing the orchestra, and a second in a loft to stage right above the players. Jordan Whitelaw, the producer, called the shots in real time by following the orchestra score himself. "The closeups of Dr. Munch's face, serene or intense as the music dictated, were an aesthetic experience in themselves. His remarkable baton technique, too, provided fascinating sequences. His technique has greatly matured since he came to Boston seven years ago."[25]

The Romanian pianist Clara Haskil, known so far in the United States only through her recordings, played Beethoven's Third Piano Concerto in the Friday-Saturday pair and Mozart's D-Minor Concerto, K. 466, the following Sunday and Tuesday. Both programs were taped for broadcast and, owing to the scant documentation of her work, have subsequently been issued on CD. They are gripping accounts, and the orchestral work is especially lovely at the end of the slow movement of the Beethoven, suggesting a much longer musical partnership than was actually the case. Munch and Haskil had, however, known each other since a salon concert at the home of the Princesse de Polignac in July 1939, where she and Dinu Lipatti played the Mozart Concerto for Two Pianos.

Guido Cantelli's sudden death on November 24, 1956, at age thirty-six in an airplane crash while taking off from Orly near Paris, came just a week after he had been appointed music director at La Scala. He was on his way to New York to conduct the Philharmonic. Since his successful Boston debut in January 1953, he had introduced the Verdi Requiem into the BSO repertoire (December 1954) and gone on to lead a total of five subscription pairs. He was widely assumed to be a candidate for the succession in either New York or Boston. Munch suggested as much on more than one occasion.

For the best soloists, appearing with the Boston Symphony often included a recording date with RCA squeezed into the one of the few remaining flexible spots in the orchestral calendar. The results, as recorded and published in the RCA Living Stereo series, which began in 1958, document another component of the Munch allure: the easy intimacies he was able to forge during short-term visits by luminaries who doubtless expected to have the stage essentially to themselves. This was the case with the Beethoven Violin Concerto recorded with Jascha Heifetz at the end of 1955, treasured by Bostonians as an artifact of a memorable artistic intimacy. In January 1957 Gregor Piatigorsky came to premiere and then record William Walton's Cello Concerto (LSC 2109), as well as Ernest Bloch's *Schelomo.* The 1956 Christmas-week reprise of *L'enfance du Christ* featured the cast that was to make the beloved recording (LM 6053) released later in the season: Cesare Valletti as narrator, Florence Kopleff as Mary, Gérard Souzay as Joseph, and Giorgio Tozzi as Herod and the *père de famille.*

Munch never prevailed on Toscanini to come to Boston. In November 1951 he had written "daring to dream" that the maestro might agree to conduct the Boston Symphony Orchestra, perhaps at Tanglewood in a *Missa solemnis* that RCA could record—closing his letter with this handwritten courtesy: "*Avec mon inexprimable admiration et si profonde affection, votre vieux violoniste, Charles.*"[26] Toscanini replied to "Dear Munch" with thanks for renewing an old invitation but feeling that at eighty-five he was so old that it was presumptuous to book future activities. Besides, he wrote, he did not like to conduct outdoors.[27] Still, their paths continued to cross. On the occasion of Toscanini's eighty-seventh birthday and the fraught circumstances surrounding his last appearances in March and April 1954, Munch had gone to New York to help out.

After Toscanini's death on January 16, 1957, a requiem mass was said by Cardinal Spellman at Saint Patrick's Cathedral in New York, a dignified if plain service with ordinary church music. The name Charles Munch led the published

list of dignitaries attending, which continued with Fritz Kreisler, Leonard Bernstein, Nathan Milstein, singers and composers and pianists, and of course the
orchestral players. On February 3 Munch joined Bruno Walter and Pierre Monteux to conduct the Symphony of the Air—the remnant of an NBC Symphony
that had "refused to fade away"—at Carnegie Hall in a memorial concert: the
Eroica with Walter, *La Mer* with Munch, and the *Enigma Variations* with Monteux. To judge from the CD released in 2007, the performances were scrappy,
but this was of no consequence to the audience, which was there to relive treasured memories in discreet silence.[28] Wanda Toscanini Horowitz had expected
to go, but, she wrote Munch, "this afternoon when I entered Carnegie Hall to
hear our old friend Nathan Milstein play I realized that I was not up to entering
the theatre emotionally restrained. Over the years so many days have been enliv-
ened with my father in Carnegie Hall and I hope with all my heart that you will
understand if tonight I don't join with you. Believe me I will try."[29]

Toscanini's death effectively elevated Munch to the deanship of American
symphony orchestra conductors, though few understood either how deeply his
personal admiration ran or the extent of his artistic bereavement. Later, when he
complained of losing touch with the household, Walter Toscanini dispatched an
unusually warm letter urging him to come to Riverdale any day, any time, where
he would always be welcome.[30]

Munch's first concert with the Philadelphia Orchestra in March 1957, part of
an exchange that took Eugene Ormandy to the BSO the same weekend, reminds
us that repertoire now taken for granted in Boston—Roussel's Third, excerpts
from *Roméo et Juliette,* Honegger's Second—was a novelty even in so orches-
trally driven a city as Philadelphia. So was his appearance—"tall, silver-thatched,
and looking youthful for his 65 years"—and his preferred arrangement of the
orchestra, string-quartet style. According to reviewer Edwin Schloss, "The running series of ovations given Munch far exceeded in warmth merely the polite-
ness due a guest."[31] Munch was obviously delighted with the virtuosity of the
Philadelphia, and he went on to say so on numerous occasions—leaving little
doubt, in the end, that it was the only orchestra he considered a rival to his own.
The exchange was successful enough that another was soon scheduled.

In Boston the new music for the 1956–1957 season included Leo Smit's
Symphony no. 1, David Diamond's Sixth Symphony, Emil Kornsand's *Metamorphosis,* and a Te Deum by Henry Barraud in memory of Koussevitzky—as well
as a major new work by William Walton, the Cello Concerto with Gregor Piatigorsky (January 25, 1957). Munch himself focused on Prokofiev, with *Romeo
and Juliet* suites performed and recorded in February, and Nicole Henriot in the
G-Minor Piano Concerto, no. 2. One also senses the gradual emergence of a
serious Wagnerian component of the Munch repertoire, soon to result in some
good recordings. For the pension fund concert in April 1957 he yielded the

podium, after *The Sorcerer's Apprentice,* to comedian Danny Kaye for a program of Pops favorites—so successful an evening that it was rerun that summer in Tanglewood and later duplicated by other major orchestras. It was the only time anyone remembered seeing the typically dour concertmaster Burgin play with tears of mirth running down his face.

Before Tanglewood, Munch called at the Strasbourg Festival to conduct a high-brow, all-French program including the *Symphonie de Numance,* from Henry Barraud's 1952 opera. The concert had, unusually, not sold out, owing in large measure to the competing draw of Carl Schuricht and Samson François in the Liszt E-flat Piano Concerto. By the closing bars of the Franck Symphony, Munch had nevertheless whipped his public up into what was described as a frenzy: Strasbourg was still his fiefdom. At Tanglewood, he added a significant new work to his repertoire just as it became available to performers at large, Stravinsky's *Canticum sacrum* (1956); then, in a reverse of the usual practice, he conducted it again in Boston and New York the following November. He grew to consider *Canticum sacrum* his central discovery of the mid-1950s, and the critics saw "deep introspection" in his reading. Tanglewood itself was in the news that summer owing to a screenplay, *A Tanglewood Story,* found in the papers of James Agee (1909–1955), and both noted directors and the big-name studios were approaching the orchestra and its conductor about participating. The movie was never made.

It was typical of Munch's values and priorities to have accepted a summer engagement far beneath his prestige level on the basis of its intrinsic humanity. This was the Baalbeck International Festival in the Roman acropolis some two hours from Beirut. Baalbeck, or Heliopolis, was the Roman City of the Sun, site of temples to Jupiter and Bacchus, two of the most spectacular ever built. The orchestra was positioned on the steps of the Temple of Jupiter. The festival's leading patron was Camille Chamoun, French-educated, Christian president of Lebanon. At the close of the three concerts with the Santa Cecilia Orchestra of Rome, Chamoun presented Munch with the Order of the Cedars of Lebanon.

The press reveled in this flamboyant, one might say colonial, display of European art in a region many continued to believe would be saved by England and France. This was a year before Gamal Nasser's nationalization of the Suez Canal in July 1956; Chamoun's government did not survive the civil war that broke out in 1958. The details did not much matter to Munch, who saw the Middle East as an obvious place to prove the healing power of music. He has been by no means the only conductor to think so.

He conducted the same orchestra in similar surroundings and with similar repertoire—Berlioz, Roussel, Franck—at the Athens Festival. To Robert Kemp of *Le Monde,* just elected to the Académie Française, Munch's dramatic profile and robust stance in the coliseum of Herod Atticus, backlit by the illuminated Parthenon, made him seem Zeus-like, as he defined his domain with lightning bolts from an all-powerful baton.[32] Since Maria Callas had cancelled her festival appearance, Munch was the uncontested star. After his concert, he was led around the Acropolis by its chief curator, viewing the monument by moonlight. "Now I can die," said Munch, transfixed. He took two weeks of vacation in Nice, led Samson François in a performance of the Schumann Piano Concerto at the Montreux Festival in Switzerland on September 17, spent a week in Paris, and was on the midnight flight from Orly airport in Paris to Logan in Boston, where he arrived in time for an official luncheon on September 28, 1957.

The press of events and his own inclination to consign personal turmoil to the recesses of his mind. The solitude was nonetheless real, and the demise of an artistic and intellectual intimacy that extended back to his early adulthood disrupted the foundations of his worldview. To Anne-Rose Ebersolt he confessed that "there are times when I don't know anymore why or for whom I work like this." As winter descended on Milton he would try to walk every day along a path his wife had loved during her year in Boston, now alone in his grief.[33]

That summer he closed the apartment in the rue Alfred Dehodencq and brought his wife's companion and cook, Alice Latorre, back to Boston with him. Arriving without a visa, she managed to tell the customs and immigration officials she meant "to work for M. Munch" and was detained at the airport for questioning, while he went to the office and made a scene. At length she was released into his custody pending a hearing. President Eisenhower's cabinet chief was alerted, and eventually an official scrawled "White House says forget it." Tod Perry later wrote his contact in Washington with thanks for clearing up "the misunderstanding: As a contribution to the music of this city, it is without precedent; as a service to a distinguished and wonderful man it is a special kindness for which we are all warmly grateful."[34]

Munch in his mid-60s had kept his looks. At 5'11" he struck his admirers as tall. The silver hair and dancing eyes were as alluring as ever. His bespoke evening wear, tailored in Paris by Chauvet, Dior, and Cardin and adjusted on site by Roger the chauffeur, considerably outstyled that of his musicians and guest soloists. (For rehearsals he favored the light-colored smock jackets in which he is frequently photographed; at home he enjoyed, like Monteux, New England plaid flannel.) His voice had grown deeper and gravelly—one effect of a lifetime of cigarette smoking.

The musicians grew accustomed to his several women friends: He had, after all, arrived with a stage-idol's reputation and with handsome women always in his entourage. His trysts were facilitated by the chauffeur; additionally, I was told, "Jimmy [Stagliano, the horn player] got him girls." Among these was Sylvia Sandeen (1935–2005), the youngest of his American suitors. At the time their relationship began, she was a student at Radcliffe and a member of the Harvard-Radcliffe chorus. She was smitten by his authority, looks, and, above all, it is fair to say, his artistry. Five decades later she was able to describe to me the particulars of performances that had seduced her. Like many others who were there, she went out of her way to insist on the primacy of the non-French works in his repertoire. Beethoven, Brahms, and Tchaikovsky, she believed, were the composers closest to his heart. Sandeen was in the Tanglewood performance of *L'enfance du Christ* in July 1957 and in those weeks conceived the idea of arranging a meeting with him. Roger drove her to the house in Milton sometime that fall, where Munch mistook her for someone desiring an audition. "What do you want to play for me, my dear?" he inquired. "The piano perhaps, the violin?" She replied, "I just came to keep you company."

She spoke affectionately and proudly of their time together, and it was clear both from her tale and from the commemorative treasures in her home the degree to which they had been devoted companions. She said, quite simply, she made him happy.[35] Though she learned very little about his past, she got to know his daily life and that of his musicians as well as anyone in or out of Symphony Hall; as a sometime journalist (for the *Boston Globe*), her observations about the man and his world ring true. She seems to have worried very little about the other women in Munch's life. Of Nicole Henriot, she mostly remembered the d'Indy *Symphony on a French Mountain Air* as being tedious; the older French women in his retinue she dismissed as insufferable. Their affair lasted into the early 1960s, when the combined effect of Munch's leaving Boston and reverses in her own life ended up separating them. Later she endowed four seats in Boston Symphony Hall, including one "in loving memory of Charles Munch." She had her tombstone readied before her death with a quotation from Munch: "Music is the only thing that matters."

It was no secret from the inner circle, either, that Olga Koussevitzky thought Munch the only viable candidate to be her next husband. His was the only name for which she would trade in Koussevitzky's. Munch was not interested, and he went to enormous lengths to avoid extended time with her. He took care when they were together to treat her kindly, however, and invited her to his country house when she came to Paris.

What at length settled his domestic life was the coalescence of a real family to surround him. Sometime in 1956 or 1957, Munch introduced Nicole Henriot to his nephew, Jean-Jacques Schweitzer, an officer in the French navy; they were married on January 27, 1958, in New York. A year later their son Jean-Philippe was born. The Boston Symphony tried to explain the frequently posed question as to the family relationships by adding a clarifying sentence to the official biography: "Charles Munch's older sister [Emma] married Albert Schweitzer's younger brother [Paul]; the issue of this marriage, French Navy Commander Jean-Jacques Schweitzer, married the young French pianist Nicole Henriot. Their infant son, Jean-Philippe Schweitzer, thus has two famous great-uncles: Munch and Schweitzer." In 1959–1960, the Schweitzers lived in the United States, while Jean-Jacques was attached to the U.S. Naval War College in Newport, Rhode Island; hence, their son Jean-Philippe was able to know at least one of his famous great-uncles—whom he dubbed "Pia" as soon as he could talk—from the beginning. In a 1970 interview Jean-Jacques Schweitzer, as captain of the antisubmarine frigate *De Grasse,* visiting New York harbor before its official commissioning, recalled his uncle Albert Schweitzer on the evidence of occasional visits; of his other famous uncle he commented with touching *pudeur* that as they virtually lived together the relationship was much too close for elaboration.[36]

Yet another Schweitzer was frequently in the United States, Jean-Jacques's brother Pierre-Paul, soon to become director of the International Monetary Fund (1963–1973) and eventually, like both Albert Schweitzer and Charles Munch, featured in a *Time* magazine cover story.[37] Pierre-Paul, whom Munch had tried to protect during the Occupation, came from Washington to Boston and New York as often as he could and was, with Charles, a frequent Sunday brunch guest of the Alfred Kohns on Park Avenue.

It was Nicole Henriot and her new husband who found a property in the quaint, artsy village of Louveciennes, just outside Paris toward Versailles, and succeeded in winning Munch over to it. They established their own home on the estate and in due course helped him transform the abandoned, overgrown acreage into an inviting and protected refuge from urban hurry. Henriot, now preferring to be called Henriot-Schweitzer, was perfectly cast as the protective niece. She understood his habits, preferences, and needs—also his history, since their own acquaintance was now of two decades' duration—better than anyone else. She insulated him from his agents, whose financial interest did not lend itself to prudent management of his schedule. In a way she had all of the characteristics of a second wife, offering him a warm home, tireless hostess service, and artistic understanding. This was new territory for all three of them— Munch, his nephew Jean-Jacques, and Nicole: Until then, by inclination and professional calling, they had been vagabonds.

The seventy-seventh season of the Boston Symphony Orchestra was built around a Saint John Passion, Brahms Requiem, and Berlioz Requiem, first performances of several of the anniversary commissions, and a very ambitious recording agenda that resulted in some of the "great" recordings, including the Mendelssohn symphonies (LSC 2221), Beethoven's *Eroica* (LSC 2233), and the wonderful *Harold en Italie* with William Primrose (LSC 2228). The superb disc of music for string orchestra that offered Barber's Adagio for Strings alongside the serenades of Elgar and Tchaikovsky appeared that fall (LM 2105; LSC 2105 lacks the Barber[38]); the Adagio has remained in circulation virtually ever since and continues to earn significant royalties. Of the seventy-fifth-anniversary commissions Gottfried von Einem's Symphonic Scenes was announced for the opening concert but, because of Sibelius's death, was postponed until the second pair in order to allow Sibelius's Seventh to be heard.

Organizational changes announced at the beginning of the season included the appointment of the first African American member of the orchestra, Ortiz Walton, as double bassist, and of another woman member, Winifred Winograd, for the cello section. New York's most sophisticated radio station, WQXR, announced plans to broadcast all twenty-four Saturday night concerts in AM and FM without commercial interruption, having gained exclusive rights to the orchestra for an eighty-mile radius around Manhattan. The station installed high-quality telephone lines to bring the signal from Boston to New York and engaged Martin Bookspan as host. During the Boston Symphony broadcasts WQXR enjoyed the largest audience share of any New York station.

For his January "vacation," Munch was in Israel again, primarily to celebrate the inaugural season of the Israel Philharmonic Orchestra's new venue in Tel Aviv, the Frederic R. Mann Auditorium.[39] When he had last been in the area, in April 1947, the orchestra had been playing in movie houses; his intention to return had been delayed by the war of independence and the Suez crisis. Munch, meanwhile, had kept a close, sympathetic eye on the Israeli nation, having, for instance, been a founding member—the only musician—of the America-Israel Society, established in June 1954.[40]

He was a "tremendous success" in his opening program of Schumann's Fourth, the Debussy Nocturnes with female chorus (the first complete Nocturnes to have been played in Israel), and Barber's Medea's Meditation and Dance of Vengeance. One critic considered the concert one of the "highest peaks" in the Israel Philarharmonic's short history: "If only for one year we could have . . . such a great musician . . . as the permanent conductor of the Israel Philharmonic! In only three rehearsals he brought about a revolutionary change in the playing of our orchestra."[41] The Jerusalem Post wrote with similar enthusiasm, especially of the "vehement" and "impetuous" Bacchus et Ariane.

Sensing political and social capital in the news from Israel, Henry Cabot invited several dozen prominent citizens, including the local Jewish leaders, to Symphony Hall to hear Munch report on his trip; his remarks were published in a press release and, a few weeks later, the program book:

> What remarkable things had happened in Tel Aviv since I was last there! My small
> hotel by the sea has almost disappeared into the shade of a magnificent new one.

The desert that was a few hundred yards away is now streets of beautiful apartments or newly covered with green. Outside the city there is a forest of orange trees, grapefruit, olives! The Israel Philharmonic Orchestra no longer repeats each concert seven times in a movie theatre but has a beautiful new hall.[42]

No wonder that he reserved a special place in his memory for the girls: His *sirènes* for the Debussy *Nocturnes* were two dozen young *kibbutzniks*, "blonde or red-haired or brunette. Their eyes were blue or brown. They spoke English or French or German or nothing but Hebrew. What sirens they were!" On closing night they brought him a basket of two dozen perfect yellow roses, each accompanied with a handwritten note from one of the girls. Munch continues:

> Driving to Haifa we left the main highway to cross Mount Carmel, the "Mountain of God," that was already a sacred place in prehistoric times. With what emotion you take the long road that rises gently to the city of Jerusalem, Jerusalem the Golden! How sad that Jerusalem must be divided into two cities—divided between two nations! What sentiment to feel the mystic return of the Jewish people to Jerusalem, the six-thousand-year-old city where David and Solomon reigned three thousand years ago, the spiritual capital of the world![43]

Many, perhaps most, of Munch's public remarks read and sound like they were first drafted by others. This address, replete with Frenchisms ("what sentiment," for instance, for *quel sentiment*) and characteristic wonder, sounds altogether like him and provides a splendid example of his ability to find simple beauties in the most troubled of circumstances.

He returned to Boston in a series of high-profile events in February and March 1958: the French saxophone star Marcel Mule introducing local audiences to the Concertino of Ibert and the *Ballade* of Henri Tomasi, the first Boston performance of Stravinsky's *Agon*, Bruckner's Seventh (with a formidable cut in the last movement), and another benefit for Albert Schweitzer in Lambaréné, again with Ernst Toch's Second Symphony. On the program for March 7–8, 1958, were premieres of both Henry Barraud's Third Symphony and Walter Piston's new Viola Concerto for Joseph de Pasquale, followed a week later by Nicole Henriot in d'Indy's *Symphony on a French Mountain Air,* recorded later in the month (LSC 2271).

On April 1, 1958, as his tenth-anniversary season was coming into view, Munch surprised the trustees with a lawyer-drafted letter announcing his intent to resign effective August 31, 1958.[44] Ten years was enough, he reasoned. "Twelve would be better," Cabot was quick to respond, and he was equally quick to secure from Munch a promise to continue indefinitely until a successor could be found.[45] There were both medical and personal reasons, Munch noted, the former certainly having to do with recurring chest pain and the latter almost as surely being pressure from Nicole to return to France to enjoy his old age. Munch assured his colleagues that he meant to continue his affiliation with the orchestra after his formal retirement and, as importantly, to enjoy in a variety of ways the warm personal relationships he had built in Boston.

He provided the details in a face-to-face meeting with Henry Cabot. However happy he was in Boston, he said, the duties had grown too oppressive: With each new season came ever more difficult scores to prepare (and a greater number—his own fault), more (and more demanding) recording sessions, and the weight of difficult personnel issues. How seriously Cabot and the management took the threat of losing their conductor is not clear: Certainly they were alarmed enough to make him immediate salary and contract concessions. It is telling that Cabot, who had so obviously not wanted Koussevitzky's help in naming a successor, now began a series of conversations with Munch as to the possibilities: Robert Shaw, Thomas Schippers ("cold, and he makes the musicians nervous"), Ferenc Fricsay (soon discovered to have leukemia), Martinon.[46] The BSO thus embarked on a deliberate course of action, hoping that the status quo would survive a few more years. For his part, Munch noted in a letter to Joseph Calvet that the 1958–1959 Boston season would "certainly be one of my last."[47]

Almost immediately, and with back-to-back first performances on the billing (Alexei Haieff's Second Symphony for April 11–12 and Easley Blackwood's First for the next weekend), Munch's health worsened dramatically. During the first pair he suffered severe angina; by the end of the following week he had decided to leave the Blackwood premiere to Richard Burgin. In the interim he was evaluated by his personal physician, Paul Withington of Milton, and Paul Dudley White, who diagnosed acute exhaustion but no new damage to the heart.[48] The prescribed treatment was anticoagulants and complete rest—however unlikely that might have been. The two physicians issued a joint statement on April 22, 1958: "Earlier this month, Dr. Munch developed some symptoms which indicated the need for rest for a few weeks and from which the chance for a satisfactory recovery is favorable. He is ambulatory and plans soon to [go to] France to continue resting there. His general condition is good otherwise." Cabot, who did not want to take responsibility for what might happen if Munch failed to slow down, reluctantly ordered the cancellation of the Berlioz Requiem planned to close the season—much to the disappointment of Lorna Cooke de Varon and the New England Conservatory forces. Richard Burgin conducted a program of Haydn, Beethoven, and Stravinsky instead.

Munch rested in Paris less than a month before he was back on the podium and canceled only his appearance at the Prague Spring Festival. By mid-June he was at the Strasbourg Festival, working as hard as ever—four concerts in short succession. Henry Cabot wrote twice in May, begging him to have his French physicians report their findings to Drs. Withington and White and to return to White's care as soon as possible.

He became increasingly, though grudgingly, aware of his own limitations. At a dinner given by the players a few months later to mark his ten-year anniversary in Boston, his remarks focused on his health. The prepared notes read, in part, as follows:

> To have been able to stay with you during 10 years I consider to be one of the great-est chances of my life. You know that during this 10 years I have tried always to protect your interest and to make your hard work as agreeable, easy and interesting as possible. Frankly I can say that I have been a happy man and that means quite a lot: . . . If I have been happy it was thanks to your kindness, your good will and won-derful spirit. . . . If for reasons of health I shall be obliged to leave you, you can be sure that it will be to my greatest regret and if you have some affection for me I can tell you that I love you with all my heart.[49]

The conditional scenario is striking, as though Munch has concluded that his career is nearing its end. He took to wearing a copper bracelet for his arthritic pain and to carrying a Russian icon in his back pocket for good luck and good health.[50]

Full-page newspaper advertisement for the RCA recordings and BSO tour appearances,
The Billboard (April 18, 1953)

BSO

With President
and Mrs. Truman,
following the
performance in
Constitution
Hall, November
16, 1950

*World Wide Photos,
Inc. BSO*

With Arthur Honegger, following
the performance of Honegger's
Second Symphony by the Boston
Symphony Orchestra at the Paris
Opéra, May 6, 1952

BSO

With Albert Schweitzer, Strasbourg Festival,
June 20, 1954

Photo Klein. Festival de Musique de Strasbourg

With the BSO in
the Great Hall of
the Leningrad
Conservatory,
September 6,
1956

BSO

With Jean-Jacques Schweitzer,
Nicole Henriot-Schweitzer, and
Fritz Munch at the Lido, circa 1957

Collection Schweitzer

With Benny
Goodman in the
Mozart Clarinet
Concerto at
Tanglewood, July 6,
1956

BSO

With John Pfeiffer and Bernard
Zighera during playback of a
recording session, January 1956

John Cook, BSO

With Henri Dutilleux, preparing for
the first performance of the Second
Symphony, December 1959

Ed Fitzgerald, BSO

With the BSO in Tokyo, May 4, 1960

BSO

With Seiji Ozawa and Eleazar de Carvalho at Tanglewood, summer 1961

Walter H. Scott, BSO

With Leonard Bernstein, preparing for the first performance of Bernstein's Symphony no. 3 (*Kaddish*), January 1964

Milton Feinberg, BSO

With the New Philharmonia
in Albert Hall, London,
January 3, 1965

*Eric Auerbach. Hulton Archive,
Getty Images*

With the Orchestre de Paris in the Théâtre de la Gaité-Parisienne, October 18, 1967

Gérard Neuvecelle

Portrait by Constantine
Manos, autumn 1958

Constantine (Gus) Manos, BSO

Portrait by Henri Cartier-Bresson,
Théâtre de la Gaité-Parisienne,
November 1967

Magnum Photos

Portrait by Gaby (Gabriel Desmarais), Montreal, circa 1962

Gabriel Desmarais heirs

CHAPTER 8

ᴄ\ᴏ

Shifting Perspectives in Boston

September 1958–April 1962

C harles Munch arrived in Boston for his tenth season, 1958–1959, in late September, sporting new glasses and looking rested and fit, ready for a packed season that would take the orchestra on the road at the very beginning and conclude with the postponed Berlioz Requiem. He had not been seen in Symphony Hall since April. Cyrus Durgin thought the first concert outstanding: "I have never heard such a performance of *La Mer.*"[1]

A new round of technological advances accompanied the season launch. The Boston Symphony Transcription Trust would distribute recorded tapes for delayed rebroadcasts to stations all over the country—some fifteen metropolitan stations in 1958–1959—thereby substantially increasing the radio audience. The related American International Music Fund Recording Project, commonly called the Recording Guarantee Project, began in earnest that fall, funded by the Rockefeller Foundation with the support of the American Federation of Musicians.[2] Kinescopes of the Cambridge concerts, now routinely televised, were to be deposited in the Educational Television and Radio Center.

October 24 is celebrated as United Nations Day in recognition of the 1945 signing of the charter. Since Munch's arrival in the United States, he and the BSO had tried to encourage the tradition of October concerts at the General Assembly Hall of the UN in New York despite the fact that the orchestra's usual touring schedule had it on its annual "western swing" to Toledo, Ann Arbor, and Detroit in the holiday week. The United Nations Day concert on October 24, 1958,[3] drew even more attention than usual, not so much for the BSO's contribution—Honegger's Fifth at the beginning and Brahms's Fourth at the end—but because Pablo Casals was to make his first American appearance since the Spanish Civil War. (Casals objected to the United States' recognition of the Franco regime.) He played a Bach sonata with piano accompaniment before an audience of 3,000 seated and another 500 standees, all of whom were so enraptured with his performance that the tight schedule was extended for an encore. After the intermission, Munch and the BSO offered the Brahms—the whole played to a huge radio and television audience in the United States. Afterward, as if that were not enough celebrating, a transmission from Paris featured Menuhin and Oistrakh—one American, one Russian—in the Bach Double Concerto. Back in New York Ravi Shankar played the sitar, and then portions of the finale from Beethoven's Ninth were beamed in from Geneva, played by the Orchestre de la Suisse Romande: a simulcast heard on four continents. Secretary-General Dag Hammarskjold welcomed and thanked the musicians, "who speak to us today of those things that can [only] be told in music's universal tongue."[4]

The diplomatic advantages of this universal tongue seemed to be invoked with every new twist of international politics. Van Cliburn, having won the first Tchaikovsky Competition in April 1958, thereby in some ways assuaging the American *amour propre* after it had been wounded by the Soviets' launching of Sputnik, came to Boston to play two pension fund concerts with Munch, Sunday afternoon and Monday night, October 5 and 6. Both sold out; between the two concerts, a four-hour recording session for the Schumann Piano Concerto (and a movement of the Rachmaninov Third)—breathlessly reported by the press— was squeezed in from midnight until 4:00 a.m.[5] John Pfeiffer, the producer, recalled editing the early-morning takes all day Monday; a photograph of the playback that night shows Van Cliburn in full concert dress with Munch and the producers in the Old Instrument Room, dominated by a portrait of the BSO's founder, Henry Higginson.

But the recording went unapproved, and Cliburn's Schumann for RCA was with Fritz Reiner and the Chicago Symphony. (His recording of the Tchaikovsky, with Kondrashin and the Symphony of the Air, was the first classical record to sell a million copies.) Van Cliburn, who came across as a callow Texan, offered an attractive new face to the kinds of values—art without boundaries, musicians as ambassadors of peace—Munch and the Bostonians had wanted to espouse in Russia. So formidable an adversary as Anastas Mikoyan saw this and said to him, "You've been a good diplomat. . . . I wish America would send more like you."[6]

Easley Blackwood's First Symphony and Haieff's Second won the first Recording Project awards, and recording sessions were set for November. Munch, who had been ill the previous year, now relearned both works and programmed them early in the season. In December Alexander Tcherepnin flew in from a sojourn in France for the first performance of his Symphony no. 4, completed in 1957 and dedicated to Munch. The program note, by the composer's son Serge, a Harvard student, observed that among the elements of the work were an authentic Russian requiem chant, a nine-pitch scale, use of a polyphonic technique called "interpoint" by the composer, and certain serial passages—all of these characteristics of the kind of progressive approach to conservative models Munch always found inviting. Tcherepnin's work had already been awarded the Glinka Prize in Russia, another moment of warmth during the Cold War.

Munch conducted Mahler for the first time with the BSO when Bruno Walter's protégée Maureen Forrester, pregnant with her first child, came for *Kindertotenlieder* and the *Lieder eines fahrenden Gesellen,* with a recording made at the end of December (LSC 2371). This left him in Boston for Christmas, which he shared with the Cabots. Henry Cabot's holiday greeting reflected fondly on their decade together: "After having known and heard you for ten years I realize that I was fortunately instrumental in giving the Boston Symphony and the music lovers of Boston the greatest musician and conductor as well as one of the finest men ever to come into this community. Your friend, Harry." The winter "vacation" in France included a trip to Monaco to open the season of the Monte-Carlo Orchestra in the presence of its patrons Prince Rainier and Princess Grace. A "notably cordial" burst of applause greeted his return to Symphony Hall in early February 1959.

Coming on top of so many advances in technology, the overseas broadcasts of the BSO programs that began in January 1959 (January 23 with Monteux, February 13 with Munch) seem almost parenthetical, but in fact the result was the addition of yet another new bloc of fans. These were direct transmissions by transatlantic cable to BBC and on to stations in Belgium, Switzerland, and Yugoslavia. Listeners in London wrote back to compliment a superlative technical achievement: "no mush, no interference, and in perfect tonal balance. The full range is coming through beautifully—from percussion to triangle—and I can't see how you can improve on this in the next concert except to hire an extra cable and do it stereophonically. It's quite impossible to believe that this broadcast is coming from 2000 miles away and not from the West End."[7] After the first broadcast WGBH received congratulations from the French radio service and the BBC, and one official wrote that "The splendid feast you have just given us has, I hope, finally buried the memories of the Tea Party."[8]

These advances were not achieved without incident. During the WQXR broadcast in April 1959, Rudolf Serkin leaned over to Munch between movements of the Brahms Second Piano Concerto to complain of a broken pedal. The audience of 2,600 waited patiently while the piano technician was summoned onstage to effect his repairs as tens of thousands of radio listeners were given the play-by-play by Martin Bookspan and network programming delayed for the rest of the evening.[9]

The banquet honoring Munch for ten years of service to the BSO took place in February 1959; Monteux sent a charming letter of regret that he could not be there, wishing to be counted "among your children and to say face-to-face how much I admire you and what affection I have for you," and concluding in simple English "I love you. —Pierre."[10]

The Parables, in mid-February, was the second of two works Munch had personally commissioned from Bohuslav Martinu at more or less the same time as the seventy-fifth-anniversary commissions from the Koussevitzky Foundation. The three parables (of a sculptor, a garden, and a labyrinth) were fashioned after Saint-Exupéry's *Citadelle* ("The Wisdom of the Sands") and *Le voyage de Thésée* (The Voyage of Theseus) by Georges Neveux—atmospheric movements deemed "impressionistic" by a largely sympathetic audience. Martinu, in failing health, was unable to make the trip from his home in Switzerland, and Munch knew they were lucky to have played it and to have sent him a tape while he was still alive.

A parade of important guests passed through in February and March: Henryk Szeryng, in his Boston debut, with the Tchaikovsky Violin Concerto; Eugene Istomin with the Schumann Piano Concerto; the young French violin virtuoso Christian Ferras in the Brahms. Again the pace caught up with Munch, and he canceled appearances in early March owing to a "severe cold." He was able to return for the Saint Matthew Passion at Easter and, by virtue of leaving half programs to Carlos Chávez and Aaron Copland, was fit for the season close on April 24–25. This was the Berlioz Requiem, postponed from the year before, with the New England Conservatory Chorus under Lorna Cook de Varon. It was both televised and broadcast nationwide and to Europe by radio.

The newspapers—encouraged by the orchestra's press department, which had prepared a ten-year retrospective—took the Berlioz as an occasion to review Charles Munch's stewardship of 240 concert pairs (and a total number of concerts conducted during that period approaching 1,400). The high points were clear: the tours of 1952, 1953, and 1956; the seventy-fifth-anniversary commissions; the RCA recordings. Broadcasting—live radio over American networks and cable link to Europe, delayed retransmission by recorded transcription, television—had made Munch and the Boston Symphony Orchestra familiar to the world at large. The Berkshire Festival was attracting record-breaking crowds with each new season. The open rehearsals had been welcomed by everyone. In terms of frequency of programming, the lists showed 65 performances of Beethoven, 53 of Mozart, 45 of Bach, 44 of Brahms, then Ravel, Tchaikovsky, Debussy, Richard Strauss, Stravinsky, Berlioz, and Wagner.

Noting "a certain opposition to Munch's programming," Cyrus Durgin referred to the ongoing menu of first performances. But he did not agree:

> His personal reputation has continued high, and under him the orchestra has con-
> tinued one of the best in the world. . . . Twice in the decade (1951, 1958) Munch
> has suffered from what has had the appearance of cardiac illness, though to my
> knowledge precise diagnosis of it as such has not been made in public. Munch has
> served music, the Boston Symphony, and the city well. I, for one, salute him.[11]

In Israel for his fourth visit (May–June 1959), he was able to renew his acquaintance with an old protégé, the resident music director, Jean Martinon. Munch took an interest in Martinon's compositions and invited him to submit a new work for consideration in Boston. This was the Prelude and Toccata, op. 50, premiered in the 1959–1960 season.

In Tanglewood that summer, a new acoustical canopy was unveiled at the Music Shed, named after its principal donor, Edna Betta Talbot. Munch him-self had made the lead gift of $10,000 some five years before. Acoustic con-sulting was provided by the up-and-coming leaders in the classical music business, Bolt, Beranek, and Newman of Cambridge, Massachusetts.[12] The capacities of the new structure were tested by both Beethoven's Ninth and the Berlioz Requiem—also by much smaller aggregations—and found to be admirable. The Beethoven program, which had Rudolf Serkin in the Fourth Piano Concerto, saw Munch at the peak of his form, responding to the new equipment with nuanced, authoritative readings that seemed to enhance the architecture and vice versa.[13]

When Ernest Bloch died in Portland, Oregon, the Tanglewood program of July 25 was rearranged at the last minute to feature Samuel Mayes in a memorial performance of *Schelomo*. Martinu died in August, and Munch played the French premiere of *The Parables* in his memory that September in Besançon.

The annual Besançon Festival included an important conducting competition, to which Munch lent his prestige as a member of the jury. The winner in Sep-tember 1959 was Seiji Ozawa, who at twenty-four was in Europe traveling by corporate-sponsored motor scooter. Lorin Maazel introduced him to Munch, and Ozawa naturally suggested taking a few lessons. Munch counterproposed that he come to Tanglewood in the summer of 1960 to work with Monteux, Bernstein, and the other distinguished members of the faculty. Ozawa's situa-tion, he sensed, meshed perfectly with the Berkshire Music Center's mission.

"Here is a name to remember," wrote Harold Schonberg the next August: "Seiji Ozawa . . . Japanese, 23 [recte: 24] years old, and . . . studying conducting at the Music Center this summer." His performance of the last movement of

Tchaikovsky's Fifth "left no doubt that he is a major talent. . . . He also has, and this will do him no harm at all, showmanship. His gestures are à la Bernstein, and that includes the most swivel-hipped action since that great man himself. What with his talent, exotic good looks, flair and choreographic ability, Mr. Ozawa is a young man who will go far."[14] Ozawa took the Koussevitzky Prize that summer, and three decades later, when the Berkshire Festival turned fifty, Schonberg remembered it vividly: "Just as Bernstein was Koussevitzky's pet, so the young Seiji Ozawa was Munch's. This writer remembers wandering into the Shed one morning and seeing a slip of a Japanese boy conducting a stirring Tchaikovsky Fourth [*sic*]. News about the young star spread rapidly. Tanglewood could help make reputations."[15]

Ozawa characterizes Munch as one of his three mentors, the most obvious source of his own passion for Berlioz. The closeness of their artistic affection was evident again in the late 1960s, when Munch invited Ozawa to conduct the new Orchestre de Paris during its first season, an engagement he was unable to accept. As music director in Boston, Ozawa programmed the Berlioz Requiem in 1976 in memory of Charles Munch, taking it to both New York and Paris. A photograph taken in September 1959 of Munch, Bernstein, Ozawa, Carvalho, and Dutilleux together in Besançon thus says a good deal about the crosscurrents of Munch's life as the new decade approached.

Munch returned to Boston in late September to a season that would include William Steinberg, Eugene Ormandy, Ferenc Fricsay, and Thomas Schippers as guest conductors—some of whom, it had been agreed in internal correspondence, were candidates for his succession. But the particular spice of the season came from international guests. In October 1959 a delegation of important Soviet composers arrived to begin their American sojourn in Boston: Shostakovich, Kabalevsky, Tikhon Khrennikov, Fikret Amirov, and others. Khrennikov was the powerful secretary-general of the Composers Union of Soviet Composers, between the infamous 1948 "Party Resolution" on compositional ideals and the fall of the Soviet Union. The group was reciprocating a visit to the USSR the year before by Ulysses Kay, Roy Harris, Roger Sessions, and Peter Mennin.

The sixth pair of BSO concerts, on November 13–14, featured Amirov's symphonic *mugam* [rhapsody] *Kurd Afshari*, Kabalevsky's Cello Concerto with Samuel Mayes (who had played the work for the composer once before, in 1953), and the Boston premiere of Khrennikov's First Symphony. In the spirit of Cold War exchange, Copland conducted his own *Tender Land Suite*. After the Friday afternoon concert the Leonard Burkats hosted a party at their home in Brookline, copiously photographed, for the Russians, the Burgins, Mrs. Koussevitzky, Copland, Piston, and Munch.[16] Kabalevsky, finding toys upstairs, first realized to his amazement that he must be in a private home, not a governmental showplace. "There were millions of toasts that evening," Burkat recalled. "Munch was at the head table. Richard Burgin . . . spoke in Russian and was very emotional. Friendship and music and cities: you can imagine what was said. Washington wasn't anything in the arts in those days, it was the political capital, and no one drank to New York, which was the business capital. So Boston—we all agreed—was the cultural capital of America."[17]

In art music circles, such "cultural exchange" was becoming routine; in January 1960 the Moscow State Symphony under Konstantin Ivanov and Kiril Kondrashin was to make its first visit to the United States. The Soviet delegation was succeeded in Boston by the Vienna Philharmonic with von Karajan, on November 18, in a program of Mozart's *Eine kleine Nachtmusik* and Bruckner's Eighth. Munch followed up, on December 4–5, with two unfinished Viennese symphonies, Schubert's Eighth and Mahler's Tenth—that is, the Adagio and Purgatorio movements in the version of Ernst Krenek, who had married Mahler's daughter.

Yet the featured work on that intrinsically fascinating concert was the *Pagan Poem* after Virgil by Charles Martin Loeffler (1861–1935), noted Boston violinist-conductor who had sat at the front desk of the violins in the BSO's first years. Loeffler, in fact of Prussian birth, had successfully established the myth that he was of Alsatian heritage, thereby making his work seem appropriate to sending a "Salute to Strasbourg" on tape from the Voice of America that spring. The French consul described Boston's many attractions (for instance, a local chapter of the Amis d'Albert Schweitzer) to Alsatian listeners but suggested that Boston was proudest of its conductor, "your prestigious countryman." The Strasbourg Radio Orchestra, under Charles Bruck, sent a corresponding musical "Salute to Boston," and between March and May 1960 the two city councils and mayors, John F. Collins in Boston and Pierre Pflimlin in Strasbourg, effected the twin cities/*villes jumelles* agreement, which is still in effect.[18]

At the following pair, December 11–12, 1959, Munch and his orchestra premiered the Second Symphony of Henri Dutilleux ("Le Double," for large and small orchestra), the most recent—if by no means the last—of the seventy-fifth-anniversary commissions to arrive and (with the possible exception of Poulenc's *Gloria* the following season) the most significant first performance of Munch's last decade. By the composer's own admission, the delay had surpassed "all decent limits," and its original billing for the previous season had proved once again too optimistic, thus also postponing the Besançon premiere. ("In the future," wrote Dutilleux, "I'll limit myself to a single orchestra at a time.") For Dutilleux, in his early forties, it was a first trip to the United States, prompting a flood of emotions as he entered Symphony Hall, a sanctuary where Messiaen had walked and the *Turangalila-Symphonie* had been born. He watched Munch rehearse nothing but his new symphony for a full week:

exalting hours, during which I watched him draw this work out of nothingness, take its form, find its own life from his wand, Munch as skittish and impatient as I was myself. There, playing on an instrument tailored to his measure—the Boston Orchestra—I discovered that that great man of instinct, of vision, also had all the qualities of an artisan, as careful to respect the letter as to convey the spirit of a musical text.[19]

Encouraged by Munch to extend to Dutilleux the same courtesies that had already been shown Henry Barraud and other European guests, management covered his travel and living expenses, while Mrs. Koussevitzky sent him a personal check to be added to whatever he might be getting from the BSO. Dutilleux returned home with good tapes of both performances. Hearing one of these, Milhaud, who had so far remained unconvinced by the young composer's earlier work, became a partisan and for weeks went about telling anyone who would listen how Dutilleux had undergone enormous change. Portions of movements 2 and 3 were recomposed before the French premiere in Besançon, and in that form the Second Symphony remains one of the BSO's signature works. Munch, meanwhile, considered Dutilleux "my best discovery since Arthur" [Honegger].[20]

During his winter interval he conducted seven concerts with the Concertgebouw in a repertoire recognized by *Het Parool* as being inspired, diversified, and "in high degree a self portrait": symphonies of Honegger and Dutilleux, a Walton concerto, Copland's suite from *The Tender Land,* a Berlioz overture, and the Schumann Concerto with Nicole Henriot.[21] His cover in Boston was another figure correctly reckoned to be of future interest, William Steinberg, who succeeded Erich Leinsdorf at the BSO in 1969. The spring saw multiple performances of Lopatnikov's Music for Orchestra, op. 39, and was the occasion for Piatigorsky's visit to play and then record the Dvořák Cello Concerto (LSC 2490). For Monteux's eighty-fifth birthday, a Ninth Symphony seemed fitting. Munch listened while Monteux conducted.

In March 1960 Jay S. Harrison of the *New York Herald Tribune* published an interview with Charles Munch that addressed in unusual detail his "current views," among them that American music criticism was more accepting of new music than European and that the Boston audiences were considerably warmer than the New York ones.[22] Munch seems very keen on Boston: He praises everyone from the musicians "right down to the last secretary" for their involvement in the mission of fine music. He says he knows every great orchestra in the world, and nowhere is the conductor's job more rewarding. When he mentions Boston and Philadelphia in one breath, the interviewer presses him on the comparison. "I think the Philadelphia is more brilliant, while the Boston is more sensitive."

He salutes the American music establishment, especially the virtuoso teachers in the conservatories, for producing a caliber of musicians found nowhere else. He sees big music (orchestras, festivals, ambitious new compositions), as it was playing out in the United States, as a miracle with no end in sight.

When asked to name names of the better contemporary composers, he comes up with Honegger first and Piston second. "Everything Piston does is perfectly organized; nothing is left to chance. It is all logical, as music should be." Then he adds Stravinsky, saying that the *Canticum sacrum* has moved him deeply. He has no preference among the younger composers: Each of them deserves whatever support he can muster.

Asked about his preferred conductors, he names only the ones he had played for: Monteux, Walter, Furtwängler, and—at the top—Toscanini, "my idol, my hero. We were not always in artistic agreement, but no orchestra ever sounded again the way it did under him." Munch denies the rumor that he is to resign from the BSO and assures readers that, as long as his health and strength remain, he means to continue. "Leave Boston? Not until they drag me away."

His new contract, signed on April 13, suggested that this was the shared position of both conductor and management, with handsome per-concert arrangements for Tanglewood and any future tours outside the United States and Canada. Significantly, however, half of all his earnings were to be withheld for his retirement.

Plans had been released for a Far-Eastern tour of perhaps eight weeks in the spring of 1960, an extravagant affair that would take the BSO to Taiwan, Korea, Japan, the Philippines, Australia, and New Zealand. The particular goals were to recognize the Centennial Year of American-Japanese Relations and to boost the young but promising Osaka Festival. Subvention funding came from the President's Special International Program for Cultural Presentations, administered, as the 1956 European journey had been, by ANTA, the American National Theatre and Academy. Sponsorship in the destination countries was from the radio and television services: NHK (Japanese Broadcasting Corporation), the Australian Broadcasting Company, and the New Zealand Broadcasting Service.

For a time, a series in India had been considered, and since Pierre Monteux, at eighty-five, was forbidden by his physicians from performing in so hot a climate, it was agreed that the conducting on the Eastern tour would be rotated among Munch, Richard Burgin, and Aaron Copland, the latter leading his First Symphony (i.e., the Organ Symphony refashioned for orchestra alone) and the *Tender Land Suite*.[23] The other American works would be Piston's Sixth Symphony, Norman Dello Joio's *Variations, Chaconne, and Finale,* Easley Blackwood's First Symphony, and Leon Kirchner's 1955 Toccata—all of them closely associated with the orchestra.

These arrangements went over poorly with the Japanese hosts. The NHK, sponsoring the majority of the concerts, said it felt "pushed around like in the days of the Occupation" by the Boston management. They objected to the notion that Munch would conduct only twelve of twenty-two concerts in their country and disliked the choice of American works "unknown in Japan." The organizers of the Osaka Festival, meanwhile, complained that the BSO would appear in Tokyo before coming to Osaka—and would arrive after the formal conclusion of the festival. Michi Murayama, the Osaka impresario, was livid: She had traveled to Europe to secure a famous orchestra to anchor her festival and canceled that engagement when the Boston was proffered. In the end she brought the Czech Chamber Orchestra to open her series and extended the festival by two days for the BSO to appear on May 7 and 8. She was also distressed that Copland and not Munch would conduct the first of the pair. Still, the Bostonians had recognized Japanese predilections by centering their repertoire on the *Eroica,* and Munch had surefire hits with *Daphnis et Chloé* and *Bacchus et Ariane,* plus his popular excerpts from *Die Meistersinger,* act III. The presenters' hostility could likely be overcome by Bostonian art.

Another last-minute change was made when, because of riots in Seoul, a pair of concerts in Korea had to be cancelled the week before the orchestra left Boston. On April 25, then, the players assembled in Los Angeles from their various departure points, along with their equipment, and were packed into three large airplanes for the second leg of their ten-thousand-mile journey—"just a routine moving chore for us," Burkat told the *Los Angeles Times.* Munch expressed formulaic confidence in what was ahead but was on the whole more interested in inspecting a helicopter on the tarmac.[24]

The BSO arrived in Japan on May 1 after a long flight from concerts the night before in Taipei, Taiwan, and were happy to find the sun after the pelting Formosan rain. By Japanese custom the first concert was presented by the corporate sponsor, NHK, in its television studio to an invited audience of 650, among them Crown Prince Akihito and Princess Michiko, Ambassador Douglas MacArthur II (nephew of the general) and his wife, and the typical cast of officials, patrons, and cultural leaders. The ninety-minute concert, broadcast over the radio and to viewers in a nation that owned an estimated eight million television sets, included the national anthems, *Eroica,* and *Daphnis et Chloé,* Suite 2. (A 2006 DVD of this concert, *Charles Munch: Boston Symphony Orchestra Live in Japan 1960,* captures the drama of the evening, especially in the anthems, and includes a good deal of newsreel footage of the group on tour.[25]) At the first public concert, in the Hibya Hall on May 5, a capacity audience of 2,400 threw local custom to the winds and cheered *Bacchus et Ariane,* the *Fantastique,* even the Piston. Munch granted two encores from the *Water Music* Suite. Nevertheless, at a press conference early in the tour, the questions were largely about the lack of Japanese music in the BSO's repertoire.

They reached Osaka on May 8, their third concert in Japan, to end the festival that had so far presented the Czech Chamber Orchestra from Prague, the Paganini String Quartet from the United States in an all-Beethoven program, Spanish dancers, and harpist Nicanor Zabaleta. A production of "the first Japanese opera," Yamada Kosaku's *The Black Ships*, to a libretto by the first American consul to serve in Japan, Townsend Harris, drew considerable attention in the press. Madeleine Renaud and Jean-Louis Barrault's theater company presented Shakespeare's *Hamlet* and its particular version of Paul Claudel's *Christophe Colombe*, with music by Milhaud (1953).[26]

Ross Parmenter of the *New York Times* went out to hear the Japan Philharmonic (with its American concertmaster, Broadus Earle) and the Tokyo Symphony, and concluded that the difference between the guest and the resident orchestras was largely a question of the simple power of the BSO and the corresponding lack of "sonority" in the local groups. He noted the vogue in Japan for string playing and string-instrument building, soon to resonate in the United States with the Suzuki Method. Parmenter also observed that the wind instruments were still being imported from Europe and the United States. Here the tables soon turned when, in 1965, the eighty-year old Yamaha corporation introduced its hugely successful line of band instruments.

All twenty-two concerts in Japan sold out, and single tickets were often split between two people who would exchange places at the intermission. At the end of each evening, little girls in kimonos would bring flowers to the stage. Encores, usually two, followed, and then Munch would pick up the flowers and gesture goodbye. Some fifty thousand people came to the concerts while many times that number listened on the radio. Hundreds more came to the informal meet-and-greet sessions with individual players and sections.

The musicians bought cameras, transistor radios, and pearls. Soon exhausted by the intense scheduling and long travel times, they often napped instead of sightseeing, skipping Mount Fujiyama and the volcanoes of Honshu. Nearly everyone visited the new Peace Museum in Hiroshima (1955), finding it sobering and, for some, traumatic. Several players sat quietly and wept.

In addition to a mild earthquake in Matsuyama while they were there, the musicians, traveling along the coast from Sapporo to Sendai, saw firsthand the devastation of the tsunami that followed the great earthquake in Chile on May 22, 1960. They played *La Mer* in Sendai, aware of its particular meaning that night, then collected among themselves one hundred thousand yen to donate to the provincial relief fund.

Munch's prepared farewell statement mentioned "many new friends" made in Japan:

The people of our nations have helped to prove once more that international understanding is strengthened through a mutual appreciation of music and the common language of art. For all members of the Boston Symphony and for myself I want to thank the thousands of Japanese who have been so wonderfully kind. The countless acts of individual thoughtfulness and the enthusiastic reception of our music by concert audiences will long be remembered by all of us who return to our homes in Boston.[27]

After three programs played in shirtsleeves to crowds of five thousand in Manila's Sports Coliseum, Munch and his players reached Australia on June 6 and New Zealand ten days later. In Australia they were joined by the manager of the Sydney Symphony Orchestra, Ernest Gibb (father of the Bee Gees); conductor Nicolai Malko; and concertmaster Ernest Llewellyn, all known to the players either from their Edinburgh Festival concerts or through Tanglewood. In addition, RCA of Australia, Ltd., had issued a special commemorative LP of the BSO and Pops; ads had been inserted in bills from the two biggest department stores in Sydney. In Melbourne, Munch conducted in the flamboyant, five-thousand-seat Swimming Stadium built for the 1956 Olympic Games. After only a few days, in short, Munch had worked his magic on still another continent.

It was a long and tedious trip, and almost no one in the orchestra remembered it as a success. The advance work had been ineffective: The result was impossible timetables and uncomfortable accommodations. Only Munch and his party had Western hotels; the musicians stayed in "traditional" tiny rooms and slept on floormats. They were given, because the Japanese had been so instructed, steak and French fries for every evening meal—"invariably cold." The box lunches came with chopsticks and no forks, and those who wanted to strike out on their own discovered that restaurants were closed by the time the concerts let out. The fifty hours of outbound travel from Boston to Taiwan began the tour by bringing more than one member to the point of collapse. The budget had been underestimated by nearly half; this effectively marked the end of Harry Kraut's rise in the BSO management. (He went on to become Leonard Bernstein's manager.) Tod Perry thought his own job on the line.

For everyone it was too much too frequently. John Fiasca, thirty-seven, was one of two musicians who died, having had a heart attack in Fukuoka. Doriot Anthony Dwyer, who had unsuccessfully pleaded with Munch for permission to travel with the group as far as Japan despite her pregnancy, had a particular reason to be grateful she had not gone. The delivery of her daughter had been complicated, and in retrospect she was grateful to have had Massachusetts General Hospital close by.

Returning to Boston, the orchestra split in two to cover the delayed Esplanade Pops concerts and the Tanglewood opening simultaneously. Munch was content to reestablish himself at Tanglewood, where he wrote to Nicole and Jean-Jacques Schweitzer with memories of the pleasant times they had spent there together: "even the *woodchok* wants to hear from you. . . . On the terrace where we used to eat there's a nest of swallows who don't seem bothered by my presence: the mother sits there roosting tranquilly. . . . The duck on the pond had twelve babies. Only one is left: the turtles ate the others."[28] Fritz, in Strasbourg, encouraged such idyllic pleasures, hoping that after Besançon his brother would come to the country house in Niederbronn—the *boîte à musique*—"where your room waits for you. . . . You'll vacation here instead of on the Mediterranean. . . . The trees are in bloom, the work on the fence advances."[29]

But within a few days Munch had caught cold, "as usual," wrote Judd, "and it settled into his bladder and he is having some discomfort." Two physicians looked him over and said "there is nothing to be alarmed about."[30] Munch went on about his business as the staff kept a wary eye on him. On July 15, 1960, he developed what was described as an "anginal pressure type of pain," and an impending heart attack was feared. The physicians there and in Boston were alerted, but since his EKG was normal, they began to suspect a variety of disorders, including gallstones, hiatal hernia or, in the worst-case diagnosis, "creeping coronary failure."[31] A round of X-rays in early August returned normal results for gall bladder and stomach; there was some evidence of narrowing of the coronary arteries, though. "Still he really looks very well," his doctor reported, "and not the least bit tired as he did at this time last year. His resting between concerts has been the answer."[32]

The new generation of critics, notably Harold C. Schonberg of the *New York Times* and soon Michael Steinberg of the *Globe,* found the Munch style overly predictable and often *passé.* Eric Salzman thought his Mozart showed a disturbing tendency "to alter tempos for expressive purposes" and that speeding up slow movements was "an annoying trick."[33] Allen Hughes considered Munch's Bach "objectionable" but conceded that:

> at this late stage, however, it scarcely seems worthwhile to protest Mr Munch's Bach style very strongly. Year after year, both here and at Tanglewood, he has clung to the notion that the orchestral suites contain pieces to be toyed with, to be made cuter, or lusher, or more dazzling than almost anything you could imagine. The idea, presumably, is that poor Bach simply did not have the wit to include all the ritards, high-speed metronome markings, diminuendos, and so forth, that it takes to make his masterpieces palatable.[34]

Schonberg, who tended to harp anyway, took strong exception to the Berkshire Festival programming announced in April 1961 for the following summer.

He complained that Tanglewood had become routine, its offerings "warmed over" from the main Boston season, their calendars "inbred . . . intermated." It was a "sorry showing . . . slapdash . . . unenterprising," for which there was no excuse—"just as there is no excuse for allowing on the Tanglewood grounds squealing young women dressed in very brief shorts and halters. Tanglewood is beginning to look like Coney Island, and, on Sunday afternoons, to smell and sound like it."[35]

He went on to make a devastating comparison: While Koussevitzky's "presence made itself felt and was an inspiration," Schonberg claimed, "nobody of that stature is around Tanglewood nowadays." In a subsequent letter the distinguished music professor H. Earle Johnson, though noting Munch's stewardship of certain key compositions, complained that "the orchestra has no point of view any more" and that "the few American works, though well selected, were chosen by others than the conductor; no group of composers or performers has had the encouragement and support of a great orchestra as was the case in Koussevitzky's day. We have abandoned national leadership for local titillation. A change is long overdue."[36] It is from this point—not before—that Koussevitzky's shadow begins to darken Munch's reputation.

A certain amount of this critique is simply false and the vocabulary grossly unfair; a certain amount of it, white noise; and a certain amount the inevitable grousing of summer campers. Mutations of taste and performance practice do leave senior conductors behind. And we do sense, beginning perhaps with the return from Japan, Munch suffering from increasingly dramatic episodes of boredom and fatigue, exacerbated by the change in critical climate. (In a photograph published that fall, wearing what is presumably a souvenir Filipino *barong*, Munch seems substantially overweight and looks drawn and puffy.) This retreat from unconditional approval, along with a corresponding rise in American hegemony over the arts, rekindled his feelings of being an outsider. In his morose turns, he could see little reason for not thinking of himself as old, unwell, and away from home.

Yet from other perspectives the role of challenging new work was as robust as ever, the decidedly Munchian choice of new repertoire for 1960–1961 sharply countering Professor Johnson's argument as to point of view. The autumn season opened with the Poulenc Organ Concerto and Stravinsky's *Jeu de cartes*, recorded soon afterward (LSC 2567). Among the premieres were works by two leading American composers: William Schuman's Seventh Symphony in October and Barber's *Die Natali*, three chorale preludes on Christmas carols in December—a seventy-fifth-anniversary commission.

The soloist who filled out the Samuel Barber program was the young Jaime Laredo, who over the course of two weeks played both the Bach A-Minor and the Mendelssohn concertos. He found Munch "sweet, nice, amazing in his talent. Immediately we understood everything about each other." However, he also thought Munch not easy when he became impetuous and much preferred his calmer, slower modes. (Joseph Silverstein told Laredo there was a six-minute difference between two consecutive performances of the Mendelssohn.) He remembers being surprised at how typically Munch would defer to Richard Burgin on matters of string rehearsal and how determined Munch was to use the entire string section for the Bach recording. (The producer, Max Wilcox, talked him out of that.) Laredo remembers thinking that the two recording sessions squeezed in around the Christmas holiday, on the twenty-fourth and twenty-sixth, seemed to define the relentless pace of his newfound celebrity.[37]

In Boston and on the road there were multiple performances of Piston's *Three New England Sketches,* Martinu's Concerto for Two Pianos with French duo pianists Janine Reding and Henry Piette, and the Bartók Viola Concerto as completed by Tibor Serly with Joseph de Pasquale. In January came the premiere of Tcherepnin's *Symphonic Prayer* and the occasion for what proved to be one of Munch's great first performances, the Poulenc *Gloria.*

Munch and Poulenc had had little enough to do with each other since the Piano Concerto a decade before, and it is not clear how much he was aware of the new, perhaps more serious, direction Poulenc's style had taken in the interim. *Le dialogue des Carmélites* and *La voix humaine* had redefined Poulenc and turned, some thought, his impishness into piety. Nevertheless, he continued to adopt an arch tone in his correspondence with Munch: "I would have liked for you to lead my *Stabat* [*mater,* 1951] in Boston, but, *hélas,* you doubtless forgot. You understand that the extraordinary success of my *Carmélites* makes me no less sensitive to these kinds of slights, but I admire and love you anyway."[38]

He was genuinely pleased for Munch to "present my last-born at the baptismal font,"[39] and Munch was looking forward to the European premiere as well, scheduled for the following summer in Strasbourg. Instead, that honor was reassigned by the composer to Georges Prêtre and Rosanna Carteri, with the Orchestre National, in order to have it heard in Paris as early as February. Poulenc blamed the *contretemps,* which both annoyed and offended Munch, on the fact that the commission had come from Mrs. Koussevitzky and the Library of Congress instead of directly from the Boston Symphony—in which case its conductor would have had a stronger claim on the right to introduce the *Gloria* to the French. Poulenc was all the more embarrassed because the best recording of his Concerto for Organ, Strings, and Timpani (Zamkochian, Firth, BSO, Munch) had just been released.[40]

The weather made for a chaotic weekend, and the Friday night of the pair had to be postponed until Sunday because of the snow, but in elegant circles it was the event of the season, drawing Marlene Dietrich, "the Bernstein crowd," and their admirers to Symphony Hall. To open the concert Poulenc had chosen to play his Concerto for Two Pianos with Évelyne Crochet as his second.

The story is best told by the glib-lipped Poulenc in descriptions to Bernac, "*mon petit Pierre*":

Tuesday, 17 January 1961: The forecast is very favorable. [Crochet] is excellent and Monique-like [a reference to Monique Haas], young, likeable, totally seductive, and loves the Concerto. As for the Gloria, if I hadn't come, what curious music they would have heard. Dear, adorable, exquisite Charlie hadn't understood a thing.

Arriving late to the first chorus rehearsal I heard something so unlike my work that my legs collapsed under me in the stairwell. *Excellent* chorus, but Patterson [Alfred Nash Patterson, director of the Chorus pro Musica] isn't the intuitive Shaw, and these good Protestants sing on tiptoe (especially the women) like in London, with an "Oh My Lord" perspective. *All* Munch's tempos were *wrong* (too fast, of course). A volunteer sang Addison's part (she hadn't yet arrived) like an out-of-tune goat. A paleface pianist tickled away at wrong notes. In sum, something to run from, and my poor offspring was about to be stillborn. What a scoundrel music is!!!

I didn't say anything before the break, then I explained all. Patterson, hearing me sing, said, "So, you want it sung like Chevalier." "Exactly." When we began again, I took the piano, the soloist didn't sing anymore, Munch relaxed, and it was perfect. Aaargh. Basically Charlie doesn't understand anybody but Arthur [Honegger] and Roussel. As he's from Strasbourg, dear thing!! I had lunch at his house; it was exquisite. Everybody is adorable here but what a dreary town, where I'm bored stiff despite the radio, TV in my room. New York, quick!

Thursday morning, 19 January 1961: The rehearsal yesterday was *wonderful.* Munch suddenly *friendly;* as for Addison, she's to die for, heavenly, with that warm purity of Negroes. . . . The Gloria is without a doubt the best thing I've done. Not a note to change in the chorus, and at least the women have no trouble with the high B. . . . Here everybody is thrilled and I'm finally emerging from my jet-lag.

Monday, 23 January 1961: And so, my dear, for a triumph it was *a triumph!* You know that because of the snow, the Friday concert was postponed until yesterday, Sunday. Saturday night was OK. Very good, very lovely, success, but Munch less inspired than usual. Yesterday, by contrast, with the critics there, a *sublime performance.* Charlie in a trance, but careful; the chorus amazing, La Addison *unbelievable,* and thus ovation on ovation. They told me this morning that the press was excellent. Marlene Dietrich was there: kisses, photos, and all.

I'm *thrilled,* because this terrific public *gave me points.* I'm already feeling the beneficial effects from the Bernstein camp. . . . Yes, we'd have gone soon enough to your funeral if you'd accepted a Boston engagement. Munch has had enough of it.

And on Friday, January 27, 1961, Poulenc wrote from New York to Munch himself:

> Dear great friend:
>
> Before leaving this snowy land for what I hope will be the sunny Midi, I want to tell you again of my gratitude for the admirable performance. I've rarely been more satisfied. Everything was beyond what I might have hoped for. New York, jealous, hopes it can be arranged for April.[41]

It was, indeed, arranged for April in New York, and before the season was over the Music Critics Circle recognized the Poulenc *Gloria* as the outstanding orchestra-and-chorus work of the year.

On a Tuesday-night concert, January 24, 1961, Roger Shermont, a section violinist, was featured in the Brahms Violin Concerto, the occasion on which Munch lent him the 1734 Stradivarius. The tape suggests a stunning performance, sinuous and resonant: A huge round of "bravos" erupts after the first movement. The offer of the performance was in some measure a goodwill offering to a countryman, since in March the orchestra was scheduled to recognize its twenty-eight-year-old Naumburg Award–winning violinist, Joseph Silverstein—formerly Shermont's stand partner—with multiple performances of the Prokofiev Second Violin Concerto. Munch lent the same instrument to the Polish violinist Henryk Szeryng for performances of the Schumann Violin Concerto, also in March. Szeryng bought the instrument in January 1962 for $40,000. In 1972 he presented it to the city of Jerusalem as the Kinor David Stradivarius—the lyre of David.[42]

Munch attended neither the inaugural reception that President and Mrs. John F. Kennedy gave for 150 leading artists in the nation nor, later, President de Gaulle's glittering reception for the Kennedys at the Élysée Palace—though he had been invited to both. While he went to Montreal for concerts and a vacation, Erich Leinsdorf covered those three weeks in Boston with a dramatic repertoire that included his selection of eleven interludes from *Die Frau ohne Schatten,* the Variations for Orchestra by Luigi Dallapiccola (a sometime visitor to Tanglewood), and Prokofiev's majestic Fifth Symphony—none of these in the Munch repertoire—plus Mozart, Beethoven, Brahms, and extended excerpts from Wagner's *Götterdämmerung.* Leinsdorf was as well received during the February road trip to New York and Washington as he was in Boston. It was this visit, and specifically the enormous impact of the Strauss, that first drew the trustees to the notion that Leinsdorf was well qualified to become Munch's successor. Here was the breath of fresh air many were seeking: new and different, progressive without being avant garde—in a word, Bostonian.

Munch returned in late February with a blockbuster program of his own: Milhaud's *La création du monde* and the complete *Daphnis et Chloé* with the New England Conservatory Chorus. This was one building block of a season focused in part on Milhaud, culminating in a recording of the *Suite provençale* and *La création du monde* (LDS 2625) for the *de luxe* Soria series; the *New York Times* praised the New York performance of the jazzy *Création* for its "Back Bay gentility." In March Byron Janis played both Liszt piano concertos in conjunction with the 150th anniversary of the composer's birth, followed the next week by the return of the Harvard-Radcliffe singers, now under Elliot Forbes, in the Bruckner Te Deum and the Fauré Requiem; the Fauré was offered in memory of the celebrated Harvard music professor Archibald T. Davidson (1883–1961), Forbes's distinguished predecessor. Berlioz's *Roméo et Juliette* closed the season, again followed up with a recording for the RCA Soria label (LDS 6098).[43] Munch had been late in deciding on the soloists for the project—Rosalind Elias, Cesare Valletti, and Giorgio Tozzi; and it had taken both the coincidence of having the Metropolitan Opera in town and Rudolf Bing's intervention in the scheduling details to make the singers available for the concerts on April 21–22 and the recording on April 23 and 24.

Poulenc was correct in his assessment that "Munch has had enough." In March Munch began notifying his inner circle of his irrevocable decision to retire from the Boston Symphony Orchestra. Cabot was distressed: One might even say he was never again the same. On April 2 he wrote:

> Dear Charles:
>   It is very difficult for me to put in words my feelings about your retirement. Your music has given me some of my deepest experiences. The Fauré last night was one. No other conductor has done for me quite what you have. I suspect it comes in large part from you yourself. After all a composer or a performer is best revealed in the music he makes. So you see that when the BSO loses you I lose something very personal. I comfort myself that I shall, if for shorter periods, hear you lead the BSO for many years to come.
>   I am proud of the job I did in getting you to come to Boston. Here is hoping we can find a worthy successor.
>   Your friend,
>   Harry[44]

Olivia Cabot had "hoped that you might reconsider. . . . I am sure that Harry will never be able to feel the same confidence in anyone else. . . . I think you know how much we both admire you, as a man and as a conductor. Come back often. That is our one comfort."[45]

Thus, the 1961–1962 season began, said Harold Rogers, "with the unhappy realization that Dr. Munch will remain but one more year in Boston."[46] Major advances in programming are not to be expected in a valedictory year, though Munch premiered Irving Fine's new symphony and gave a first Boston performance of Haieff's Third. Walter Piston's Seventh, although announced, was not performed until Leinsdorf's first season; Lukas Foss conducted his own *Time Cycles*.[47] By contrast, as though their sinecure would soon expire, a parade of French soloists appeared: Évelyne Crochet (returning from her successful appearance the previous season with Poulenc), Jeanne-Marie Darré, Nicole Henriot-Schweitzer, the great cellist André Navarra in his American debut—and the legendary Viennese violinist, Erica Morini. Otherwise, the signature Munch fare was doled out in one farewell after another: Berlioz and Debussy and Ravel, Honegger and Martinu, Rameau (the *Dardanus* Suite, as arranged by d'Indy) and Handel, Mozart, the Brahms First. In venue after venue, journalists struggled to express the *frisson:* his music as "the antidote to a lot of world problems" (Rochester), Munch as "one of the greatest" (Lexington), "one of the world's greatest living conductors" (Cincinnati), and "the tall, white-haired, benign Director of the Orchestra [who] manages to draw from the orchestra such overwhelming sounds" (Detroit), as well as a "sweeping, powerful performance of Brahms' [First] that doubtless will be long remembered by those present" (Detroit).[48] Harold Schonberg's eloquent, nostalgic essay on the last New York concert—the *Fantastique, La Mer,* and *Daphnis,* three scores in which, "it safely can be said, he is unexcelled"—praised the Berlioz as sinuous and hair raising and the others as in the best traditions of the BSO. "The phrasing is so idiomatic, the textures so right, that the music falls right into place."[49] At the end, in the tumult, he brought Doriot Anthony Dwyer forward to take a bow for her work in the Ravel, but gave no remarks or encores. "Mr. Munch bowed and bowed and then left the stage."

Two significant losses in what was already a year of transition were the deaths of composer Jacques Ibert in Paris on February 5, 1962, from influenza at the age of seventy-one, and of Bruno Walter in Beverly Hills on February 17, 1962, at the age of eighty-five. Ibert had been working on a symphony that Munch had commissioned for the orchestra. Its finished movement, called *Bostoniana,* was premiered in January 1963 during Munch's first return visit to the BSO after his retirement.

In February, March, and April Munch and the Boston Symphony Orchestra made their last recordings together in Symphony Hall, each of them, for different reasons, a treasure of the final months: Franck's *Le chasseur maudit* and the Chausson Symphony (LSC 2647), the haunting Tchaikovsky *Pathétique* (LSC 2683), favorites of Debussy and Ravel (LSC 2668, 2664), and a new *Symphonie fantastique* (LSC 2608).

Planning for the farewell dinner began in December 1961. Invitations were extended to the Munch clan in Europe. Jean-Jacques and Nicole Schweitzer responded with their intent to come; her parents, however, were too old, Schweitzer wrote, and Charles's older brothers were "not too well these days, and the young one [Hans], as a doctor, hesitates to leave his patients."[50]

Menus were solicited from various prestigious restaurateurs, noting always "French service." Foster's, the Boston landmark, was chosen as caterer. Among the venues considered were the Museum of Fine Arts and the Museum of Science. In January, the Isabella Stewart Gardner Museum was made available by special dispensation from the family and proved "irresistibly attractive, combining as it does intimacy, art, and the ghost of Mrs. Gardner."[51] Tod Perry's good-humored letters to the principals talk about "the good grey Dr. Munch" and tell his correspondents that "We would like this to be the most memorable dinner party ever."[52]

It may have been precisely that. On April 15, 1962, there were cocktails, eight hundred hot and cold canapés, oysters on the half shell, cold vichyssoise, filet of beef with mushroom sauce and potatoes O'Brion (deep-fried potato balls, a Boston specialty from the 1918 edition of Fannie Farmer's *Boston Cooking School Cookbook*), green beans amandine, Caesar salad, champagne, French pastry, fresh fruit and cheese, demitasse and tea, and cognac. The guest list numbered nearly three hundred: the orchestra trustees, staff, musicians and their spouses, the museum trustees, and, among the celebrities, Munch, the Schweitzers, the Fiedlers, the Judds, Olga Koussevitzky, the Monteux, and the Leinsdorfs.

The budget of $5,000—"This was mentioned at the Trustees Meeting and generally felt to be reasonable and certainly a jolly good party and worth it"— had included the cost of gifts for Burgin and Munch.[53] A Paul Revere bowl was presented to Burgin "in grateful recognition of the 42 years as concertmaster, 1920–1962, and in warm appreciation of his continuing services as Associate Conductor, 1935– ." For Munch, who loved and collected fine silver, there was a George II silver pie service, London 1734, by John Tuite, chosen from a large selection sent by the leading vendors to the BSO offices on approval.

The speeches included words of welcome from Mr. Gardner, George Zazofsky for the players' organization (that same year Zazofsky had helped organize the ICSOM—International Conference of Symphony and Opera Musicians— and was its first chairman), and two of the trustees. Cabot, of course, presented the principal address:

> We are here tonight to express our admiration and affection for you, Charles Munch, and to tell you in a way as simple and earnest as we can how deeply grateful we are for the thirteen years you have dedicated to the making of music with the Boston Symphony Orchestra.

There are those who have loved your direction because you have opened new vistas which many of us did not know existed in the great music of France; there are those who have been stirred by your zeal in presenting the works of our contemporaries, especially American contemporaries; those who have been exhilarated by the magnificence of your inspiration, the pace and excitement which leave your audience profoundly stirred; and those who remember with serene pleasure the countless slow passages, illuminated by your gentleness and sweetness, yet never lagging, never marred by sentimentality.

For all this and so much more we shall be forever in your debt, and if what we owe you and the Boston Symphony Orchestra cannot be summoned up in a few lines, we still can try to leave an impression and can perhaps do that by recalling what you said to your Orchestra thirteen years ago at our first rehearsal. I am told you said you hoped there would be joy.

There has been joy—joy among all your associates in our Orchestra, joy among all of us who have taken such pride in our "Symphony," a pride in this Orchestra, which we think of as ours, but which in truth has no such narrow bound, for it has won and held the admiration of the lovers of music throughout the world.

To us not the least of your qualities of greatness is that you have fixed in the memories of your players, your audiences, your trustees, the image of that tall, masterful, devoted leader, who was more than a leader. You are one whom we have come to love.[54]

Reading from a handwritten draft, Munch replied:

Dear President, Trustees, Colleagues, Ladies & Gentlemen—

Once more I am deeply moved and very much embarrassed that such a *diner* is given in my honor. (Gift.) Certainly the most precious thing in my life has been the privilege of working for 13 years with such a great institution, in such a great country. But the sad moment is coming now that I must turn this important page. Everything in this world which has a start must have an end. Only the infinite has no end and no beginning.

I thank you with all my heart: our President, Trustees, Management; my dear friends: Judd, Perry, Burkat—and last but not least my dear colleagues who have given me such a support and so much kindness.

I have no words to tell you what I think and what I feel, but you can hear, I hope, what is between my words, what is in my heart, just as I have often heard thanks to you the mysterious music who is between the notes and between the lines. But perhaps it is just this mystery that had created between us a warm and close relationship.

I do not want to evoke here souvenirs. There are so many. But for me there will be so many elements that unite me with you, that I shall certainly never be able to forget them.

I have the conviction that the Boston Symphony will always remain a united family and will keep this so important and unique role for the world of music and for the glory of this country.

Thank you very much for everything and you can be sure [it] is not easy for me to say goodbye and God bless you all.[55]

They had maneuvered successfully past the unspoken difficulty of the evening, which was that Munch was not especially happy to be sharing the spotlight with his concertmaster. An interoffice memorandum from Perry to Cabot had noted that "Leonard Burkat, with his sensitive finger on the pulse of Charles Munch, has just dropped me a memo which says 'Charles Munch . . . would be more honored by a portrait without Burgin. Watch out for shared honors on the April 15th do. I think that's what he really doesn't like about it.' . . . We may have some delicate pussy-footing to do."[56]

His final concert pair was on April 26–27 and featured a highly personal choice of programs: Honegger's *Chant de Nigamon* and Beethoven's Ninth with his preferred soloists: Adele Addison, Florence Kopleff, John McCollum, and Donald Gramm with the Chorus pro Musica. The program book, which would have summarized the season anyway, paused to take stock of Munch's thirteen seasons, as it had done after his fifth and tenth anniversaries. Now it counted 1,046 individual programs over that period, of which Munch himself had conducted 721. These included 39 world premieres, 58 American premieres, and 97 first performances in Boston. The tally of composers by frequency performed is surprising in that Bach holds third place (after Beethoven and Mozart), ahead of Brahms, Ravel, Tchaikovsky, and Debussy. Berlioz is in tenth place, just ahead of Stravinsky and Haydn. Only six of the twenty-six most frequently played composers were French: Ravel, Debussy, Berlioz, Roussel, Fauré, and Milhaud.

At Tanglewood the farewells were repeated—with another lunch, another Paul Revere bowl now presented by the governor of Massachusetts, another farewell to the trustees. His very last concert as music director was on August 26, with Copland's *Quiet City* and another Beethoven Ninth. At the end Munch was joined in final bows by the two other retirees, Richard Burgin and the venerable cellist Jacobus Langendoen. The audience of fifteen thousand broke the record for the Berkshire Festival.

The most striking characteristic of the several dozen oral histories gathered from retired members of the Boston Symphony is their spontaneous focus on Koussevitzky and the legends surrounding him. "Years after he had left, eighty percent of the conversation was about Koussevitzky," said one player,[57] and I found that to be true even in the new millennium. Eventually, or when prompted, they turn to Munch with near identical trains of thought: first, his "penchant for, you know, canceling out rehearsals," then his gentle, kind manner and natural affection for the musicians, the ease with which one played for him. How they learned and then learned to love the French repertoire. "They were peaceful, quiet years," one remarked, in part because "nobody was let go." Clarinetist Pasquale Cardillo suggested both that "maybe we relaxed too much at the beginning" but that Munch deliberately and successfully advanced the performance standards within weeks of his arrival.[58]

"He was a sad man in many ways," Cardillo continued. "He seemed to be a sad-type person. I guess he had his own personal sadness in his life." John Barwicki, double bassist from 1937 to 1987, remembered: "I loved Munch because he was more of a gentleman; he let us be more relaxed. He wanted us to be serious but at the same time to be relaxed. . . . He was the one who made us travel so much."[59]

Many remembered the Bach performances especially, thinking the Saint John and Saint Matthew Passions the most moving works they created together. Bach comes up in their recollections more than does Berlioz. Violist Eugene Lehner suggested that biblical texts particularly inspired the conductor: "Munch was great, absolutely irresistible. . . . He never conducted an oratorio or a Bach cantata but that he was carried away."[60] He remembered Honegger's *Jeanne d'Arc au bûcher* and *La danse des morts* similarly fondly.

All of them, of course, remembered the spontaneity. "You never knew what was going to happen at a concert. Actually it was an exciting thing to have. It made it spontaneous. . . . Many times [when] we played the last movement of the *Fantastic Symphony*, it was like an avalanche going down a steep mountain. . . . The adrenalin starts going and you do it. We got out of those performances and we were exhilarated, absolutely exhilarated. . . . [The Munch years] were exciting, sometimes torturous, but whoever said life is easy? Munch had a flair for conducting, which was wonderful because he got emotionally involved."[61]

The principal oboist, Ralph Gomberg, also enjoyed recalling Munch's instructions to Burgin on asking him to cover for a rehearsal when he felt ill. "What tempo do you want me to take these things in?" Burgin asked. Munch replied "Richard, I don't know myself until I'm on the podium what tempo I'm going to take." Gomberg summarizes: "That, in essence was his approach to music, which was marvelous."[62]

Willis Page, who left the orchestra to pursue a career as conductor in Boston and Japan, remembered Munch calling him in front of the orchestra to present him his ceremonial gold watch. He remarked: "I hope I will always be able to treat the musicians the way Mr. Munch has treated us." Munch responded: "Your job is here, if you'd like to come back."[63]

"He was just a wonderful human being," recalled bassist Henry Freeman. "If there was a mistake made and he made it, he'd point to himself right in the concert."[64] For Tod Perry, "He was a gentleman—I liked him a lot. I found him a very warm friend, and I liked his conducting. I liked the whole repertoire he got us into. . . . It was his thing, and he did it very beautifully."[65]

For not a few orchestral players, Munch was the first distinguished conductor they had ever worked with. Harold Farberman remembered how the Radio City conductors were

> horrendous, one . . . worse than the other. . . . So when I came with Munch, I was really impressed because I felt the electricity of his personality. He introduced me to the French repertoire, and it was a staggering musical experience. . . . I was really taken with how he conducted and what he did. . . . I was not as involved as I am now with the technical side of conducting: . . . mine was a simple reaction to what I saw and felt physically from the podium. It was a physical sensation that compelled me to want to perform to the best of my ability. There was a certain edginess and excitement to his conducting, but it was somewhat unpredictable at times. That gave one the possibility of moving into uncharted territory and actually making a musical performance from excitement and danger.[66]

Farberman was also proud that when Munch became ill and Ansermet, Beecham, Barbirolli, and Dorati filled in, the orchestra never played beneath its ability.

Winifred Mayes would never forget her first *Fantastique:*

> It was just incredible to see the excitement that went on in the orchestra as they tried to follow his excitement, his timing and pacing. . . . It was really an inspiration and a joy to play with him. I thought his timing was so incredible, and the nights when he was *really* on I thought the concerts were absolutely super, and I was swept away. I just could not believe that anyone could take over my whole soul and being, and everyone else's in the Orchestra, and sweep us off our feet the way he did, and the audience, too.

"The only thing I can compare [the Munch period] with," said Roger Voisin, "is the Impressionist period: the splash of color, the big canvas. Sometimes it was a mess, sometimes it was a little too fast. But when it worked. . . . That was a magnificent era of the orchestra." Voisin later added, "It was poetic, and it was always different. You were never bored." He was in a position to know. On one tour they took orchestral excerpts from *Roméo et Juliette.* For the love scene, during which the trumpet is tacet, "I would bring a book or a magazine, so I could read during the twenty-five minutes. But for twenty-eight days I never opened the book. I was completely riveted by that man."[67]

Robert Ripley, who came to the BSO from Cleveland and had a certain chip on his shoulder about the quality of the Boston as he found it, was a naysayer.

He was shocked by the lack of discipline at Tanglewood, by the "fooling around, not paying the slightest attention to the conductor." He thought Munch talked too softly and held his poor English to be one reason the musicians "virtually ignored him, it seemed to me. . . . I was disappointed, but mostly shocked." The interviewer suggested that the recordings told a different story. "Yes," replied Ripley, "but the concerts were something else. And of course the press got a hold of it [the alleged laxity] and New York got a hold of it and the BSO went down. Cleveland was a much better orchestra than Boston in those days. We were just about at the bottom of the big five."[68]

"The press in Boston," Ripley's diatribe continued, "would be constantly comparing Munch's performances to Koussevitzky's. One day Munch all of a sudden said 'I am sick and tired of always Koussevitzky, Koussevitzky, Koussevitzky!'"[69] A number of threads in the Ripley interview of 1999 raise not only eyebrows but also suspicion: the notion that the press was "constantly" comparing Munch and Koussevitzky, for one; for another his suggestion that Munch had hemophilia. (He took blood thinners.) But by the early 1960s there were other detractors, too. Joseph Silverstein was one, thinking Munch "a piece of work" and strenuously objecting to his habit of the closing whip-up.[70] Silverstein's loyalty was, for obvious reasons, to Leinsdorf.

Leinsdorf, for his part, was a conductor for whom the primacy of German repertoire was a matter of faith. His uncharitable assessment of his predecessor—"a musician who found the work too much and who spent thirteen years doing too many concerts and too few rehearsals"—was typical of a dismissive attitude toward colleagues that was part of the reason he and Boston did not work out. (His tenure was five seasons.) Leinsdorf's claim that "*vieux copains* from [Munch's] Paris days were permitted to remain in key musical chairs even though they were no longer able to turn pages," a remark that can apply only to the English horn player, Louis Speyer, is both unkind and untrue.[71]

For the college students from Harvard, Radcliffe, and the New England Conservatory who had the good fortune to encounter Munch over and above the already formidable experience of working with G. Wallace Woodworth, Elliot Forbes, and Lorna Cooke de Varon, the experience was usually life changing. Stephanie Friedman, noted California mezzo-soprano, recalls Munch preparing the recording of *La damnation de Faust* as "a cherub, who smiled and winked at us and didn't come off at all like the grand maestro. He cued us well, was authoritative without being tyrannical; maybe he hummed along." For Friedman and surely for most of the rest, "it was my first experience with a great conductor and was one of the best experiences of my musical life. But then all of my time with Harvard-Radcliffe was—the musical part, anyway."[72]

It was also a privilege, she said, to work with soloists such as Danco, Singher, Souzay, and Gramm, who would give the professionally inclined ones career advice during the breaks. "We knew we were lucky to be singing behind them, but being full of ourselves, thought the chorus was the star of the show. Which, in *La Damnation,* was not so far from the truth. Those choruses still echo in my mind's ear. I really think H-R did them better than [the norm today]. We had all that sublimated hormone matter and youthful (unpaid) enthusiasm."[73]

The more experienced musicians remembered the consistency of the excitement in an orchestra that thought it had already seen all, done all by the time Munch first walked in the door. This was not merely about the institutional and technical advances I have emphasized. It was also about the very way music is made. Vic Firth cast it in terms of his subsequent experience with Boulez on tour: At the outset Boulez had mightily impressed the musicians with his disciplined approach and the profundity of his concept of a work. Inevitably an unflattering connection was made with Munch, who was seemingly less technically equipped, not as smart about the layers of meaning contained in the chosen repertoire. However, said Firth, "by the end of the tour I was bored with Boulez and by contrast could not remember ever feeling that way about Munch."[74]

Charles Munch would stay in fond touch with Henry Cabot and the Perrys for the rest of his life, both on holidays and at other cornerstone life events. He would keep up with his favorite players as circumstances allowed. And he would, after all, be back in six months.

CHAPTER 9

✧

Paris, Again

May 1962–August 1966

L a Futaie (The Plantation) at Louveciennes lies on what was once royal property attached to the chateau of Marly-le-Roi. Here the last of the kings Louis would retreat from Versailles with their personal entourages to enjoy the hunt and days of leisure; here, too, Mme. du Barry, mistress of Louis XV, was given the villa, where she lived permanently after her banishment from court. The Munch estate occupies a portion of what had been du Barry's gardens, and the Schweitzers fashioned their home from one of her stable buildings.

The vine-covered *maison de maître* of three, low-ceilinged stories is not royal at all but a later construction, evocative of the Rhineland or Switzerland. Within, Munch appointed his house with French and English period furniture, and on the walls were treasures from his painting collection: Cézanne, Degas, Dufy, and Sisley in the living room, his seventeenth-century Flemish etchings in his study upstairs, and his Rembrandt and Dürer drawings. There was garden furniture, a long, narrow lawn with trees on either side, and an Airedale, the ensemble broadcasting an atmosphere of "expansive friendliness."[1]

The park overlooks, steeply below, the site of the *machine de Marly*, a miraculous contraption built in the 1680s to draw water from the Seine at Bougival and lift it over the top of the ridge to supply the fountains at Versailles; the arches of the aqueduct are still preserved and can be seen from the estate. Also in Bougival, on the national highway that runs along the Seine, was the popular inn Le Coq Hardi, to which Munch and his guests would often repair for dinner on the spur of the moment, leaving behind the work of not one but two cooks resident at La Futaie.

Nicole Henriot had found the property in the mid-1950s and bought half of it, hoping to talk Munch into retiring there. Appalled by the condition of the grounds and the relative simplicity of the chalet-style house that looked over it, he staged what she called "a big incident"—as much, one suspects, over the notion that he was meant to retire to the country as for any other reason. Eventually, with the cleverness that characterized her quiet management of his best interests, she succeeded in convincing him to buy the other half. Little by little he found himself won over and began to think of the property as a kind of dream world, hidden farther away from rehearsals and concerts, from airplanes and hotels, than was actually the case. He called it home from 1958, when he sold the apartment in the rue Alfred Dehodencq.

In some respects Charles Munch became a country baron. "He made groves; he made hills," recalled Lita Starr, remembering the estate "in all its glory." Each year she arrived from New York to find some new surprise: a fine old table, a round fountain. "Rocks. Old rocks. He even loved rocks, when they were old."

In May 1962 Jacques Lonchampt, music critic of *Le Monde,* was the first journalist to interview Charles Munch at Louveciennes. At the outset Munch focused so much on the property—since the lawn needed rain—that the journalist feared their interview would never get started, but at length he extracted some good material.

"Ici je suis chez moi," Munch began, and *"à Boston je suis aussi chez moi."* He seemed content. After six days he had made no particular effort to get in touch with things Parisian. He was looking forward to Honegger and Dutilleux concerts in Bordeaux, Basel, and Strasbourg; his return to the Besançon Festival; a trip to Japan with Nicole. He was philosophical about his uncertain health: "How can you know a year in advance what you're going to feel like?" The loss of French talent to foreign ensembles (Prêtre to Covent Garden, Baudo to Vienna and Milan) he regarded as the ordinary course of things; he imagined Jean Martinon would have "a tough time at the beginning" in Chicago: "It's a severe city, very German."

He grew animated as he described Boston, trying to explain governance by a board of trustees and the system of private donations that made the BSO stable:

In America orchestras are subventioned by groups of businesses and individuals and run by them on a volunteer basis: They collect the donations. The musicians are considered a capital investment.

Consider: In Paris, at the Société des Concerts, I had, for anything and everything, one secretary. In Boston there are 37: three managers, librarians, and so on. It's always been like that in Paris. You have only to read Berlioz. We are accustomed to getting by with derisory means and producing extraordinary things.

Yes, responded Lonchampt, but what about the notorious tradition of under-rehearsing in France?

> I did indeed have in Boston as many rehearsals as I wanted. But French musicians, who are very strong in *solfège*, often play much better on the first try, sightreading, because they pay close attention and concentrate. Why should we reproach ourselves over the limitations of our country?
>
> Not least because French orchestras are the only ones that stand out from the others. They have a certain color, an inimitable sense of light. Most of the others know how to play loud, but they don't sound as good. French winds in particular are unique: It was they who brought out the exceptional quality of the Boston orchestra: When the Société toured the United States after the War of 1914, under Messager and Gaubert, Boston succeeded in snaring several of the best stands of winds. There were still some there when I arrived.
>
> But why do the Parisians insist on everybody playing Sundays at the same time? In Boston there was a Friday series, a Saturday series, a Sunday one, with different programs. And the house was always full.
>
> In the US the conductor is the only one responsible for choosing the programs. It doesn't occur to anybody to fuss over putting this work or that one on the program. The public, it is true, is more curious and respectful of contemporary music. Thanks to that I was able to do 200 first performances of new works, most of them American.[2]

He talked more about Dutilleux ("there are musicians in whom you have confidence, and I'll do my best for him throughout his career") and Honegger, whose neglected *Chant de Nigamon* would figure in an all-Honegger program with the Orchestre National in Basel that June. Then he looked back at the lawn and upward toward the coming rain. Lonchampt wondered how anyone would succeed in keeping him at home.

Nicole Henriot-Schweitzer tried to do just that. The press failed to take her seriously as an artist, suggesting that without Charles Munch she could not survive. Her friends thought this perhaps self-fulfilling prophecy ultimately affected her playing. The relationship, rather simpler than was commonly supposed, had evolved from *maître–protégée* thirty years before to a workable artistic and domestic symbiosis. Where Munch took care of her and her family in the 1940s, now she took care of him. The goal was to establish a family circle, *tranquillité* and a proper *vie privée* being necessities of the elevated French lifestyle.

However charming this notion, as shared by Munch and the Schweitzers, it was on the whole unrealistic. Practically speaking, there was to be little relief from the star conductor's grueling schedule, little true retirement: Munch and his handlers had already seen to that. There was nothing else he much wanted or was equipped to do. Advancing age had, instead of freeing his artistry, bound him tighter than ever to the routine.

From the last Boston years until his death, Munch's companion while he was in the United States was Lita Kohn, née Starr, an avid art collector and wealthy resident of New York City. They were introduced in 1955 by Mrs. Koussevitzky; their conspiratorial friendship was sealed when they sneaked away from an aristocratic dinner party and went to the circus instead. They soon found themselves meeting for Sunday brunch when Munch was in New York and going on shopping sprees at the most exclusive New York galleries. They collected porcelains, drawings, and old master paintings. "He bought everything. But he was a sincere collector." He reckoned the price of an item in terms of the number of concerts he would need to conduct to pay for it and often used that figure in his haggling with purveyors who had opened their businesses just for him. Additionally, Starr owned the latest audio components, where Munch could come listen for the first time to his Living Stereo discs.

In 1960, while he was in New York, staying, as was his custom, at the Drake Hotel on Park Avenue, he succumbed to a serious bout with flu, and Starr suggested that he move into the apartment farther up Park Avenue, where she and her family lived. "From 1960 until he died, his home in the US was mine, and my home in France was his."[3]

In 1962, she thought, "He needed taking care of." This was the main reason she went with him on the American tour of the Orchestre National that October. She did not go on to Japan but subsequently traveled with him in the United States and Canada, visited France nearly every summer, and accompanied him to the summer festivals. Lita Starr and Nicole Henriot-Schweitzer became intimate friends, and the families are still close. The two of them handled the details of his demise. Lita Starr believed his decision to abandon Boston "a terrible mistake"—not because of their feelings for one another but for what he was giving up artistically. "I loved him, and he loved me, but after all we could go back and forth. There was nothing waiting for him in France. It was nice to be invited back to Boston, but the orchestra was no longer yours." For a year or two afterward he was, she said, "not pleasant—like somebody who gave up smoking."[4]

Munch had given his last concert in Boston on April 28, 1962. On May 8 in Paris, at the head of the Orchestre National, he conducted the anchoring *concert de gala* in the citywide festival commemorating the centenary of Debussy's birth: Hommage de Paris à Claude Debussy. There was a major exhibition at the Bibliothèque Nationale and a published catalogue by the eminent *debussiste*

François Lesure, numerous commemorative volumes, dozens of concerts and recordings, and, of course, a deluxe printed program for the inaugural concert. Nicole Henriot-Schweitzer took the solo part in the Fantaisie for Piano and Orchestra, identified since its inception with her teacher, Marguerite Long, who was no longer appearing in public. The broadcast tape has since been published on compact disc.[5]

Then in late May, still in his first month of "retirement," he headed for nine concerts with the Israel Philharmonic. Following these were the Honegger program in Basel, the Dutilleux Second Symphony in Strasbourg, and, after August in Tanglewood, late-summer festivals—still focused on Debussy—in Besançon and Montreux. Two weeks later he was in New York to begin the American tour of the Orchestre National.

The Debussy centennial concert thus effectively marks Charles Munch's adoption of a new orchestra. This outcome had been carefully plotted in France from the moment it became known that he was thinking of leaving Boston. At the ORTF (French national radio-television) the composer Henry Barraud, who had resurrected the Orchestre National after the war, wooed Munch publicly and privately. As early as December 1961 there had been a recording session of Munch and the National performing Barraud's Third Symphony and the *Bacchus et Ariane* Suite, released by Véga in 1963 (after the clauses that bound Munch to RCA had begun to relax). From that point on, Munch and the National became, as he was fond of saying, family.

On the face of it, it is a strange match: What had been the Radio Orchestra was a workaday organization at best, at worst consumed by political and economic turmoil that is the downside of government involvement in broadcasting and the arts.[6] Its mission, other than a *cahier de charges* that continued to favor compositions by living composers, cannot have been especially attractive to Munch, and it could not approach, organizationally or musically, the sophistication of the Boston Symphony. On the other hand, he could not really pursue an exclusive relationship with one of the venerable concert associations since he was permanent honorary president of the Lamoureux, longtime guest conductor at the Colonne, and ex-president of the Société des Concerts du Conservatoire. (The Société had gone without a permanent conductor since the 1960–1961 season.)

And Munch needed a Paris orchestra as much as the nation needed him. Gavoty noted that "in daily life Munch seems like a person in distress. He floats, he wanders, melancholy and disoriented, like someone deprived of his favorite activity. Onstage, he has his revenge—or, rather, he finds his true nature: . . . he swims, finally, totally happy, and communicates to his musicians his torrential vitality."[7] The theory of his appointment with the Orchestre National was that he would do gala events like the Debussy concert and the bulk of the high-profile traveling and festival appearances. In short succession there would be a Berlioz Requiem to celebrate the fiftieth anniversary of the Théâtre des Champs-Élysées (the historic venue that had seen the first performance of *The Rite of Spring* and by that time many hundreds of orchestral concerts, including those of Koussevitzky, Monteux, and Toscanini), a concert inaugurating the auditorium in the Maison de Radio-France, now called the Salle Darius Milhaud, and so on. He eventually led the orchestra on tours to the United States and Japan and all over Europe.

A robust recording schedule with the Orchestre National was not in the scenario originally presented to Munch—nor was the commercial market central to the mission of the orchestra. By the end, however, there were a half dozen published records of substance, including a prize winner—and after his death, when there was opportunity to mine the archive of broadcast tapes, a major repertoire of "live" recordings began to circulate.

The musicians were his compatriots, all of them French, and hence heirs to a national practice Munch had described as "a certain color, an inimitable sense of light."[8] A few of the players were *vieux copains;* all of them took fond memories of Charles Munch forward to the generation of Paris musicians who would see out the twentieth century. In that respect alone, his affiliation with the Orchestre National is of enormous cultural importance.

The American tour of the Orchestre National in October 1962 began and ended in the new Philharmonic Hall in Lincoln Center, New York, from where it circled to Ottawa, then down through New England and south to Washington, D.C., Norfolk, and Raleigh, on into the Midwest, north to Ann Arbor, and back to New York via Toledo, Detroit, and Syracuse. Following custom, by now long established, he alternated concerts with other conductors, in this case Lorin Maazel and Maurice Le Roux; his program consisted of the Berlioz overture *Le Corsaire,* Milhaud's Serenade for Orchestra, and one or more of his standbys: *Bacchus et Ariane, Daphnis et Chloé, La Mer,* or *La Valse.*[9] This tour was long on drudgery and short on luxury: Lita Starr remembered a motel called The Blue Goose and, in a green room somewhere, a portrait of Mata Hari. One night Munch passed her his baton: "They'll never know the difference."

"Goddamn that Arthur Judson," she remarked of the impresario who had organized the tour.

During the rehearsals in France, Munch had alarmed the organizers by complaining of fatigue and seeming rather distant. As the days went on, however, he caught fire and was soon restored to form. The reviewer in Ottawa said that his concert in the Capitol Theatre was the most extraordinary she had heard in her thirty-four-year career.[10] In Washington, D.C., there was yet another iteration of the Franco-American diplomatic display that had greeted him on nearly every visit, with the dignitaries and socialites enumerated by breathless society columnists. In Raleigh, as the Cuban missile crisis reached its height, admirers sought out Munch at intermission and asked him to substitute the national anthems for the Berlioz *Marche hongroise:* the applause for the *Star-Spangled Banner* drowned out the opening of the *Marseillaise.* For the rest of the tour Munch took particular delight in the anthems, waving his left arm behind him to cue the audience to sing, then turning fully around to conduct the enchanted crowd.

At the closing concert in New York, the French broadcasting service, ORTF, presented Lincoln Center an autographed letter by Berlioz to one of his favorite correspondents, Princess Carolyne Sayn-Wittgenstein, which spoke about American lore. In response the president of the New York Philharmonic observed, correctly, that Berlioz's popularity in the United States was owing largely to the work of Charles Munch. (Ross Parmenter, in the *New York Times,* noted that even so climactic a work as *La Mer* sounded "somewhat thin" in Philharmonic Hall, foreshadowing the long debate on acoustics that would later ensue.[11]) The musicians returned home pleased by their success and surprised at the discovery that nearly every city they had visited had its own professional orchestra. They suspected their draw was merely that they came from old Europe, so it was pleasing that the papers routinely suggested that with Munch they were to be counted among the world's best orchestras.

Munch went on to Montreal in mid-November, since a first priority of his new life was to be able to continue his romance with the Montreal Symphony Orchestra. He had first conducted this group in 1948 and 1949 during his earliest conquests of the New World and had frequently insisted to the BSO trustees that he be allowed to conduct in Canada. He considered the orchestra, said Lita Starr, "a great bunch of guys" and felt at home there—though only half, by his estimation, spoke decent French. The orchestra liked him, too: Starr overheard a group of the men remarking to one another how much better they played when he was in town. Later he agreed to help the organization find a successor to the resident conductor, Zubin Mehta.

Incredibly, for a man supposedly avoiding fatigue, Munch then went directly back to Europe for a concert with the Orchestre de la Suisse Romande in Geneva (December 5, 1962, a first performance of the Dutilleux in Switzerland) and left two weeks later for the Far East. Over a period of twelve weeks he conducted more than two dozen concerts on three continents.

In December 1962 he and Nicole Henriot-Schweitzer were in Tokyo for four concerts with the Japan Philharmonic Orchestra, Akeo Watanabe's young but thirsty new ensemble. The programs covered much of his usual territory—Liszt and Brahms, *Bacchus et Ariane,* the *Fantastique, La Valse*—as well as a Beethoven Ninth with all-Japanese soloists. These concerts, fundamentally different from the tour appearances with the BSO in 1960 and the Orchestre National in 1966, represent the closest interaction between Munch and the orchestral establishment in Japan, thus a moment of substantial cultural exchange, which has since been commemorated in retrospective CDs and a DVD. Jean-Philippe Schweitzer notes the natural affinities that drew Munch toward Japanese culture: his love of ancient civilizations, his knowledge of Eastern painting and ceramics, his admiration for fast-lane technology, and belief in the centrality of recording and broadcasting to modern life.[12]

The television broadcast on December 20, 1962, featured Nicole Henriot-Schweitzer and Charles Munch together in the Liszt E-flat Piano Concerto, the best visual record we have of them.[13] She is, in her late thirties, an altogether handsome woman, almost regal as she sweeps in and out in a glittering, European-style evening gown. The performance is impressive, not just technically proficient in its negotiation of the Lisztian demands but also thoughtful and well shaped, making of the work something considerably more important than a display piece. It is also cool, just short of mechanical as the two of them deliver up one of "their" pieces as they had done so many times before. During the curtain calls they do not acknowledge each other at all, and she takes nearly all the focus. He seems in peak condition. When, at the beginning of the concert, there is to-do about adjusting the height of his stand, he eventually slides it away and goes on. At the end, in a custom he had come to relish, two little girls in kimonos come out with flowers.

Charles Munch returned to Boston as conductor emeritus for the first time in mid-January 1963. (He canceled January dates with the National Orchestra in Washington, D.C., presumably in order to recuperate from Japan.[14]) He was booked for four Friday/Saturday pairs and the associated extras, for a total of thirteen appearances. In the end he canceled March 29–30 and April 2, leaving his place to Monteux.

Inevitably this period of transition brought up delicate matters: gossip, for instance, as to the reasons for his departure. A local physician wrote to *Time* magazine to protest its coverage: "There are many who believe that his retirement was not justified musically and that it represented the political manipulation of a powerful American recording company [RCA]. . . . There are even more who feel that the appointment of Mr. Leinsdorf has thus far brought with it adynamic qualities and lackluster which have been foreign to this great orchestra."[15] Management responded that Munch's retirement had been entirely his own doing. "There was no manipulation or hanky-panky by recording companies or anyone else."[16]

Yet the players, too, speculated as to exactly what had happened. Robert Ripley thought the whole story had never been told, though in the end believed "it was mainly his decision." The goals of the principals—the BSO, Columbia Artists Management, RCA, and, of course, Munch himself—now varied considerably. Munch believed his primary responsibility was to program and create the seventy-fifth-anniversary commissions that had failed to arrive during his tenure: the Leonard Bernstein work and the one movement left behind by Jacques Ibert at his death and now called *Bostoniana*. Munch premiered the Ibert to polite reception on his second program, January 25, 1963.

Also, Munch and his agents were demanding top dollar for his appearances, even in Boston. That summer he required $2,000 for each of four Tanglewood concerts, plus travel and lodging, plus expenses for Nicole Henriot-Schweitzer and $1,500 for her appearance. Tod Perry began to keep notes of his dealings with Ronald Wilford, Judson's successor as head of the conductor division at CAMI: "I told Wilford it was up to him to settle the fee—we'd pay what Wilford asked, but that in my opinion Mr. Munch was being simply an ingrate in asking such fees." In March 1963 Perry left a note in the file indicating his frustration: "I also gave Wilford a little speech on his preventing Munch from being so irresponsible and thoughtless as to lose his friends. . . . We would be hard to lose, but that CM was pushing us pretty hard. The transitional period of an honorable visit this season and next summer was very important. After this summer it really isn't important for him or us whether he comes again, and Wilford should protect Munch from making himself unwelcome or unemployable."[17]

Perry also told Wilford of the advice he had given "our dear friend, Charles Munch" when he canceled his last concerts. "We don't believe that Munch any longer has the stamina to do more than two weeks at a stretch."[18] Wilford responded: "As I believe I mentioned to you on the phone, we have arranged Munch's schedule next year so that he will have at least a one-week rest between each two-week engagement and in most of the two-week engagements he will not have more than five or six concerts."[19]

Wilford, for his part, pushed his clients hard. Lita Starr thus began to attend their conferences so that she could later advise Munch on stumbling blocks: Two pairs of ears were better than one when it came to contract negotiations. (In earlier periods, his wife and then Mme. Margot-Noblemaire had served this function.) During a conference at the Drake Hotel in March 1963, Munch agreed to limit himself to two pairs of programs with the BSO in 1963–1964 but then surprised everyone present by returning to the question of premiering Leonard Bernstein's *Kaddish* Symphony—a leftover obligation he took seriously.

No one knew much about where the *Kaddish* symphony stood or what performing forces it would require. Perry consulted Bernstein's secretary, Helen Coates: "We don't seem to know a great deal about Lenny's piece commissioned by Mr. Munch."[20] She replied to the effect that she did not, either: "On some days Lenny thinks there may be a boys' chorus, too, but on other days he doesn't."[21] In any event it would be in Hebrew.

The Bernstein situation left everyone in a quandary. Cabot wanted Munch to conduct one of the major Berlioz works during his 1964 Boston visit. The New England Conservatory Chorus had to be accommodated, having prepared Debussy's *Le martyre de St.-Sébastien* only to see it canceled when Munch withdrew from his last Boston concert. Bernstein wanted to conduct his own premiere and was being as uncommunicative as Munch at his worst. By May it was still unclear how, when, and by whom *Kaddish* would first be performed—"too many *cuisiniers* in the *potage*," remarked Perry.[22] At length the decision was made to waive the customary right of first performance so that Bernstein might premiere it in Tel Aviv, which he probably would have done with or without permission. Munch would conduct the American premiere at his first Friday-Saturday pair, January 31 and February 1, 1964.

From Boston he continued that February and March 1963 to Chicago, Pittsburgh, and Philadelphia with a repertoire, now all but exclusively French, of the *Dardanus* Suite by Rameau and d'Indy, Fauré's *Pelléas et Mélisande*, the *Valses nobles et sentimentales* and *La Valse*, as well as the symphonies of Berlioz, Franck, and Saint-Saëns. A new generation of radio and television broadcast tapes began to accrue. A Chicago Symphony television broadcast, published on DVD, preserves the *Dardanus* Suite; the stunning Philadelphia radio broadcast of *Daphnis et Chloé* and material from a New York appearance with the Philadelphia Orchestra both now circulate on CD.

His conquest of Philadelphia in March 1963 was thorough. A previous visit in 1957, with a program of Honegger and Roussel, had convinced him of the elevated tastes of the audience there. He thus chose two sophisticated programs that featured not only the Honegger again but also Dutilleux's Second and Barber's *Die Natali*. Harold Schonberg reported a solid match: Going from the Boston to the Philadelphia was, for Munch, like slipping from a Cadillac into a Continental: "two high-priced and luxurious pieces of machinery that operate much the same way."[23] Moreover, Munch and the Philadelphia Orchestra recorded three of his core works for Columbia Masterworks (MS-6253) during the second week of his residency: the *Pelléas et Mélisande* Suite, *Valses nobles et sentimentales,* and the three famous excerpts from *La damnation de Faust.* The result is, indeed, as luxurious as it is unique.

He went home via England and Italy, recording Bizet and Tchaikovsky with the Royal Philharmonic in London, followed two days later by an all-French program in Florence. The Italian market, too, was clamoring for Munch, and it was probably during this visit that officials first promoted their notion that he might lead Debussy's *Pelléas et Mélisande* for the Maggio Musicale. In France he joined up again with the Orchestre National for the Berlioz Requiem in Paris—this made the front page of *Le Figaro*—and a tour to Spain, Portugal, and Chartres Cathedral.

With the Orquesta Nacional de España an important new connection blossomed that summer, as did a personal friendship with its engaging conductor, Rafael Frühbeck de Burgos, later an important guest at the Orchestre de Paris. Nicole Henriot-Schweitzer was popular in Spain, and Munch enjoyed the weather and the lifestyle. The orchestra had its limitations, but it responded quickly and by several accounts profited mightily from his tutelage. His appearances with the Orquesta Nacional continued through December 1967.

The only hint of any tapering off in the 1963–1964 season was that it began a few weeks later than usual. At the behest of André Jolivet, president of the Lamoureux orchestra, Munch had agreed to do the French premieres of Ibert's last works, *Bostoniana* and the *Symphonie marine,* that October: An advance piece in the *Figaro* pictures him with Madame Ibert. In December there was the inauguration of the new auditorium in the flamboyant Maison de l'ORTF on the quais of the Seine beyond Passy. The first half of the program premiered Beethoven's *Consecration of the House* and Seventh Symphony, the latter commemorating the 150th anniversary of the first performance in December 1813. The second half premiered *Pacem in terris,* a ninety-minute work for contralto, baritone, chorus, and orchestra commissioned from Darius Milhaud with text drawn from the papal encyclical of John XXIII—featuring an ecumenism (the composer a Jew, the librettist a Catholic, and the conductor a Protestant) admittedly contrived by the promoters to feed the press. One journalist was put off by the whole event: Owing to the damp, uninteresting acoustics of the new auditorium, the Seventh Symphony was not a success. "Steel attics are not for Beethoven, however functional they may be." The balance was poor, as were Munch's tempos: too fast for the Allegretto, too slow for the finale, where "one's feet never left the ground." He considered *Pacem in terris* a monotonous failure but agreed that Munch had tried to make the best of it.[24]

Yet another elegant woman had emerged as a prominent member of the Munch circle during the 1950s and '60s: Gabrielle Pasquier-Monduit, called Gaby, descended on both sides from important families in architecture and design. (For two centuries the house of Monduit had done the metalwork for architectural monuments, including the Statue of Liberty.) A student and intimate of Marguerite Long, Pasquier emerged from the war a capable and experienced promoter of concerts, especially for Jacques Thibaud, whose mistress she became. At Thibaud's instigation she joined the artist-management firm of Marcel de Valmalète, taking only four clients: Thibaud, the mercurial pianist Samson François, the cellist Bernard Michelin, and Long's protégée, Nicole Henriot;

additionally, in 1946 she became administrative director of the Long-Thibaud Competition. In 1947, again at Thibaud's instigation, she was called, in part owing to her impeccable English, to serve as the French liaison in organizing the Orchestre National's long, troubled tour of the United States (fall 1948): "Not always organized to the satisfaction of the musicians," she admitted, "but superb anyway."[25]

She had thus often encountered Munch in her multiple professional capacities, and after Thibaud's tragic death in a 1953 airplane disaster, she began to take on Munch's travel arrangements. Pasquier met the requirements for keeping him comfortable—wealth, breeding, discreet but undeniable public presence, better English than his own—and she was soon a fixture in the entourage. She was especially fond of Nicole Henriot-Schweitzer and her son, Jean-Philippe Schweitzer, about whom she writes in her 2001 memoir *Chère Marguerite Long*. She told intimates that toward the end of his life they had discussed marriage but that she had mixed feelings about the possibility. Then it was too late.

A three-month sojourn in the United States and Canada in early 1964 was meant by his management to complete Munch's conquest of the American orchestral establishment. In addition to a Boston set in early February, there was a return engagement with the Los Angeles Philharmonic (his first since the 1940s), debuts in Houston and San Francisco (both long put off) and in Toronto—thus effectively locating him in all the major markets since his retirement from Boston. Dallas would come in 1966 and Detroit in 1967. In Boston he was scheduled to premiere the Bernstein symphony and complete his sweep of the local universities by collecting an honorary degree from the New England Conservatory on February 5, 1964.

Readying the *Kaddish* symphony would have been a challenge even in ordinary circumstances: Munch later said the score had the most difficult rhythms he had ever encountered. Given Bernstein's thorough dominance of the New York–Boston axis and the press surrounding his own premiere of the work in Tel Aviv the previous December, there was some degree of anticipation that the Munch version would disappoint. Additional nuance came from the Kennedy assassination, which had occurred while Bernstein was finishing his orchestration. He had added "to the beloved memory of John F. Kennedy" at the head of the autograph score,[26] thus effectively upping the stakes for both Munch and the Bostonians. Bernstein's favorite, Jeannie Tourel, who had sung the premiere, was to have the soprano solo, and Bernstein's wife, actress Felicia Montealegre, would narrate (as she did for the rest of her life). The New England Conservatory Chorus and the Columbus Boychoir of Princeton, New Jersey, completed the cast.

In a move characteristic of his personality, Bernstein cut a week from his New York Philharmonic schedule in order to show up in Boston for the rehearsals, a gesture read negatively by musicians and the press in two ways: its neglect of his own orchestra when he had already been away most of the fall, and his evident doubt as to what Munch might be up to.[27] It was on this occasion that he famously—*Time* magazine gleefully reported it—called down "*Beaucoup mieux, Charles,*" from a balcony in Symphony Hall to a stage full of top-of-the-line players. Then he insisted on taking one of the general rehearsals himself. The performance came off well enough, and the scene onstage at the end, as the musicians engulfed Bernstein, was, according to the *Times*, frenetic.[28]

But the critics found the *Kaddish* symphony rather silly. Michael Steinberg, writing his first essay for the *Boston Globe* and untroubled by the thought of taking on Munch, Bernstein, and the BSO—all three sacred cows if ever there were any—thought the work of "unashamed vulgarity . . . a lava-flow of clichés."[29] His review appeared on Saturday morning. By Sunday night the editors of the *Globe* had accrued dozens of angry demands for Steinberg's dismissal: This they understood to be a good argument for continued appointment. (Steinberg went to work for the BSO in 1976, after twelve years on the attack and having once been banned from Symphony Hall by a vote of the players.) The *Boston Herald,* the *Christian Science Monitor,* and the *Nation* were more positive—the *Herald* commented on "the release of a talent freed from the lashings of its own facility."[30]

Bernstein's thank-you letter managed to be charming and supercilious at once: He hoped Munch would conduct his work often *in French,* "in which case you will find, I'm sure, significance in the text that, you say, escapes you for now."[31]

Munch had been of two minds about taking on the work and had agonized over the decision for months. In the end, his loyalty to the idea of the anniversary commissions held sway. He and Bernstein had never been especially close, but nearly fifteen years had passed since Bernstein had been passed over for the Boston job, and no one could deny the commitment Munch had brought the *Kaddish.* This was the beginning of a perhaps carefully orchestrated *rapprochement.* A few months later they were found staying up all night drinking and singing Berlioz's *Faust* at Lita Starr's piano.

For the next pair at the BSO, Munch had chosen the *Fantastique,* Nicole Henriot-Schweitzer in the Ravel G-Major Concerto, and Roussel's Third. Harold Rogers, in the *Christian Science Monitor,* took the opportunity to address the question everyone was asking:

Was the Boston Symphony disintegrating under Dr. Munch's 13-year tenure as its music director? Now when he returns as a guest we learn that it was a glorious period, that the ghost he strained not at—the disintegration truly went no deeper than a gnat's wing. . . . His concert Friday should go down in history as one of his brightest hours. . . . He has reached that point in his career where he has earned the right to play only the music he loves, the music he does best.[32]

Michael Steinberg, in sharp contrast, wrote:

When I was living in New York in the fifties, I used to imagine Symphony Hall as the scene of a more or less perpetual performance of the Berlioz "Symphonie fantastique," relieved now and again by "Daphnis and Chloe" and "La Mer." A touch of the old days returned with the second week of Charles Munch's recent engagement. . . . All in all, I found [the *Fantastique*] abominable. However, for the benefit of the lady who wrote in last week to object to my failure to report that the audience had liked that which I had not, I append the information that 27 persons shouted "Bravo" and that Munch had four recalls.[33]

Stenberg's essay caused considerable drama offstage. The next day Perry alerted Cabot that:

We may be in some difficulties with Munch. Yesterday he was terribly upset by the Globe review, photostat enclosed. The other reviews which were totally favorable and enthusiastic, as was the audience, were swamped in his mind by this one, and he muttered "abominable, they think I'm abominable" to the Kohns [i.e., Lita Starr and her husband], his New York friends, and said he'd never come back here again, and so on and so on. In the evening when I saw him he said nothing of this, but he fled the hall immediately after the concert, seeing no one and being almost rude.[34]

Perry and his wife went with Munch to the airport and proffered the more-or-less routine invitation to return next year. "He gave me one of those Gallic 'we'll see' sorts of shrugs. I've asked Nicole and the Kohns not to let this idea settle into him, for it would be an outrage for him either not to come back because this twerp wrote in this manner, or that he have the feeling of not having been totally welcome." Perry hoped Cabot would write with reassurances that Boston loved Munch even if one journalist did not. "I must say I am appalled at the brutal, insensitive, presumptuous review. It has been clear that Steinberg was out to show the yokels what a real reviewer is like, but this sort of crudity makes me wild."[35] The overall assessment in Boston was more like Rogers's: pleasure to see him again, with a goodly dose of nostalgia for the joys of a simpler past. (Leinsdorf was already unpopular with the musicians and some of the trustees and made no secret that would not long tolerate the grueling BSO schedule.)

The concerts with the San Francisco Symphony in the War Memorial Opera House were his first as guest conductor there, the long-put-off tit for tat with Monteux. Here, too, critical reaction was mixed. Alexander Fried, in the *Examiner*, "deplored" the all-French program of *Pelléas*, the Ravel Concerto, and the Franck D-Minor: "Munch Concert Goes Pop," as the headline put it. Dean Wallace, in the *San Francisco Chronicle*, wondered of the Franck how Munch could seem "totally convinced that it was the lost masterpiece of the ages. Moreover, he managed to sell this preposterous idea to most of the orchestra and virtually all of the audience." Still, Fried concluded, "On Wednesday, whether he conducted brilliantly or badly (and he did both), there was no question he provided his listeners with a remarkably individual, warm view of the music." A graduate student from San Francisco State booed *La Valse*. When corrected by a patrician, he replied "You can boo a baseball umpire. Why not a conductor?" The shocked lady replied, "But Mr. Munch is a guest in this city."[36]

Earlier in Los Angeles, on the other hand, things had been entirely amicable. Munch had chosen to introduce Walter Piston's Sixth Symphony, following his promise to President Kennedy. Piston had encouraged him by writing that the orchestra consisted of "musicians of the first order, extremely well-seasoned, and who will like you a lot."[37] Munch for his part found the LA Philharmonic under Zubin Mehta much improved and was pleased by the reception of the Piston, which he admired. "It is one of the best of American symphonies. It has a construction, an organism. So often modern composers have no architecture. They build a nice house but not the kind one wants to live in."[38]

Los Angeles Times critic Albert Goldberg, in a full-page feature called "The New Life, Freedom of Charles Munch," had found Munch relaxed and positive at the interview. He was glad to be free to conduct anywhere and to be relieved of the all-night study that preceded first performances. He said he preferred the singles and pairs to the Boston system. "How can you play the Cesar Franck Symphony five times in succession with intensity?"

But this was exactly what he kept agreeing to do. Here we encounter a central dilemma of the orchestra business in the 1960s: Economics demanded many more repetitions of the same event. Doubles became triples, with runouts and festivals. In Boston there were often five or six playings of the same work in ten days. He was to face the same situation with the Orchestre de Paris. Orchestras introduced variety with frequent changes of conductors; conductors like Munch jetted from ensemble to ensemble. This only masked the problem of keeping a program as alive and a reading as spontaneous at the end of the run as at the beginning.

Munch told Albert Goldberg that he was delighted by the opportunity to visit important new cities in his world since that meant new art galleries: He had just been to the Prado and the Escorial for the first time. He said he would decline invitations from the Hollywood Bowl, Ravinia, and Lewisohn Stadium because he did not like outdoor concerts—but then appeared at all of these and at other festivals like them.

He talked broadly of conductors and conducting, what he had learned from Furtwängler, what he himself liked to teach, and his approach to contemporary music. Goldberg led him into one of his few pronouncements on the biggest compositional question of those decades: serialism. "Yes, I play serial music. Why not? This music exists and is important in the development of the art. Whether anything will come of it remains to be seen. I find that it goes against a wall. I cannot go behind it."[39] Finally, with a long trip still before him, he talked wistfully about Louveciennes and his paintings.

He returned home via Toronto and Montreal, with a Saint Matthew Passion, and England, for a Berlioz Requiem at the Leeds Festival in April 1964. There were reservations. The great Berliozian David Cairns described a performance that "narrowly missed being marvellous, but turned out to be no better than a frustrating occasion full of uplifting moments":

> The ingredients were there: a superb and lion-hearted choir; acoustics giving a noble, reasonably clear sonority throughout and an overwhelming one in the two or three places that are meant to be overwhelming; and a conductor, Charles Munch, with long experience of Berlioz's works behind him. It is characteristic of him that this performance was in many ways strikingly different from the recording he made a few years ago. Munch is a byword for unpredictability on the night. When excitement takes hold of him he may do anything. Excitability controlled and shaped can produce a great performance; excitability by itself may produce no more than a lively one.[40]

The spring and summer of 1964 continued at this typically relentless pace: eight concerts in Israel; a second reading of Milhaud's Pacem in terris, this one at Notre Dame Cathedral in Paris; and a trip to the Helsinki Festival with the Orchestre National. In Strasbourg, showing symptoms of overwork, he withdrew from a Ninth Symphony (June 19, 1964) but a week later was in Spain with Nicole and by August was once again on the festival circuit with the Orchestre National: Edinburgh, San Sebastián, Besançon, Montreux. In October 1964 he gave two concerts in Palermo.

If the majority of Munch's touring repertoire was now immutable, by preference of his management and his public alike, he was as interested as ever in travel and discovery. New cities and their orchestras—Naples, Rotterdam, Budapest; the Orquesta Nacional de España, the Royal Philharmonic, the New

Philharmonia—gave him an opportunity not only to proselytize but also to learn new local works: several premieres were still to come. With the major orchestras and the most sophisticated audiences, he would look beyond the steady diet of Berlioz and Roussel and the impressionists. In Chicago he programmed Alexander Tcherepnin's Fourth Symphony; in Los Angeles, the Poulenc *Gloria* (both in March 1965).

Meanwhile, Europeans vied to add him to their recording programs. This was the period of projects for *Reader's Digest,* Erato, London/Decca, and the Deutsche Grammophon Gesellschaft (DGG), leaving us significant works he had not yet recorded, as well as signature pieces with orchestras other than the Boston. Advances in sound engineering and technology were being introduced every few weeks, which meant that each new disc sounded more modern than the last. One had to keep buying his LPs.

The BSO recognized the good sense of allowing Munch to record elsewhere, as it was in everyone's best interest for him to be satisfied with his new situation. On the other hand, RCA Victor meant to insist on its exclusivity clauses. This problem came to the fore when Paris impresario Charles Kiesgen asked the BSO to waive contractual arrangements so that Munch could record the major French repertoire—interestingly, not to include Ravel—for the Guilde Internationale du Disque, an important subscription club of the period. Since RCA did nothing to promote Munch in Europe, Kiesgen noted, the BSO recordings were simply not to be found in the record shops. Munch would be five years beyond his separation by the time the proposed recordings began to appear in 1967. "Being in a good deal of demand for recording in Europe he is eager to do what he can," Tod Perry reported to RCA, "although I am sure he doesn't want to rock the boat on our end."[41] At length RCA secured a legal opinion granting Munch the freedom to record whatever he had not done with the BSO (hence, Bizet, Offenbach, and the Albéniz *Ibéria*). For the rest RCA intended to retain exclusive rights until after 1970. Such findings were honored in the breach: The revelatory Albéniz/Debussy *Ibéria* appeared even though the Debussy work was still in print at RCA. Moreover, off-air semipiracies were creeping into the market: In 1966 a Budapest rehearsal of the *Symphonie fantastique* was published by Hungaroton; the licensed Melodiya live recording of the BSO in the Soviet Union began to circulate in the West. By the mid-60s the exclusivity clause with RCA effectively had little hold.

With Henri Dutilleux there were two red-letter events: the creation of *Métaboles,* a work dedicated to Munch, in January 1965 by the Cleveland Orchestra under George Szell; then a recording in February 1965 of the Second Symphony by Munch and the Lamoureux Orchestra. In August Dutilleux finally wrote with "news of the recording of my Second Symphony, edited last week in my presence":

The engineering, on the whole, seemed to me excellent, and the stereo version gives considerable relief to the two orchestral groups. The soloists are all excellent: Delmotte [Roger Delmotte, trumpet player] really outstanding in his phrase.

The first and second movements are, in my view, especially successful, but even though we had a little more difficulty in editing the third movement, the results are nevertheless quite satisfying. Now it will be necessary to oversee the manufacturing, which should be done in a few weeks. Perhaps we can listen to the first sample together, in September.

What more is there to say, other than my great pleasure at being reminded by this recording of the magic you brought to this work in Boston, and which is yours alone? I was curious to hear the tape recording from Symphony Hall, rather fearing the comparison (since the Paris version was done in record time!). But the Erato recording is not unworthy of the other, and I imagine that you will be happy with it.[42]

Munch had declined his fee "*par amitié pour Dutilleux.*" In 1967 he would record *Métaboles* himself, again for Erato.

Of similar consequence was the November 1965 premiere of the Second Symphony by Marcel Landowski, part of a gala to benefit the rebuilding of the pipe organ in Chartres Cathedral. President Georges Pompidou, André Malraux, and diplomat/scholar Alain Peyrefitte served as the patrons—the very clique that would lure Munch into the next stage of his career a few months later.

To all appearances, then, by the mid-1960s his life had stabilized into a routine built around an extended annual visit to North America, the festivals, and the duties incumbent on a French patriarch. In 1964, for instance, he was appointed, to no one's surprise, president of the École Normale de Musique, where he had once been on the faculty, succeeding Cortot. In May and June 1965 he took the Orchestre National on a widely covered journey to the Soviet Union, attracted as always to the possibility of lessening political difference through live music.

This is not to say that the sharp edges had been dulled or the anxieties softened by some new, reliable serenity. The managers found him more difficult to pin down than ever, and organizational lapses became increasingly common. When no one came to meet him at the train station in Aix-en-Provence, he tongue-lashed the hapless Gabriel Dussurget—the "magician of Aix"—only to be reminded that he had never told anyone he was coming. Offstage, he could be petty over anything from his paycheck to where he stood in a photograph. On two different occasions in film coverage of the BSO in Japan, he can be seen nudging others (Richard Burgin, Leonard Burkat) out of the camera range.

After threatening to skip Boston in 1964–1965 he went back anyway, pairing Honegger's Fourth with Roussel's Fourth. The New York Philharmonic's French-American Festival in July, produced by Lukas Foss, brought summer audiences the Poulenc *Gloria,* a complete *La damnation de Faust,* and both *Daphnis et Chloé* suites. "Mr. Munch, of course, has this music in his blood," wrote Harold C. Schonberg, "being more familiar with it than any other conductor."[43] After Tanglewood, he came back to the New York Philharmonic, thereby helping to guarantee the success of the third Long Island Festival, in August 1965, with a Brahms Second that the audience of thirty-five hundred "adored," responding to the "snorts and foot stamps" to be heard from the podium during the concluding whirlwind.[44]

There was again political significance when Munch and the Orchestre National embarked together for the Federal Republic of Germany in January 1966. France and West Germany were by then staunch allies, the economic powerhouses of Western Europe. Frankfurt, Stuttgart, and Baden-Baden were hardly Leipzig and Berlin, his old stamping grounds. Still, there was something epochal—and very different from the BSO in 1952—about Munch at the head of this quintessentially French organization making its way across the Rhine, playing Beethoven and Schumann as they went.

In February he was off for his annual swing to America: Los Angeles, Dallas, and Boston. Returning to Boston, on the occasion of the orchestra's eighty-fifth-anniversary season, he was greeted with standing ovations before and after the music. The Saint-Saëns Organ Symphony drew wild applause. ("What did Charles play this week?" Monteux asked Harold Rogers backstage at the Met. "He conducted the Saint-Saëns Third." "Well," Monteux replied, "the critics don't like it very much, but Munch and I like it because it is so wonderful for the conductor.") Rogers thought the performance wonderful for the critic, too.[45]

Munch, unusually, turned and addressed the audience, reading from a handwritten draft, as to "the great privilege it has been for me during these many years to conduct the Boston musicians and to feel how they have always shared with me my deep love of music."[46]

The really daring venture of his third period was a production of Debussy's *Pelléas et Mélisande* in Florence during the Maggio Musicale of 1966: four performances at the Teatro Communale during the week of June 18, just weeks before the devastating summer flood. The cast, including Françoise Ogéas, Jacques Jansen, Gérard Souzay, Suzanne Danco, and André Vessières, was perfect for him and for the work. According to Geneviève Honegger, however, he was unable to achieve ensemble in the unfamiliar stage-to-pit array and harbored bad memories of the experience. Nevertheless, one reviewer wrote of "a wonderful performance," and another of a "perfect" account, where Charles Munch kept the orchestra "in a state of nervous reserve, in which there were some moments of extraordinarily effective sound." Both writers seemed impressed that the work was sung in French.[47] From Florence he flew directly to

the Ravinia Festival with the Chicago Symphony, his spirits lifted by the ceremonial, boisterous fanfare he was offered by the Chicago brass—the orchestra's
traditional salute to its favorites.

After Ravinia he disappeared from view for ten weeks, canceling appearances in Israel that were to have included a Berlioz Requiem. The *New York
Times* reported he was having surgery; his intimates suggested a recurrence of
heart trouble. He reappeared in Besançon in mid-September with a virtuoso
program of the *Benvenuto Cellini* overture, Roussel's Fourth, and the French premiere of Dutilleux's *Métaboles*. *Cellini* was later released as recorded live, and
Métaboles was scheduled for a studio recording. At the end of the month Munch
and Nicole Henriot-Schweitzer were in Cologne for a concert with the radio
orchestra, the Kölner Rundfunk-Sinfonie-Orchester. Here Munch had played as
journeyman violinist four decades earlier; whether this and the Berlioz Requiem with DGG the following summer constituted the beginnings of a *rapprochement* with Germans and Germany, he did not say.

CHAPTER 10

c✔ა

The Orchestre de Paris

September 1966–November 1968

M unch turned seventy-five on September 26, 1966. Lita Starr flew to
Europe to surprise him for the occasion and was pleased by his appearance. She was also shocked to learn that he had undertaken to organize and conduct the all-new Orchestre de Paris. It was to be the centerpiece of a national
plan for music in France being developed in André Malraux's cabinet, primarily
by the government's director of music, composer Marcel Landowski. Music in
France was "gravely ill," its symptoms ranging from the conspicuous absence of
the established French conductors, including Pierre Boulez, to the lack of venue,
to the notorious habit the overbooked Paris professionals had of sending substi-
tutes along to rehearse for them.

Charles Munch had so far stayed comfortably at the sidelines of this national
debate since reestablishing himself in France. At the Société des Concerts and
around the Conservatoire, it was known as early as 1963–1964 that a new
national *orchestre de prestige* was on the horizon; by the 1965–1966 season there
had been work actions and political manifestos related to the idea, and early in
1966 the more or less formal commitment emerged to proceed with a plan by
which the Société des Concerts du Conservatoire would dissolve itself and then
reemerge in radically modernized guise as the Orchestre de Paris. It appears that
Landowski approached Munch sometime in the late spring of 1966 with the
proposal. (In one account Landowski places this visit in May 1967, but that
seems too late by a year.) He told Munch of his desire to have an orchestra worthy of France, that only Munch could lead it, and that the nation and his many

disciples in the profession were counting on him. Landowski's polite version of the story suggests that Nicole Henriot was enlisted to help, and during a conversation at Louveciennes, Munch merely smiled "maliciously" in agreement and said, "Let's have a little whiskey."[1]

In fact, Nicole was thoroughly against it and had put up a fuss. He had succeeded in enjoying his new home; his health was uncertain; and he deserved a tranquil old age. The notion that he would return to the Société des Concerts under any guise at all, given his abrupt departure—or dismissal, depending on one's point of view—in 1946 was conceptually dubious, though from the government's point of view it was just as clear that the project could not survive without him. According to Nicole, Malraux and Landowski overtly threatened Munch that if he did not accept, the orchestra would go to von Karajan. This was the turning point: "I'll be damned," he told Lita Starr, "if any Boche will conduct this orchestra."[2]

In all probability it never occurred to him to say no. His ongoing addiction to his work is obvious from the calendar he accepted: By 1964–1965 the raw number of concerts was down—just over two dozen between the summer festivals of 1964 and 1965—but recording dates and the fatiguing international tours were up. He hardly needed the money and by this time in his career was comfortably beyond needing the recognition. Of late, on the other hand, his work had drawn its share of negative criticism, and he may well have had an occasional sense of being put out to pasture. Flattery is a powerful tool, and for anybody with his psychological makeup, the gesture of stepping forward to inaugurate something great because you are the only one who can do it is natural. It seemed in his nation's best interests, perhaps music's best interests, to accept.

With Georges Sebastian, meanwhile, he shared the podium of the Orchestre National for its tour to Japan, enviously following on the conspicuous success of the Société des Concerts under André Cluytens in 1962—the first visit of a French orchestra to Japan. They played *Daphnis* and the *Fantastique,* which Munch had already done in Japan, and *Pictures at an Exhibition,* a work Munch did not conduct. (Simultaneously, Malraux had sent the Venus de Milo to Tokyo.)

The National's three-week tour began in the Metropolitan Festival Hall of Tokyo, on October 8, 1966, with *La Mer* and *Daphnis et Chloé,* preceded by Schumann's Fourth Symphony and the Prokofiev Second Piano Concerto with Nicole Henriot-Schweitzer. The Prokofiev turned out to be a first performance in Japan, and Nicole returned home with an official certification to that effect. The English-language reviewer waxed eloquent over the Ravel and made an intriguing geological observation: "Throughout Ravel's marvelous score—the sumptuous orchestration, the lyrical solo entries, and the tense rhythmic crescendo—Munch sensitively balanced the spectacular and poetical, with the proper amount of tone and intensity to keep our listening imagination completely hypnotized at every turn of the music. (Was anyone aware that an earthquake occurred during the 'Pantomime'?)"[3]

It was clear that Munch, Debussy, and Ravel were the stars. The Prokofiev was held to be at "a lower level of musical distinction" and "less gripping," and the reviewer took Sebastian to task, at the next evening's concert, for a number of shortcomings. He was especially harsh on the *Phèdre* ballet suite by Georges Auric, who, as administrator of the ORTF, was along for the ride:

> One would have desired a less contrived and less pretentious work and certainly one more rewarding. But I suppose it was something of an occasion to have the composer, who traveled to this country with the orchestra in an official capacity, present in the flesh in the Festival Hall. I must not forget to add that Sebastian and the orchestra performed this piece of Kitsch as if it were the "Coriolanus" overture.[4]

Seiji Ozawa, happy to encounter Munch in Japan, remarked, with some insight: "And now your life is easy, you only conduct your favorite music, no more work." Munch replied, "Ah, but there you are wrong. Every day I must study these scores for many hours. Even now I learn something new."[5]

His month of repose, scheduled for November 1966, was interrupted by a memorial concert for the great Marguerite Long, who had died in February. Both piano soloists, Nicole Henriot-Schweitzer and Jean Doyen, had been her students. The program also included *Métaboles* and Henry Barraud's *Offrande à une ombre,* a stark commentary on Paris during World War II—a past shared by Barraud, Long, and Munch.

The American visit began in December in order that Boston, and particularly Henry Cabot, could finally have *L'enfance du Christ* for the Christmas season. The video artifact of this last appearance with the BSO is thus greatly poignant, with more than a hundred old comrades on the cramped stage revisiting a work Munch had first brought them in 1953.[6] John McCollum, the tenor, had been in that first performance; Florence Kopleff, as Mary, was on the RCA recording; Donald Gramm, as Joseph, had appeared dozens of times with Munch and the BSO, notably as Brander in *La damnation de Faust.* The Harvard-Radcliffe ensemble, prepared by Elliot Forbes, exudes the look and sound of the Ivy League in the mid-60s; their collegiate seriousness of purpose is much to be savored. So, too, is the famous Trio of the Young Ishmaelites for two flutes and harp, with Doriot Anthony Dwyer, James Pappoutsakis, and Bernard Zighera. Munch smiles with satisfaction, lets them play it, and, assuming he is off camera, slips a digitalis tablet under his tongue.

His one-day debut in Minneapolis was followed by three sets in Montreal, which included Copland's *Tender Land Suite* and a new Fantasia for Orchestra by the Toronto composer Harry Somers (1925–1969). The Montreal orchestra had been much in the press: Zubin Mehta, overworked with two orchestras, was leaving, and his successor, Franz-Paul Decker, had just been announced. It was noted that the consulting committee had consisted of Mehta, conductor laureate Wilfrid Pelletier, and Munch.

Top-of-the-line soloists fleshed out the winter concerts: Rostropovich and Stern in Montreal, Francescatti in Chicago. The New York Philharmonic concert of February 27, 1967, his fifty-fifth with that ensemble, proved to be his last. "With Charles Munch leading the New York Philharmonic in a French program," Howard Klein asked in the *New York Times*, "how could anything go wrong?" He thought the music making, especially Roussel's Third, "glorious," and the evening as a whole "irresistible."[7]

By the time Munch got back from the United States in March 1967, it was publicly known that he would take on the new Orchestre de Paris. He would be ably seconded by Serge Baudo, with the title of *chef permanent*, and the young conductor Jean-Pierre Jacquillat as assistant. Both Baudo and Jacquillat were percussion players with the Société des Concerts. Baudo had favored Jacquillat as a good solution to overcome the intrigue of a "clot of mediocrities" vying for an assistant conductor position, the better to be in the line of succession should Munch not survive.[8] Among those petitioning for Munch's attention was Roberto Benzi, the former child star, just turning thirty.

For Baudo it was a singular opportunity to work alongside a hero of his youth; indeed, Munch had once tried to woo him to Boston. Baudo recalled:

> During the auditions leading up to forming the new Orchestre de Paris, we were always together, and the days usually ended at his estate in Louveciennes, where we would savor a delicious dinner. During those marvelous evenings, I got to know him better, this generous man, very sincere, and who, despite his age, was fully living out this new adventure. So many plans he had for his orchestra!
>
> His happiness could not mask the deep wounds left by the Parisian musical establishment before he went to Boston. [Not even this task] could overcome this secret anxiety. Doubtless he sensed intuitively the opposition of a certain highly placed administrator at the Orchestre de Paris [almost certainly Georges Tessier, called behind his back the Prince of Darkness], whose collaboration was not thoroughly scrupulous, [a situation that] affected his morale and possibly his already fragile health.[9]

Together Baudo and Munch heard more than three hundred auditions for the new *orchestre de prestige*.

Winner of the competition for concertmaster, or *1r violon solo*, of the new orchestra was Luben Yordanoff, who occupied that seat in the Monte-Carlo Orchestra. He and Munch had met there in the course of an appearance where the rehearsals were superb but the outdoor performance compromised by a *mistral* that kept the musicians lunging after their music as it blew away. Once the appointment was won, Landowski and Munch applied to Prince Rainier of Monaco, who in the kind of ritual played out by European musicians and their patrons for centuries, accorded his concertmaster leave "to represent the glory of Monaco to the world at large."[10] Munch always had a healthy respect for his concertmasters, having been one himself, but seldom sought a personal friendship. Yordanoff, by contrast, entered his inner circle largely by virtue of living not far from La Futaie. The chauffeur would take them to Yordanoff's after rehearsals and concerts, where the conversation that went along with the whiskey was never about the music but mostly about national and international politics.[11]

Disengaging from the Orchestre National could be done only gradually and delicately, for Munch was popular with the players. He was already booked to travel with them to Montreal for the international exposition widely called Expo 67 (the occasion when Charles de Gaulle famously cried "Vive le Québec libre!") and then on to New York, where Stravinsky, eighty-five, was supposed to have conducted *Le sacre du printemps*—a tour shared with resident conductor Maurice Le Roux. (*Le Sacre* was eventually conducted by Martinon.) There were commercial recording sessions with the National scheduled on through February 1968.

Jean Douay, the orchestra's new principal trombonist—who had decided to become a professional musician on hearing Munch and the BSO in Metz in 1952—remembers an atmosphere of jealousy and annoyance among the musicians, who felt they were being abandoned. Munch sensed this, too. "Forgive me," he pleaded during a rehearsal. "They are my friends; you are my family."[12] And from that moment the "stupefying" Munch regained his control. "No one," said Douay, "was remotely like him. *Homme fabuleux*."[13]

The members of the Orchestre National went on to elect Charles Munch their honorary president for life, the traditional mark of respect for a beloved conductor on his departure. Deeply touched, he responded in April 1967, nostalgic about the memories they shared and assuring the players that he regarded the gesture as a signal honor: another strand in a relationship of "deep affection and admiration."[14]

He finished the season with visits to both Israel and Egypt, a long set in Tel Aviv, followed by a concert to inaugurate the new Sayed Darwish Concert Hall near the pyramids of Giza, home of the new Cairo Symphony Orchestra. The performance of a symphony for chorus and orchestra by Abu-Bakr Khayrat (1910–1963) represents what appears to have been the last new work he added to his repertoire. The summer festivals took him to Strasbourg (with Jean-Pierre Rampal) and the very outdoor events in the United States he had said he would decline: Ravinia with the Chicago Symphony, Meadow Brook with the Detroit, and Saratoga with the Philadelphia, then Santander with the Orquesta Nacional de España. In Paris, the Société des Concerts du Conservatoire formally disbanded on June 21, 1967.

Charles Munch was decorated on October 5, 1967, as Grand Officier of the Legion of Honor at his home in Louveciennes. Louis-Pasteur Vallery-Radot (1886–1970), member of the Academy, distinguished physician, and Debussy enthusiast, presided. His grandiose *discours*, taking wing from *Je suis chef d'orchestre*, analyzed the profession from the Munchian point of view: "You can't just study for ten years and have the gift. You have to work from the morning you first set foot in the conservatory until the evening when, exhausted, you have completed the last concert of your career. . . . To be a conductor is not a *métier* but rather a sacred rite." The catalogue of accomplishments noted that Munch himself was proudest of his honorary degrees from Harvard and Boston University and of his new orchestra. "But all these are lesser distinctions. You deserve *la gloire,* and you have it. We admire you, and we love you passionately. On behalf of all of us I say: stay longer among us. Share with us your enthusiasms, your dreams, your feelings. We will be the richer for it."

But it was the remarks of Jean-Jacques Schweitzer, representing the relatives, that captured the family spirit:

> Dear Charry:
>
> Your brother Fritz should be here tonight. But that's not possible, and I'm the one he wanted to replace him on this occasion to express your family's sentiments.
>
> From the very beginning, countless times, you've had it explained to you that you were the runt of the litter. Nobody, happily, took that seriously—certainly not your parents, who were never all that worried about you. But there's a huge difference between not worrying and the joy they would have had tonight.
>
> We should recall your father's happiness, the pleasure and the pride he showed, when in the 1920s he was himself admitted to the Legion of Honor.
>
> As for Grandmother [Charles's mother], one only needed to talk with her a few minutes to learn the latest news you regularly sent. It was easy to see that in her affection "little Charry," as she called you, had a particular place. We can imagine that her looking down on you here today, a high dignitary of our French order, is some compensation for not having been able to be present at the liberation of Alsace, as she had so fervently wanted.

I think also, tonight, of Aunt Vivette [Geneviève Maury, Mme. Munch]. Everybody who knew her understands that the happiness and satisfaction she enjoyed in life owed to the success, the distinctions, you earned.

Dear Charry, you're awfully discreet about the things you have done. Even so, little bits of truth come to light now and then. I remember a few years ago, you had the flu, and you were huddled in your bed with a high fever. I heard you talking to yourself, saying, "I nevertheless helped many people during my life." That sort of thing you would never say in your normal state. I have no idea how many people you have helped across the world, but I know that there's not a single member of the family to whom you haven't, one time or another, one way or another, given a hand.

When I was very small—during the war years—and my father was in a somewhat delicate financial situation, we had a car of which it was said that the chassis was Father's but the rest was yours. It was the first car I ever climbed into.

Not to dwell on me—but that's the case I know the best: without you I would never have met Nicole and we would not have married. And my life today wouldn't have much sense.

From the other end of the spectrum, I remember reading a moving letter from Uncle Albert thanking you for all you had done to help the hospital in Lambaréné.

All of which is to say, my dear Charry, that all your family, and I think particularly of your big sister [Jean-Jacques's mother], rejoices tonight with you.[15]

It was precisely the kind of apotheosis he loathed, but having it take place in the warm surroundings of La Futaie and the intimacy of his family made it more acceptable. And it was good to have these things said to his face while there was still time.

Throughout the summer, the talk in musical circles was that the new organization would never take wing. Orchestral playing had declined too far in France, and Munch was too old and too ill to be able to fix it. Munch himself had his doubts and said merely, "I will do what I can."

Yet a visitor to La Futaie in those weeks suggested that Charles Munch was anything but fragile: "Hale and hearty at 75, he is under no doctor's orders. He enjoys food, wine, and smokes freely."[16] On the auspicious occasion of the first rehearsal for the new orchestra, Bernard Gavoty joined Munch for an interview during the break. Gavoty says he knows better than to ask Munch about the Paris orchestral associations, but what does he think of their work habits? Munch flinches at the word *associations*, then grins as a flood of memories occurs to him. "Well, in any case they could often use more rehearsal: no doubt about that." Then his face softens. "The style of French musicians is—perfection: their sense of sonority, their . . . *solfège*. . . . Give me a little time." Gavoty tries to turn his thoughts to Boston, but Munch deflects the attempt. "I'm convinced, I always thought, that France was the only nation that could create a national sonority and," his excitement rising, "has been able to *keep* it."[17]

The birth of a new *orchestre de prestige* in Paris, which I have described at length elsewhere, was certainly the biggest single event in the arts since the resumption of concert life after the liberation. Every step of the way was covered in a modern press blitz. The *New York Times* suggested that France was at last getting serious about music; Janet Flanner wrote a piece in the *New Yorker* that, in her fashion, managed to co-locate the fiftieth anniversary of the Russian Revolution, the dawn of color television in France and the conundrum of the conflicting SECAM and PAL broadcasting systems, Charles de Gaulle's one-seat majority in Parliament—and the Orchestre de Paris. The fashion magazines made a great to-do over the blue Nehru jackets that Pierre Cardin designed for the orchestra. Munch was said to be "looking plump and fit."[18] *Time* magazine concluded its account with the wry detail that "As one astounded member noted after a rehearsal, some of the men even take their music home to practice."[19]

There were television cameras at the first rehearsal. Virtually every player is dressed in a jacket and tie, and the front desk players rises as Munch enters and shakes their hands. He looks dazzling in a dark sweater and white shirt.

They begin with the second movement of the *Fantastique*. After sixteen bars of introduction he stops, looks to the winds, and suggests: "I think the nuances are marked a little too softly; you can play out a little more, especially at [the scalar fall: he sings to illustrate]; give me the maximum. But the beginning is *beaucoup trop fort. Beaucoup trop fort.*" They respond correctly, and he remarks during the music: "*Voilà.*" Then: "Sssssh. Not yet." . . . [at the falling scale:] "Now. *Now!*"

He stops after the first phrase. "I hear that [in my mind] prettier. You have good violins? *Non?* I recommend that." As a second thought: "*Que voulez-vous?* In Boston there were ten Strads. It makes a difference." Pause. "OK. We do what we can. I start over."[20]

There was a full month of daily three-hour general rehearsals before the first concert, a schedule Munch found to be at the outer limits of his physical strength. (There were to be eight rehearsals and five performances of each set, including runouts to suburbs and schools.) Though he seldom kept the orchestra the whole three hours, he made very nearly every rehearsal. Eight rehearsals and five performances were too much, too, for Francescatti, who would be playing the Brahms Concerto later in the season, with the result that concertmaster Yordanoff had the opportunity to play the solo in three rehearsals and two runout concerts. "We made a party out of it," he said.[21]

On the birthday itself, Tod Perry sent a telegram: "BOSTON FANS CHEER DEBUT ORCHESTRE DE PARIS STOP MERDE DEAR UNCLE CHARLES."[22] Despite a driving rainstorm over Paris, the inaugural concert of November 14, 1967—the

Fantastique, Stravinsky's Requiem Canticles, and *La Mer*—went off without a hitch, an evening Yordanoff cherishes as "one of the most beautiful memories of my life."[23] The front page of *France-Soir* noted "Orchestre de Paris Stupefying for a Newborn" on the left—and on the right,"Johnny Hallyday Breaks His Guitar over His Knee. Before 6,500 Screaming Spectators."[24]

How thoroughly Munch figured in the very identity of the Orchestre de Paris needs emphasizing. The Société des Concerts and the Boston Symphony Orchestra, even the Orchestre National, were well established when he took them over. The Orchestre de Paris was, as the journalists noted, his personal garden, his valedictory masterpiece. He had chosen the musicians and shaped the working arrangements. "He was the source of the fervor, the discipline, and the enthusiasm that was the most important characteristic of the Orchestre de Paris." "He gave us a soul," remarked one of his players.[25]

Many in France believed that the association of a permanent conductor with a frontline orchestra was precisely what was lacking in France. (The Société des Concerts had been one of the last organizations to give in to the vogue of guest conductors.) The concept of the master-sculptor, they held, was what had made the American orchestras great—the long-term associations of Stokowski and Ormandy with Philadelphia, Szell with Cleveland, Bernstein with New York. The same was true in the Germany of Furtwängler and Karajan (whose title in Berlin was "conductor for life"). Both that and the problem of getting the musicians to rehearsal had been fixed.

Almost immediately an executive of the Orchestre de Paris was corresponding with Boston to inquire about methods of moving a major symphony orchestra around the United States, noting that "M. Charles Münch greatly admires your personal manner of administration, which is what prompts me to write."[26] (One journalist reported that an American tour was discussed even before the orchestra was actually founded: It was always imagined that a new Paris orchestra would earn its reputation not in town but on the road.) Clearly Munch was expecting to lead such an expedition.

Yet his engagements with the new orchestra were strictly limited, and his principal associate, Serge Baudo, took many of the runout concerts, while the frequent guests included Martinon, Karl Münchinger, and Paray. Altogether he conducted only five sets with the new orchestra in France, a total of thirty-two concerts. Baudo's assistant, Jean-Pierre Jacquillat, not especially popular with the musicians, took an increasingly prominent role. At times Munch seemed obsessed with his mortality by making repeated references to wanting Fauré's *Pelléas et Mélisande,* with its intimate death march for Mélisande, at his funeral. Rehearsing Debussy, he was prone to observe, *"La Mer, c'est la mort."*

Outwardly he appeared a tower of strength. In December 1967 he traveled to Spain to help the Orquesta Nacional de España celebrate its thirtieth anniversary; in January 1968 he did a complete *Roméo et Juliette* in Boston and a set in Houston; and at the beginning of February came the stunning Debussy session with the Orchestre National, later released as Debussy / Albéniz: *Ibéria*. Leaving one of the rehearsals, however, he suffered a chill that rapidly developed into a pneumonia so acute that he was forced to abandon plans to conduct at the Winter Olympics in Grenoble and, more significantly, to lead his new orchestra on its eighteen-day tour of the Soviet Union (Moscow, Leningrad, Minsk, Riga), accompanied by André Malraux. He was replaced by Paray, Baudo, and Jacquillat. Still fragile, he traveled with Nicole Henriot-Schweitzer to Montreal. In April he made the acquaintance of a last orchestra, the Vienna Symphony, but afterward canceled his appearances, including a planned all-Roussel festival, until Tanglewood in August.

In late September and the first days of October, Munch and the Orchestre de Paris recorded a Ravel cycle with EMI that became "His Last Recordings" (EMI / La Voix de Son Maître CVB 2281–82). There was an almost macabre presentiment in the room that the Ravel Piano Concerto would be the last time Munch and Henriot-Schweitzer would work together, and people remember the sessions as painful and melancholy. The photographs taken of them in the studio that day by are the last ones.

The second season of the Orchestre de Paris, which opened on October 9, 1968, with Isaac Stern in the Brahms Violin Concerto, naturally brought out the tensions that had been masked by the necessity for good behavior in the first. What had at first been deemed an opportunity to rehearse seriously, a proper *travail,* was now thought to be too many rehearsals and recording sessions. (In addition to the Munch recordings there had been sessions with Baudo, Prêtre, and others.) Few guest conductors of note had been successfully booked. There were disagreements between labor and management on many fronts, a curious lack of Beethoven and Mozart on the programs, a single first performance, and no prospects for a proper hall. Above all, the musicians were "haunted" by the question of Munch's succession: They feared him "used up, fragile."[27]

Nevertheless, the Orchestre de Paris was full of courage as it departed on its campaign to secure international approval by virtue of winning over the New World. The ensemble, including Serge Baudo and Jean Martinon, with whom he would share the podium, was photographed at the airplane. It landed in Ottawa on October 16; on October 18 Munch conducted in Quebec City.

Munch had personally chosen Boston as the point of entry for the U.S. portion of the journey. The Orchestre de Paris reached Boston with exactly the same style as the BSO had reached Paris and Strasbourg in 1952. As he took the stage the house rose as one in still another magnificent ovation. "Munch Returns in Triumph," wrote Harry Neville in the *Boston Globe,* while the article in the *Boston Herald Traveler* was headed "Orchestre de Paris, Munch Excel." Neville began his column by citing Virgil Thomson: "French orchestras are the best in the world when they are good and the worst when they are not." He continued:

> The Orchestre de Paris is very good indeed. I am also prepared to believe it is one of the best in the world. Chief among [its particular characteristics] were a beautifully blended, balanced sound and an admirable unanimity of attack and release. Impressive also were the players' very precise intonation and a method of sound production that was never forced, even in moments of climax. The string-sound was decidedly brilliant, and the woodwind sound was characterized by a great deal less vibrato than American audiences are used to. The net result was to achieve a clarity to which we are not invariably accustomed.[28]

McClaren Harris found the Brahms too full of "misplaced Gallic passion" and "leaving too little to understatement" but agreed that Munch was firmly in command and noted that his late-career pairing with the virtuoso Orchestre de Paris was reminiscent of the vintage years of Toscanini with the NBC and Walter with the Columbia. "Its collective tone shimmers with the brilliance one is inclined to associate with the French musical manner—the brass bright, the woodwinds sweet and well-focused, the strings having an almost tangible lushness and incandescent warmth."[29]

New York was widely predicted to be the acid test of the new orchestra. The doubtful, and there were many, thought the orchestra should have had another year to ripen. Munch, too, had his doubts but in post-concert glow proclaimed that "The orchestra has already found its personality, its *sensibilité sonore.*"[30] The black-tie gala at Carnegie Hall, with the *Fantastique, Daphnis et Chloé,* and *Medea's Meditation,* was everything the promoters had desired: Samuel Barber bowed from his box; there was a prolonged standing ovation. Edgar Feder, critic of *France-Amérique,* wrote of a magnificent concert by one of the best orchestras in the world. "It's a good lesson, even for Americans, to hear an orchestra of this quality, with the genial *maître* Charles Munch at its head." However, it was Munch's old friend Alexander Tcherepnin, responding to Bernard Gavoty and his film crew in carefully delivered French, who seemed the most moved:

"I have never heard a public react so directly to music as we have seen tonight in New York. I assure you I never heard such an ovation. My heart trembled with joy: for France, for Charles Munch," whom he reaches over to grasp by the shoulder in a last embrace that carries three decades of warmth, "for French music, and for New York, which had the good sense to recognize it all."[31]

Karajan, at intermission, had been giddy on camera: "It's absolutely fabulous. Munch has had the good fortune to create an orchestra that was already
ripe at the beginning and is of such a perfection that I have but a single desire: to
conduct it. *Fa - bu - leux!*" Munch, reflecting on this singular formulation, was
pleased. "*Ah, ça alors.* From a colleague it's an immense compliment. Worth all
the words of all the critics in the world." What, Gavoty asked him, did Munch
himself think? "Well, *voyez-vous,* I had the impression that we actually made
music."[32]

In Philadelphia, Ormandy said "Marvelous! Absolutely marvelous!" And as
though with limitless vigor, the orchestra continued strong in Washington, D.C.,
with a post-concert reception at the French embassy. Munch was pictured with
the U.S. ambassador to France and his wife, Charles and Claire Booth Luce, and
among the guests were the glamorous Nicole Alphand, who during the Kennedy era had made the embassy the focal point of Washington society (and had
her picture on the cover of *Time*), and Pierre Cardin.

Paul Hume's junior colleague at the *Washington Post,* who found the orchestra "an almost-but-not-quite-great ensemble," got pretty much everything else
wrong. The Munch beat was "never a model of clarity"; his interpretation of the
Fantastique was "too consistent." "I prefer, however, a Fantastic not held so
closely to the leash. Berlioz's turbulent phantasmagoria, it seems to me, deserved
a little histrionic overstatement." He thought Munch perfect for a *Daphnis et
Chloé* that was "overwhelmingly evocative." Then he went on to dismiss the
Métaboles as "a piece of such brilliantly crafted surface, it almost makes you forget that below the surface lies nothing."[33]

In Raleigh on Saturday and Sunday, November 2 and 3, Munch conducted
for the last time: the *Fantastique, Medea's Meditation and Dance of Vengeance,* and
Daphnis et Chloé. The orchestra played in Charlottesville on November 4, while
Munch and his chauffeur-valet went ahead to Richmond and ensconced them-
selves in the landmark John Marshall Hotel. Lita Starr, who had met Munch in
Boston and been "with him every moment of that tour," had flown home to New
York from Raleigh to celebrate her fortieth birthday with her family.

Tuesday afternoon, November 5, he took in the film of *West Side Story,* then
invited Serge and Madeleine Baudo, Luben Yordanoff, and the chauffeur for
dinner. "It was a lovely evening, very gay. He was quite happy, and we had a very
good time."[34] He told Serge Baudo that he wanted to establish an annual Berlioz
Festival in France, and Baudo went on to "regard it as his sacred duty to fulfill the
master's wishes" (which he did).[35] It was election night, and Munch stayed up
late to watch the results, as Richard Nixon narrowly defeated Hubert Humphrey
to become president of the United States. He called Lita Starr in New York at 11
to say happy birthday.

When the valet went to wake him on Wednesday, November 6, he was dead. The medical examiner announced that he had suffered a heart attack in the early morning hours. Munch, he said, had a history of heart attacks and was carrying several prescriptions prescribed by his physician in Paris. The valet's first call was to Lita Starr: "*C'est fini avec M. Munch.*" Starr pleaded with the management not to notify the musicians until she had had time to telephone the Schweitzers in Louveciennes, and it was Nicole who alerted the French government.

Michel Debost learned of the situation in a phone call from a reporter. The oboist Malgloire and the violinist Ollu, walking on the street, were hailed by the timpanist from a passing cab: "*Rentrez vite à l'hôtel. Le patron est mort!*" The orchestra was gathered in the lobby of the hotel and told of the situation. Some of them went to the funeral home to view the body—a memory Debost has a hard time forgetting: "It was terrible to see this beautiful man who had been Munch, so full of life, now all made up to look like some theater person. It was surreal."[36] Ollu thought otherwise: "He was magnificent."[37] From Richmond the casket was flown to New York, where Lita had engaged Frank E. Campbell's funeral chapel to supervise the transfer to Paris on the Air France flight that Thursday night at 10:00 p.m.

The orchestra played its Richmond concert in the Mosque Theater under Baudo and requested that there be no applause. The stricken trombonist Guy Destangue wrote the following back to Paris:

6 November 1968, 11:00 pm

[Richmond, Virginia]

My dear Robert:

I've just finished the most painful concert I've ever played in 30 years in the business. I know that the Orchestre National was also playing tonight and that the terrible news has already reached you.

Our great Charles Münch is gone! He passed away during the night at about 2:30, and his chauffeur discovered the body this morning at 9:30.

At first we were going to decline to play, but then came a message from Madame Nicole Henriot asking us to play the *Symphonie fantastique* because it was the first work the *maître* had conducted with his new orchestra. So we played it for him, with all our hearts. The American public, informed by an announcement, shared our grief perfectly by maintaining an impressive silence.

Imagine how poignant: the ordinary progress of a concert, except that there was no applause, not a single murmur. Same things for the second half, with *Daphnis:* both performances followed by a minute of meditation. Never, I think, has the total silence of the stage and the audience together had such nobility, such power.

Owing to the lack of a second tuba, I played that part in the *Fantastique:* so it fell to my colleague [Fernand] Lelong and me to play the theme of the dead. I thought I would never make it.

During this frightful day, I recalled that I had the honor of belonging to the Orchestre National that he so loved. I was with him all the way and would have followed him to the end of the world.

This afternoon, we went to bid him a last farewell at the funeral home where he had been taken. He was lying there, serene, dressed in his evening clothes. He seemed to be sleeping, and that good smile, his eternal smile, softened his face.

In those moments of enormous grief, I sensed a silent message from you. I felt your thoughts extending to the American soil, and I prayed, there beside him, in your name.

To think that we will never again play *La Mer, Bacchus,* the *Fantastique,* or *Daphnis* together with him breaks my heart. He was the greatest, the best, and nothing, no one, can ever erase his memory. His immense shadow will hover over the stands of dark halls, and we will always sense his presence, no matter what.[38]

It was agreed that the tour would continue under Baudo, Jacquillat, and Martinon and would return from Mexico at the end of the month. In Birmingham, Alabama, on November 14 there was to have been a large birthday cake with a single candle to celebrate the orchestra's first anniversary.

Nicole Henriot-Schweitzer had come to New York and gone with Lita Starr to the funeral parlor. Luben Yordanoff joined them to accompany the casket back to Paris. Once it had reached the salon at La Futaie, the Schweitzers had to return to the airport immediately to complete the customs declarations; Nicole telephoned Gaby Pasquier to come to the house, where she sat alone with "this man who was accustomed to being surrounded by crowds from every corner of the world."[39] The funeral was set for November 12 at the Oratoire du Louvre, the Protestant church where Édouard Maury had once been the pastor and where Honegger's memorial service had been held.

In Boston, on Thursday, November 7, and for the Friday-Saturday pair the programs began with the "Death of Mélisande" from Fauré's *Pelléas et Mélisande* as Munch had so often said he wanted. The audience stood, as of late, noted one journalist, it had whenever he entered the hall. The BSO's press release summarized Munch's American career, alongside a personal if rather stiff statement by Erich Leinsdorf. Tod Perry and Leinsdorf booked passage to Paris, leaving on November 10 and returning on November 13.

Leonard Burkat, who had become a vice president of CBS, went with Tod Perry and Ronald Wilford to call on the Schweitzers at La Futaie. They gathered in the salon, "a room where none of us has ever before known anything but great joy. This time candles, flowers, and a coffin occupied most of it."

"It is so good of you three to come," said Schweitzer. "He so much loved Boston and the spirit of life of all your country."[40]

Speaking at the funeral were André Malraux, Georges Auric for the Orchestre National, Erich Leinsdorf for the Boston Symphony Orchestra, and Marcel

Landowski for the Orchestre de Paris. Luben Yordanoff, in the concertmaster's seat, played the Mozart Adagio and Fugue in C Minor with an orchestra of musicians from the Orchestre National, the Opéra, and the Opéra-Comique. As a *grand officier* of the Legion of Honor, Munch was given full military honors.

Outside the Oratoire afterward, the Americans wondered aloud at the French officials' conspicuous omission of references to Munch in Boston. Leinsdorf reminded them that this had been a state ceremony in the presence of cabinet ministers and other officials of a civilization more ancient and honorable than even Boston's. Munch was after all a French citizen who had died in the service of his country. He had been buried not as a private individual or even as a renowned public figure but as a national hero.

In Boston Henry B. Cabot wrote a lovely essay for the *Boston Globe*, noting that he had had "a part" in choosing Munch:

> He was a truly remarkable man and to my mind a great one: the sort of person whose friendship one coveted and which, I think, I finally achieved in spite of his deficiencies in English and mine in French. . . . He taught us the treasure of French music in general and of Berlioz in particular. It was a wonderful thirteen years. . . . He left us largely, I think, because he could not tell any player he was not up to BSO standards. . . . He was the worst correspondent imaginable.[41]

Cabot would cherish Munch's remark in Boston just ten days earlier that the thirteen years there were among the happiest of his life. Nadia Boulanger, also writing in the *Boston Globe*, took consolation at the thought that he had "departed at the height of his activity, in full glory." It was fitting, in fact, that Munch had died in the United States—and, moreover, on a tour. Jean-Jacques Schweitzer agreed: "This is also the way I feel."[42]

The Boston memorial service was at noon on Thursday, November 14, at Trinity Church in Copley Square, not far from Symphony Hall. (The heavy machinery working next door at the John Hancock building was silenced for the occasion.) Charles Wilson, then assistant conductor at the BSO, led the Barber Adagio, "The Shepherd's Farewell" from *L'enfance du Christ* with the Harvard-Radcliffe singers, and "How Lovely Is Thy Dwelling Place" from the Brahms Requiem with the New England Conservatory Chorus. Those attending included Arthur Fiedler, the Perrys, the board of trustees, the French consul general, Mrs. G. Wallace Woodworth, a delegation from the New York Philharmonic, and retirees from the BSO—along with hundreds of ordinary music lovers.

The primary eulogy was given by the Rev. Theodore P. Ferris, rector of the Trinity Church and a former trustee of the orchestra. Ferris gets a fact or two wrong, but the tone of his remarks rings true:

We are here to remember Charles Munch, the kind of man he was, the music he made for us, and the place he made for himself in our hearts.

He never came very close to many of us. He didn't have to. Music mattered more than anything else to him, and if we loved the music and listened to it, that was all he asked and all we needed.

We could see that he made music for the joy of making it; we could tell that by watching him when he was conducting. His back and shoulders rose and fell with the music when it began to surge and when the climax came, his face, if you could see it, was like the shining sun.

He was a simple man. He went to the peak of fame but was never a prima donna. He had thousands of admirers but never held court and never had a cult of idolizers.

He was a shy man and was never at ease in a crowd. But he loved people and enjoyed the company of his friends, especially if they spoke French or loved music. They were his family and glowed in the warmth of his affection and fun.

He was a quiet man, but in his own way he loved life—not noisily, boisterously, but quietly, heartily. He enjoyed a good meal, a good story, and above everything else a good trip—especially with the orchestra. Every four years the spirit moved him, and the road called, first to France, then to Russia, finally to Japan. But never alone; always his music-makers went with him and shared his excitement and joy.

He was a gentle man. He could be stern if he had to be, but he didn't like to be. It wasn't his nature. It was natural for him to be kind, thoughtful, considerate, and understanding. Seldom has a great artist been at the same time so tender and so gentle.

There is no regret, no sadness in our memories of this man, only gratitude. We are thankful that he came our way; that for thirteen seasons, under increasing difficulties, he gave us the music he loved. We like to think the longer he stayed with us, the better he liked us. We know that our affection for him grew with the years.

We cannot be sad for him. He had no fear of death, and he died quietly without a single distortion of his body or soul. He had put down his baton after the final chord of D major and walked off the stage of life onto the wings where he is free to be himself, to sing, to soar.[43]

The congregation joined the performers for the closing chorale of the Saint John Passion, sung in Arthur Mendel's translation: "Lord, thy little angel send." As though giving full circle to a life that had begun in the lineage of Bach, the BSO's organist, Berj Zamkochian, played the chorale prelude *Wenn wir in höchsten Nöten sein*, BWV 641.

CHAPTER 11

✧

An Eternal Smile

Between Munch and an orchestra there would develop a loving connivance, which would lead to miracles. His smile was irresistible: a smile to encourage a soloist before some difficult passage. A smile in New York, as though to say, "I'm the one with stage-fright, so you'll need to help me out as usual." A smile—pleated face draping down from the silver mane—simply from happiness, radiating the music he loved. And a whole orchestra would be transfigured.

Sylvie de Nussac, in *L'Express*, November 1968

There were loose ends, especially with regard to his bookings. The centenary of Hector Berlioz (1803–1869) was looming large, and with it should by rights have come the opportunity for Munch to savor the fruits of his Berlioz stewardship. The French commemorations were to have opened with Munch conducting a Requiem at the Palais des Sports jointly with his two ensembles: the Orchestre de Paris and the Orchestre National. He was expected in Boston for a week in February. The Orchestre de Paris under his direction was booked for European circuits as well as a full-blown foray to Japan.

Both in France and abroad, the grief of professional musicians was palpable. In a splendid televised tribute to Munch that aired in France on November 14, 1968—a year to the day after the inauguration of the Orchestre de Paris, two days after the funeral—Bernard Gavoty presented the last film clips of Munch, together with recollections from pianist Jacques Février, Landowski, and Dutilleux, then his own lovely eulogy. Dutilleux, weeping, is unable to conclude his remarks; Gavoty's own eyes glisten at the end. There follow sixty minutes' worth of tape from the Orchestre National's appearances in Tokyo (October 1966):

three movements of Brahms's First and *Daphnis et Chloé*. Munch seems to be enjoying himself, smiling at his favorite passages and fine playing, flirting as usual with the kimono-clad flower girls at the end.[1]

Doriot Anthony Dwyer, deeply moved by what Henry B. Cabot had written in his letter to the *Boston Globe* ("Music to him was the breath of life. . . . When [he] took fire and kindled the orchestra, the results were unforgettable."), sent her condolences directly to the Cabots. "As he doesn't have 'family' that I am acquainted with, at least well enough, I am writing to you as a substitute, and I know you are in pain. I wish one would not have to go through this . . . [but] the pain will turn to further enrichment of feeling if you can just stand it for a while. At least I think so."[2]

The Orchestre de Paris tailored its December 7, 1968, concert to his memory: Fauré's *Pelléas et Mélisande;* Martinů's Sixth Symphony / *Fantaisies symphoniques,* composed for and premiered by Munch and the Boston Symphony; and Rostropovich in the Dvořák Cello Concerto, reflecting not only the affection Munch had long entertained for that particular work but also his artistic diplomacy in the homelands of both the cellist and the composer.

Roger Toureau, the beloved chauffeur and factotum, died less than two months later, on December 31, 1968, at his home near the French Riviera. Tod Perry notified the Boston musicians, and the *Boston Globe* published an obituary.[3]

Events thus dictated that Herbert von Karajan did indeed get his hands on the Orchestre de Paris—an outcome strongly favored in influential Paris circles. In Aix that September Karajan conducted the *Symphonie fantastique* and appeared with Jörg Demus and Christoph Eschenbach in Mozart's Concerto for Three Pianos, a program billed as a Munch memorial. Karajan continued as figurehead "advisor" for two seasons, 1969–1971. Daniel Barenboim, Munch's real successor as chief conductor in Paris, from 1975–1976, invested widely in the orchestra's connections with its founder, though he had not known him well. His creation of the Chœurs de l'Orchestre de Paris, under Arthur Oldham, made *La damnation de Faust, Roméo et Juliette,* and *Daphnis et Chloé,* with proper forces, possible—indeed, almost routine. Barenboim was like Munch, too, in keeping his distance from the historically driven performance practices then in vogue, caring little about Beethoven's metronome and continuing to play Bach on the piano.

Barenboim's contribution was not lost on the players. Maurice Bourgue, the oboist, wrote tellingly that the early days of the Orchestre de Paris were a "deceptive hybrid" of young musicians in the presence of a titan: The Munch mystique "masked some real problems: a lack of discipline, poor pitch, imperfect attacks. It became a great orchestra thanks to Barenboim."[4]

In Boston Erich Leinsdorf was, at least in public, sensitive to nuance and *politesse* but disinclined to emphasize the lineage. The usual take on Leinsdorf's brief tenure in Boston was that he was returning drill and discipline to the BSO and leading the repertoire back toward Germany and Austria. When William Steinberg and Michael Tilson Thomas took the BSO to Europe in April 1971, the featured work was Mahler's Eighth, far outside the Munch repertoire.

Nevertheless, the BSO's visit to France in 1971 was the occasion of a memorable reception given by the Schweitzers in Louveciennes for what Munch called *mes trois orchestres:* the Boston, the Orchestre de Paris / Société des Concerts, and the Orchestre National. The players and their spouses, American and French, recall the event as crystallizing their understanding of his legacy: They had been aware of his role in their own careers and outlook but had not stopped to consider how the same personality might have played itself out in groups other than their own. There were agendas, too—for one, the hope of resurrecting an American career for Nicole Henriot-Schweitzer. The members of the inner circle had stationed themselves about the house to discourage souvenir hunters. "It was so hard to hear, again and again that day, how the men worshiped his memory, while Nicole and I had felt so alone in our grief all that time," said Lita Starr, tears welling up in her eyes for the only time in our interviews.[5]

It was Seiji Ozawa, appointed to the Boston podium in 1973, who reconfirmed the Munch tradition there, notably by establishing the Berlioz Requiem as a standard of the repertoire. In 1976–1977 he presented the work in Boston, New York, and Tanglewood (where he appeared for the work in formal black instead of his usual summer whites), then in Paris. He placed a portrait of Munch in the Shed's green room that summer and liked to think: "Maestro Munch is there. I still believe that Maestro Munch listened to this."[6]

Ozawa, who appreciated "the wonderful finesse of color that was the creation of Charles Munch and that was still there ten years after he had left,"[7] kept the Bostonians focused on Berlioz, and for the world at large there were new records (now with Deutsche Grammophon) and television broadcasts. Ozawa recorded the Requiem twice in Boston, and it was to that work that he spontaneously turned after the September 11, 2001, attacks on New York City. He kept Dutilleux's Second in the repertoire as well, and the Poulenc *Gloria,* thus in some way trademarking all these works as Bostonian, like the Bartók Concerto for Orchestra. The personal affinities linking Munch and Ozawa were several, and in terms of longevity and public appeal, wanderlust, and deepening criticism that characterized the last Boston seasons, their stories are quite similar. Ozawa's successor, James Levine, was acutely sensitive to the Boston lineage and drew the public's attention to his orchestra's long association with Berlioz during gala performances of *Les Troyens* in 2008.

The Orchestre de Paris survived and by many measures prospered. Daniel Barenboim led a Berlioz Requiem at the Invalides during the weeklong tenth anniversary of Munch's death, and that fall the four discs the orchestra and its founder had prepared together were released as a boxed set, *Charles Munch et l'Orchestre de Paris*. The post-1969 Berlioz fever was reaching its peak, and the orchestra and its chorus were on the verge of returning to the United States for Paris: The Romantic Epoch, a festival at the Kennedy Center. In the dozens of public papers on Berlioz presented on that occasion, the recorded examples were taken mostly from the Colin Davis Berlioz Cycle for Philips, but the Munch precedents were nearly always referenced. Everybody had learned their Berlioz from Munch.

For Landowski ten years of the Orchestre de Paris meant nothing less than the "renaissance" of musical life in France:

> Without Charles Munch this wouldn't have been possible. For we needed at the time his example of work ethic, technical quality, and discipline, topped off by that spark of genius that, as [actor-director] Charles Dullin said, "lets God settle in." Without Charles Munch French music could never have become what it is today. Such enthusiasm, such respect he brought to scores that needed to establish themselves: Roussel, Milhaud, Messiaen, Jolivet, Rivier! Dutilleux, for instance, was carried to triumph by Munch. . . . As for Honegger, whose humanitarian vision he shared, along with a deep faith that the ritual of live performance was the very *raison d'être* of music, he conducted all the works and created several, always stamping them with that contagious joy he had whenever he was leading something he loved—this giant of a musician who always kept himself above squabbles between schools, thinking always that music could not survive unless it were in accord with the human spirit.[8]

Messiaen and Dutilleux expressed many of the same sentiments. Messiaen, noting that Munch was "taciturn in private life, electric in public," recalled captivating performances of Berlioz but was grateful above all for the export of French contemporary music to the United States. "Orchestral musicians loved him and venerated him. His presence on the podium linked his musicians and listeners to music's encompassing power. One would say of him what the Delphic Oracle said to Alexander the Great: 'no one can resist you.'"[9]

Dutilleux recalled on multiple occasions the Munch credo: "We have to live and work every day as though it's our last."[10] He evoked Munch's bringing his Second Symphony to life in Boston:

> thoroughly happy . . . breathing into it his exceptional sense of phrase, of respiration. It's that same sigh of the visionary Munch, the one left to us, happily, by the recordings of *La Mer*, that he brought just yesterday to the Théâtre des Champs-Élysées in his performance of the *Fantastique* with the Orchestre de Paris. That night, the

young musicians told me how they owed him their understanding of Berlioz the modernist. And the same thing had happened to me, long before, in the Salle du Conservatoire.[11]

Arthur Rubinstein's reflections went back to October 1938, when he joined Munch and the Société Philharmonique in the Second Piano Concerto of Brahms, noting again Munch's role in proving to the Parisians the merit of Brahms, a composer they had not yet understood.[12]

If Munch's return to France in 1962 was rather less heralded than Boulez's in 1976, that was in part because he wanted it that way. It was no less significant, because France really was at a crossroads in art music, and no single celebrity or approach could have resolved it. Charles Munch played his part well: reigning monarch of the podium, guardian of the patrimony.[13] Even Boulez seems to have become resigned to the Orchestre de Paris (though never to the underlying principles of the Landowski plan) and eventually showed up himself to conduct it. What separated Munch and Boulez, who had much in common when it came to philosophy of programming, was largely the difference in their generations: Munch did not look much past Dutilleux, and that idiom was no longer, for Boulez and his followers, anything of great interest. How even to define classical music in France is still much debated: whether the government should be involved in programming and whether there should be subventions to orchestras (or to the radio station France-Musique) at all. Yet Munch clearly would have approved of the robust health of the French compositional establishment today, whose work is now exported widely and followed closely in the world at large. One might hazard the suggestion that there are more living French composers of international stature today than ever before.

By the twentieth anniversary of the Orchestre de Paris, 1987–1988, the founding of the organization and memory of its founder could reasonably be celebrated in a single season. The anniversary concert, on November 14, 1987, conducted jointly by Solti and Barenboim, featured the *Fantastique*. A small exhibition was set up in a gallery adjoining the lobby of the Salle Pleyel, and a team headed by Nicole Salinger published a commemorative book, *Orchestre de Paris*. The poster-sized photographs of Munch with his new orchestra—conducting the first rehearsal in his natty sweater, standing with his players in front of a jetliner on the morning of the fateful trip to the United States—still hang in the office suite. Musicians in the Orchestre de Paris proclaimed that his charisma remained central to their approach, while commemorative issues of *Le monde de la musique* and *Diapason* reviewed his accomplishments and sent readers off to purchase his work on compact disc, the new medium of choice. That season Philippe Olivier presented his *Charles Munch: Une biographie par le disque*, a freewheeling combination of informal historical essays and discography, savaged by Leonard Burkat in *Notes,* the journal of the Music Library Association in the United States,[14] but full of primary documentation nevertheless. It was a decent—and an innovative—first solution to describing the scope of the recorded legacy, insofar as that could be established, from Paris, at the time.

On the occasion of the Charles Munch centenary, in 1991, the Strasbourg musicologist Geneviève Honegger, assisted by the Schweitzers, developed a major exhibit with published catalogue for the sister cities of Strasbourg (November 1992–January 1993) and Boston (Symphony Hall, February–March 1993). Significant retrospectives of the recorded legacy began to appear on compact disc in the late 1990s. Dante LYS offered the substance of the early recordings in twelve volumes (1997–1999), and a *Charles Munch Edition /* *Hommage à Charles Munch* consisted of nine discs from the vaults of the Orchestre National at the ORTF (Auvidis/Valois, 1998). The Japan Victor Company (JVC) developed new techniques for processing the master tapes that made details of the Boston/RCA recordings clearer than before. In 2006 the new conglomerate label Sony BMG Red Seal, Japan, published a forty-volume set, essentially the complete run of stereo recordings with Munch and the BSO. In 2004 Marc-Mathieu Münch, a nephew and well-known professor of comparative literature, wondered whether anyone was still much interested in his uncle. But the ongoing publication and sale of these records, to say nothing of the dozens of web reviewers who treasure one or another of the Charles Munch accounts as their all-time favorite, suggest that his concern was unfounded.

Admiral Schweitzer, who as sole legatee oversaw the disposition of the estate, died in 1993. Nicole Henriot-Schweitzer had gone on to teach at the University of Liège (1970–1973) and the Royal Conservatory in Brussels. She died unexpectedly in 2001, much as Charles had done: quietly, in her sleep. All three rest together in the cemetery at Louveciennes beneath a simple bleached-white headstone, a five-minute walk from La Futaie.

The poetic nature of those last eighteen months, a kind of real-life apotheosis where the so-called retiree found himself again at the center of the nation's musical interests, was not lost on Munch. The Orchestre de Paris was his last artistic testament, and he liked that notion. He was happy enough with the role and to some degree savored the rekindling of long-dormant passions for Paris and its glamour. That this amounted to returning to the bosom of orchestral art in France—the new ensemble was officially the Orchestre de Paris / Société des Concerts du Conservatoire—could easily enough have been promoted as a signal personal victory. Those few who remembered the whole story were too polite to dwell on the details, however, and pretty well everybody was, so far as

I can tell, grateful to see the de facto end of the simultaneous Sunday afternoon concerts. In the *New Yorker,* Janet Flanner wrote:

> For years Paris has been the Sunday seat of four ill-paid, mostly ill-rehearsed orchestras, which all played at the same matinée hour and often played the same programs. . . . Now the outcast Sunday orchestras, on small subsidies, are to be drafted for service in the outer provinces, which have for years been bereft even of such provincial opera-house troupes as used to exist.[15]

In fact, little was left of the old Société des Concerts du Conservatoire except a handful of its best players, most of whom would be gone within a few seasons, and nothing at all of the administrative principles that had hamstrung the organization since 1918. The sound was that of a modern hundred-piece orchestra, with only a few pockets of its old sonority and strategies. The new Orchestre de Paris had breadth and depth and, as Munch soon observed, personality, especially in the woodwinds. The horn playing is proficient as always but newly refined: The Lucien Thévet-like vibrato has disappeared, but the Karajan style of dominating brass, becoming pan-European, has yet to take hold. The percussion is round and tubby, seldom flagrant. Munch's pointed focus on the first violins is unusual, as though the full resonance of the cellos and basses had yet to be achieved.

Not the least of his legacies is *Je suis chef d'orchestre / I Am a Conductor* (1955), which attracted wide attention in the press at the time of its publication. Nothing like it had appeared before, at least in the United States. That kind of volume is no longer in vogue, and the English version, with Leonard Burkat's elegant biographical portrait of Munch and his methods of work, has long been out of print. (The French has been republished twice.) Nevertheless, music lovers of that generation still tend to have a copy on their shelves, into which they've tucked clippings, obituaries, and other souvenirs of Munch at work. In those circles his little book continues to enjoy a certain presence.

With few specifics on Beethoven or Berlioz, very little consideration of technique, and almost nothing by way of musical analysis, the book dwells on the human factors of music making. The players keep turning out to be the main characters. Here is where Munch best articulates his understanding of how an orchestra actually functions:

> Musicians come to play, not to listen to lectures. Say what you must in as few words as possible. Experienced professionals hate to be given lessons. Let them retain some sense of responsibility. Never discourage them. Restore the confidence of those who are in trouble. Do not make much of their errors. Correct them without embarrassing them before their comrades.[16]

That passage was thought, at the time, to make specific reference to Koussevitzky in Boston, but many, maybe most, of the conductors in Munch's direct past—which Koussevitzky was not—might have figured in the train of thought. The brief autobiographical portion is in most specifics reliable. Like any good teacher, Munch warns aspiring conductors against following his own almost haphazard career path, but this is mostly device. His example of long years in the violin section and committing the canonic repertoire to heart amounts to precisely the education prescribed.

Tucker Keiser, in the *Boston Sunday Post,* found all this supercilious and contradictory, complaining that "many of the principles which he sets forth earnestly he ignores consistently"—the written insistence on "perfect clarity of gesture" turning out instead a "frequent spectacle" of movements "that have lost all definition." He denied the magic that audiences found in the Munch concerts and complained about the routine "violence which he brings to non-violent music." He found it self-contradictory of Munch to speak out against "festivals" (single-composer concerts, in the French manner), while "Last year we nearly drowned in Berlioz both in Boston and the Berkshires."[17]

That was thoroughly to confuse fair and unfair critique. More interesting is Munch's essential admission that he prefers inspiration to accuracy—just at the time when the concept of abject fidelity to the published score joined up with musicological theories of "correct" performance practice. Lawrence Morton, in *Notes,* deplored Munch's belief that objectivity without sentiment could not be art and lamented the shortage of conductors "who are eager to *use* musicology where it can be helpful rather than sneer at it because it challenges their comfortable ignorance." Where, he wondered, was such empirical music taking place? ("Certainly not Boston.") But wherever it was happening, "that is where I want to go to hear a few concerts. Just for a change, I would like to hear performances that are only correct."[18]

For the layperson, on the other hand, *I Am a Conductor* offers an inside (and bracingly brief) view of what a conductor actually does. Toscanini worship, extended by then to veneration of Bernstein and Karajan, had elevated the *maestri* to near divinity. Here an avuncular craftsman recounts sleepless nights hovering anxiously over new manuscripts, "face to face with the score." And with stage fright. He dwells at some length on the all-important task of programming. He is broadminded, too, about criticism: how inevitably it wounds but how, in the end, it is up to the public to decide. Albert Goldberg of the *Los Angeles Times* wrote that *I Am a Conductor* gets closer to the heart of the matter than the previous efforts, the work of Berlioz, Richard Strauss, Felix Weingartner, Hermann Scherchen, and Max Rudolph having been either polemics or textbooks.[19]

The overarching theme is by now familiar: the conductor as humble servant, the vocation as a sacred calling—a life of hard labor, ecstasy, and sacrifice.

Charles Munch continued generous to the end, even while he worried incessantly about his income and the cost of things. His Renoir red-chalk drawing, a study of a female nude, had gone to the Fogg Museum at Harvard in 1959. He had sent two fine porcelain figurines by Joseph Hannong to the Boston Museum of Fine Arts in 1951. Other pieces he gave away on the spur of the moment. Because a certain amount of the Maury family art had become mingled with his own, he offered Vivette's sister, Juliette Ebersolt, anything she might want from his collections, but she was too embarrassed to respond at all. He gave a niece three fine *objets d'art*, including a Ming-dynasty vase. (Not all of his treasures were, in the end, authentic.)[20] These gestures and countless like them were, like the story of the family car in wartime, not meant to be noticed. His Lamoureux fees he returned since the ensemble was in financial straits; when asked to help a nascent or struggling orchestra—the New Philharmonia, the Japanese establishment, and, of course, the Orchestre de Paris—his instinct was always to say yes.

After all, his personal code held that music is the only thing that matters.[21] He articulated this point to the students at Tanglewood in 1954:

> The spirit of music that unites us here is not an illusion, but rather a revelation. The power of Music lies in the fact that it reveals to us beauties which we cannot find in any other sphere, and the comprehension of these beauties is not transitory, but rather a reconciliation with life itself. Art is the essence of the consciousness of man; it is the "élan vital" of his realization. And Music, more than any other art, contributing directly to the happiness of human beings, must occupy the highest place in life.
>
> The aim of educators, schools, conservatories is to have an exchange of experience.... There must be a persistent sense of dedication to the causes we live for. The Artist, in every branch of art, thought, and science, is the bearer of inspiration and strives for beauty, joy, and goodness.[22]

These values, he believed, are the most meaningful thing we have to pass on to future generations: music and musicians better our daily lives. Artistic expression, he thought, was "the true language of Life." Music, he knew, would "elevate us over our miserable human condition." It would restore our faith in humankind if only we would listen closely for its messages, always "with that marvelous amazement of a child dazzled by the lights of a Christmas tree."

Faith in humankind also meant establishing liberty and peace for common people. Munch was as significant a voice as any conductor's in advocating political and social advances for ordinary people. Some of his specific actions were courageous: his covert activities in Paris during the Occupation; choosing a woman and then a black man for the Boston Symphony. Some were audacious (the trip to the Soviet Union); some simply symbolic (the concert in Cairo). The principles behind them were elementary. They cost him no second thought at all.

Too often his smile gave way to the loneliness that was never far off. Nobody, even those who loved him and whom he loved in return, got deeply enough into his psyche to know all the reasons for it. Obviously there was the trauma of two wars between his native cultures; there must have been regret, too, over the nature of his marriage. His religious faith had been sorely tried by real life. What would always bring him out of these anxious musings was the game afoot: musicians in pursuit of beauty. Without a live orchestra, he was restless and irritable.

Being loved in return, though not a necessary commodity for a conductor, was in his case not an inconsequential dividend. He did not seek the adulation that draws lesser spirits to the podium, but that is often where he found the energy to go on. Toscanini and Bernstein and Karajan left behind much larger personae. Nonetheless, seeing and hearing Munch play Berlioz and Debussy and Brahms again reminds us that on the podium he was always their equal. His amiable human approach brought results. John Corigliano Sr., longtime concertmaster of the New York Philharmonic, put it simply: "When he conducts, I feel that I'm looking into the face of God."[23]

ABBREVIATIONS

BNUS	Bibliothèque Nationale et Universitaire, Strasbourg
BSO	Boston Symphony Orchestra archive
BSO programs	program booklets for Boston Symphony Orchestra, published weekly, paginated continuously, bound annually by season
ChimP	Francis Poulenc, *Correspondance 1910–1963*, ed. Myriam Chimènes. Paris: Fayard, 1994.
CM	Charles Munch
CM, *Conductor*	Charles Munch, *I Am a Conductor* (New York: Oxford University Press, 1955)
CSM	*Christian Science Monitor*
GHCM	Geneviève Honegger, *Charles Munch: Un chef d'orchestre dans le siècle: correspondance*. Strasbourg: Nuée Bleue, 1992.
HBC	Henry B. Cabot
HCS	Harold C. Schonberg
int.	interview
let.	letter
NJJS	Collection Nicole and Jean-Jacques Schweitzer
NYHT	*New York Herald Tribune*
NYT	*New York Times*
OD	Olin Downes
TDP	Thomas D. (Tod) Perry Jr.

NOTES

INTRODUCTION

1. Gilles Cantagrel and Claudette Douay, *L'Orchestre National de France: L'album anniversaire, 1934–1994* (Paris: Radio-France / Van de Velde, 1994), 60. This version places the incident in Edinburgh with the Orchestre National.
2. G. Y. Loveridge, "Munch, New Conductor, Brings Joy to the Boston Symphony," *Providence Sunday Journal* (Jan. 29, 1950).
3. See www.musicinthemail.com/classicalconducting/munch.html.
4. Let. Poulenc to Pierre Bernac, Jan. 23, 1961, GHCM 323–24.
5. Marcel Landowski, "Preface," GHCM 5.
6. CM, *Conductor*, 13.
7. Int. Michel Debost, Sept. 20, 2004.
8. Philadelphia Orchestra, *The Centennial Collection: Historic Broadcasts and Recordings, 1917–1998*, 12 CDs (Philadelphia Orchestra Association 1999), vol. 4, track 3 (rec. Mar. 4, 1963).
9. Virgil Thomson, "The Koussevitzky Case," *NYHT* (Feb. 23, 1947), in Virgil Thomson, *Music Reviewed, 1940–1954* (New York: Vintage, 1967), 106–109. Claude Samuel, "Charles Munch, vingt ans après," *La lettre du musicien* 65 (November 1988), 11.
10. "Charles Munch Answers a Letter," *Boston Herald* (Nov. 3, 1957) (from mimeographed press release, BSO); rpt. in BSO programs 1957–1958, 323–24.
11. Cyrus Durgin, "Turangalîla, or Love in the East Indies, or a Messiaen Afternoon," *Boston Globe* (Dec. 3, 1949).
12. Michel Debost, "Charles Munch, ou le don de soi," *Diapason* 221 (October 1977), 30–31.
13. Andrew L. Pincus, *Scenes from Tanglewood* (Boston: Northeastern University Press, 1989), 15.
14. Yves Dentan, "Avec le maître," *Réforme* (Mar. 23, 1968).
15. CM, *Conductor*, 94.
16. Int. Agnès Schoeller, Aug. 29, 2007.
17. Janet Baker-Carr, *Evening at Symphony: A Portrait of the Boston Symphony Orchestra* (Boston: Houghton Mifflin, 1977), 136.
18. See Eric Salzman, "Shell Dedicated at Tanglewood," *NYT* (July 13, 1959); see also "Charles Munch and the Boston Symphony Orchestra: Brief Fact Sheet," mimeographed (obituary) press release, Nov. 6, 1968, with one version of how the Charles Munch Fund was established, BSO.

19. Jacques Lassaigne, *Dufy: Étude biographique et critique* (Geneva: Skira, 1954), 81.
20. Let. CM to Fritz Munch, Dec. 10 [1945], GHCM 168–69.
21. Samuel, "CM, vingt ans après."
22. *Charles Munch Conducts NY STEREO*, February [23,] 1967, CD Disco Archivia 1357 [off air] [n.d., c. 2005].
23. Let. HBC to editor, *Boston Globe* (Nov. 7, 1968).
24. CM describes this system in a letter to Martini, Sept. 3, 1940, GHCM 135–36. The dossier marked "Compositeurs" remains more or less intact.
25. See D. Kern Holoman, *The Société des Concerts du Conservatoire, 1828–1967* (Berkeley: University of California Press, 2004).

CHAPTER 1

1. Henri Strohl, *Le Protestantisme en Alsace* (Strasbourg: Editions Oberlin, 2000), 413 (citing Robert Will).
2. Albert Schweitzer, "Ernest Munch, as I Remember Him," in *Music in the Life of Albert Schweitzer*, ed. Charles R. Joy (New York: Harper, 1951), 37.
3. Ibid., 38.
4. Ibid., 39.
5. Ibid., 40–41 (translation edited).
6. Strohl, *Protestantisme,* 414.
7. A. Schweitzer, "Ernest Munch," 35–45.
8. Jean Daltroff, "Quatre grandes figures de la maison de musique S. Wolf à Strasbourg (1825–1960)," *Annuaire de la Société des Amis du Vieux Strasbourg* 29 (2002), 137.
9. See Geneviève Honegger, *Le Conservatoire et l'Orchestre Philharmonique de Strasbourg* (Strasbourg: Oberlin, 1998), 25–47.
10. Ibid., 28.
11. Ibid., 55.
12. CM, *Conductor,* 17. Clarification from G. Honegger.
13. Ibid., 20.
14. Ibid., 18, 19, 20.
15. Let. Célestine Munch to Fritz Munch, May 29, 1919, GHCM 32.
16. Sophie Maury-Monnerat, *Du Léman au Limousin: Journal de Sophie Maury-Monnerat, femme de pasteur, entre 1888 et 1919* (Paris: Pensée universelle, 1989).
17. Maury, *Journal,* 112–15.
18. Ibid., 139 (often acts out), 141–42.
19. Ibid., 184.
20. Lili sold it to Yehudi Menuhin, who passed it on to Herbert Axelrod; it was played for a time in the late 1990s by Leila Josefowicz.
21. Geneviève Maury, *L'enfant à la charrue: Huit contes Limousins du temps de guerre* (Paris: Meynial, 1918).
22. Maury, *Journal,* 281.
23. Ibid., 237.
24. Ibid., 141.
25. Int. Agnès Scholler, Aug. 29, 2007.
26. See, for instance, "Boston Symphony 75th-Anniversary Press Book," mimeographed press release 1958, BSO.

27. Maury, *Journal,* 242.
28. CM, *Conductor,* 20.
29. Let. Ernest Munch to CM, June 29, 1918, NJJS.
30. Ibid.
31. Let. CM to Albert Schweitzer, Sept. 17, 1938, GHCM 113–14.
32. Ibid., 196.
33. Ibid., 196–97.
34. Munch, "Albert Schweitzer," x.
35. Let. Célestine Munch to Fritz Munch, Feb. 10, 1919, GHCM 29–30.
36. Ibid.
37. Ibid.
38. Let. Ernest Munch to Guy Ropartz, Apr. 2, 1919, GHCM 31–32.
39. CM, *Conductor,* 21.
40. Ibid., 20.
41. Ibid., 21.
42 *Les Dernières Nouvelles d'Alsace,* Apr. 4, 1922.
43. Ibid.
44. Munch, *Conductor,* 21.
45. In 1964 he told a journalist he had served nearly twenty years as a concertmaster: "nine years in Strasbourg, one year in Cologne, and nine in Leipzig" (Albert Goldberg, "The New Life, Freedom of Charles Munch," *Los Angeles Times,* Jan. 26, 1964). The correct figure is four in Strasbourg (beginning as principal second), one in Cologne, and six in Leipzig.
46. Let. Célestine Munch to CM, March 20 and 22 [1925], GHCM 43–44. Honegger has this pair a year too late, in 1926, but Friday was March 20 in 1925. The correctly dated later from Ropartz to CM, June 3, 1926, refers to his decision to resign definitively from his Strasbourg positions, from which he had until then been on leave.
47. Wilhelm Furtwängler, *Notebooks 1924–1954,* ed. Michael Tanner (London: Quartet, 1989), 32 (Boston and Philadelphia), 36 (prized dogs).
48. Goldberg, "New Life, Freedom," Jan. 26, 1964.
49. Let. Karl Straube to Fritz Munch, July 4, 1925, GHCM 40–42.
50. Ibid.
51. Let. Guy Ropartz to CM, June 3, 1926, GHCM 45–46.
52. Let. Célestine Munch to CM, June 18, 1926, GHCM 46.
53. Let. Otto Klemperer to CM, Aug. 31, 1927, GHCM 50–51.
54. Kurt Hessenberg, "A Brief Autobiography" (English translation of the "Kleine Selbstbiographie"), which opens *Kurt Hessenberg: Beiträge zu Leben und Werk,* ed. Peter Cahn (Mainz: Schott's Söhne, 1990); see http://cassandrarecords .com.
55. Let. Célestine Munch to CM, May 26, 1929, GHCM 58.
56. Bruno Walter, *Theme and Variations,* trans. James Austin Galston (New York: Knopf, 1946), 288.
57. ZED, "Le Concert du Gewandhaus de Leipzig au Palais des Fêtes," *Les Dernières Nouvelles d'Alsace,* June 2, 1931.
58. See Harry Lapp, *Livre d'or du Festival de Musique de Strasbourg: 51 années de festivals* (Strasbourg: Société des Amis de la Musique de Strasbourg, 1989).

59. CM, *Conductor,* 22.

60. Ibid., 23.

61. Let. Wilhelm Furtwängler to CM, Dec. 28, 1931, GHCM 67.

62. Let. Leipzig Gewandhaus Orchestra management to CM, Aug. 31, 1932, GHCM 71–72.

63. Let. Célestine Munch to CM, May 26, 1929, photocopy BNUS.

64. Let. Célestine Munch to CM, Aug. 11, 1932, photocopy BNUS.

65. Let. Célestine Munch to Fritz Munch, Sept. 5, 1932, GHCM 72.

66. Charles Munch, "Address of Charles Munch at the opening exercises of the Berkshire Music Center, Tanglewood, 5 July 1953," handwritten mss. in French and English, typescript, and version published in *1953 Berkshire Festival* program book, p. 6, NJJS.

67. CM, *Conductor,* 23.

CHAPTER 2

1. Virgil Thomson, "Kusevitsky, Conductor: The Risen Russian Suggested for Boston," *Boston Evening Transcript,* Feb. 8, 1922; in Anthony Tommasini, *Virgil Thomson: Composer on the Aisle* (New York: Norton, 1997), 103.

2. Suzanne Demarquez, "M. Charles Münch" [rev. of Nov. 1, 1932], *Courrier musical,* Dec. 1, 1932, 438–39; in GHCM 73–74.

3. CM, *Conductor,* 23–24.

4. Célestine Munch to CM, Jan. 1, 1933, photocopy BNUS.

5. Célestine Munch to CM, Jan. 29, 1933, photocopy BNUS.

6. Thomas Mann, *Tonio Kröger, suivi de Le petit monsieur Friedemann, Heure difficile, L'enfant prodige, Un petit bonheur,* trans. Geneviève Maury (Paris: Stock, 1924); Hermann Hesse, *Knulp, suivi d'Un Conte et de La fontaine du Cloître de Maulbronn,* trans. Geneviève Maury (Montrouge: Schmied, 1949); Waldemar Bonsels, *Maïa l'abeille et ses aventures,* trans. Geneviève Maury (Paris: Librairie Stock, 1925); Karin Michaëlis, *Bibi: Vie d'une petite fille,* trans. Geneviève Maury (Paris: Stock, 1930).

7. Alfred Szendrei, *Dirigierkunde* (Leipzig: Breitopf & Härtel, 1932).

8. See Israel J. Katz, "Alfred Sendrey (1884–1976): In Memoriam," *Musica judaica* 1 (1976): 106–108. Aladár Szendrei / Alfred Sendrey is not to be confused with his son, Al (Albert) Sendrey (1911–2003), who became a sought-after Hollywood arranger and orchestrator.

9. CM, *Conductor,* 24.

10. Let. Paul Bastide to CM, August 1939, GHCM 129–30.

11. On Irène Aïtoff's recollections see GHCM 141–42; see also Philippe Olivier, *Charles Munch: Une biographie par le disque* (Paris: Belfond, 1987), 59–60.

12. Henri Dutilleux, *Music—Mystery and Memory: Conversations with Claude Glayman,* trans. Roger Nichols (Burlington, Vt.: Ashgate, 2003), 40. These include the Dance of Ariadne and Bacchus (reh. 111–3 to 113+4; note the interesting misprinted meter signature 19/8 for 10/8) and a big chunk of the Bacchanale (118–4 to 128+6) and other details.

13. Let. Roussel to CM, Apr. 12, 1933, GHCM 77.

14. GHCM 77 (citing *Diapason,* 1965).

15. Let. Roussel to CM, Jan. 14, 1934, GHCM 81–82.

16. Let. Roussel to Yvonne Gouverné, Nov. 30, 1936, GHCM 97.

17. Let. Roussel to CM, Jan. 30, 1937, GHCM 101–02.

18. Yvonne Gouverné, "Les échos du temps passé," *Zodiaque: Cahiers de l'atelier du Cœur Meurtry,* April 1959, 21–22; see GHCM 102–103.

19. Charles Bouvet, "Concerts Siohan (13 janvier)" [1934], *Le Ménestrel,* Jan. 19, 1934, 21.

20. Charles Bouvet, "Concerts Siohan (17 février)" [1934], *Le Ménestrel,* Feb. 23, 1934, 71.

21. Jean Lobrot, "Concerts Siohan (24 février)"[1934], *Le Ménestrel,* Mar., 1934, 82.

22. Joseph Baruzi, "Concerts Siohan (samedi 24 mars)" [1934], *Le Ménestrel,* Mar. 30, 1934, 129.

23. Maurice Imbert, "Les concerts symphoniques à Paris" ["chez Siohan," Jan. 13, 1934], *Courier musical,* Feb. 1, 1934, 70–71.

24. Maurice Imbert, "Les symphoniques" [Lamoureux, Jan. 12–13, 1935], *Courrier musical,* Feb. 1, 1935, 58.

25. Ibid.

26. Arthur Honegger, "Le festival Claude Debussy," *Comœdia,* June 13, 1941, 3.

27. Suzanne Demarquez, "Orchestre de la Société Philharmonique de Paris," *Courrier musical,* Jan. 1–15, 1935, 22.

28. Denyse Bertrand, "Société Philharmonique de Paris (8 décembre)" [1935], *Le Ménestrel,* Dec. 13, 1935, 382–83.

29. Denyse Bertrand, "Société Philharmonique de Paris (21 décembre)" [1935], *Le Ménestrel,* Dec. 27, 1935, 398.

30. Review of Munch-Levy recital, Mar. 11, 1936, *Les Dernières Nouvelles d'Alsace,* Mar. 12, 1936.

31. See let. Albert Schweitzer to CM, June 30, 1936, GHCM 96.

32. Arthur Honegger, in his 1954 address called "The Musician in Modern Society," in Geoffrey Spratt, *The Music of Arthur Honegger* (Cork: Cork University Press, 1987), 469.

33. GHCM 109, quoting *La nouvelle revue française* (1941).

34. Fred Goldbeck, "*Oriane la sans égale,* de Florent Schmitt (concert Münch)" [Feb. 12, 1937], *Revue musicale,* no. 172 (February 1937), 123–25; in GHCM 103–104.

35. See Jacques Feschotte, biographical notice on CM in program for concert of Mar. 31, 1939, BNUS.

36. Michel-Léon Hirsch, "Hommage à Roussel (13 octobre)" [1937], *Le Ménestrel,* Oct. 22, 1937, 278; in GHCM 107–108.

37. F., "London Concerts: BBC Contemporary Concert," *Musical Times* 79(1139), (January 1938): 58.

38. Fred Goldbeck, "Concert Münch" [Dec. 2, 1937], *Revue musicale,* no. 179 (December 1937), 424–28; in GHCM 108.

39. See *Kapralova Society Journal* 4, no. 1 (Spring 2006): 8.

40. Munch, *Conductor,* 33–34.

41. Henri de Curzon, "Société des Concerts du Conservatoire" [Mar., 1938], *Le Ménestrel,* Mar. 11, 1938, 71.

CHAPTER 3

1. GHCM 111.
2. CM, remarks to Orchestre Philharmonique de Paris, May 1938, ms., NJJS.
3. Antoine Elwart, *Histoire de la Société des Concerts du Conservatoire Impérial de Musique* (Paris: Castel, 1860), 287.
4. Paul Bertrand, "Le 'Requiem' de Berlioz (16 juin)" [1938], *Le Ménestrel,* June 24, 1938, 171.
5. Jean-Philippe Mousnier, *Paul Paray* (Paris: L'Harmattan, 1998), 43.
6. "Menu du dîner offert à Leurs Majestés Britanniques Le Roi George VI et La Reine Elizabeth, jeudi 21 Juillet 1938," BNUS.
7. Let. Albert Schweitzer to CM, July 16, 1938, GHCM 113.
8. Let. CM to Albert Schweitzer, Sept. 17, 1938, GHCM 113–14.
9. Henri de Curzon, "Société des Concerts du Conservatoire" [Mar. 11, 1938], 71.
10. Jacques Feschotte, biographical notice on CM in program for concert of Mar. 31, 1939, BNUS.
11. Saint Louis Symphony Orchestra program, Dec. 29, 1939. The *New York Times* was unaware of the change. See "With Some Orchestras," *NYT* (Oct. 8, 1939), and "Notes Here and Afield," *NYT* (Dec. 24, 1939).
12. Let. CM to Martinu, Sept. 3, 1940, GHCM 136.
13. CM, remarks to Société des Concerts, September 1938, ms., NJJS; see GHCM 136–37.
14. Deirdre Bair, *Simone de Beauvoir: A Biography* (New York: Summit, 1990), 251; cited by Kate Fullbrook and Edward Fullbrook, *Simone de Beauvoir and Jean-Paul Sartre: The Remaking of a Twentieth-Century Legend* (New York: Basic Books, 1994), 145.
15. See, for instance, Jeffrey Mehlman, "The Boston/Vichy Connection," *Salmagundi,* no. 135/136 (Summer 2002): 213–25.
16. Int. Agnès Schoeller, Aug. 29, 2007.
17. The Noblemaire Principle of 1921, treating fair pay for foreign employees of international organizations, is named for an uncle, Georges Noblemaire (1867–1923), chair of the commission of the League of Nations where it was formulated.
18. Let. Furtwängler to CM, Feb. 28, 1939, GHCM 124–25.
19. Let. Furtwängler to CM, Apr. 6, 1940, GHCM 134.
20. Let. Furtwängler to CM, Aug. 4, 1941, GHCM 142–43.
21. Let. Furtwängler to CM, Sept. 25, 1942, GHCM 148–49.
22. Rossenthal and Dutilleux, in interviews long after the fact, said they could not remember Munch taking an active part in the clandestine meetings, but this stands to reason, given his disinclination to take an active part in any kind of meeting; see Guy Krivopissko and Daniel Virieux, "Musiciens: Une profession en résistance?" in *La vie musicale sous Vichy,* ed. Myriam Chimènes (Brussels: Editions Complexe, 2001), 333–51.
23. Minutes, Nov. 16, 1941; see Holoman, *Société des Concerts,* 452–53.
24. Let. Pierre Capdevielle to CM, July 4, 1942, GHCM 148.
25. Dany Brunschwig, "Hommage de la Société des Concerts du Conservatoire au Maréchal Pétain," *L'information musicale,* Dec. 22, 1942, and as a separate leaflet distributed at Conservatoire concerts.
26. Let. Ropartz to CM, Nov. 23, 1946, GHCM 179. Honegger, "Le festival Guy Ropartz" [Jan. 24, 1943], *Comœdia* (Jan. 30, 1943): 5.

27. Honegger, "Concerts du dimanche" [Feb. 28, 1943], *Comœdia* (March 6, 1943): 5.
28. Let. Martinon to CM, July 23, 1943, GHCM 153–54.
29. Harry Halbreich, *Arthur Honegger: Un musicien dans la cité des hommes* (Paris: Fayard, 1992), 179.
30. Included in *Charles Munch Conducts NY STEREO, February* [23,] *1967*, Disco Archivia 1357 [off air], n.d. [c. 2005].
31. Robert Magidoff, *Yehudi Menuhin* (New York: Doubleday, 1955), 232.
32. "Famous Foreign Conductor in London," *London Times* (Nov. 9, 1944).
33. "French Musicians in London," *London Times* (Nov. 13, 1944).
34. Pvt. Edwin L. Richmond (writing on Nov. 7, 1944), "News of Casals," *NYT* (Dec. 24, 1944). The *New York Times* had already reported on Casals: See "Menuhin Returns," *NYT* (Oct. 13, 1944).
35. Let. Lincoln Kirstein to Virgil Thomson, Oct. 4, 1944, Virgil Thomson papers, Irving S. Gilmore Music Library, Yale University.
36. Let. Kirstein to Thomson, Nov. 9, 1944, Yale.
37. L. D., "Paul Paray a fait une rentrée en fanfare" [Oct. 23, 1944], unidentified newspaper clipping, NJJS.
38. Ibid.
39. CM, statement on wartime activities, typescript, Dec. 4, 1944, NJJS.
40. Ibid.
41. Ibid.
42. Olin Downes, "A Visit with Paul Paray," *NYT* 18 (Nov. 18, 1945). See also "Friend and Foe," *Time* (Oct. 25, 1945).
43. Let. Ropartz to CM, Jan. 1, 1945, GHCM 164.
44. Let. Arthur Honegger to a Portuguese correspondent, Apr. 24, 1945, GHCM 164.
45. Charles Stuart, "The Edinburgh Festival," *Musical Times* 88, no. 1256 (October 1947): 327.

CHAPTER 4

1. Lewis Foreman, *Arthur Bliss: Catalogue of the Complete Works* (Sevenoaks, Kent, UK: Novello, 1980), 70.
2. "Paris Orchestra in London," *London Times* (Nov. 5, 1945).
3. ZED, rev. of Nov. 28, 1945, *Les Dernières Nouvelles d'Alsace* (Nov. 29, 1945).
4. Holoman, *Société des Concerts*, 458.
5. Minutes of the Comité d'Épuration, Chambre Syndicale des Artistes-Musiciens de Bordeaux, Nov. 23, 1944; copy NJJS.
6. Let. W. W. Caswell Jr. to George Judd and HBC, Feb. 10, 1949, BSO.
7. Int. Agnès Schoeller, Aug. 29, 2007.
8. Minutes of June 30, 1946; see Holoman, *Société des Concerts*, 463–65; also GHCM 174–76.
9. See, for instance, Jan Lowenbach, "Prague's First Post-War Festival," *NYT* (June 30, 1946).
10. William McNaught, "London Concerts: An Orchestra from Paris," *Musical Times* 87, no. 1245 (November 1946): 347.
11. Let. Ropartz to CM, Nov. 23, 1946, GHCM 179.
12. "Muench, Conductor, Arrives," *NYT* (Dec. 20, 1946).
13. "Le Beau Charles," *Time* (Feb. 3, 1947).

14. OD, "Muench Conducts the Philharmonic," *NYT* (Jan. 24, 1947).

15. "Muench, Departing Guest, Honored by Philharmonic," *NYT* (Feb. 3, 1947).

16. Howard Taubman, "Rodzinski's Resignation Accepted by Philharmonic, Effective at Once," *NYT* (Feb. 5, 1947).

17. Ibid.

18. "Muench Due on Podium of Philharmonic," *Los Angeles Times* (Mar. 2, 1947).

19. "Cheers Tribute Unique Concert Led by Muench," *Los Angeles Times* (Mar. 7, 1947).

20. Raymond Gérôme may be heard in the 1943 Brussels production now available on compact disc: *Jeanne d'Arc au bûcher*, Opera d'Oro 1223, 1999.

21. Virgil Thomson, "Joan of Arc in Close-Up," *NYHT* (Jan. 2, 1948); in Thomson, *Music Reviewed, 1940–1954* (New York: Vintage, 1967), 229–30.

22. Noel Straus, "Muench Conducts Handel Concerto," *NYT* (Nov. 17, 1947).

23. Ibid.

24. OD, "Miss Neveu Scores as Violin Soloist," *NYT* (Nov. 14, 1947).

25. Let. Richard E. Myers to George Judd, Apr. 15, 1948, BSO.

26. Let. Frank Perkins to George Judd, Feb. 21, 1945, BSO.

27. "List of Recordings Made by Charles Munch" [before his appointment in Boston], 1948, BSO. James North noted the Munch recording of Haydn's *Sinfonia concertante* in Koussevitzky's collection before it went on the market.

28. Humphrey Burton, *Leonard Bernstein* (New York: Doubleday, 1994), 158.

29. "Discord in Chicago," *Time* (Feb. 9, 1948).

30. Let. George Judd to M. A. DeWolfe Howe, Jan. 22, 1948, BSO.

31. Let. Susan B. Irving to George Judd, Mar. 31, 1948, BSO.

32. Cyrus Durgin, "What Sort of Man Is Charles Munch?" *Boston Globe* (Apr. 1, 1948).

33. Let. HBC to Geneviève Munch, Apr. 8, 1948, BSO.

34. Let. Bernstein to Koussevitzky, May 21, 1948, Leonard Bernstein collection, Library of Congress.

35. Text GHCM 186.

36. Concert of June 20, 1948, Strasbourg; see Orchestre National, *Livre d'or*, I, 117, at Documentation Musicale, Radio France.

37. Isaac Stern, *My First 79 Years* (New York: Knopf, 1999), 69–70.

38. *Radiodiffusion-Télévision Française / Orchestre National / Tournée de Concerts / Etats-Unis et Canada / 1er Octobre au 5 Novembre 1962,* mimeographed press-book with itinerary, copy NJJS.

39. *Detroit Times* (Oct. 25, 1948), in dossier assembled by a clipping service, BSO.

40. "IU Goes Continental," *Indianapolis Star* (Nov. 3, 1948), citing G. W. Rogers.

41. Virgil Thomson, "French Loveliness," *NYHT* (Oct. 18, 1948); in Thomson, *Music Reviewed, 1940–1954,* 255–56.

42. Virgil Thomson, "France at Its Best," *NYHT* (Oct. 24, 1948); in Thomson, *Music, Right and Left* (New York: Holt, 1951), 21.

43. GHCM 188.

44. "Dirty Linen Is Aired in Orchestra Dispute," *NYT* (Dec. 18, 1948); see also "French Orchestra Asks Arbitration" *NYT* (Dec. 5, 1948); "Arbitrators Hear Musicians' Dispute," *NYT* (Dec. 15, 1948).

45. "French Orchestra Asks Arbitration."

46. *Charles Münch volume 12* / New York Philharmonic-Symphony Orchestra / Robert Casadesus, piano / Mozart, Liszt, d'Indy, Chabrier, Dante LYS 543, 1999; *Ginette Neveu Historic Public Performances*, 2 CDs Music and Arts CD-4837, 1998.
47. Let. W. W. Caswell Jr. to George Judd and HBC, Feb. 10, 1949, BSO.
48. Let. CM to George Judd, Feb. 23, 1949, BSO.
49. Let. George Judd to HBC, Apr. 27, 1949, BSO; citing a telephone conversation from George Kuyper.
50. See James H. North, *Boston Symphony Orchestra: An Augmented Discography* (Lanham, Md.: Scarecrow, 2008), 267.

CHAPTER 5

1. Cleveland Amory, *The Proper Bostonians* (New York: Dutton, 1947), 115–16.
2. Int. William Moyer, by Robert Ripley, typescript from tape, Jan. 29, 1993, BSO. Moyer was trombone II in the BSO from 1952 to 1966 and personnel manager from 1966 to 1987.
3. Let. George Judd to HBC, Apr. 27, 1949, BSO.
4. "Munch Arrives in Boston," *NYT* (Sept. 21, 1949).
5. "Charles Munch / Music Director / Boston Symphony Orchestra," mimeographed statement for the press, 1950, BSO.
6. Ibid.
7. Let. William Judd to George Judd, Sept. 27, 1949, BSO.
8. HBC, "Remarks of Henry B. Cabot," dittographed press release, Oct. 7, 1949, BSO.
9. Let. Albert Schweitzer to HBC, 8 December 1949, BSO programs 1949–1950, 563–64.
10. Typescript NJJS; pub. in Charles R. Joy, *Music in the Life of Albert Schweitzer* (New York: Harper, 1951), ix.
11. Cyrus Durgin, "Turangalîla, or Love in the East Indies, or a Messiaen Afternoon," *Boston Globe* (Dec. 3, 1949).
12. See handwritten English texts for CM public appearances in NJJS. In addition, Mrs. Hirschmann was an intimate of Koussevitzky and Nicholas Nabokov: See, for instance, let. Aaron Copland to Serge Koussevitzky, Sept. 27, 1947, Aaron Copland collection, Library of Congress.
13. Henri Dutilleux, *Music—Mystery and Memory: Conversations with Claude Glayman*, trans. Roger Nichols (Burlington, Vt.: Ashgate, 2003), 51.
14. Int. Jean-Philippe Schweitzer, Apr. 27, 2006.
15. Contract with CM, Apr. 7, 1948, para. 3, BSO.
16. Ibid., para. 6.
17. Let. HBC to Lucien R. Le Lievre, Apr. 20, 1948, BSO.
18. Let. HBC to Lucien R. Le Lievre, Apr. 28, 1948, BSO.
19. Let. Lucien R. Le Lievre to HBC, July 20, 1950, BSO.
20. Let. Bernard Zighera to George Judd, May 23, 1951, BSO.
21. Let. HBC to CM, May 19, 1950, BSO.
22. Francis Poulenc, *Entretiens avec Claude Rostand* (Paris: Julliard, 1954), 133–34.
23. Let. Francis Poulenc to CM, 24 February 1950, GHCM 202.

24. CM, responses prepared (in English) for interview by Martin Bookspan, WBMS, Boston, Feb. 1, 1950 (typescript), NJJS.

25. Rudolph Elie, "The First Season: Munch Wins Over a Strange City," *Boston Sunday Herald* (Apr. 23, 1950).

26. Ibid.

27. Poulenc's scrapbook of (minimally identified) press clippings, Bibliothèque Nationale de France, Musique, notably Claude Rostand, "Le Concerto de Poulenc à Aix-en-Provence," *Paris-Presse* (July 26, 1950).

28. Let. Leonard Burkat to George Judd, Sept. 11, 1950, BSO.

29. Let. HBC to CM, Nov. 28, 1950, BSO.

30. "Seating Plan, Stage of Symphony Hall," BSO programs 1950–1951, 624.

31. "About the Chorus," BSO programs 1950–1951, 419.

32. Rudolph Elie, "Charles Munch Returns, and the Symphony Season Looms," *Boston Herald* (Oct. 1, 1950).

33. See Jann Pasler, *Composing the Citizen: Music as Public Utility in Third Republic France* (Berkeley: University of California Press, 2009), 451–60.

34. "The Student Rehearsals Catch On in a Hurry" (rpt. of Rudolph Elie in *Boston Herald,* Dec. 21, 1950), BSO programs 1950–1951, 471–72.

35. Ibid.

36. Cabot's remarks transcribed in "Prospects for the Orchestra," BSO programs 1951–1952, 923–24.

37. Harold Rogers, "Trustees Ask Support by Businessmen," *Christian Science Monitor* (Jan. 23, 1953); rpt. in BSO programs 1952–1953, 675–76.

38. Ibid.

39. Let. HBC to CM, Apr. 12, 1950, BSO.

40. Let. HBC to CM, Nov. 7, 1950, BSO.

41. Let. Monteux to CM, Jan. 23, 1950, GHCM 200.

42. *Boston Globe* (Jan. 24, 1951); cited by Canarina, 209–10.

43. Let. CM to Monteux, Mar. 8, 1951.

44. Steven Lowe, notes accompanying *David Diamond: Symphony no. 3, Psalm, Kaddish.* Seattle Symphony / Gerard Schwarz. CD Naxos 8.559155 (2002).

45. K. Robert Schwarz, "A Lost Generation of Americans Is Coming Home," *NYT* (July 1, 1990).

46. Let. HBC to CM, Feb. 14, 1951, BSO.

47. Warren Storey Smith, rev. of Apr. 27, 1951, *Boston Post* (Apr. 28, 1951).

48. OD, "Boston Symphony in Work by Bartok," *NYT* (Feb. 15, 1951).

49. Let. CM to Arthur Honegger, Mar. 10, [1951], GHCM 225.

50. OD, "Work by Honegger Introduced Here," *NYT* (Mar. 15, 1951).

51. Henri Weill, rev. of June 25, 1951, in *Les Dernières Nouvelles d'Alsace,* cited GHCM 230.

52. Let. Schoenberg to CM, Nov. 22, 1950, GHCM 215.

53. CM, *Conductor,* 42–43.

54. CM, "Address of Charles Munch, Director of the Berkshire Music Center, at the opening exercises of the Twelfth Session, July 1954," typescript (carbon copy), NJJS. Ed. by DKH.

55. "Charles Munch Answers a Letter," *Boston Herald* (Nov. 3, 1957) (from mimeographed press release, BSO); rpt. in BSO programs 1957–1958, 323–24.

CHAPTER 6

1. Let. George Judd to Bernard Zighera, May 23, 1951; "Mr. Judd's conversation with Mr. Zighera from Paris," note to file, May 26, 1951, BSO.

2. HBC, "Notes for telephone conversation with CM," ms., June 12, 1951, BSO.

3. Wire-service photograph, July 2, 1951, BSO.

4. James R. Holland, *Tanglewood* (Barre, Mass.: Barre, 1973), 12–13.

5. Let. CM to Henri Weill, Mar. 23, 1951, GHCM 227.

6. Andrew L. Pincus, *Scenes from Tanglewood* (Boston: Northeastern University Press, 1989), frontispiece caption.

7. Let. Koussevitzky to CM, July 11, 1950, NJJS. Further on this affair, Peggy Glanville-Hicks wrote Virgil Thomson, Aug. 23, [1950]: "From Cecil [Beaton] I get the lowdown on the Boston Affair. It seems that Munch IS remaining with the orchestra according to contract. All the fuss was about two weeks of Tanglewood, which Kousse was supposed to take and felt he couldn't handle in addition to his overseas adventures. Munch took them over, found Judd a menace, and when he found he was asked to play Judd-planned programs refused to do so. Sabata was hired by Judd without Koussevitzky being consulted. Now Kousse is being very polite to Sabata in public but is carefully staying away from his concerts." James Murdoch, *Peggy Glanville-Hicks: A Transposed Life* (Hillsdale, N.Y.: Pendragon, 2002), 65.

8. "Address of Charles Munch, Director of the Berkshire Music Center, at the opening exercises of the Twelfth Session, July 1954," typescript, NJJS.

9. "Address by Charles Munch at the opening exercises of the Berkshire Music Center, Tanglewood, 5 July 1953," handwritten ms. in French and English, typescript, and version published in 1953 Berkshire Festival program book, NJJS.

10. Ibid.

11. "Aaron Copland's Message," BSO programs 1951–1952, 55–56.

12. "Munch Illness," dittographed press release, Nov. 7, 1951, BSO.

13. Let. Piston to CM, Jan. 4, 1952, GHCM 239–40. (The Fourth Symphony was premiered on Oct. 10, 1952.) Let. CM to Harsányi, early 1952, Bibliothèque Nationale de France.

14. Let. HBC to Ernest Ansermet, Feb. 10, 1952, BSO; pub. in BSO programs 1951–1952, 683.

15. Lucien Price, "Words of Welcome" on WGBH during the broadcast intermission features, Mar. 28–29, 1952; in BSO programs 1951–1952, 971–72, 994.

16. Let. Geneviève Munch to George Judd, May 8, 1952, BSO.

17. Let. George Judd to CM, June 11, 1952, BSO.

18. Let. HBC to CM, Apr. 8, 1952, BSO.

19. Let. HBC to Conrad Oberdorfer, Apr. 24, 1952, BSO.

20. Theodore P. Ferris (rector of Trinity Church), eulogy for Charles Munch, Nov. 14, 1968, published in *Boston Globe* (Nov. 15, 1968).

21. "The Orchestra to Play at Paris Exposition," BSO programs 1951–1952, 439–40 [December 1951].

22. Rudolph Elie, "Paris in the Spring for the Boston Symphony," *Boston Herald* (Jan. 23, 1952); rpt. in BSO programs 1951–1952, 635–36, 654.

23. Ibid.

24. "Orchestra to Play."

25. Point men: ibid. Couldn't spend it all: Frances Stonor Saunders, *Who Paid the Piper? the CIA and the Cultural Cold War* (London: Granta, 1999), 105; her source was Gilbert Greenway.

26. "The First European Tour by the Boston Symphony Orchestra," BSO programs 1951–1952, 684.

27. "The European Itinerary," BSO programs 1951–1952, 875–76.

28. Cyrus Durgin, "With the Boston Symphony in Europe," *Saturday Review* (May 31, 1952), 37–41. Two BSO players, the double bassist Henri Girard and the English hornist Louis Speyer, had played in the first performances of *Le sacre du printemps*.

29. Thomas Heinitz, "Letter from London," *Saturday Review* (June 28, 1952).

30. Let. George Judd to CM, Sept. 3, 1952, BSO.

31. Int. Doriot Anthony Dwyer, Sept. 7, 2005. Women's toilets, she took care to note, were in short supply on "ladies' day."

32. Quoted in "Boston Picks a Woman," *Time* (Oct. 13, 1952).

33. Int. Margo Miller, May 19, 2005.

34. Janet Baker-Carr, *Evening at Symphony* (Boston: Houghton Mifflin, 1977), 125.

35. Int. Roger Shermont, Apr. 5, 2006.

36. "Touring Bostonians," *Time* (May 25, 1953).

37. Int. Roger Voisin, by Robert Ripley, typescript from tape, Aug. 22, 1992, BSO.

38. Cited in "Classic Popularity," *Time* (June 1, 1953).

39. Rudolph Elie, "Charles Munch Returns 'Home,'" *Boston Herald* (Oct. 11, 1953).

40. "Year's Best Records," *Time* (Jan. 3, 1955).

41. OD, "Ernest Bloch, Now over 70, Is Writing Music That Is Living and Important," *NYT* (Mar. 7, 1954).

42. "Munch Conducts 5 Bach Concertos," *NYT* (July 10, 1954).

43. OD, "A Mass by Haydn Heard at Lenox," *NYT* (July 24, 1954).

44. Ross Parmenter, "Lenox Week-End," *NYT* (Aug. 8, 1955).

45. Howard Taubman, "Healing Strains of Beethoven," *NYT* (July 23, 1955).

46. *In Memory of Arturo Toscanini / Munch, Walter, Monteux,* 2 CDs, Music and Arts 1201, 2007.

47. Mark Schubart, "Behind the Baton," *NYT* (April 3, 1955).

48. M. A. DeWolfe Howe, "Schweitzer," BSO programs 1954–1955, 697.

49. Let. Leonard Bernstein to Helen Coates, Apr. 11, 1955, Leonard Bernstein collection, Library of Congress.

50. OD, "New Symphony by Martinu," Jan. 13, 1955; "Boston Symphony Orchestra Heard Here," *NYT* (Jan. 16, 1955).

51. OD, "Monteux at 80," *NYT* (Apr. 3, 1955); "Monteux, at 80, Directs Concert," *NYT* (Apr. 5, 1955).

52. CM, "Pierre Monteux: I am not going to make a speech," Apr. 4, 1955, typescript, NJJS.

53. Canarina, *Monteux,* 249–50; Baker-Carr, *Evening at Symphony,* 69.

54. Ross Parmenter, "Boston Symphony Will Play in Russia," *NYT* (June 8, 1956). Koussevitzky had aspired to such an undertaking; the Philadelphia Orchestra was forced to decline the invitation owing to a labor action. See Katerina Frank, "Looking at Both Sides of the Iron Curtain: Boston Symphony Orchestra's Tour

of the Soviet Union," graduate seminar paper, University of California, Davis, 2007.

55. Let. TDP to HBC, Oct. 12, 1955, BSO.
56. Let. Copland to Olga Koussevitzky, Aug. 27, 1954, Aaron Copland collection, Library of Congress.
57. Let. Copland to Irving Fine, Feb. 12, 1956, Aaron Copland collection, Library of Congress.
58. Alexander Tcherepnin, "Charles Munch and Symphony no. 4 by Alexander Tcherepnin," typescript (New York, January 1970), NJJS.
59. Margo Miller, "Memories of BSO's Russia Trip," *Boston Globe* (Mar. 6, 1988).

CHAPTER 7

1. "Boston Musicians Off," *NYT* (Aug. 15, 1956).
2. "Mme Munch Dies in Paris Home," *Boston Globe* (Aug. 25, 1956); also carried on the Associated Press wire service that day.
3. Let. CM to Anne-Rose Méhu-Ebersolt, Aug. 28, 1956, GHCM 277–78.
4. Dmitri Kabalevsky, rev. of the BSO in Moscow, *Pravda* (Sept. 14, 1956); trans. as "An Opinion from Moscow," BSO programs 1956–1957, 115–16, 147.
5. Stephen Williams, "Boston Symphony in Edinburgh Bow," *NYT* (Aug. 27, 1956).
6. Hugh Smith, "Boston Symphony Opens in Ireland" (dateline Cork, Aug. 24, 1956), *NYT* (Aug. 25, 1956).
7. Felix Aprahamian, "Varied Reactions to Programs in Scotland," *CSM* (Sept. 8, 1956).
8. Colin Mason, *Manchester Guardian* (Sept. 16, 1956); in "European Impressions," BSO programs 1956–1957, 59–60.
9. Janet Baker-Carr, *Evening at Symphony* (Boston: Houghton Mifflin, 1977), 87.
10. "Gay Soviet Tour Begun," *CSM* (Sept. 6, 1956).
11. Jack Phipps, "Boston Visits Moscow," *Tempo* no. 41 (Autumn 1956): 15–17; in BSO programs 1956–1957, 284, 315. Two photographs by United Press photographer Ed Fitzgerald, in Mary Smith's tour scrapbook (BSO archive), verify this incident: In one Monteux can be seen backstage with Munch and his valet Roger Toureau; in the next, Munch, alone, is bowing to the crowd, the orchestra having left the stage.
12. "Gay Soviet Tour Begun."
13. Cited in Margo Miller, "Memories of BSO's Russia Trip," *Boston Globe* (Mar. 6, 1988).
14. Leonid Gesin, int. by Katerina Frank, May 5, 2007; cited in Katerina Frank, "Looking at Both Sides of the Iron Curtain: Boston Symphony Orchestra's Tour of the Soviet Union," graduate seminar paper, University of California, Davis, 2007.
15. Let. trombone section of the Moscow State Symphony Orchestra to CM, Oct. 11, 1957, NJJS; published as "A Message from Moscow," BSOP 1957–1958, 579–60.
16. Kabalevsky, rev. *Pravda.*
17. Rudolf Klein, "Visitors from U.S. in Vienna," *CSM* (Sept. 22, 1956).
18. "The Orchestra Honored in Vienna," BSO programs 1956–1957, 451–52.
19. "7 Centuries Bridged as Boston Symphony Presents Concerts at Chartres Cathedral," *NYT* (Sept. 22, 1956).

20. Émile Vuillermoz, "Two Travelers in Paris," *CSM* (Oct. 13, 1956).
21. "Boston Symphony in London," *CSM* (Sept. 25, 1956) (from a Reuters wire story).
22. Erwin Stein, "Boston Symphony in London," *CSM* (Oct. 6, 1956).
23. Let. Dwight D. Eisenhower to HBC, Sept. 28, 1956, BSO; facs. rpt. in BSO programs 1956–1957, 109; also in "Eisenhower Lauds Boston Symphony," *NYT* (Oct. 6, 1956).
24. "An Official Welcome," BSO programs 1956–1957, 171–72, 203.
25. Harold Rogers, "Charles Munch on Podium for Telecast in Cambridge," *CSM* (Oct. 31, 1956).
26. Let. CM to Toscanini, Nov. 8, 1951, BSO.
27. Let. Arturo Toscanini to CM, Nov. 28, 1951, GHCM 236–37.
28. Canarina, *Monteux,* 263.
29. Let. Wanda Toscanini Horowitz to CM, Feb. 3, 1957, GHCM 282.
30. Let. Walter Toscanini to CM, Mar. 19, 1958, GHCM 289.
31. Edwin H. Schloss, rev. of Philadelphia concert of March 1, 1957, *Philadelphia Inquirer* (Mar. 2, 1957); in "Dr. Munch in Philadelphia," BSO programs 1956–1957, 975.
32. Robert Kemp, "Charles Munch à Athènes," *Le Monde* (Sept. 7, 1957).
33. Let. CM to Anne-Rose Méhu-Ebersolt, Nov. 27, 1956, GHCM 279–80.
34. The cabinet secretary was Maxwell M. Rabb (1910–2002), later ambassador to Italy (1981–1989). Let. TDP to Maxwell M. Rabb, Oct. 15, 1957, BSO. Attached to the carbon copy is the interoffice note of Oct. 14, 1957: "White House says forget it."
35. Int. Sylvia Sandeen, Sept. 8, 2005. She died the following December; see Gloria Negri, "Sylvia Sandeen, 70, a Lover of the Symphony and the Sox," *Boston Globe* (Dec. 22, 2005).
36. Werner Bamberger, "French Navy Captain Recalls Two Talented Uncles," *NYT* (Oct. 14, 1970).
37. "It Could Be Dawn," *Time* (Mar. 29, 1968).
38. North, BSO discography, 59.
39. Frederic R. Mann (1903–1987) was the Philadelphia industrialist and philanthropist after whom the Mann Music Center (1976), summer home of the Philadelphia Orchestra, is also named.
40. "New Group Urges Ties with Israel," *NYT* (Jan. 24, 1954).
41. Review from *Haaretz,* rpt. in "Reports from Israel," BSO programs 1957–1958, 835–36.
42. CM, address on trip to Israel (Symphony Hall, Boston, Feb. 6, 1958), typescript, BSO; in "Dr. Munch's Impressions of Israel," BSO programs 1957–1958, 963–64, 1003.
43. Ibid.
44. Let. CM to HBC, Mar. 29, 1958, BSO.
45. Henry B. Cabot, "Note to file re: conversation with CM on resignation," Apr. 1, 1958, BSO.
46. Ibid.
47. Let. CM to Joseph Calvet, Aug. 14, 1958, GHCM 291.
48. Let. HBC to TDP, Apr. 15, 1958, BSO.

49. CM, address at tenth-anniversary banquet, February 1959, ms., NJJS.
50. Int. Lita Starr, Oct. 7, 2005.

CHAPTER 8

1. Cyrus Durgin, "Munch Begins 78th Season," *Boston Globe* (Oct. 4, 1958).
2. "The Recording Project," BSO programs 1958–1959, 196, 231.
3. "The Return of Casals" (citing Paul Henry Lang in the *New York Herald Tribune*), BSO programs 1958–1959, 260, 287, 295.
4. Lindesay Parrott, "Throng at U.N. Hails Performance by Casals," *NYT* (Oct. 25, 1958).
5. James H. North, *Boston Symphony Orchestra: An Augmented Discography* (Lanham, Md.: Scarecrow, 2008), 64; subsequent review by North and the author shows the early morning times to be correct, confirmed by the Monday press ("Van Cliburn Keeps Symphony Up Late," etc.).
6. Van Cliburn, statement to United Press from Moscow, Apr. 14, 1958, rpt. in "Van Cliburn," BSO programs 1958–1959, 4, 39.
7. Let. H. G. Wonnacott, manager of the London office of Filene's, to Harold D. Hodgkinson, trustee of the BSO, January 1959, in "Overseas Broadcast," BSO programs 1958–1959, 963–64.
8. Cable G. R. Lewis, head of Planning, Home Service, BBC, to WGBH, in "The First International Broadcast," BSO programs 1958–1959, 835.
9. "Broken Pedal Prolongs Piano Concerto Pause," *NYT* (Apr. 12, 1959).
10. Let. Monteux to CM, Feb. 2, 1959, GHCM 298.
11. Cyrus Durgin, "Munch's First Decade as Conductor of Boston Symphony," *Boston Globe* (Apr. 26, 1959).
12. Eric Salzman, "Shell Dedicated at Tanglewood," *NYT* (July 13, 1959). In that period Bolt, Beranek, and Newman also provided the acoustical design for the United Nations Assembly Hall, Kresge Auditorium at MIT, and Philharmonic Hall in New York.
13. Ross Parmenter, "Final Week-End at Tanglewood Begins with Beethoven Concert," Aug. 8, 1959.
14. HCS, "Berlioz' 'Damnation of Faust' Led by Munch," *NYT* (Aug. 15, 1960).
15. HCS, "As Tanglewood Marks a 50th, Let the Cavils Not Be Sounded," *NYT* (July 4, 1990).
16. Photographs, Nov. 13, 1959, Leonard Burkat home, Brookline, Mass., in the Leonard Burkat papers, Yale University, box III.
17. Margo Miller, "Memories of BSO's Russia Trip."
18. BSO program book 1959–1960, 451–52.
19. Let. Dutilleux to CM, Sept. 21, 1958, GHCM 296 (one orchestra at a time); GHCM 307 (exalting hours; transcribed from televised "Hommage à Charles Münch," Nov. 14, 1968).
20. Jose Bruyr, "Bonsoir, Monsieur Charles Munch," obituary clipping from unidentified magazine, NJJS.
21. Bertrus van Lier, "Gasdirigen Concertgebouworkest Charles Munch," *Het Parool* (Jan. 11, 1960).
22. Jay S. Harrison, "Munch and Music: His Current Views," *NYHT* (Mar. 6, 1960); rpt. in BSO programs 1960–1961, 1247–55.

23. Copland calls this late-career call to serious conducting, as well as his association with Munch and the BSO, "one of my fondest memories." See *Aaron Copland, a Reader: Selected Writings, 1923–1972,* ed. Richard Kostelanetz (New York: Routledge, 2004), xxx.

24. "Boston Symphony Off for Tour of Far East," *Los Angeles Times* (Apr. 26, 1960).

25. *Charles Munch: Boston Symphony Orchestra Live in Japan 1960,* DVD NHK Classical NSDS-9486, 2006.

26. Eloise Cunningham, "From Townsend Harris to Charles Munch," *CSM* (Apr. 6, 1960).

27. "Victories and Vicissitudes of the Boston Symphony Orchestra in Japan," *CSM* (June 11, 1960).

28. Let. CM to Jean-Jacques Schweitzer and Nicole Henriot-Schweitzer, July 2, 1960, GHCM 313. The house was rented from the Miller family, publishers of the *Berkshire Eagle.*

29. Let. Fritz Munch to CM, Apr. 12, 1960, GHCM 311–12.

30. Let. TDP to HBC, July 6, 1960, BSO.

31. Let. Franklin K. Paddock MD to TDP, July 15, 1960, BSO.

32. Let. Dr. Pelton to TDP, Aug. 4, 1960, BSO.

33. Eric Salzman, "Shell Dedicated at Tanglewood," *NYT* (July 13, 1959).

34. Allen Hughes, "Boston Symphony Gives 2d Concert," *NYT* (Dec. 4, 1960).

35. HCS, "Routine Winter Works Fill Berkshire Lists," *NYT* (Apr. 30, 1961).

36. H. Earle Johnson, "Leadership Needed," *NYT* (May 14, 1961).

37. Int. Jaime Laredo, Feb. 17, 2008.

38. Let. Poulenc to CM, May 23, 1959, GHCM 200; ChimP 59-10.

39. Let. Poulenc to CM, Oct. 17, 1960, GHCM 315–16, ChimP 60-27.

40. Let. Poulenc to CM [Jan. 15, 1961], GHCM 317–18 [dated December 1960], ChimP 61-2.

41. Lets. Poulenc to Bernac and CM, ChimP 61-2, 61-3, 61-4, 61-6, and 61-8.

42. Tad Szulc, "1734 Violin Given Israel by Szeryng," *NYT* (Dec. 19, 1972).

43. LDS is the designation for RCA's Soria series, named for the legendary record producer Dario Soria (1912–1980), at the time vice president of RCA's international record operations. It designates signature performances in de luxe presentation.

44. Let. HBC to CM, Apr. 2, 1961, NJJS.

45. Let. Olivia Cabot to CM, Apr. 2, 1961, NJJS.

46. Harold Rogers, "Initial Program Brilliant under Munch's Baton," *CSM* (Sept. 30, 1961).

47. On the works by Fine and Piston, see North, BSO Discography, 76–77.

48. All cited in "A Tour of Farewells," BSO program book 1961–1962, 261–62.

49. HCS, "Munch Leads French Scores," *NYT* (Apr. 5, 1962).

50. Let. Jean-Jacques Schweitzer to HBC, Dec. 29, 1961, BSO.

51. Let. TDP to Perry Rathbone, Jan. 8, 1962, BSO.

52. TDP, dossier "Testimonial Dinner / 15 April 1962," BSO.

53. Ibid.

54. Henry A. Laughlin, "Trustees' Resolution," read by HBC at banquet, Apr. 15, 1962, BSO programs 1961–1962, 1483–84.

55. CM, address at farewell banquet, Apr. 15, 1962, ms., NJJS.

56. Let. TDP to HBC, Feb. 16, 1962, BSO.
57. Int. William Moyer, by Robert Ripley, typescript from tape, Jan. 29, 1993, BSO.
58. Int. Pasquale Cardillo, by Robert Ripley, typescript from tape, Dec. 9, 1991, BSO.
59. Int. John Barwicki, by Robert Ripley, typescript from tape, Jan. 26, 1993, BSO.
60. Int. Eugene Lehner, by Robert Ripley, typescript from tape, July 31, 1993, BSO.
61. Int. Ralph Gomberg, by Robert Ripley, typescript from tape, July 28, 1992, BSO.
62. Ibid.
63. On Willis Page, see North, BSO Discography, 255–58.
64. Int. Henry Freeman, by Robert Ripley, typescript from tape, July 21, 1992, BSO.
65. Int. Thomas D. (Tod) Perry, by Robert Ripley, typescript from tape, Aug. 21, 1992, BSO.
66. Int. Harold Farberman, by Robert Ripley, typescript from tape, Aug. 5, 2002, BSO.
67. Int. Roger Voisin, Sept. 19, 2005.
68. Int. Robert Ripley, by Joel Moerschel, typescript from tape, June 1, 1999, BSO.
69. Ibid.
70. Int. Joseph Silverstein, Dec. 5, 2005.
71. Erich Leinsdorf, *Erich Leinsdorf on Music* (Portland, Ore.: Amadeus, 1997), 316–17.
72. Int. Stephanie Friedman, May 22, 2005.
73. Ibid.
74. Int. Vic Firth, Apr. 6, 2006.

CHAPTER 9

1. Raymond Ericson, "France Boosts Music," *NYT* (Nov. 12, 1967), citing Thomas Quinn Curtiss, noted critic with the *International Herald Tribune.*
2. Jacques Lonchampt, "Entretien avec Charles Munch," *Le Monde* (May 9, 1962).
3. Int. Lita Starr, Oct. 7, 2005.
4. Ibid.
5. Charles Munch edition CD 4: *Debussy: Ibéria, Fantaisie, La Mer,* in Charles Munch and Orchestre National de France, *Hommage à Charles Munch / Tribute to Charles Munch.* 9 CDs. Auvidis Valois, 1998.
6. See Joseph E. Potts, "European Radio Orchestras (III)," *Musical Times* 96, no. 1353 (November 1955): 584–86.
7. Bernard Gavoty, "Les dix plus grands chefs d'orchestre," *Réalités femina* (July 1962), 22–28.
8. Lonchampt, "Entretien."
9. *Orchestre National / Tournée de Concerts / États-Unis et Canada / 1er Octobre au 5 Novembre 1962,* mimeographed tour itinerary, in red cover, 1962, NJJS.
10. Loretta Thistle in the *Ottawa Citizen,* cited by Pierre Dellard, "La Tournée de l'Orchestre National aux États-Unis et au Canada," *R.T.F. Informations–Documentation* (la vie de la R.T.F.), December 1962.
11. Ross Parmenter, "Munch Conducts French Program," *NYT* (Nov. 1, 1962).
12. Jean-Philippe Schweitzer, "Japanophile, Munch," in program book accompanying *Charles Munch: Boston Symphony Orchestra Live in Japan 1960,* DVD NHK Classical NSDS-9486, 2006.
13. *Liszt: Piano Concerto no. 1 / Brahms: Symphony no. 1,* DVD Fuji Television / Exton OVCB-00017, 2003.

14. "Symphony Guest Unable to Appear," *Washington Post* (Jan. 6, 1963); this suggests he had conflicting engagements in Europe.
15. Let. F. James Rybka, MD, to editor, *Time* magazine (Mar. 3, 1963), BSO.
16. Let. TDP to F. James Rybka, MD, Mar. 5, 1963, BSO.
17. TDP, note to file re: phone conversation with Ronald Wilford, c. Mar. 10 and 12, 1963, BSO. Concerning the transition from Judson to Wilford at CAMI, see Ross Parmenter, "Music World: Parting Is No Sweet Sorrow," *NYT* (Oct. 20, 1963).
18. Let. TDP to Ronald Wilford, Feb. 5, 1963, BSO.
19. Let. Ronald Wilford to TDP, Feb. 19, 1963, BSO.
20. Let. TDP to Helen Coates, Mar. 5, 1963, BSO.
21. Let. Helen Coates to TDP, Mar. 11, 1963, BSO.
22. Let. TDP to CM, May 3, 1963, BSO.
23. HCS, "Munch in Form," *NYT* (Mar. 21, 1963).
24. Antoine Goléa, "L'Orchestre National (Maison de la Radio, le 20 décembre)" [1963], *Guide du concert* 412(Jan. 18–24, 1964), 19.
25. Gaby Pasquier, *Chère Marguerite Long (1874–1966): Souvenirs personnels de Gaby Pasquier* (Nogent-le-Rotrou, 2001), 60.
26. See Ross Parmenter, "Bernstein's Symphony no. 3," *NYT* (Feb. 1, 1964).
27. HCS, "Too Much Hoopla," *NYT* (Feb. 2, 1964).
28. Ross Parmenter, "Bernstein's Symphony no. 3."
29. Michael Steinberg, "Bernstein's 'Kaddish' in Premiere Here," *Boston Globe* (Feb. 1, 1964).
30. Robert Taylor, "'Kaddish' Reveals Bernstein Genius," *Boston Herald* (Feb. 1, 1964).
31. Let. Bernstein to CM, Feb. 3, 1964, GHCM 344.
32. Harold Rogers, "Munch Back in Boston," *CSM* (Feb. 11, 1964).
33. Michael Steinberg, "Munch Conducts Berlioz 'Fantastique,'" *Boston Globe* (Feb. 8, 1964).
34. Let. TDP to HBC, Feb. 9, 1964, BSO.
35. Ibid.
36. Alexander Fried, "Munch Concert Goes 'Pop,'" *San Francisco Examiner* (Feb. 21, 1964); Dean Wallace, "Munch Conducts 'Lost' Masterpiece," *San Francisco Chronicle* (Feb. 21, 1964); Fried, "All in the Life of a Music Critic," *San Francisco Examiner* (Feb. 23, 1964).
37. Let. Walter Piston to CM, Jan. 5, 1964, GHCM 343.
38. Albert Goldberg, "The New Life, Freedom of Charles Munch," *Los Angeles Times* (Jan. 26 1964).
39. Ibid.
40. David Cairns, "Leeds Festival," *Musical Times* 105, no. 1458 (August 1964): 445–46.
41. Let. TDP to John T. Noon, attorney at law, Dec. 12, 1966, BSO.
42. Let. Dutilleux to CM, Aug. 3, 1965, GHCM 348–49.
43. HCS, "French and American Festival," *NYT* (July 15, 1965).
44. Howard Klein, "3,500 Are Drawn to L. I. Festival," *NYT* (Aug. 7, 1965).
45. Harold Rogers, "Freewheeling Sounds," *CSM* (Mar. 16, 1966).
46. CM, handwritten remarks, tucked into eighty-fifth-anniversary scrapbook (and photocopy in CM dossier 1965–1966), BSO.

47. Cited in liner notes for *Charles Munch en Italie* (concert of June 8, 1951, Turin), off-air, CD Tahra TAH-590, 2006.

CHAPTER 10

1. Marcel Landowski, *Batailles pour la musique* (Paris: Éditions du Seuil, 1979), 43.
2. Int. Lita Starr, Oct. 7, 2005.
3. "Brilliant Performances by the French National Orchestra," *Japan Times* (Oct. 12, 1966).
4. Ibid.
5. Janet Baker-Carr, *Evening at Symphony: A Portrait of the Boston Symphony Orchestra* (Boston: Houghton Mifflin, 1977), 80.
6. *Berlioz / L'enfance du Christ / McCollum, Kopleff, Upman, Gramm / Boston Symphony Orchestra / Charles Munch / 1966*, VAI DVD 4303, 2004.
7. Howard Klein, "Munch Conducts French Program," *NYT* (Feb. 24, 1967).
8. Let. Serge Baudo to CM, Apr. 27, 1967, GHCM 354.
9. Ibid., 355–56.
10. Int. Luben Yordanoff, Apr. 25, 2006.
11. Ibid.
12. Gilles Cantagrel and Claudette Douay, *L'Orchestre National de France: L'album anniversaire, 1934–1994* (Paris: Radio-France/Van de Velde, 1994), 60.
13. Int. Jean Douay (trombonist, Orchestre National), Apr. 18, 2006.
14. Let. CM to members of the Orchestre National, Apr. 4, 1967, in Orchestre National *livre d'or*, vol. 2; Documentation Musicale, Radio France.
15. Jean-Jacques Schweitzer, "Allocution de J. J. à l'occasion de la décoration de Charry," typescript, Oct. 5, 1967, NJJS.
16. Raymond Ericson, "France Boosts Music," *NYT* (Nov. 12, 1967).
17. Television broadcast with Bernard Gavoty, "Hommage à Charles Münch," Nov. 10, 1968 (Paris: ORTF), INA.
18. Janet Flanner (Genêt), "Letter from Paris: 15 November," *New Yorker* (Nov. 27, 1967).
19. "Together at Last," *Time* (Nov. 24, 1967).
20. Televised "Hommage à Charles Münch." The exchange is recounted also by Jean-Louis Ollu, "Jean-Louis Ollu, un Français à Bayreuth (1): L'Orchestre de Paris," int. by Yannick Millon, Aug. 8, 2007, www.altamusica.com.
21. Int. Yordanoff.
22. Telegram TDP to CM, Nov. 13, 1967, BSO. Perry also sent birthday cables: for instance, on Sept. 27, 1968: A HAPPY BIRTHDAY WISH TO DEAR UNCLE CHARLES FROM CABOTS TRUSTEES AND ALL THE BOSTON SYMPHONY /S/ PERRYS.
23. Int. Yordanoff.
24. Jean Cotti, "L'Orchestre de Paris: stupéfiant de maturité pour un nouveau-né," *France-Soir* (Nov. 16, 1967).
25. Sylvie de Nussac, "Triomphe et mort de Charles Munch," *L'Express* (Nov. 11, 1968).
26. Let. Lucien Wesmaël to TDP, Dec. 4, 1967, BSO.
27. Nussac, "Triomphe et mort de Charles Munch."
28. Harry Neville, "Munch Returns in Triumph," *Boston Globe* (Oct. 24, 1968).

29. McLaren Harris, "Orchestre de Paris, Munch Excel," *Boston Herald Traveler* (Oct. 24, 1968).
30. Nussac, "Triomphe et mort de Charles Munch."
31. ORTF television footage from New York, Oct. 26, 1958, included in televised "Hommage à Charles Münch."
32. Ibid.
33. Alan M. Kriegsman, "French Orchestra Suffers Birth Pangs," *Washington Post* (Oct. 31, 1968).
34. Int. Yordanoff.
35. Let. Serge Baudo to David Cairns, described by Cairns to DKH, Feb. 8, 2009.
36. Int. Debost, Sept. 20, 2004.
37. Millon, "Jean-Louis Ollu, un Français à Bayreuth."
38. Let. Guy Destangue to Orchestre National, Nov. 6, 1968, pasted into Orchestre National *livre d'or*, vol. 2.
39. Gaby Pasquier, *Chère Marguerite Long (1874–1966): Souvenirs personnels de Gaby Pasquier* (Nogent-le-Rotrou, 2001), 55.
40. Leonard Burkat, "At Charles Munch's Funeral," *Boston Globe* (Dec. 7, 1968).
41. Let. HBC to editor, *Boston Globe* (Nov. 7, 1968).
42. Let. Jean-Jacques Schweitzer to TDP, Jan. 7, 1969, BSO.
43. Theodore P. Ferris (rector of Trinity Church), eulogy for Charles Munch, Nov. 14, 1968; published in *Boston Globe* (Nov. 15, 1968).

CHAPTER 11

1. Televised "Hommage à Charles Münch." Concert videos later issued as DVD: Brahms: Symphony no. 1; Ravel: *Daphnis and Chloé*, Suite no. 2, EMI Classics (Classic Archive 55), 2007.
2. Let. Dwyer to HBC and Mrs. Cabot, Nov. 11, 1968, NJJS.
3. "Roger Toureau" (obituary), *Boston Globe* (Jan. 14, 1969).
4. Cécile Reynaud, Cathérine Massip, and D. Kern Holoman, *L'Orchestre de Paris: De la Société des Concerts du Conservatoire à l'Orchestre de Paris, 1828–2008* (Paris: Centre des Monuments Nationaux / Éditions du Patrimoine, 2007), 143–44.
5. Int. Lita Starr, Oct. 5, 2007.
6. Andrew L. Pincus, *Scenes from Tanglewood* (Boston: Northeastern University Press, 1989), 27.
7. Richard Dyer, "In His Own Words: The Maestro Reflects," *Boston Globe* (Apr. 14, 2002).
8. Marcel Landowski, "Hommage à Charles Münch," Orchestre de Paris program booklet, Mar. 10, 1969.
9. Olivier Messiaen et al., "Charles Munch" [on the tenth anniversary of his death], *Échos de l'Orchestre* (newsletter of the Orchestre de Paris), September 1978.
10. "Il faut travailler chaque jour comme si nous allions mourir demain," cited by Dutilleux (passim) and in Jacques Lonchampt, "Charles Munch" (obituary), *Le Monde* (Nov. 8, 1968). Alternative expressions along similar lines are attributed to Benjamin Franklin and Mahatma Gandhi. In a 1954 news conference in Boston, Munch offered the same sentiments in English, attributing them to "a letter that the composer Rameau wrote to his nephew: 'Live as though you had all eternity, and work as if you were to die tomorrow'" (*Boston Globe*, Oct. 7, 1954).

11. Televised "Hommage à Charles Munch," Nov. 14, 1968.

12. Messiaen et al., "Charles Munch."

13. See Bernard Gavoty, "Les dix plus grands chefs d'orchestre," *Réalités femina* (July 1962). The other nine, in order, were Karajan, Maazel, Markevitch, Ansermet, Benzi, Bernstein, Sebastian, Paray, and Cluytens. (Gavoty names as nearly their equal Pierre Dervaux and Georges Prêtre and, as stars on the rise, Serge Baudo, Louis Frémaux, and Jean Périsson.)

14. Leonard Burkat, rev. of Olivier, CM; *Notes* 46, no. 2 (December 1989): 382–85.

15. Janet Flanner (Genêt), "Letter from Paris: 15 November," *New Yorker* (Nov. 27, 1967).

16. CM, *Conductor,* 61.

17. Tucker Keiser, "New Book by Munch on Music," *Boston Sunday Post* (Apr. 10, 1955).

18. Lawrence Morton, rev. of *I Am a Conductor* by Charles Munch [with] Leonard Burkat, *Notes* 12(3) (June 1955): 440–41.

19. Albert Goldberg, "Charles Munch Writes a Penetrating and Witty Book about the Art of Conducting," *Los Angeles Times* (April 17, 1955).

20. Pierre-Auguste Renoir, *Study of a Female Nude,* drawing: red chalk on off-white antique laid paper, 62.1 × 46.1 cm, 1890, Fogg Art Museum, Harvard University. Ebersolt gift: int. Jérôme and Annie Kaltenbach, July 30, 2007. Schoeller gift: int. Agnès Schoeller, Aug. 29, 2007. A Rembrandt and a Caravaggio proved to be forgeries, Lita Starr recalled.

21. Int. Sylvia Sandeen, Sept. 8, 2005.

22. CM, "Address of Charles Munch, Director of the Berkshire Music Center, at the opening exercises of the Twelfth Session, July 1954," typescript, NJJS.

23. Corigliano to Margo Miller, int. Margo Miller, May 19, 2005.

BIBLIOGRAPHY

Note: The list of recordings appears at the companion website.

INTERVIEWS

By the author:

Gustav Barth and Marc Boss, Louveciennes, September 5, 2007. Suzanne Danco, Aldeburgh, April 23, 1993. Michel Debost, by telephone, September 20, 2004. Lorna Cooke de Varon, by telephone, January 26, 2007. Jean Douay, by telephone, April 18, 2006. Doriot Anthony Dwyer, Cambridge, Mass., September 7, 2005. Vic Firth, Boston, April 6, 2006. Stephanie Friedman, by email, May 22, 2005. Jérôme Kaltenbach and Annie Kaltenbach, Villefavard, July 30, 2007. Jaime Laredo, Davis, Calif., February 17, 2008. Margo Miller, Boston, May 19, 2005. Sylvia Sandeen, Boston, September 8, 2005. Agnès Schoeller, Paris, August 29, 2007. Jean-Philippe Schweitzer, Louveciennes, September 8, 2005, July 29, 2008, Paris, April 27, 2006. Roger Shermont, Hyannis, Mass., April 5, 2006. Joseph Silverstein, December 5, 2005. Lita Starr, Carlsbad, Calif., October 7, 2005, April 10, 2006. Michael Steinberg, San Francisco, December 1, 2004. Roger Voisin, by telephone, September 19, 2005; Newton, Mass., April 6, 2006. Ronald Wilford, New York, September 16, 2007. Luben Yourdanoff, by telephone, April 25, 2006. Barbara Zighera, by email, September 19, 2007.

By Katerina Frank:

Leonid Gesin, May 5, 2007; see Frank, "Looking at Both Sides," see under Books and Articles.

By Robert Ripley:

typescript transcriptions from tape, Boston Symphony Orchestra archive

John Barwicki, January 26, 1993. Pasquale Cardillo, December 9, 1991. Harold Faberman, August 5, 2002. Henry Freeman, July 21, 1992. Ralph Gomberg, July 28, 1992. Eugene Lehner, July 31, 1983. William Moyer, January 29, 1993. Thomas D. (Tod) Perry Jr., August 21, 1992. Robert Ripley (interviewed by Joel Moerschel), June 1, 1999. Roger Voisin, August 22, 1992.

LETTERS

Bibliothèque Nationale de France, Paris

Charles Munch: to Harsányi, early 1952; to Guy Ropartz, November 2, 1946. Ernest Munch: to Guy Ropartz, April 2, 1919, February 20, 1920.

Bibliothèque Nationale et Universitaire, Strasbourg (photocopies, largely of Munch family correspondence)

Célestine Munch: to CM, March 20, 1925, March 22, 1925, June 18, 1926, May 26, 1929, August 11, 1932, January 1, 1933, January 29, 1933; to Fritz Munch, February 10, 1919, May 29, 1919, September 5, 1932. CM: to Joseph Calvet, August 15, 1958; to Arthur Honegger, March 10, 1951; to Bohuslav Martinu, September 3, 1940; to Anne-Rose Méhu-Ebersolt, August 28, 1956, November 27, 1956; to Fritz Munch, December 10, 1945; to Albert Schweitzer, September 17, 1938; to Henri Weill, March 23, 1951. Albert Roussel: to Yvonne Gouverné, November 30, 1936. Karl Straube: to Fritz Munch, July 4, 1925.

Boston Symphony Orchestra

Leonard Burkat: to George Judd, September 11, 1950. Henry B. Cabot: to Ernest Ansermet, February 10, 1952; to editor, Boston Globe, November 7, 1968; to editor, Boston Herald, November 19, 1950; to Lucien R. Le Lièvre, April 20, 1948, April 28, 1948; to CM, April 12, 1950, May 19, 1950, November 7, 1950, November 28, 1950, February 14, 1951, April 8, 1952; to Geneviève Munch, April 8, 1948; to Conrad Oberdorfer, April 24, 1952; to Tod Perry, April 15, 1958. W. W. Caswell Jr.: to George Judd and Henry B. Cabot, February 10, 1949. Helen Coates: to Tod Perry, March 11, 1963. Dwight D. Eisenhower: to Henry B. Cabot, September 28, 1956. Susan B. Irving: to George Judd, March 31, 1948. George Judd: to Henry B. Cabot, April 27, 1949; to M. A. DeWolfe Howe, January 22, 1948; to Richard Mohr, September 28, 1949; to CM, March 31, 1950, June 11, 1952, September 3, 1952; to Bernard Zighera, May 22, 1951, May 23, 1951. William Judd: to George Judd, September 27, 1949. Lucien R. Le Lièvre: to Henry B. Cabot, July 20, 1950. Richard E. Myers to George Judd, April 15, 1948. Pierre Monteux: to CM, January 23, 1950, February 2, 1959. CM: to Henry B. Cabot, March 29, 1958; to George Judd, February 23, 1949; to Pierre Monteux, March 8, 1951; to Arturo Toscanini, November 8, 1951. Geneviève Munch: to George Judd, May 8, 1952. Richard E. Myers: to George Judd, April 15, 1948. Franklin K. Paddock, MD: to Tod Perry, July 15, 1960. Dr. Pelton: to Tod Perry, August 4, 1960. Frank Perkins: to George Judd, February 21, 1945. Tod Perry: to Helen Coates, March 5, 1963; to Henry B. Cabot, October 12, 1955, July 6, 1960, February 16, 1962, February 9, 1964, October 12, 1965; to CM, May 3, 1963, September 27, 1968, November 13, 1967; to John T. Noon, December 12, 1966; to Maxwell Rabb, October 15, 1957; to Perry Rathbone, January 8, 1962; to F. James Rybka, MD, March 5, 1963; to Ronald Wilford, February 5, 1963. F. James Rybka, MD: to editor, Time, March 3, 1963. Jean-Jacques Schweitzer: to Henry B. Cabot, December 29, 1961; to Tod Perry, January 7, 1969. Lucien Wesmaël: to Tod Perry, December 4, 1967. Ronald Wilford: to Tod Perry, February 19, 1963. H. G. Wonnacott: to Harold D. Hodgkinson, trustee, January 1949. Bernard Zighera: to George Judd, May 23, 1951.

Library of Congress

Leonard Bernstein: to Koussevitzky, May 21, 1948; to Helen Coates, April 11, 1955; to CM, February 3, 1964. Aaron Copland: to Koussevitzky, September 27, 1947; to Olga Koussevitzky, August 27, 1954; to Irving Fine, February 12, 1956.

Orchestre National, Documentation Musicale, Radio France
see under Manuscripts and Documents.

Collection of Nicole and Jean-Jacques Schweitzer, Louveciennes (all to CM unless noted)
Paul Bastide, August 1939. Serge Baudo, April 27, 1967. Leonard Bernstein, February 3, 1964. Henry B. Cabot, April 2, 1961 (with Olivia Cabot). Pierre Capdevielle, July 4, 1942. Alfred Cortot, October 6, 1943, October 13, 1943. Henri Dutilleux, September 21, 1958, August 3, 1965. Doriot Anthony Dwyer to Mr. and Mrs. Henry B. Cabot (forwarded to Schweitzers): November 11, 1968. Wilhelm Furtwängler, December 28, 1931, February 28, 1939, April 6, 1940, August 4, 1941, September 25, 1942. Otto Klemperer, August 31, 1927. Serge Koussevitzky, July 11, 1950. Leipzig Gewandhaus Orchestra, August 31, 1932. Jean Martinon, July 23, 1943. Pierre Monteux, February 2, 1959. Moscow State Symphony Orchestra trombone section, October 11, 1957. Charles Moses, January 13, 1960. CM to Jean-Jacques Schweitzer and Nicole Henriot-Schweitzer, July 2, 1960. Ernest Munch, June 29, 1918. Fritz Munch, April 12, 1960. Walter Piston, January 4, 1952, January 5, 1964. Francis Poulenc, February 24, 1950, May 23, 1959, October 17, 1960, December 1960. Guy Ropartz, June 3, 1926, November 23, 1946. Albert Roussel, April 12, 1933, January 14, 1934, January 31, 1937. Arnold Schoenberg, November 22, 1950. Albert Schweitzer, June 30, 1936, July 16, 1938. Arturo Toscanini, November 28, 1951. Walter Toscanini, March 19, 1958. Wanda Toscanini Horowitz, February 3, 1957.

Yale University: Virgil Thomson papers, Irving S. Gilmore Music Library
Lincoln Kirstein: to Virgil Thomson, October 4, 1944, November 9, 1944, November 12, 1944, February 2, 1945.

MANUSCRIPTS AND DOCUMENTS

Boston Symphony Orchestra. "Australasian Tour 1960." Mimeographed guide for musicians, 1960. BSO archive.

———. "Boston Symphony 75th Anniversary Press Book." Mimeographed press release. Boston, 1958. BSO archive.

———. "Charles Munch / Music Director / Boston Symphony Orchestra." Mimeographed press release, 1950. BSO archive.

———. "Charles Munch and the Boston Symphony Orchestra: Brief Fact Sheet." Mimeographed press release (obituary), November 6, 1968. BSO archive.

———. "Charles Munch to Retire as B.S.O. Music Director at Conclusion of the 1962 Berkshire Festival / Erich Leinsdorf to Succeed Doctor Munch as Music Director in September 1962." Mimeographed press release, April 21, 1962. BSO archive.

———. Contracts with Charles Munch, April 7, 1948, and following. BSO archive.

———. "European Tour 1956." Mimeographed guide for musicians, 1956. BSO archive.

———. "First Transcontinental Tour, April–May 1953, as Reviewed by Music Critics of 16 Cities." Mimeographed press release. BSO archive.

———. "List of Recordings Made by Charles Munch" (before his appointment in Boston), 1948. BSO archive.

———. "Munch Illness." Dittographed press release, November 7, 1951. BSO archive.

———. "Press Comments on the Retirement of Serge Koussevitzky (Summer of 1949) and the Engagement of Charles Munch (Autumn of 1949) as Conductor of the BSO." Mimeographed press release. BSO archive.

———. *Transcontinental Tour, 1953.* Souvenir program. BSO archive.

Cabot, Henry B. "Note to file re: conversation with CM on resignation," April 1, 1958. BSO archive.

———. "Notes for telephone conversation with CM," June 12, 1951. BSO archive.

———. "Remarks of Henry B. Cabot." Dittographed press release, October 7, 1949. BSO archive.

Ferris, Theodore P. (rector of Trinity Church, Boston). Eulogy for Charles Munch. Mimeographed text for press release, November 14, 1968. BSO archive. Published in *Boston Globe,* November 15, 1968.

Judd, George. "Mr. Judd's conversation with Mr. Zighera from Paris," note to file, May 26, 1951. BSO archive.

"Menu du dîner offert à leurs Majestés britanniques le roi George VI et la reine Elizabeth, jeudi 21 Juillet 1938," Strasbourg Bibliothèque Nationale et Universitaire.

Munch, Charles. Address at farewell banquet, Boston Symphony Orchestra, given April 15, 1962. Handwritten manuscript. Collection Nicole and Jean-Jacques Schweitzer.

———. Address at his 10th anniversary banquet, Boston Symphony Orchestra, given February 1959. Handwritten manuscript. Collection Nicole and Jean-Jacques Schweitzer.

———. "Address by Charles Munch at the opening exercises of the Berkshire Music Center, Tanglewood, 5 July 1953." Handwritten manuscript in French and English, typescript, and version published in *1953 Berkshire Festival* program book, p. 6. Collection Nicole and Jean-Jacques Schweitzer.

———. "Address of Charles Munch, Director of the Berkshire Music Center, at the opening exercises of the Twelfth Session, July 1954." Typescript (carbon copy). Collection Nicole and Jean-Jacques Schweitzer.

———. Address on trip to Israel, given February 6, 1958. Typescript. BSO archive. Published as "Dr. Munch's Impressions of Israel," BSO Programs 1957–1958: 963–64, 1003.

———. "Pierre Monteux: I am not going to make a speech," given April 4, 1955. Typescript. Collection Nicole and Jean-Jacques Schweitzer.

———. Remarks to audience for BSO 85th anniversary season, 1965–1966, given March 11–12, 1966. Handwritten manuscript. BSO archive.

———. Remarks to Orchestre Philharmonique de Paris, given May 1938. Handwritten manuscript. Collection Nicole and Jean-Jacques Schweitzer.

———. Remarks to Société des Concerts, given September 1938. Handwritten manuscript. Collection Nicole and Jean-Jacques Schweitzer.

———. Responses prepared for interview by Martin Bookspan, WBMS, Boston, February 1, 1950. Typescript. Collection Nicole and Jean-Jacques Schweitzer.

———. Statement on wartime activities, December 4, 1944. Typescript. Collection Nicole and Jean-Jacques Schweitzer.

Orchestre National de France. *Livre d'or.* 2 vols. Documentation Musicale, Radio France. Includes letter from CM to members of the orchestra, April 4, 1967.

———. *Radiodiffusion-Télévision-Française. Orchestre National / Tournée de Concerts / États-Unis et Canada / 1er Octobre au 5 Novembre 1962.* Mimeographed pressbook with tour itinerary, in red cover, 1962. Collection Nicole and Jean-Jacques Schweitzer.

Perry, Thomas D., Jr. Note to file re: phone conversation with Ronald Wilford c. March 10, 1963, and March 12, 1963. BSO archive.

———. "Testimonial dinner / 15 April 1962." Dossier of notes and correspondence with providers, December 1961–April 1962. BSO archive.

Schweitzer, Jean-Jacques. "Allocution de J. J. à l'occasion de la décoration de Charry." Typescript, October 5, 1967. Collection Nicole and Jean-Jacques Schweitzer.

Smith, Mary H. "Remembrances of BSO Things Past." Public lecture text: Kimball Farms, Lenox, Mass., 2009. Typescript.

———. Scrapbook from the 1956 tour, including documentation of her work with the flight manifests and personnel and a number of United Press photographs. BSO archive.

Société des Concerts du Conservatoire. Minutes of administrative committee meetings and general assemblies. Bibliothèque Nationale de France, Mus. D17342, D17343, D17345.

Tcherepnin, Alexander. "Charles Munch and Symphony no. 4 by Alexander Tcherepnin." Typescript. New York, January 1970. Collection Nicole and Jean-Jacques Schweitzer.

Vabres, Renaud Donnedieu de. "Discours de Renaud Donnedieu de Vabres prononcé à l'occasion de la remise des insignes de Chevalier dans l'ordre national de la Légion d'Honneur à Samuel et Paul Josefowitz." Mission du Mécénat, Ministère de la Culture et de la Communication, Paris, October 24, 2005. http://www.mecenat.culture.gouv.fr.

BOOKS AND ARTICLES

Amory, Cleveland. *The Proper Bostonians.* New York: Dutton, 1947.

Bair, Deirdre. *Simone de Beauvoir: A Biography.* New York: Summit, 1990.

Baker-Carr, Janet. *Evening at Symphony: A Portrait of the Boston Symphony Orchestra.* Boston: Houghton Mifflin, 1977.

Barblan, Guglielmo. *Toscanini e la Scala.* Milan: Edizioni della Scala, 1972.

Benson, Robert E. "A Four-Decade Friendship with Charles Gerhardt." *Classical CD Review,* c. 2000. http://www.classicalcdreview.com.

———. "RCA SACDs." *Classical CD Review* (February 2005). http://www.classicalcdreview.com.

Bernard, Elisabeth. *Le concert symphonique à Paris entre 1861 et 1914: Pasdeloup, Colonne, Lamoureux.* Paris: Bernard, 1978.

Boston Symphony Orchestra Programs by season. Boston: Boston Symphony Orchestra. Program bulletins published weekly, paginated continuously, bound annually by season. See under "Magazines."

Bowen, José. *The Cambridge Companion to Conducting.* New York: Cambridge University Press, 2003.

Bret, Gustave. "Bach, Schweitzer, et la Société J. S. Bach de Paris." *Saison d'Alsace* 2 (1950): 155–60.

Burian, K[arel] V[ladimir]. *Charles Munch.* Prague: Edition Supraphon, 1971.

Burkat, Leonard. Review of Philippe Olivier: *Charles Munch. Notes* 46, no. 2 (December 1989): 382–85.

Burton, Humphrey. *Leonard Bernstein.* New York: Doubleday, 1994.

Canarina, John. *Pierre Monteux, Maître.* Pompton Plains, N.J.: Amadeus, 2003.

Cantagrel, Gilles, and Claudette Douay. *L'Orchestre National de France: L'album anniversaire, 1934–1994.* Paris: Radio-France/Van de Velde, 1994.

Chimènes, Myriam, ed. *La vie musicale sous Vichy.* Brussels: Éditions Complexe, 2001.

Copland, Aaron. *Aaron Copland, a Reader: Selected Writings, 1923–1972,* ed. Richard Kostelanetz. New York: Routledge, 2004.

Daltroff, Jean. "Quatre grandes figures de la maison de musique S. Wolf à Strasbourg (1825–1960)." *Annuaire de la Société des Amis du Vieux Strasbourg* 29 (2002): 135–43.

Dutilleux, Henri. *Music—Mystery and Memory: Conversations with Claude Glayman.* Trans. Roger Nichols. Burlington, Vt.: Ashgate, 2003.

Elwart, Antoine. *Histoire de la Société des Concerts du Conservatoire Impérial de Musique.* Paris: Castel, 1860.

Erismann, Guy. *Martinů: Un musicien à l'éveil des sources.* Arles: Actes Sud, 1990.

Feschotte, Jacques. Biographical notice on CM in program for concert of March 31, 1939. Strasbourg: Bibliothèque Nationale et Universitaire.

Flesch, Carl. *Memoirs.* New York: Macmillan, 1957.

Foreman, Lewis. *Arthur Bliss: Catalogue of the Complete Works.* Sevenoaks, Kent, UK: Novello, 1980.

Frank, Katerina. "Looking at Both Sides of the Iron Curtain: Boston Symphony Orchestra's Tour of the Soviet Union." Seminar paper. University of California, Davis, 2007.

Fullbrook, Kate, and Edward Fullbrook. *Simone de Beauvoir and Jean-Paul Sartre: The Remaking of a Twentieth-Century Legend.* New York: Basic Books, 1994.

Furtwängler, Wilhelm. *Notebooks 1924–1954,* ed. Michael Tanner. London: Quartet, 1989.

Gandin-Morlet, Dominique, ed. *Orchestre National de France 1934–2004.* 2 vols. for the 90th anniversary of the orchestra. Cahiers de la Doc 154. Paris: Documentation Musicale, Radio France, 2004.

Gavoty, Bernard. *Chroniques de Clarendon: Au bonheur des soirs (1945–1981).* Paris: Éditions Albatros, 1990.

Gouverné, Yvonne. "Les échos du temps passé." In *Zodiaque: Cahiers de l'atelier du Cœur Meurtry / Abbaye Sainte-Marie de la Pierre-qui-vire* (April 1959): 2–28.

Graffman, Gary. *I Really Should Be Practicing.* New York: Doubleday, 1981.

Halbreich, Harry. *Arthur Honegger: Un musicien dans la cité des hommes.* Paris: Fayard, 1992. Trans. Roger Nichols as *Arthur Honegger.* Portland, Ore.: Amadeus, 1999.

Hessenberg, Kurt. "Kleine Selbstbiographie." In *Kurt Hessenberg: Beiträge zur Leben und Werk,* ed. Peter Cahn. Mainz: Schott's Söhne, 1990. English translation at http://www.cassandrarecords.com.

Holland, James R. *Tanglewood.* Barre, Mass.: Barre, 1973.

Holoman, D. Kern. *Berlioz.* Cambridge, Mass.: Harvard University Press, 1989.

———. *The Société des Concerts du Conservatoire, 1828–1967.* Berkeley: University of California Press, 2004.

Honegger, Geneviève. *Charles Munch: Catalogue de l'exposition Strasbourg, B.N.U.S., du 23 Novembre 1992 au 31 Janvier 1993, Boston Symphony Hall, du 19 Février au 31 Mars 1993.* Strasbourg: Bibliothèque Nationale et Universitaire de Strasbourg, 1992.

————. *Charles Munch: Un chef d'orchestre dans le siècle: Correspondance.* Preface by Marcel Landowski. Strasbourg: Nuée Bleue, 1992.

————. *Le Conservatoire et l'Orchestre Philharmonique de Strasbourg.* Strasbourg: Oberlin, 1998.

Hunt, John. *A Gallic Trio: Charles Munch, Paul Paray, Pierre Monteux: Discographies.* London: Hunt, 2003.

J.O.C. Review of *I Am a Conductor* by Charles Munch with Leonard Burkat. *Music and Letters* 36(4) (1955): 401–402.

Joy, Charles R., ed. *Music in the Life of Albert Schweitzer.* Preface by Charles Munch. New York: Harper, 1951.

Jung, Erik. *Le Chœur de St.-Guillaume de Strasbourg: Un chapitre de l'histoire de la musique en Alsace.* Strasbourg: Heitz, 1947.

Kaltenbach, Laurent. *Cinquante concerts spirituels au temple de Villefavard en Limousin: 150 ans de présence protestante en Basse-Marche.* Dieulefit: La Neft de Salomon, 1995.

Katz, Israel J. "Alfred Sendrey (1884–1976): In Memoriam." *Musica judaica* 1 (1976): 106–108.

Kazdin, Andrew F. "The Boston Symphony Orchestra Changes Its Conductors: A Case Study" (master's thesis, MIT, 1953).

Krivopissko, Guy, and Daniel Virieux. "Musiciens: Une profession en résistance?" In *La vie musicale sous Vichy*, ed. Myriam Chimènes, 333–51. Brussels: Éditions Complexe, 2001.

Landowski, Marcel. *Batailles pour la musique.* Paris: Éditions du Seuil, 1979.

Lapp, Harry. *Livre d'or du Festival de Musique de Strasbourg: 51 années de festivals*, ed. Henri Weill. Strasbourg: Société des Amis de la Musique de Strasbourg, 1989.

Lassaigne, Jacques. *Dufy: Étude biographique et critique.* Geneva: Skira, 1954. Also simultaneous English version, trans. James Emmons.

Leinsdorf, Erich. *Erich Leinsdorf on Music.* Portland, Ore.: Amadeus, 1997.

Lowe, Steven. Notes accompanying *David Diamond: Symphony no. 3, Psalm, Kaddish.* Seattle Symphony / Gerard Schwarz. CD Naxos 8.559155 (2002).

Magidoff, Robert. *Yehudi Menuhin.* New York: Doubleday, 1955.

Maury, Geneviève, trans. *Bibi: Vie d'une petite fille*, by Karin Michaëlis. Paris: Stock, 1930.

————. *L'Enfant à la charrue: Huit contes limousins du temps de guerre.* Paris: Meynial, 1918.

————, trans. *Knulp, suivi d'Un Conte et de La fontaine du cloître de Maulbronn*, by Hermann Hesse. Montrouge: Schmied, 1949.

————, trans. *Maïa l'abeille et ses aventures*, by Waldemar Bonsels. Paris: Librairie Stock, 1925.

————, trans. *Tonio Kröger, suivi de Le petit monsieur Friedemann, Heure difficile, L'enfant prodige, Un petit bonheur*, by Thomas Mann. Paris: Stock, 1924.

Maury-Monnerat, Sophie. *Du Léman au Limousin: Journal de Sophie Maury-Monnerat, femme de pasteur, entre 1888 et 1919.* Paris: Pensée universelle, 1989.

Mehlman, Jeffrey. "The Boston/Vichy Connection." *Salmagundi* 35/136 (Summer 2002): 213–25.

Monteux, Doris. *It's All in the Music: The Life and Works of Pierre Monteux.* New York: Farrar, Straus, and Giroux, 1965.

Morton, Lawrence. Review of *I Am a Conductor* by Charles Munch with Leonard Burkat. *Notes* 12(3) (June 1955): 440–41.

Mousnier, Jean-Philippe. *Paul Paray.* Paris: L'Harmattan, 1998.

Munch, Charles. *I Am a Conductor.* New York: Oxford University Press, 1955. In French as *Je suis chef d'orchestre.* Paris: Éditions du Conquistador, 1954.

Murdoch, James. *Peggy Glanville-Hicks: A Transposed Life.* Hillsdale, N.Y.: Pendragon, 2002.

North, James H. *Boston Symphony Orchestra: An Augmented Discography.* Lanham, Md.: Scarecrow, 2008.

Olivier, Philippe. *Charles Munch: Une biographie par le disque.* Paris: Belfond, 1987.

Paolacci, Claire. "Serge Lifar and the Paris Opera during World War II." *Journal of the Oxford University Historical Society* 2 (2004): 1–9.

Pasler, Jann. *Composing the Citizen: Music as Public Utility in Third Republic France.* Berkeley: University of California Press, 2009.

Pasquier, Gaby. *Chère Marguerite Long (1874–1966): Souvenirs personnels de Gaby Pasquier.* Nogent-le-Rotrou, 2001.

Pfeiffer, John. "The Age of Living Stereo." Liner booklet in *The Age of Living Stereo: A Tribute to John Pfeiffer.* CD, 2 vols. RCA 09026-68524-2, 1996.

Pincus, Andrew L. *Scenes from Tanglewood.* Boston: Northeastern University Press, 1989.

———. *Tanglewood: The Clash between Tradition and Change.* Boston: Northeastern University Press, 1998.

Potts, Joseph E. "European Radio Orchestras (III)." *Musical Times* 96(1353) (November 1955): 584–86.

Poulenc, Francis. *Correspondance 1910–1963,* ed. Myriam Chimènes. Paris: Fayard, 1994.

———. *Entretiens avec Claude Rostand.* Paris: Julliard, 1954.

Reynaud, Cécile, Cathérine Massip, and D. Kern Holoman. *L'Orchestre de Paris: De la Société des Concerts du Conservatoire à l'Orchestre de Paris, 1828–2008.* Paris: Centre des Monuments Nationaux / Éditions du Patrimoine, 2007.

Salinger, Nicole, ed. *Orchestre de Paris.* Paris: Hachette / van de Velde, 1987.

Saunders, Frances Stonor. *Who Paid the Piper? The CIA and the Cultural Cold War.* London: Granta, 1999.

Schweitzer, Albert. "Ernest Munch, as I Remember Him." In *Music in the Life of Albert Schweitzer,* ed. Charles R. Joy. New York: Harper, 1951: 35–45.

Schweitzer, Jean-Philippe. "Japanophile, Munch." Liner booklet for DVD *Charles Munch: Boston Symphony Orchestra Live in Japan 1960.* NHK Classical NSDS-9486, 2006.

Simeone, Nigel. "Messiaen and the Concerts de la Pléiade: 'A Kind of Clandestine Revenge against the Occupation.'" *Music and Letters* 81(4) (2000): 551–84.

Spratt, Geoffrey. *The Music of Arthur Honegger.* Cork: Cork University Press, 1987.

Stern, Isaac. *My First 79 Years.* New York: Knopf, 1999.

Strohl, Henri. *Le Protestantisme en Alsace.* Strasbourg: Oberlin, 2000.

Szendrei, Alfred. *Dirigierkunde.* Leipzig: Breitkopf & Härtel, 1932.

Thomson, Virgil. *Music Reviewed, 1940–1954.* New York: Vintage, 1967.

———. *Music, Right and Left.* New York: Holt, 1951.

———. *Virgil Thomson: A Reader: Selected Writings, 1924–1984,* ed. Richard Kostelanetz. New York: Routledge, 2002.

Tommasini, Anthony. *Virgil Thomson: Composer on the Aisle.* New York: Norton, 1997.
van Bart, Jan. *Discografie van het Concertgebouworkest.* Zutphen: Walburg Pers, 1989.
Walter, Bruno. *Theme and Variations.* Trans. James Austin Galston. New York: Knopf, 1946.

MAGAZINES

Anderson, W. R. "The Edinburgh Festival." *Musical Times* 95(1340) (1954): 555–56.

Baruzi, Joseph. "Concerts Siohan (samedi 24 mars)" [1934]. *Le Ménestrel* (March 30, 1934): 129.

Bertrand, Denyse. "Société Philharmonique de Paris (8 décembre)" [1935]. *Le Ménestrel* (December 13, 1935): 382–83.

———. "Société Philharmonique de Paris (21 décembre)" [1935]. *Le Ménestrel* (December 27, 1935): 398.

Bertrand, Paul. "Le 'Requiem' de Berlioz (16 juin)" [1938]. *Le Ménestrel* (June 24, 1938): 171.

Boston Symphony Orchestra. Programs. Paginated consecutively and typically bound by season.

    1949–1950: "Results of the Organ Concert" (letter of Henry B. Cabot to Albert Schweitzer, conveying proceeds of $4,500 from concert of November 14, 1949), 283–84; "Letter from Africa" (Schweitzer to Cabot, December 8, 1949), 563–64, "Charles Munch: Recording of Seventh Symphony," 1124.

    1950–1951: "Student Rehearsals," 3; "The 70th Anniversary," 3; "About the Chorus," 419; "The Student Rehearsals Catch On in a Hurry" (rpt. of Rudolph Elie in *Boston Herald* [December 21, 1950]), 471–72; "Seating Plan, Stage of Symphony Hall," 624; "Boston Symphony to Play for French President," 784; "The Revival of Berlioz' Requiem," 992; "Lowell Institute Broadcasts by This Orchestra" (WGBH), 1043–44.

    1951–1952: "Aaron Copland's Messages," 55–56; "Orchestra on Television," 152; "The Orchestra to Play at Paris Exposition," 439–40; "Paris in the Spring for the Boston Symphony" (rpt. of Rudolph Elie in *Boston Herald* [January 23, 1952]), 635–36, 654; "Our Guest Conductors" (incl. letter of Henry B. Cabot to Ernest Ansermet), 683; "The First European Tour by the Boston Symphony Orchestra," 684; "The European Itinerary," 875–76; "Prospects for the Orchestra" (address of Henry B. Cabot to the Friends, March 19, 1952), 923–24; "Words of Welcome" (to CM on returning, text of WGBH intermission feature), 971–72, 994.

    1952–1953: "A Full Season," 3–4; "The Spring Tour," 627; "Trustees Ask Support of Businessmen," citing Harold Rogers in *CSM*, 675–76.

    1953–1954: "A Berlioz Season," 51–52; "Berlioz Redivivus," 579–80.

    1954–1955: "Munch to Conduct 'NBC' Orchestra," 51; "The 'Damnation of Faust' Recording" (quoting B. H. Haggin in *San Francisco Chronicle* [September 12, 1954]), 51–52; "15 New Works Commissioned for Boston Symphony's 75th Season," 435–36, 477; "For Albert Schweitzer," 675; M. A. DeWolfe Howe, "Schweitzer" (poem), 697; "Monteux Birthday," 916; "The Anniversary Season," 963–64.

    1955–1956: "Features of the 75th Anniversary Season," 3–4; "The Tour," 55–56; "The European Tour," 607–608; "Mr. Munch's Concert in Paris" (citing Suzanne Demarquez in *Guide du concert,* René Leibowitz in *L'Express,* and W. Landowski in *Le Parisien*), 775–76; "Grand Prix for 'The Damnation of Faust,'" 975.

1956–1957: "The European Tour," 3–4, 35, 46; "Welcome by the City," 59; "European Impressions" (citing Colin Mason in *Manchester Guardian,* unsigned in *NYT,* Welles Hangen in *NYT,* Jean Mistler in *L'Aurore,* Frank Kelly in *NYHT,* and Felix Aprahamian in *London Sunday Times*), 59–60, 91; facsimile of congratulatory letter from President Eisenhower, 109; "An Opinion from Moscow" (citing Dmitri Kabalevsky in *Pravda*), 115–16, 147; "An Official Welcome," 171–72, 203; "Boston Visits Moscow" (rpt. of Jack Phipps in *Tempo*), 284, 315; "The Orchestra Honored in Vienna," 451–52; "The Orchestra in New York" (citing Howard Taubman in *NYT* and Jay S. Harrison in *NYHT*), 483; "Dr. Munch in Philadelphia" (citing Max de Shauensee in *Boston Globe* and Edwin H. Schloss in *Philadelphia Inquirer*), 943–44, 975.

1957–1958: "Charles Munch Answers a Letter," 323–24 (rpt. from *Boston Herald*); "The Commissioned Works," 491; "A Message from Moscow," 579–80; "Dr. Munch in Israel," 772; "Reports from Israel" (citing *Haaretz* and *Jerusalem Post*), 835–36, 875; "Dr. Munch's Impressions of Israel," 963–64, 1003.

1958–1959: "The Tenth Season of Dr. Munch," 3; "Van Cliburn," 4, 39; "The United Nations Concert," 131; "Radio and Television Broadcasting," 167; "The Recording Project," 196, 231; "The Return of Casals" (citing Paul Henry Lang in the *NYHT*), 260, 287, 295; "The First International Broadcast," 835; "Overseas Broadcast," 963–64; "Ten Years with Charles Munch," 1481–86.

1959–1960: "The Autumn Tour," 132; "Strasbourg and Boston," 451–52, "A Tour of the Orient," 580; "Aaron Copland to Tour with This Orchestra," 643; "Transatlantic Broadcast, 836; "The Far Eastern Tour," 1283, "Pierre Monteux as Guest Conductor," 1347.

1960–1961: "Music since Last April," 5–6; "Musical Plans," 70; "Transatlantic Broadcast," 326, 340; "Paderewski Award," 340; "Reports from Overseas Broadcast," 454; "Award," 518; "The New Monday Series," 1286; "Award for Poulenc's 'Gloria,'" 1477.

1961–1962: "The UNESCO Concert," 6; "A Tour of Farewells," 261–62; "The Albert Schweitzer Medal," 710; "New York Bohemian Dinner Honors Charles Munch" (rpt. of Cyrus Durgin in the *Boston Globe,* January 23, 1962), 837–38; "The Orchestra on Television," 1372; "A 'Nostalgic' Close" (rpt. of Harold C. Schoenberg in *NYT,* April 5, 1962), 1413–14, 1436; "Trustees' Resolution" (Henry A. Laughlin, read by Henry B. Cabot, April 15, 1962), 1483–84; "Thirteen Years in Retrospect," 1486–92.

Bouvet, Charles. "Concerts Siohan (13 janvier)" [1934]. *Le Ménestrel* (January 19, 1834): 21.

———. "Concerts Siohan (17 février)" [1934]. *Le Ménestrel* (February 23, 1934): 71.

Brunschwig, Dany. "Hommage de la Société des Concerts du Conservatoire au Maréchal Pétain." *L'Information musicale* (December 22, 1942), and as a separate leaflet distributed at Conservatoire concerts.

Bruyr, José. "Bonsoir, Monsieur Charles Munch." *Guide du concert* 537 (November 23, 1968): 9.

Cairns, David. "Leeds Festival." *Musical Times* 105(1458) (August 1964): 445–46.

Courchelle, Gérard. "Charles Munch est de retour." *Diapason* 343 (November 1988): 74–76.

Curzon, Henri de. "Société des Concerts du Conservatoire" [March 6, 1938]. *Le Ménestrel* (March 11, 1938): 71.

Debost, Michel. "Charles Munch, ou le don de soi." *Diapason* 221 (October 1977): 30–31.

Dellard, Pierre. "La tournée de l'Orchestre National aux Etats-Unis et au Canada." *R.T.F. Informations—Documentation* (la vie de la R.T.F.), December 1962.

Demarquez, Suzanne. "M. Charles Münch" [rev. of November 1, 1932]. *Courrier musical* (December 1, 1932): 438–39.

———. "Orchestre de la Société Philharmonique de Paris." *Courrier musical* (January 1–15, 1935): 22.

Durgin, Cyrus. "With the Boston Symphony in Europe." *Saturday Review* (May 31, 1952).

Editor's Note. *Saturday Review* (August 30, 1952).

Flanner, Janet (Genêt). "Letter from Paris: 15 November." *New Yorker* (November 27, 1967).

F., "London Concerts: BBC Contemporary Concert." *Musical Times* 79(1139) (January 1938): 58.

Gavoty, Bernard. "Les dix plus grands chefs d'orchestre." *Réalités fémina* (July 1962): 22–28.

Goldbeck, Fred. "Concert Münch" [December 2, 1937]. *La Revue musicale* 179 (December 1937): 424–28.

———. "*Oriane la sans égale*, de Florent Schmitt (Concert Münch)" [February 12, 1937]. *La Revue musicale* 172 (February 1937): 123–25.

Goléa, Antoine. "L'Orchestre National (Maison de la Radio, le 20 décembre)" [1963]. *Guide du concert* 412 (January 18–24, 1964): 19.

Heinitz, Thomas. "Letter from London." *Saturday Review* (June 28, 1952).

Hirsch, Michel-Léon. "Hommage à Roussel (13 octobre)" [1937]. *Le Ménestrel* (October 22, 1937): 278.

Honegger, Arthur. "Concerts du dimanche" [February 28, 1943]. *Comœdia* (March 6, 1943): 5.

———. "Le festival Claude Debussy" [June 13, 1941]. *Comœdia* (June 21, 1941): 3.

———. "Le festival Guy Ropartz" [January 24, 1943]. *Comœdia* (January 30, 1943): 5.

Imbert, Maurice. "Les concerts symphonique à Paris" ["chez Siohan," January 13, 1934], *Courrier musical* (February 1, 1934): 70–71.

———. "Les symphoniques" [Lamoureux, January 12–13, 1935]. *Courrier musical* (February 1, 1935): 58.

Kolodin, Irving. "Classical LPs." *Saturday Review* (July 26, 1952).

Landowski, Marcel. "Hommage à Charles Münch." Orchestre de Paris program booklet, March 10, 1969.

Lobrot, Jean. "Concerts Siohan (24 février)" [1934]. *Le Ménestrel* (March 2, 1934): 82.

Maygarden, Tony. "London Phase 4 Stereo." *The Endless Groove.* http://www.endlessgroove.com.

McNaught, William. "Gramophone Notes: Prokofiev's 'Classical Symphony.'" *Musical Times* 89(1269) (November 1948): 336.

———. "London Concerts: An Orchestra from Paris." *Musical Times* 87(1245) (November 1946): 347.

Messiaen, Olivier, Luben Yordanoff, Arthur Rubinstein, and Marcel Landowski. "Charles Munch" [on the tenth anniversary of Munch's death]. *Échos de l'Orchestre* (newsletter of the Orchestre de Paris), September 1978.

Millon, Yannick. "Jean-Louis Ollu, un Français à Bayreuth (1): L'Orchestre de Paris" (interview, August 8, 2007), http://www.altamusica.com.

Morin, Philippe, "Discographie intégrale de Charles Munch," *Le monde de la musique* (November 21, 1988): 123–26.

Phipps, Jack. "Boston Visits Moscow." *Tempo* 41 (Autumn 1956): 15–17.

Rosenfeld, John. "A New 'Porgy' in Dallas." *Saturday Review* (June 28, 1952).

Samuel, Claude. "Charles Munch, vingt ans après." *La lettre du musicien* 65 (November 1988): 11.

Stuart, Charles. "The Edinburgh Festival." *Musical Times* 88(1256) (October 1947): 327.

Time magazine, unsigned. "Friend and Foe," October 25, 1945; "Le Beau Charles," February 3, 1947; "Baton Week," February 24, 1947; Discord in Chicago," February 9, 1948; "Boston Picks a Woman," October 13, 1952; "Symphony Traffic," March 23, 1953; "Touring Bostonians," May 25, 1953; "Classic Popularity," June 1, 1953; "Year's Best Records," January 3, 1955; "Composers: Boy with Cheek," February 7, 1964; "Together at Last," November 24, 1967; "It Could Be Dawn" (re: P.-P. Schweitzer), March 29, 1968.

DAILY NEWSPAPERS

Aprahamian, Felix. "Varied Reactions to Programs in Scotland." *CSM* (September 8, 1956).

Bamberger, Werner. "French Navy Captain Recalls Two Talented Uncles." *NYT* (October 14, 1970).

Beam, Alex. "The Real Charles Munch?" *Boston Globe* (September 29, 2002).

Bernheimer, Martin. "Charles Munch: Second Only to Churchill." *Los Angeles Times* (November 24, 1968).

Bonavia, F[erruccio]. "Report from London." *NYT* (May 13, 1945).

Boston Globe, unsigned. "Mme Munch Dies in Paris Home" (August 25, 1956).

———. "Roger Toureau" obituary (January 14, 1969).

Boston Herald, unsigned. "Charles Munch Answers a Letter" (November 3, 1957).

Briggs, John. "'St. John Passion' Offered at Lenox." *NYT* (July 16, 1956).

———. "Two Bach Suites Played at Lenox." *NYT* (July 17, 1954).

Burkat, Leonard. "At Charles Munch's Funeral." *Boston Globe* (December 7, 1968).

Christian Science Monitor, unsigned. "Boston Symphony in London" (September 25, 1956).

———. "First Group of Men Due on Friday" (September 22, 1956).

———. "Gay Soviet Tour Begun" (September 6, 1956).

———. "Leslie J. Rogers" obituary (October 13, 1956).

———. "Munch to Give Premiere of Martinu Sixth Symphony" (January 4, 1955).

———. "Soviets Ask for Another Performance" (August 30, 1956).

———. "Symphony Wins More Praise" (October 10, 1956).

———. "Victories and Vicissitudes of the Boston Symphony Orchestra in Japan" (June 11, 1960).

Cotti, Jean. "L'Orchestre de Paris: Supéfiant de maturité pour un nouveau-né." *France-Soir* (November 16, 1967).

Cunningham, Eloise. "From Townsend Harris to Charles Munch." *CSM* (April 6, 1960).

Dentan, Yves. "Avec le maître." *Réforme* (March 23, 1968).

Dernières Nouvelles d'Alsace, Les, unsigned. Review of CM recital of early April 1922 (April 4, 1922).

―――. Review of Munch-Levy recital, March 11, 1936 (March 12, 1936).

Downes, Olin. "Berlioz Estimate." *NYT* (January 31, 1954).

―――. "Boston Symphony in Work by Bartok." *NYT* (February 15, 1951).

―――. "Boston Symphony Orchestra Heard Here." *NYT* (January 16, 1955).

―――. "Ernest Bloch, Now over 70, Is Writing Music That Is Living and Important." *NYT* (March 7, 1954).

―――. "A Mass by Haydn Heard at Lenox." *NYT* (July 24, 1954).

―――. "Miss Neveu Scores as Violin Soloist." *NYT* (November 14, 1947).

―――. "Monteux at 80." *NYT* (April 3, 1955).

―――. "Munch Conducts Dutilleux Work." *NYT* (January 14, 1954).

―――. "Muench Conducts the Philharmonic." *NYT* (January 24, 1947).

―――. "Muench Is Cheered by Concert Crowd." *NYT* (January 31, 1947).

―――. "Muench Returns as Podium Guest." *NYT* (November 7, 1947).

―――. "New Symphony by Martinu." *NYT* (January 13, 1955).

―――. "Picking Up Again." *NYT* (December 13, 1953).

―――. "A Visit with Paul Paray." *NYT* (November 18, 1945).

―――. "Work by Honegger Introduced Here." *NYT* (March 15, 1951).

Durgin, Cyrus. "Munch Begins 78th Season." *Boston Globe* (October 4, 1958).

―――. "Munch's First Decade as Conductor of Boston Symphony." *Globe* (April 26, 1959).

―――. "This Time I Saw Paris: A Visit to Charles Munch's Home. *Globe* (June 27, 1950).

―――. "Touring Europe with the Boston Symphony." Near-daily enumerated reports in the *Globe* (August–September 1956).

―――. "Turangalîla, or Love in the East Indies, or a Messiaen Afternoon." *Globe* (December 3, 1949).

―――. "What Sort of Man Is Charles Munch?" *Globe* (April 1, 1948).

Dyer, Richard. "In His Own Words: The Maestro Reflects." *Boston Globe* (April 14, 2002).

L. D. "Paul Paray a fait une rentrée en fanfare" [October 23, 1944]. Unidentified clipping in collection of Nicole Schweitzer and Jean-Jacques Schweitzer.

Elie, Rudolph. "Charles Munch Returns, and the Symphony Season Looms." *Boston Herald* (October 1, 1950).

―――. "Charles Munch Returns 'Home.'" *Boston Herald* (October 11, 1953).

―――. "Paris in the Spring for the Boston Symphony." *Boston Herald* (January 23, 1952).

―――. "The First Season: Munch Wins Over a Strange City." *Boston Herald* (April 23, 1950).

―――. "The Student Rehearsals Catch On in a Hurry." *Boston Herald* (December 21, 1950).

Ericson, Raymond. "France Boosts Music." *NYT* (November 12, 1967).

Fox, R. M. "Orchestra Acclaimed in Dublin." *CSM* (September 1, 1956).

Fried, Alexander. "Munch Concert Goes 'Pop.'" *San Francisco Examiner* (February 21, 1964).

―――. "All in the Life of a Music Critic." *San Francisco Examiner* (February 23, 1964).

Goldberg, Albert. "Charles Munch Writes a Penetrating and Witty Book about the Art of Conducting." *Los Angeles Times* (April 17, 1955).

————. "Conductor Munch Revitalizes Classics." *LA Times* (January 4, 1964).

————. "The New Life, Freedom of Charles Munch." *LA Times* (January 26, 1964).

Haggin, B. H. Review of *The Damnation of Faust* (RCA). *San Francisco Chronicle* (September 12, 1954). Quoted in BSO programs, 1954–1955, q.v.

Hangen, Welles. "Boston Symphony Gets Standing Ovation at First Concert in Moscow Conservatory." *NYT* (September 9, 1956).

Harris, McLaren. "Orchestre de Paris, Munch Excel." *Boston Herald Traveler* (October 24, 1968).

Harrison, Jay S. "Munch and Music: His Current Views." *NYHT* (March 6, 1960).

Hughes, Allen. "Boston Symphony Gives 2d Concert." *NYT* (December 4, 1960).

Hume, Paul. "Auriols and Trumans Guests at Boston Symphony Concert." *Washington Post* (April 2, 1951).

————. "Boston Orchestra Concert Is Sellout." *Washington Post* (18 December 1959).

————. "Bostonians Present New Schuman Work." *Washington Post* (December 2, 1960).

————. "Conductor Charles Munch Dies." *Washington Post* (November 7, 1968).

————. "Maestro Munch to Quit Podium in August, 1962." *Washington Post* (April 22, 1961).

Indianapolis Star, unsigned. "IU Goes Continental" (November 3, 1948).

Japan Times, unsigned. "Brilliant Performances by the French National Orchestra" (October 12, 1966).

Johnson, H. Earle. "Leadership Needed." *NYT* (May 14, 1961).

Jorden, William J. "Leningrad Hails Boston Symphony." *NYT* (September 7, 1956).

Keiser, Tucker. "New Book by Munch on Music." *Boston Sunday Post* (April 10, 1955).

Kemp, Robert. "Charles Munch à Athènes." *Le Monde* (September 7, 1957).

Klein, Howard. "3,500 Are Drawn to L. I. Festival." *NYT* (August 7, 1965).

————. "Munch Conducts French Program." *NYT* (February 24, 1967).

Klein, Rudolf. "Visitors from U.S. in Vienna." *CSM* (September 22, 1956).

Kriegsman, Alan M. "French Orchestra Suffers Birth Pangs." *Washington Post* (October 31, 1968).

Léon, Georges. "Charles Munch n'est plus." *L'Humanité* (November 7, 1968).

Lonchampt, Jacques. Charles Munch obituary. *Le Monde* (November 8, 1968).

————. "Entretien avec Charles Munch." *Le Monde* (May 9, 1962).

London Times, unsigned. "A Paris Orchestra in London" (November 5, 1945).

————. "Famous Foreign Conductor in London" (November 9, 1944).

————. "French Musicians in London" (November 13, 1944).

Los Angeles Times, unsigned. "Boston Symphony Off for Tour of Far East" (April 26, 1960).

————. "Charles Munch, Noted Conductor, Dies at 77" (November 7, 1968).

————. "Cheers Tribute Unique Concert Led by Muench" (March 7, 1947).

————. "Muench Due on Podium of Philharmonic" (March 2, 1947).

————. "Munch, Piano Soloist List Three Concerts" (January 5, 1964).

————. "Munch to Conclude Visit with 4 Concerts in Area" (January 6, 1964).

Loveridge, G. Y. "Munch, New Conductor, Brings Joy to the Boston Symphony." *Providence Sunday Journal* (January 29, 1950).

Lowenbach, Jan. "Prague's First Post-War Festival." *NYT* (June 30, 1946).

Miller, Margo. "Memories of BSO's Russia Trip." *Boston Globe* (March 6, 1988).

————. "With the BSO Abroad." Reports for the *Berkshire Eagle* (August–September 1956).

Negri, Gloria. "Sylvia Sandeen, 70, a Lover of the Symphony and the Sox." *Boston Globe* (December 22, 2005).

Neville, Harry. "Munch Returns in Triumph." *Boston Globe* (October 24, 1968).

New York Times, unsigned. "Arbitrators Hear Musicians' Dispute" (December 15, 1948).

————. "Boston Musicians Off" (August 15, 1956).

————. "Boston Orchestra in New Fund Plea" (December 13, 1953).

————. "Broken Pedal Prolongs Piano Concerto Pause" (April 12, 1959).

————. "Dirty Linen Is Aired in Orchestra Dispute" (December 18, 1948).

————. "Carter, Foss, and Poulenc Works Get Music Critics Circle Awards" (April 19, 1961).

————. "Joseph Silverstein to Take Boston Symphony Post" (December 19, 1961).

————. "Eisenhower Lauds Boston Symphony" (October 6, 1956).

————. "French Bar Pianist and Dancer" (November 8, 1945).

————. "French Orchestra Asks Arbitration" (December 5, 1948).

————. "Full House Hears Philharmonic" (February 3, 1947).

————. "Kogan Will Bow Here" (August 7, 1957).

————. "Martinu Is Honored by Music Critics" (March 25, 1956).

————. "Menuhin Returns" (October 13, 1944).

————. "Monteux, at 80, Directs Concert" (April 5, 1955).

————. "Muench, Conductor, Arrives" (December 20, 1946).

————. "Muench, Departing Guest, Honored by Philharmonic" (February 3, 1947).

————. "Munch Arrives in Boston" (September 21, 1949).

————. "Munch Conducts 5 Bach Concertos" (July 10, 1954).

————. "Munch to Resume Conducting" (February 7, 1952).

————. "Musicians in Russia" (September 8, 1956).

————. "New Group Urges Ties with Israel" (January 24, 1954).

————. "Notes Here and Afield" (December 24, 1939).

————. "Seat Sale to Open for Paris Festival" (March 30, 1952).

————. "With Some Orchestras" (October 8, 1939).

————. "WQXR to Broadcast Saturday Concerts by Symphony Beginning on Oct. 5" (August 23, 1957).

————. "7 Centuries Bridged as Boston Symphony Presents Concerts at Chartres Cathedral" (September 22, 1956).

Nussac, Sylvie de. "Triomphe et mort de Charles Munch." *L'Express* (November 11, 1968).

Parmenter, Ross. "Bernstein's Symphony no. 3." *NYT* (February 1, 1964).

————. "Boston Symphony Will Play in Russia." *NYT* (June 8, 1956).

————. "Final Week-End at Tanglewood Begins with Beethoven Concert" (August 8, 1959).

————. "French Works." *NYT* (December 22, 1946).

————. "Lenox Week-End." *NYT* (August 8, 1955).

————. "Munch Conducts French Program." *NYT* (November 1, 1962).

————. "Orphans of the Storm." *NYT* (March 25, 1956).

————. "Parting Is No Sweet Sorrow." *NYT* (October 20, 1963).

———. "Program of Bach Heard at Lenox." *NYT* (July 6, 1957).

Parrott, Lindesay. "Throng at U.N. Hails Performance by Casals." *NYT* (October 25, 1958).

Richmond, Pvt. Edwin L. "News of Casals." *NYT* (December 24, 1944).

Rogers, Harold. "Charles Munch on Podium for Telecast in Cambridge." *CSM* (October 31, 1956).

———. "Doriot Anthony Dwyer Symphony Soloist in Flute Suite." *CSM* (October 13, 1956).

———. "First Complete Hearing of Score in Symphony Hall." *CSM* (January 22, 1955).

———. "Freewheeling Sounds." *CSM* (March 16, 1966).

———. "Initial Program Brilliant under Munch's Baton." *CSM* (September 30, 1961).

———. "Munch Back in Boston." *CSM* (February 11, 1964).

———. "Orchestra Welcomed Home from Tour." *CSM* (October 6, 1956).

———. "'Salute to Strasbourg' Features Loeffler Work." *CSM* (December 5, 1959).

———. "Soviet Composers in Boston Visit." *CSM* (November 14, 1959).

———. "Trustees Ask Support by Businessmen." *CSM* (January 23, 1953).

Rostand, Claude. "Le concerto de Poulenc à Aix-en-Provence." *Paris-Presse* (July 26, 1950).

Schubart, Mark. "Behind the Baton." *NYT* (April 3, 1955).

Salzman, Eric. "Shell Dedicated at Tanglewood." *NYT* (July 13, 1959).

Schloss, Edwin H. Review of Philadelphia Orchestra concert of March 1, 1957. *Philadelphia Inquirer* (March 2, 1957); quoted in "Dr. Munch in Philadelphia," BSO programs 1956–1957, 943–44, 975.

Schonberg, Harold C. "As Tanglewood Marks a 50th, Let the Cavils Not Be Sounded." *NYT* (July 4, 1990).

———. "Berlioz' 'Damnation of Faust' Led by Munch." *NYT* (August 15, 1960).

———. "French and American Festival." *NYT* (July 15, 1965).

———. "Music: Munch in Form" *NYT* (March 21, 1963).

———. "Munch Leads French Scores." *NYT* (April 5, 1962).

———. "Too Much Hoopla." *NYT* (February 2, 1964).

———. "Routine Winter Works Fill Berkshire Lists." *NYT* (April 30, 1961).

Schwarz, K. Robert. "A Lost Generation of Americans Is Coming Home." *NYT* (July 1, 1990).

Smith, Hugh. "Boston Symphony Opens in Ireland." *NYT* (August 25, 1956).

Smith, Warren Storey. Review of April 27, 1951. *Boston Post* (April 28, 1951).

Stein, Erwin. "Boston Symphony in London." *CSM* (October 6, 1956).

Steinberg, Michael. "Bernstein's 'Kaddish' in Premiere Here." *Boston Globe* (February 1, 1964).

———. "Munch Conducts Berlioz 'Fantastique.'" *Boston Globe* (February 8, 1964).

Straus, Noel. "2 Roussel Works Heard at Concert." *NYT* (February 2, 1947).

———. "Muench Conducts Handel Concerto." *NYT* (November 17, 1947).

———. "Muench Conducts Poulenc Concerto." *NYT* (January 26, 1947).

———. "Muench Conducts Saint-Saens Work." *NYT* (November 10, 1947).

Szulc, Tad. "1734 Violin Given Israel by Szeryng." *NYT* (December 19, 1972).

Taubman, Howard. "A Modern Master." *NYT* (July 22, 1957).

———. "Bad Faith Charged to Rodzinski." *NYT* (February 6, 1947).

———. "Healing Strains of Beethoven." *NYT* (July 23, 1955).

———. "Rodzinski's Resignation Accepted by Philharmonic, Effective at Once." *NYT* (February 5, 1947).

Taylor, Robert. "'Kaddish' Reveals Bernstein Genius." *Boston Herald* (February 1, 1964).

Thomson, Virgil. "France at Its Best." *NYHT* (October 24, 1948).

———. "French Loveliness." *NYHT* (October 18, 1948).

———. "Joan of Arc in Close-Up." *NYHT* (January 2, 1948).

———. "Kusevitsky, Conductor: The Risen Russian Suggested for Boston." *Boston Evening Transcript* (February 8, 1922).

———. "The Koussevitzky Case." *NYHT* (February 23, 1947).

van Leer, Bertrus. "Gasdirigen Concertgebouworkest Charles Munch." *Het Parool* (January 11, 1960).

Vuillermoz, Emile. "Two Travelers in Paris." *CSM* (October 13, 1956).

Wallace, Dean. "Munch Conducts 'Lost' Masterpiece." *San Francisco Chronicle* (February 21, 1964).

Washington Post, unsigned. "Symphony Guest Unable to Appear" (January 6, 1963).

Williams, Stephen. "Boston Symphony Ends Fete Series." *NYT* (August 31, 1956).

———. "Boston Symphony in Edinburgh Bow." *NYT* (August 27, 1956).

ZED. "Le Concert du Gewandhaus de Leipzig au Palais des Fêtes." *Les Dernières Nouvelles d'Alsace* (June 2, 1931).

———. Review of November 28, 1945. *Les Dernières Nouvelles d'Alsace* (November 29, 1945).

INDEX